SOCIAL POLICY REVIEW 24

Analysis and debate in social policy, 2012

Edited by Majella Kilkey, Gaby Ramia and Kevin Farnsworth

First published in Great Britain in 2012 by

The Policy Press
University of Bristol
Fourth Floor
Beacon House
Queen's Road
Bristol BS8 1QU, UK
Tel +44 (0)117 331 4054
Fax +44 (0)117 331 4093
e-mail tpp-info@bristol.ac.uk
www.policypress.co.uk

North American office:
The Policy Press
c/o The University of Chicago Press
1427 East 60th Street
Chicago, IL 60637, USA
t: +1 773 702 7700
f: +1 773-702-9756
sales@press.uchicago.edu
www.press.uchicago.edu

British Library Cataloguing in Publication Data
A catalogue record for this book is available from the British Library.

Library of Congress Cataloging-in-Publication Data
A catalog record for this book has been requested.

ISBN 978 1 44730 447 0 hardback
ISBN 978 1 44730 446 3 paperback SPA members' edition (not on general release)

The right of Majella Kilkey, Gaby Ramia and Kevin Farnsworth to be identified as
editors of this work has been asserted by them in accordance with the 1988 Copyright,
Designs and Patents Act.

Cover design by The Policy Press
Front cover: photograph kindly supplied by www.istock.com
Printed and bound in Great Britain by TJ International Padstow
The Policy Press uses environmentally responsible print partners

Contents

Part Three: Severe crisis: social policy in most challenging circumstances

List of tables and figures

Tables

Figures

Notes on contributors

Daniel Béland holds the Canada Research Chair in Public Policy at the Johnson-Shoyama School of Public Policy (University of Saskatchewan campus). A student of comparative social policy, he has published eight books and more than 60 peer-reviewed articles: www.danielbeland.org

Fran Bennett is a Senior Research Fellow (half-time) in the Oxford Institute of Social Policy, Oxford University, engaged in teaching and research. Her interests include social security policy, gender issues and poverty. She is also an independent consultant, writing on social policy issues for the UK government, the European Commission, NGOs, etc. She is joint editor of the *Social Policy Digest* (*Journal of Social Policy*).

Jonathan Bradshaw, CBE, FBA, is Professor of Social Policy at the University of York. He was founding Director of the Social Policy Research Unit and served two terms as Head of Department. His main research interests are child poverty and well-being, and comparative social policy. His latest book is *The well-being of children in the UK* (The Policy Press, 2011).

Karen Nielson Breidahl is a political scientist and PhD student at CCWS – Centre for Comparative Welfare Studies, Aalborg University, Denmark. Her primary research interests include comparative welfare state research and labour market reforms targeted at unemployed – in particular immigrants – in the Scandinavian countries.

Claire Callender is Professor of Higher Education at the Institute of Education and at Birkbeck, University of London. Her research focuses on student finances in higher education and related issues, including studies for the most significant UK inquiries into student funding. Claire has given evidence to various House of Commons Education Select Committees and to the Browne Review of Higher Education Funding and Student Finance.

Harriet Churchill is a Lecturer in Social Work at the University of Sheffield. Her research examines policy and practice developments in child welfare and family support, and everyday experiences of childhood, parenthood and family relations.

Mairéad Considine is a Lecturer in Social Policy at the School of Applied Social Studies, University College Cork, Ireland. She co-authored *Irish social policy: A critical introduction* (Gill & Macmillan, 2009)

with Fiona Dukelow. Her research interests include pensions policy, social protection and the impact of the contemporary crisis on the Irish welfare state.

Fiona Dukelow is a Lecturer at the School of Applied Social Studies, University College Cork, Ireland. Current research interests include aspects of the political economy of the Irish welfare state. She co-authored *Irish social policy: A critical introduction* (Gill & Macmillan, 2009) with Mairéad Considine, and co-edited *Mobilising classics: Reading radical writing in Ireland* (Manchester University Press, 2010) with Orla O'Donovan.

Kevin Farnsworth is a Senior Lecturer in Social Policy at the University of Sheffield. His recent publications include: *Social policy in challenging times*, edited with Zoë Irving (The Policy Press, 2011) and *Social versus corporate welfare* (Palgrave, 2012).

Caroline Glendinning is Professor of Social Policy in the Social Policy Research Unit, University of York. She is an Associate Director of the NIHR School for Social Care Research; an Academician of the Academy of Social Sciences and, from 2009 to 2012, was Chair of the UK Social Policy Association.

Zoë Irving is a Lecturer in Comparative Social Policy at the University of Sheffield. Her current research interests are in the social policy of small island states and comparative analysis of social policy responses to economic crisis. She has previously published in the area of gender, work and employment and is co-editor with Kevin Farnsworth of *Social policy in challenging times* (The Policy Press, 2011), and co-author with Michael Hill of the eighth edition of *Understanding social.policy* (Blackwell Wiley, 2009).

Rana Jawad is a Lecturer in Social Policy in the Department of Social and Policy Sciences at the University Bath (UK). She has two main research interests: (1) the welfare regimes and social policies of the region of the Middle East, with a particular focus on Islam and the Arab countries; (2) the influence of religion in the development of state and non-state welfare provision around the world.

Majella Kilkey is a Senior Lecturer in Social Policy at the University of Sheffield. Her current research is concerned with the examination of family policies and practices through the lens of migration in the UK and internationally

Stefan Kühner is a Lecturer in Social Policy at the University of York. His research centres on comparative and international political economy with emphasis on the politics of welfare state change in historical perspective. His publications address theoretical and methodological debates in comparative analysis. He is co-author of *The short guide to social policy* (The Policy Press, 2008).

Alan Murie is Emeritus Professor of Urban and Regional Studies at the Centre for Urban and Regional Studies at Birmingham University. He has written widely on the development of housing provision, housing policy, privatisation and issues related to cities and neighbourhoods throughout the UK and Europe.

Robert M. Page is currently Reader in Democratic Socialism and Social Policy at the University of Birmingham. His recent work has focused mainly on the approaches adopted towards the welfare state by post-1945 Labour and Conservative governments in Britain.

Theodoros Papadopoulos is a Lecturer in Social Policy at the University of Bath and has written extensively on aspects of social and family policy in Greece. His research interests are in the governance of social security, the social integration of migrants, and labour market and employment policies in the EU. Among his recent publications is *Migration and welfare in the New Europe*, co-edited with Emma Carmel and Alfio Cerami (The Policy Press, 2011).

Gaby Ramia is Associate Professor in the Graduate School of Government at the University of Sydney. His research is in comparative and international social policy.

Javier Ramos-Díaz is Visiting Professor at the E-Democracy Centre, University of Zurich, and Senior Researcher at Greds-Emconet (Employment Conditions Network), Pompeu Fabra University/ Barcelona. Previously he acted as an advisor in both Spain's Ministry of Labour and Immigration, and the Cabinet of the President of the European Parliament. His research interests are in globalisation, European integration, labour market, poverty and social exclusion, health inequality, and innovation: javier.ramos@upf.edu

Antonios Roumpakis is Visiting Fellow in the Centre for the Analysis of Social Policy at the University of Bath and has been a post-doctoral fellow at the Nordic Centre of Excellence, University of Helsinki. His research interests are in comparative governance of pension funds, and labour market and employment policies in the EU. Among his recent publications is 'Contingency in risk management: the case of pension funds in Sweden and Finland', co-authored with Ville-Pekka Sorsa in Sorsa, V-P. (ed) *Rethinking social risks in the Nordics* (Foundation for European Progressive Studies, 2011).

Sally Ruane is a member of the Health Policy Research Unit, De Montfort University, Leicester. Current research interests include the Private Finance Initiative, tax reform and health service reform, particularly political aspects of health service reform. She has been an active campaigner in opposition to the Health and Social Care Bill.

Rebecca Surender is a Lecturer in Comparative Social Policy at the University of.Oxford and a Fellow of Green-Templeton College. Her research interests and.publications are primarily in the area of health policy and 'policy and development', including a forthcoming co-edited book *Social policy in a developing world* (Elgar, 2012). She was a founding member of the Centre for the Analysis of South African.Social Policy (CASASP) in Oxford.

Marian Urbina Ferretjans is a doctoral researcher in Social Policy at Oxford University and has a background in Demography (MPhil), Sociology and Political Sciences (BA). Her current research interests are in global social policy, social policy in developing countries and South–South social cooperation. She has been a contributor and reviewer of publications by the United Nations Population Fund where she worked before enrolling in her doctorate.

Clare Ungerson is Emeritus Professor of Social Policy, University of Southampton. She retired in 2005 and lives in Sandwich in East Kent. She is a trustee of a voluntary organisation in South London and founding Chair of the East Kent Justice for Palestinians group. She is researching and writing about the rescue of 4,000 Jewish men who were refugees from Nazi Germany and housed in a camp on the edge of Sandwich in 1939. This is not strictly social policy research but raises interesting social policy issues, not least the question of rationing.

Albert Varela is a doctoral candidate and University Teacher at the Department of Sociological Studies, University of Sheffield. His research interests include comparative social policy, labour market mobility, and poverty and social exclusion measurement: a.varela@sheffield.ac.uk

Alex Waddan is a Senior Lecturer in Politics and American Studies at the University of Leicester. His most recent book is *The politics of policy change: Welfare, medicare, and social security reform in the United States* (Georgetown University Press, 2012; co-authored with Daniel Béland).

40th anniversary preface

Introduction: 40 years of *Social Policy Review*

Caroline Glendinning ACSS, Professor of Social Policy, Chair, UK Social Policy Association

As Chair of the Social Policy Association (SPA) during the 40th Anniversary year of the *Social Policy Review*, I am delighted to introduce this Preface.

Social Policy Review first appeared in 1972 in a rather different guise, as *The Year Book of Social Policy in Britain*. Jointly conceived by Professor Kay Jones and (then) publishers Routledge and Kegan Paul, the *Year Book* provided a critical review of recent developments in social policy and social work. Since then, it has moved publishers, to Longman and, most recently, The Policy Press, with a period in between when it was published 'in house' by the SPA. Indeed, one crucial development over these four decades has been the establishment of close links with the SPA. This has given the *Year Book/Review* a clear audience, of teachers and students in social policy, for whom it has become a vital source of discussion and debate on contemporary issues. It also means that the SPA can offer junior colleagues opportunities and mentoring in academic commissioning and editing. Three other developments stand out over the past 40 years: the shift from a focus on very recent developments in policy and administration to broader debates and trends; the regular rotation of editors to bring in new ideas and approaches; and, perhaps most significantly in a globalised policy environment, at least as much attention to international as to UK issues.

Some of the key turning points in the history of the *Year Book/Review* are marked in this Preface by those who were involved at the time – Jonathan Bradshaw, Clare Ungerson and Robert Page. Their accounts illustrate how much the study of social policy has changed over the past 40 years – and how the success of the *Year Book* and the *Review* has been rooted in their ability to adapt and keep pace with these changes.

The beginnings: 1972 – *The Year Book of Social Policy in Britain 1971*

Jonathan Bradshaw, Professor of Social Policy, University of York

The first edition was published in 1972 by Routledge and Kegan Paul and edited by Kathleen (Kay) Jones who was the editor of their *International Library of Social Policy*. It was called *The Year Book of Social Policy in Britain 1971*. Kay had been appointed to the new Chair of Social Administration at the University of York in 1965 and accepted, initially, graduate students from 1966 in social work and social administration. She went on to edit a further six *Year Books* up until 1976. Then, Muriel Brown and Sally Baldwin, the latter also at York, took over for three years during 1977–79 and then the editorship moved elsewhere. Kay's aspiration for the book was that it:

> would provide a critical review of the developments which have taken place over the previous year in social policy and social work.... Each volume would be in two parts: Part I will feature a subject of special interest for that year, Part II will contain papers on a range of current issues.

The special subject in the 1971 edition was the Seebohm Report. In her introduction, Kay Jones writes:

> The idea for the *Year Book of Social Policy* first occurred to publisher and editor in October 1971. As soon as it took shape we realised that there would have to be a 1971 edition, because it was a key year for social policy.

The haste to produce the volume perhaps explains why six of the 15 chapters were contributed by her staff or former students! Curiously, she also writes 'Civil servants, in particular, were not able to contribute because there was no time to obtain departmental approval.' But would civil servants ever have contributed to a year book on current social policies – have they ever? One coup was that she managed to persuade Sir Keith Joseph to allow the reprinting of an article in *The Guardian* on the Conservative social strategies.

Kay was always more interested in services and institutions than social security, education or housing policy – after all, she was a distinguished historian of the mental health services. The choices in the volume reflect this. Seven chapters on the early results of the Seebohm reforms, four on other services, nothing on housing or education, and only one (by me) on social security. Would we now look back on the Seebohm reforms to personal social services as the most important events in 1971? In fact, 1971 was a very rich year for social policy – almost all of it bad.

In 1970, the Conservatives had won the general election and Edward Heath had formed an administration after a lacklustre election. I fought the Labour cause in Thirsk and Malton, and, apart from the beauty of the countryside and the perfect weather, I can only remember Heath's repetition of the claim by Frank Field (then Director of the Child Poverty Action Group) that 'The poor get poorer under Labour!' and my opponent's single refrain about hyperinflation, which then was running at 6%. In 1971, it rose to 11%.

Sir Keith Joseph became Secretary of State for Social Services and Margaret Thatcher became Secretary of State for Education. Sir Keith immediately increased health services charges, scrapped the massive Crossman National Superannuation scheme, which was on its way to the statute books, and set about replacing it with a pale shadow, which in turn was scrapped by Labour when they returned to power in 1974, and so the yo-yo on pensions went on – as it still does today. However, he did lift from the Bill the Attendance Allowance and Invalidity Benefit – both now being emasculated by Iain Duncan Smith. Mrs Thatcher increased the price of school meals, famously snatched free school milk from primary schoolchildren and told local authorities that they could keep their grammar schools (and there is talk of a state funeral for her as I write). Joseph also reneged on the election promise to increase family allowances and instead introduced Family Income Supplement (FIS), the first means-tested benefit for the working poor since Speenhamland, and the precursor to Family Credit, Child Tax Credit, Working Tax Credit and now the dreaded Universal Credit coming in 2013. All were administrative disasters in their way, but Universal Credit will be the greatest ever – mark my words.

Another notable event in 1971 that might have been chosen to be included as a chapter was the Housing Finance Bill, designed by Peter Walker to shift housing subsidies from bricks and mortar to tenants in the form of means-tested national rent rebates, and covering private tenants for the first time. It led to higher rents, rent strikes and Clay Cross councillors being surcharged.

Perhaps the most significant policy-related event of all in 1971, which might have featured in the book, was the massive increase in unemployment – it rose from 600,000 to over a million during the year. To its credit, and unlike subsequent Tory governments, this increase caused much alarm in the Cabinet and led to the famous Heath U-turn.

The increase in charges and the introduction of FIS and Rent Rebates created the poverty trap, described for the first time by Frank Field and David Piachaud (1971). Richard Titmuss, as Chair of the Supplementary Benefits Commission, published his famous essay in defence of discretion (Titmuss, 1971), arguing that it provided an element of flexible, individualised justice in the social security system. I remember that he came to York to give a seminar on it and I am ashamed to report that this great man of social policy was roundly attacked by the young staff and postgraduates who were by then working on the weekly welfare rights stall in York marketplace.

My chapter in the *Year Book* was my first publication. I had forgotten it – for some reason it does not appear on my publications list. I, and the many hundreds of social policy academics who have since published in the *Year Book* and the *Review*, should be grateful to Kay Jones for starting it all 40 years ago.

Transition: from *Year Book* to *Review*

Clare Ungerson, Emeritus Professor of Social Policy, University of Southampton

It is over 25 years since I took on the joint editorship of what was then called *The Year Book of Social Policy in Britain*. It was the first time that I had worked with Maria Brenton, so that was an unknown quantity – which turned into a real pleasure over the four years we worked together. In order to write this preface, I sneaked into the University of Kent Library (I am afraid my own copies have long since been given away) and went through the *Year Books* and *Reviews* that I had jointly edited. On the whole, I was pleasantly surprised. I thought many of the articles stood the test of time: it seemed to me that historians of social policy would find the articles contained within the covers of this periodical a helpful summary of the main issues of that era and a well-informed, thoughtful and thorough analysis of what their meanings were. And much of what was happening in the 1980s seemed very familiar: it was a period of long Conservative government and very important shifts in the welfare state were taking place during the mid- to late 1980s. The arguments that the welfare state is an unsustainable burden and that the privatisation and marketisation of public services are the efficient routes forward are now well embedded and rehearsed daily. It was also a period of cuts, though nothing like as draconian as currently in 2011. There were even riots in Handsworth, Birmingham in September 1985, which we noted in our preface to the 1985/86 edition. *Plus ça change* ...

But reading these old issues reminded me how precarious the publication was. For a start, it kept changing its name. At first it was called *The Year Book of Social Policy in Britain*, then in 1987 we dropped the two words 'in Britain', and the following year we changed the name to *Social Policy Review*. We also kept changing publishers. Almost as soon as Maria and I started working together, Routledge and Kegan Paul, the publishers who had published the *Year Book* since its inception wrote to us saying that they no longer wished to do so. Fortunately, we found another publisher, Longman, fairly quickly. But all this toing and froing indicated a basic problem – nobody, not even the editors, really knew who the readers of the *Year Book* were. It was, as a volume, very expensive to buy; hence, its main buyers were university libraries rather than individuals. Moreover, the words 'Year Book' were misleading. One might have expected to find a digest of the main events in social policy for the previous year and an almanac-style list of policy departments and policy research institutes (the kind of thing one can find these days with the click of a mouse but which in the 1980s was still a question of finding the right publication on an obscure library shelf). But this periodical was a collection of articles that tried to present current issues in a way that was *both* topical *and* did not date – it was a potentially impossible mission coupled with a demonstrably small readership.

Longman were determined to shift the focus. Their mantra was 'practitioners'. They wanted to see the *Year Book* sitting on the shelves of senior social workers and directors of social services, civil servants in the main social policy departments of government, and directors of voluntary organisations, and they thought that one of the ways of doing this was to get 'practitioners' to write the articles. We agreed to do our best. Looking at the list of authors that we commissioned, I see that we largely failed in getting practitioner contributors but that we did commission articles that might substantively appeal to readers 'in the field' rather than in academe. We also moved to a paperback, which was much better priced. But, as I remember it, our readership numbers did not really increase enough to make a profit for Longman, and towards the end of my stint as joint editor (my last year was jointly edited with Nick Manning) we were moving towards a much closer connection with the Social Policy Association, which in the long run has proved so fruitful. A new readership of teachers and students of social policy, and, given the international section now a regular part of the *Social Policy*

Review, a wider readership globally has stabilised the publication and given it an international standing.

The experience of being an editor of this particular publication was, and I am sure remains, rather special. It is unlike editing the usual kind of collection of papers organised around a single theme, or editing a journal where the editors are generally relatively passive. In my day, most of the articles for the *Social Policy Review* were commissioned, and this meant that, on an annual basis, we had to think about the issues that had characterised the year in question and consider the way in which a commissioned author might present an overview and an analysis that would have a lasting utility. I can remember having quite fierce arguments with Maria about our selection of the issues we wanted to cover in any one volume. Often those arguments amounted to 'What is Social Policy?', a question I still find very difficult to answer because the boundaries of our subject matter seem to shift so easily. But returning to these foundational questions on an annual basis was always stimulating – and somehow or other we always found a compromise. It is terrific that the *Social Policy Review*, despite its early vicissitudes, has continued to flourish and to develop. I particularly enjoyed dipping into its latest issue – back to hardback, and, to my delight, an index. Long may the *Social Policy Review* continue!

Saving the *Social Policy Review*: Nick Manning to the rescue!

Robert M. Page, Reader in Democratic Socialism and Social Policy, University of Birmingham[1]

At the end of the 1980s, *The Year Book of Social Policy*, which had first been published in 1972, faced an uncertain future. The then publisher Longman had found it necessary to make hefty increases in the cover price to cover falling revenue, with the result that individual sales were in steady decline. It seemed almost inevitable that the *Year Book* would become at best a limited hardback edition aimed solely at the institutional market.

It was the intervention of SPA Executive member Nick Manning in late 1989 that eventually saved the *Review*. With his customary entrepreneurial flair (many of his closest colleagues detect similarities to Alan Sugar, albeit with extra charm), Nick attempted to persuade the Executive that the SPA should take full responsibility for the contents, production and distribution of the *Year Book*. As he recounts in *Social*

Policy Review 4 (SPR 4), such a 'revolutionary' idea was initially thought to be overambitious and a three-year compromise deal was struck with Longman, which involved a new title (*Social Policy Review*), a broader thematic structure and an agreement that the book would be offered to members at a discounted rate. By the end of this three-year period, the Executive were finally persuaded of the merits of self-publishing. Nick agreed to take on responsibility for the entire production process of *SPR 4* with John Baldock 'ready' in the wings to take over this role for *SPR 5* and *SPR 6*. Robert Page was to act as co-editor for all three editions, focusing on the academic content of the *Review* and its distribution.

Getting *SPR 4* to market on time proved to be a Herculean task. The aim was to have copies available for purchase at the annual SPA conference at the University of Nottingham in July 1992. In preparation for this endeavour, Nick had to devote many a long hour to mastering the intricacies of desktop publishing with the assistance of rudimentary hardware and software.

One of the commercial problems with the *Year Book* identified by Longman was that the emphasis on contemporary developments within the volume restricted its shelf life and long-term viability. Indeed, one of the main reasons for changing the title of the publication to *Social Policy Review* was to persuade prospective readers that the contents had a 'sell-by' date that extended beyond the advertised years on the front cover. In recognition of this 'perishability' factor, the editors of *SPR 4* continued with the more recent practice of commissioning a broader range of essays than had been traditionally the case with the *Year Book*, not least because this would ensure that there was less 'time-sensitive' content. It was also decided to omit any reference to the current year on the front cover. It was hoped that this strategy would increase the appeal and impact of the book as well as enhance sales.

The editors were mindful of the fact that *SPR 4* was due to be published shortly after the 1992 general election. In order to be as up to the minute as possible, one editor (who shall remain nameless) suggested that we might take a calculated 'gamble' on the outcome of the general election and refer to Labour's election 'victory' in the joint introduction. The other editor, who was convinced that John Major would return to Downing Street and was also keen to avoid the possibility of an SPA 'Dewey defeats Truman' moment[2] was not so enamoured by this idea. The resultant compromise was to leave space in the opening paragraph for a 'stop-press' insertion referring to the 'actual' election result.

The production schedule proved to be an extremely tight one, which required Nick Manning to drive at breakneck speed from Canterbury to

Nottingham on the eve of the conference with the precious cargo in the car boot. Effective pre-publicity, a competitive price and an enthusiastic conference 'marketing' team ensured a brisk level of sales and a useful financial 'surplus' for the SPA.

The cover design and fonts inherited from Longman were retained until the last self-published edition rolled off the presses eight years later in 2000 (*SPR 12*). Since 2001, the *SPR* has been published by The Policy Press, which under the leadership of Alison Shaw and her dedicated team, has played such a prominent role in promoting the subject in recent decades. Intriguingly, one of the first changes The Policy Press made was to reinstate the time period of the edition on the front cover! The decision to rotate the editors of the *Review* on a regular basis has also proved to be an astute one, allowing as it does for an infusion of new ideas, perspectives and contributors as well as providing some new colleagues with an opportunity to gain editorial experience.

The new arrangement with The Policy Press has proved highly successful for the SPA and the *Review* now forms part of the annual membership package. As you browse through this 40th edition, it is worth remembering, however, that none of this would have been possible without the resolve and drive of Nick Manning in the late 1980s.

Notes

[1] Thanks to Nick Manning for clarifying points of information.

[2] Faced with a tight publishing deadline, *The Chicago Tribune* decided to run a banner headline declaring (inaccurately as it transpired) that the Republican challenger for the White House, Thomas Dewey, had secured victory in the 1948 Presidential election over the Democrat incumbent Harry S. Truman even though many results from the east coast states had yet to be declared. There is a famous picture of a triumphant Harry S. Truman holding up the front page of the paper for the camera!

References

Field, F. and Piachaud, D. (1971) 'The poverty trap', *New Statesman*, 3 December, 82, 2124.

Titmuss, R. (1971) 'Welfare rights, law and discretion', *Political Quarterly*, vol 42, no 2, pp 113-32.

Introduction

Majella Kilkey

The 'long view' offered in the contributions to the '40th anniversary preface' offers scant consolation to a social policy analyst today in the UK, and one suspects in much of Europe and beyond. Jonathan Bradshaw notes the alarm 40 years ago from the then Tory government when unemployment reached one million. At the end of 2011, one million was the level of *youth* unemployment in the UK! Total unemployment stood at 2.64 million. And this is before the bulk of the public expenditure cuts committed to by the 2010 Conservative–Liberal Democrat Coalition government take effect; cuts that Clare Ungerson, reflecting on what was happening during her editorship of the *Year Book/Social Policy Review* in the 1980s, acknowledges are unprecedented.

The implications of the planned public expenditure cuts and the Coalition's broader 'reform agenda' for specific areas of social policy are addressed in Part One of this collection, which focuses on current developments in the UK. In her introduction to the anniversary preface, Caroline Glendinning identified the increasing internationalisation of the *Year Book/Social Policy Review* as one of its most significant developments. In keeping with that trend, the remaining two parts of the collection turn their focus to other countries. Part Two includes an examination of social policy in 'developing' countries, including in Africa and the Arab nations. Part Three considers the fate of social welfare in countries among the worst hit by the 'economic crisis', including Ireland, Greece, Spain, Portugal and Iceland.

Part One: Current developments

Majella Kilkey

Part One analyses developments during 2011 in five key areas of social policy – social security, housing, higher education, family support and health. Unsurprisingly given that it was the first year of the Conservative–Liberal Democrat Coalition government, 2011 has been a busy one in all of those policy areas. As we see across the chapters, the 'politics of coalition' per se has contributed to the ground upon which developments have been taking place. So too has the continuing global economic crisis and the cutbacks in public expenditure that, for some at least, this is deemed to have necessitated. In all areas examined, though, it is Conservative ideology that seems the dominant component in the developments that have occurred.

In the first chapter in Part One, Fran Bennett employs an impressive volume of evidence from a wide range of sources to provide a thorough critique of the Coalition's proposals for Universal Credit (UC) – a new means-tested benefit amalgamating in- and out-of-work benefits/tax credits, due for introduction for new claimants in 2013. The proposals – designed to simplify the benefits system and improve work incentives – are based on the scheme proposed by the Centre for Social Justice established by Iain Duncan Smith (IDS) in 2004 after stepping down as leader of the Conservative Party, and have been championed by IDS as Secretary of State for Work and Pensions in the 2010 Coalition government. Following an overview of the proposals for UC – which, at the time of writing, were still making their way through Parliament – Bennett focuses on the gendered implications of UC. Her 'gendered impact assessment' includes analysis of the implications for gender roles and relationships, the potential for individuals' financial autonomy and gender inequalities within the household. On those indicators, Bennett's analysis suggests that UC scores badly. Of particular concern, she suggests, is the risk of greater economic dependence within the family arising from changes to non-means-tested benefits, payment provisions for UC and the likely decreased incentives for 'second earners'. Bennett concludes by arguing that when UC is considered alongside the Coalition's public expenditure cuts, it seems that gender equality is not a Coalition priority.

Harriet Churchill broadens the analysis of welfare reform under the Coalition in her examination of policy developments in the field of 'family support' (the term she adopts to capture a wide range of social policies and provisions that seek to assist families in caring for and raising children). As Churchill notes, 'the family' had become a key site of government intervention during New Labour's years in government, and she begins by examining the legacy they left, which she suggests included significant reductions in child poverty on the one hand, and rising economic and social divisions on the other. Churchill moves on to focus on the Coalition's work in this area during its first 18 months in government. She argues that developments have been significant and have been driven by austerity measures, social mobility initiatives, public service reforms and the government response to the 2011 summer 'riots'.

These, in turn, Churchill suggests, have been framed by two agendas – that of the Conservatives' 'smaller state, bigger society', and the Liberal Democrats' 'fairness and civil liberties' agenda. Churchill's review of developments highlights a number of trends, which include the erosion of financial support for families, cutbacks in children's services and an intensification of discourses that root poverty and social exclusion in poor parenting and family breakdown.

The first two chapters touch on changes to the housing benefits system in their analysis of the new UC and reforms to 'family support', respectively. In Chapter Three, Alan Murie develops the account in greater detail and locates it within a broader analysis of the direction of travel for housing policy under the Coalition government, as compared with its longer-term historical trajectory. Murie outlines a number of elements to the Coalition's approach to housing, which began to emerge shortly after it took office and which has been finalised with the 'Housing Strategy' published in November 2011. The approach includes, among other things: cuts in capital expenditure for new home-building; a cap on the amount of Housing Benefit available to private sector tenants; greater marketisation of housing association rents; reduction of tenants' rights in the social rented sector; incentives for private house-building and home-ownership; and the resurrection of the Right to Buy. Taken together, Murie suggests that the measures represent 'another redesign of housing in the welfare state'; a remake affected by the credit crunch, economic recession, level of government debt and the Conservatives' long-standing ambition to reduce the role of the state in housing. As such, it is a design characterised by residualisation and marketisation, within which, Murie argues, the poorest households will be most vulnerable in terms of living standards and housing security.

As discussed by Claire Callender in her chapter, the marketisation and privatisation agendas are also central to the changes to student financial support and funding for higher education (HE) institutions in England introduced by the Coalition government, which come into effect in 2012/13. As Callender argues, the changes are in line with the direction of reform of student financial support since 1990, which, under both Conservative and New Labour governments, has followed a 'cost-sharing agenda' involving shifting responsibility from the state to students and/or their families. However, the 2012/13 changes, she suggests, are the most radical and far-reaching to date, in part because they have been framed by the Coalition's austerity agenda, which meant that HE also had to take a share of public expenditure cuts. The changes centre on a reduction of 80% in government support for undergraduate teaching, with lost income to be replaced by an increase in maximum tuition fees from £3,290 to £9,000 per year, still payable up front with a government loan. The government has also taken measures to ensure that the level of fees is more variable across institutions. Having outlined the changes, Callender assesses them against the government's stated aims: 'putting HE on a sustainable financial footing', delivering 'a better student experience' and 'increased social mobility'. As she argues, while it will be years before we can fully evaluate the consequences of the changes, it is possible to identify a number of risks, including the potential for the exclusion of some from HE altogether, and the growing polarisation among those who do go to university based on the level of fees they are willing/able to tolerate.

Having pledged prior to the 2010 general election not to raise university tuition fees, their subsequent increase to a £9,000 maximum caused much embarrassment for the Liberal Democrat partners in the Coalition government, and exposed some of the tensions inherent in coalition policymaking. The politics of coalition is taken up more directly in the chapter by Sally Ruane, which focuses on the contemporary politics of health policy. The chapter centres more specifically on the Coalition's White Paper 'Equity and excellence: liberating the NHS' – issued weeks after the creation of the Coalition government and containing a package of proposals that had not figured in either coalition partners' general election manifestos or in the 'Coalition agreement'. Ruane argues that the first peacetime coalition government since the 1930s, combined with an official opposition that has just lost power after a lengthy period in office, provides a fairly unique political context for what she terms the 'NHS reform process' – 'that series of actions and developments relating to the launch and progress of the government's health reform package before and during the formal legislative process'. Ruane goes on to analyse the reform process through an examination of the responses to the White Paper of three institutions – the Liberal Democrat Party, the British Medical Association and the Labour Party. She concludes the chapter by delineating and discussing four interlinked themes around the contemporary politics of health care to have emerged from her analysis: the character and implications of institutional divisions and tensions; the influence of the medical process; the contradiction of between-party differences and the tightening of the neo-liberal grip on policy; and the absence of the public.

Part Two: Social policy in the developed and developing worlds

Gaby Ramia

In scholarship, as in practice, social policy is constantly internationalising. In contemporary times, there is a need for researchers within the field to come to terms with the adaptation of developed welfare states to financial and environmental crises and, in many countries, to the political responses by civil society and researchers to cutbacks in public services and expenditures. In the international arena, it is necessary to understand the challenges faced not only by developed countries, which for so long have been the mainstay of social policy scholarship, but also by the countries of the developing world. In addition, we must consider the interaction between developed and developing countries as they increasingly intermesh in the realms of trade, investment and various forms of partnering for development. It is imperative that we ask questions at this crucial time about how far social policies, as commonly understood in the richer countries, can be seen in the agendas of governments in countries not traditionally considered either 'models' or 'regimes' of social policy. Finally, social policies stemming from relationships within and among developing countries – which some have termed 'South–South' interactions – have become important, although are thus far neglected in research.

Collectively, these themes are taken up by the chapter authors of Part Two. This section of the *Social Policy Review* showcases strategically selected papers presented at the Social Policy Association Conference of July 2011 in Lincoln, UK. The chapters do not deal specifically or extensively with financial or environmental crisis management. They engage with social policy issues faced by both developed welfare states and developing countries and, in the case of one chapter, relations between and among countries. In doing so, the chapters assist in the process of extending social policy research, even comparative research, from the traditional focus on rich countries towards transnational questions and developments.

Part Two begins in Chapter Six with the analysis of a set of countries commonly considered relatively generous and well-developed welfare states, those of Scandinavia. Specifically, author Karen Nielsen Breidahl applies a comparative lens to examine the 'immigrant-targeted activation policies' of Norway, Sweden and Denmark. Asking if there is 'a fundamental contradiction between inclusive welfare policies and immigration', she first discusses the conceptualisation of activation policies and then conducts a comparative analysis of the three comparator countries. Finally, she explores the factors that may explain the similarities and differences between them. Briedahl's central finding is that the three countries differ in their treatment of immigrants, and that the relative welfare generosity of the Scandinavian welfare states cannot easily predict or underpin the progressive or regressive treatment of immigrants. More nuanced frameworks are required. In coming to this conclusion, she cites various explanatory factors, including 'country-specific political constellations' and 'national and transnational policy-learning mechanisms'.

In Chapter Seven, Stefan Kühner maintains the European focus, but of the Scandinavian countries he includes only Denmark. His other three comparators are Germany, France and the Netherlands. Thematically, he analyses whether Left or Right party incumbency matters to governmental approaches to welfare retrenchment. In doing so, he marshals fresh evidence to explore parties and retrenchment through an extensive scholarly review of perspectives and country case studies. Specifically, Kühner discusses accounts of 'why, when and how policymakers, particularly on the Left of the political spectrum, engage in "treacherous" welfare state retrenchment'. He probes three common conceptual perspectives and assesses the potential to consolidate them into one framework. Using his case study countries, he argues that there is analytical value in consolidation, mainly for the facilitation of 'a more holistic understanding' of the party–retrenchment relationship.

Moving away from Europe, in Chapter Eight, Rana Jawad changes geographical focus by analysing the social policy approaches of the Arab countries. She acknowledges the salience of evidence from the United Nations Development Programme (UNDP) of continuing serious shortfalls in social welfare across the region, including: 'youth unemployment, illiteracy and a poor record of democratisation and human capital'. Yet Jawad argues that the time is ripe for the social policy research community to consider the Arab countries as 'coming of age', and moving 'from black hole to spring'. Here, she refers to the recent movement in several countries towards democracy through popular protest and revolution in some cases, albeit in as yet evolving forms and with as yet hard to identify effects in the long term. Further, she contends that 'it has long been possible to examine the institutional and political discourses shaping social policy in the region'. It is also both possible and necessary to conceive of welfare and human well-being through social institutions and policies in the Arab world.

In the final analysis of the section, Chapter Nine considers the question of South–South interaction. This is somewhat novel in social policy, given that scholarly accounts in the field examining developing countries generally involve either only the countries of the South or their relations with countries, regions or multilateral institutions of the North. Specifically, authors Marian Urbina-Ferretjans and Rebecca Surender analyse the contribution of China's foreign policies and social investments to the development of Africa; or, as they describe it in the title, 'China's developmental model in Africa'. In doing so, the authors ask whether 'a new era in global social policy' is currently being ushered in, given that a nominally still-developing country such as China is able to (and does) provide social and economic carrots and sticks for African countries' development, primarily through transnational aid and social assistance interventions in and for the region. They discuss the 'instruments and mechanisms' used by China to deliver its foreign interventions and compares this with Western donor approaches, arguing that doing so helps to renew efforts to understand the contemporary nature of the social policies that cross and transcend the borders of the nation-state. This should, in turn, benefit the more encompassing and interdisciplinary study of globalisation.

Part Three: Severe crisis: social policy in most challenging circumstances

Kevin Farnsworth

As the dust has begun to settle on the economic crisis that began in the US in 2007, it is possible to stand back and begin to survey its impact on welfare states. The chapters that appear in this section of the *Review* summarise the impact of the crisis in five of the worst-hit economies. The overriding lesson is that the impact has been huge but that, three years after the collapse of Lehman Brothers in the US, which gave birth to the global economic crisis, the economic crisis is clearly not yet over.

The impact of the 'global' crisis was felt in almost every economy, although not to the same degree. And 'the' crisis turned out to be at least three distinct, but related, crises. The first began with the US banking crisis and the contagion that spread to a number of economies, but hit the UK, Ireland and Iceland especially hard. The chapters on the US, Ireland and Iceland in this volume capture the rapidity with which the banking crisis took hold and immediately began to shape the social policy responses within these economies. Ireland began to impose cuts in social expenditure immediately. The US pursued expansionary social policies in order to try to boost macro-economic demand. In both countries, the crisis was severe enough to force through change, but not severe enough to totally destabilise the economy. The case of Iceland was different, however, as Irving illustrates. In some ways, Iceland was unique in facing the most serious crisis of all the states here – a crisis of such magnitude that it could not realistically resolve. Here, its 'smallness' was actually helpful in pushing it towards the only possible response – voluntary bankruptcy. This, in turn, helped to facilitate a radical departure from previous neo-liberal solutions. In this respect, Iceland remains one of the few countries where the crisis appears to have led to a more favourable social policy environment. And only in Iceland does there appear to have been full recognition in mainstream politics that fundamental problems in the operation and management of capitalism was a major cause of the crisis. This is made clear in the chapters by Ramos-Diaz and Varela, Considine and Dukelow, and Papadopoulos and Roumpakis. They all point to the particular vulnerability of their country case studies as a result of the pursuit of pre-crisis neo-liberal measures – especially in property markets in the case of Spain and in chasing free-floating capital in the case of Ireland – but each one has pursued more of the same as an attempt to address their own crisis.

The second crisis – the rapid global economic slowdown, or Great Recession as it has come to be known – again spread to engulf a number of economies that had dodged the worst aspects of the initial banking crisis. This second crisis added to the financial woes of those hurt by the first wave, as Considine and Dukelow show in respect of Ireland and Béland and Wadden illustrate in the US, but it also had a heavy toll on the strong exporting nations. While the likes of Finland, Germany, Sweden and China escaped the first-wave 'crisis', they suffered the effects of the global economic slump. Germany and China, in particular, suffered major downturns in export markets, but in both countries, pre-emptive measures to boost demand, including through social policy measures, appear to have staved off deep recessions. Similarly, the Nordic countries appear to have survived the worst of the crisis and are dealing with recession rather than crisis management. They were also better positioned to forestall economic slowdown given their already large public policy infrastructure, not to mention their interventionist histories. For these reasons, Germany, Finland and Sweden have adjusted far more painlessly to the changed circumstance than countries that bore heavy costs during the first wave of the crisis.

The third crisis began to hit in 2009 and it is still being played out. It was caused by a combination of: (1) the costs borne by governments in their attempts to protect their industries (primarily banking, but also non-banking); (2) the costs associated with attempts to boost domestic demand and/or provide the growing number of unemployed with benefits; and (3) fiscal crises and the difficulties of servicing public debt. The extent to which economies have suffered in this third crisis again depends on a number of factors, but the effects have been especially marked in the worst-affected economies in the Eurozone. These economies have been affected by a combination of Eurozone-imposed macro-economic constraints, weak domestic demand, growing instability caused by financial speculation, and precarious borrowing environments. The option of quantitative easing, or printing money, which has been effectively employed in the US and the UK, has been denied to the Eurozone economies. In this scenario, the cost of borrowing has become prohibitively expensive. Only intervention by the European Central Bank and the International Monetary Fund (IMF) during 2010 and 2011 has saved these economies from total collapse. This combination of events applies especially to the three Eurozone countries included in this section. Each of the three economies, in fact, exhibits different macro-economic environments. They have different levels of debt and they have different welfare systems. But here the judgements of 'financial markets' have also proven to be important. Spain and Greece represent higher risks according to international credit-rating agencies, Ireland less so and the US least of all. As an illustration of the additional 'risks' imposed by membership of the Euro, Iceland's rating is above that of Greece despite the fact that it alone has so far actually defaulted on outstanding debt. But there are also some clear differences between these economies, and the pursuit of neo-liberal programmes tells only part of the story. The vulnerability of Greece, in particular, is traced by Papadopoulos and Roumpakis to the errors and misjudgements not just of the Greek government, but also of the Eurozone and the IMF some years prior to the crisis.

All the countries here have elected new political parties to government since the onset of the crisis. President Obama in the US is the longest serving and he came to power in the wake of the US banking crisis. It is clear that he faces an uphill battle to gain re-election in November 2012. Spain swung to the Right with the election of the Conservatives in 2011. Ireland has swung moderately to the Left with the election of a social democratic coalition in 2011. Iceland swung to the Left in 2009 and, in 2011, Greece, along with Italy, broke new ground with the 'installation' of unelected governments orchestrated by the European Union. But, with the exception of Iceland, political leadership appears not to matter to the key debates and outcomes. The chapters here illustrate that a range of external pressures, primarily the EU but also the IMF and the actions of the finance sector, have forced Greece, Spain and Ireland to adopt severe austerity measures. The US has also faced severe economic constraints but, as Béland and Wadden illustrate, these have largely been imposed by internal politics – the rise of the Right has succeeded in pushing through spending cuts and opposing tax rises. In Iceland, the decision not to bail out its major financial institutions has reduced the external and internal constraints, creating opportunities for new economic thinking and even welfare expansion.

Despite the enormity of the economic crisis on the worst-hit welfare states, therefore, there are some small signs of hope. While the success story of Iceland could yet become unravelled by challenges from governments that have lost as a result of its default, for now it points the way towards an alternative future, as Irving illustrates. Béland and Wadden also reveal a somewhat positive picture as far as the US is concerned. Although there is an ongoing ideological battle between Left and Right in the US, this is at least a more positive development than the pre-crisis neoliberal consensus. The apparent 'conversion' of the US to an enthusiastic supporter of Keynesianism is also a positive step. In addition to this, opposition to austerity in the US, Ireland, Greece and Spain has given some hope that politics may yet challenge the new austerity consensus. On this note, the IMF and the EU are beginning to waver on their positions on austerity as the impact of deep cuts are stalling international economic recovery.[1] The chapters here support the view that austerity measures are having a negative impact not only on the poorest and most vulnerable, but also on their wider economies.

What is also clear is that, without the buffer of national welfare states, the global economic crisis would have been deeper, more prolonged and even more damaging. Perhaps the most important lesson from the chapters presented here is that the struggle over welfare has to be as international as the economic crisis and that a failure to help defend welfare provision in the worst-hit economies will have negative consequences for all welfare states.

Note
[1] The speeches of Christine Lagarde (head of the IMF) and José Manuel Barroso (President of the European Commission) illustrate the tensions between public spending cuts and economic growth. Contrast the

reports of speeches by Lagarde in September 2011 in the *New York Times* (available at: www.nytimes.com/2011/08/31/opinion/christine-lagardes-tough-message.html), the *Daily Telegraph* (available at: www.telegraph.co.uk/finance/financialcrisis/8766381/Christine-Lagarde-hints-UK-pushing-too-hard-with-austerity-cuts.html) and the *Financial Times* (available at: www.ft.com/cms/s/0/dec1e60a-da39-11e0-bc99-00144feabdc0.html#axzz1jEnzYG3p).

José Manuel Barroso stated in a speech delivered in October 2011 that 'fiscal consolidation has to be part of wide-ranging reform to how the European public sector operates. It can work and it is working.' But later in the speech he stated: 'As you may have guessed, dear friends, the Commission does not believe that cutbacks are the solution to Europe's challenges' (available at: http://europa.eu/rapid/pressReleasesAction.do?reference=SPEECH/11/663&type=HTML).

Part One

Current developments

ONE

Universal Credit: overview and gender implications

Fran Bennett

Introduction and background[1]

A simpler benefits (or tax/benefits) system has always been the 'holy grail' of social security reform in the UK.[2] New social security ministers tend to come into office unable to fathom why their predecessors have been unable to achieve this – and leave office older and wiser. But after the introduction of the new tax credits in 2003 by the Labour government, critiques of the existing system as complex and confusing for claimants increased (eg Community Links et al, 2007; Bennett et al, 2009); and think tanks, and the government itself, developed variations on the idea of a 'single working-age benefit' (Freud, 2007; Brewer et al, 2008). The proposals from Left and Right often shared similar preoccupations and proposed similar benefit structures (Sainsbury and Stanley, 2007; Martin, 2009; Kay, 2010; Taylor et al, 2010). The core suggestion in most was to merge means-tested benefits/tax credits for adults in and out of employment, and often payments for some additional costs (such as for children and housing) as well.

It was the scheme proposed by the Centre for Social Justice (CSJ, 2009), however, that proved most influential with the Conservative–Liberal Democrat Coalition government taking office in May 2010. In part, this was because of a shared ideological perspective – in itself hardly surprising, as the Secretary of State for Work and Pensions, Iain Duncan Smith MP, had set up the CSJ before coming into government. This perspective included an abhorrence of so-called 'welfare dependency' (Lister and Bennett, 2010) – a concept that seems to have expanded to include reliance on tax credits in work, not just benefits out of work. The Secretary of State did identify the more pragmatic issue of disincentives to work (when commenting on why migrants rather than British-born claimants had taken many of the newly created jobs).[3] But a simultaneous focus on 'welfare dependency' and cultural habits handed down through the generations appeared to contradict this rationalist perspective, and formed the backdrop to the government's welfare reform proposals (Duncan Smith, 2011).

Other key elements in the context for 'welfare reform' were the financial crisis and recession, and the Coalition government's determination to reduce the deficit as fast as possible. The social security budget bore a significant proportion of the immediate cuts and spending review plans (IFS, 2010), and ministers highlighted this explicitly to demonstrate that they were protecting other areas of expenditure: 'particular focus has been given to reducing welfare costs and wasteful spending' (HMT, 2010a, summary, p 5). This was, to say the least, a challenging time for a major reform of the benefits system.

This chapter examines this reform of the benefits system in order to draw out its gender implications in particular. It outlines the major aims and elements of the government's proposals for 'Universal Credit' (UC) (the new means-tested benefit amalgamating benefits in and out of work, to be introduced from 2013), highlighting some general claims made about it and concerns expressed by its critics. It proceeds to a gender analysis of the proposals, focusing on the implications for women in couples, drawing on the work of the Women's Budget Group. It is argued that it is not only the impact of policy changes in terms of the numbers of men and women affected – often the focus of formal gender impact assessments – that is important, but also the implications for gender roles and relationships; the potential for individuals' financial autonomy; and gender inequalities within the household. From this perspective, the introduction of UC and other policy proposals in the Welfare Reform Bill 2011 raise a number of concerns.

Proposals for reform: overview

On taking office, the Coalition government was quick to develop its proposal to introduce a 'Universal Credit'. The government's two central aims were to create a simpler system and to improve work incentives. The rationale for the changes, and the outline proposals themselves, were outlined in a consultation document (DWP, 2010a), followed by a White Paper (DWP, 2010b) and the Welfare Reform Bill 2011, which was still being debated in Parliament at the time of writing. 'Universal' Credit was a misnomer, as this was to be a super-means-tested benefit that incorporated others. There did not, however, seem to be any recognition by the government that the predominance of means testing in the UK benefits system was integrally related to the two problems it had identified as key – complexity and disincentives. Indeed, the proposals will lead to a further extension of means testing, by time-limiting or abolishing some forms of the Employment and Support Allowance, paid to those too ill or disabled to work.

UC will be phased in from October 2013, starting with new claimants. It will amalgamate benefits/tax credits that currently have varying purposes and that for couples may be claimed by, and paid to, one partner or the other. Instead, UC will be claimed and owned by couples jointly, and usually paid to one partner. The closest parallel is joint claims for income-based Jobseeker's Allowance, introduced recently for childless couples and now being extended. But the absorption of help with housing costs into UC in addition makes decisions about the payee even more significant.

Currently, benefits/tax credits are paid at different intervals, and withdrawn at different rates in a certain order. For example, tax credits reduce entitlement to Housing and Council Tax Benefit, and Child Tax Credit is withdrawn after Working Tax Credit. UC, instead, is one benefit, and will be withdrawn simultaneously across all its elements. The government has stated (Department for Work and Pensions [DWP] press release, 13 September 2011) that UC will be paid monthly, though it recognises the need for some exceptions, with interim and bridging loans and the provision of budgeting support (DWP, 2011b). Payments on account will replace budgeting loans from the discretionary Social Fund, and there will also be interim and bridging payments for some.

This amalgamation of benefits and tax credits can be seen as one 'simplifying' element of UC. The other is to withdraw benefit at a single taper rate, of 65% (higher than the 55% suggested by the CSJ in its proposed scheme). The single taper is also seen as improving work incentives. Earnings will reduce UC by 65% of each (net) pound above a certain level of disregarded (ignored) income. The disregard amount will vary depending on the family unit, with higher amounts for those with children, increasing with each additional child.[4] However, help with housing costs will reduce this to a 'floor' (minimum) disregard, also varying with the type of family.

The goal is to make every hour of work pay, including 'mini-jobs' of a few hours per week. The government is critical of the current system, in which single unemployed claimants can earn only £5 a week before their benefit is reduced pound for pound, and in which at least 16 hours' work per week is necessary to qualify for the more generous Working

Tax Credit (with a bonus at 30 hours). In recent years, this issue had also been taken up by think tanks and lobby groups (eg Bell et al, 2007) and formed part of the context for the government's reforms.

A radical feature of UC is to abolish the distinction between being 'in' and 'out' of work – and also, in theory at least, to extend conditionality to everyone within its range. The positive incentive of additional help to those in employment for a certain numbers of hours per week, described earlier, will be replaced by the extension of conditionality for those in work until their (family) earnings reach a certain level. Conditionality will be more varied in nature, rather than being tied to receipt of particular benefits. It will apply to both partners in a couple on UC, but will be modified for the partner designated by the couple as the 'lead carer' for children; for those with significant caring duties for disabled/elderly people, or very young children, conditionality will be waived altogether.[5]

Claims for UC will be 'digital by default'; the government expects the majority of claimants to apply and manage their claim online, including reporting changes of circumstances. Couples will apply jointly, and either one, or both, can manage the claim. Changes in earnings, however, will be reported instead via a new HM Revenue and Customs computer system for employers (PAC, 2011). This 'real-time' information in theory means quick adjustments of UC on a monthly basis to reflect changes in earnings. Help with childcare costs will be delivered via the UC monthly in arrears.

Child Benefit and other non-means-tested benefits will continue outside UC, at least for now – although Child Benefit is being frozen for three years until 2013 and the non-means-tested Disability Living Allowance (for additional costs) will be replaced by a more restricted 'Personal Independence Payment'. Council Tax Benefit will be devolved to local authorities, who will be asked to devise their own schemes, albeit with a 10% cut in the budget; pensioners are to be protected from any shortfall in benefit, which presumably means that working-age benefit claimants may see more than a 10% cut. At the time of writing (December 2011), the government had not yet announced its plans on 'passported' benefits (such as free prescriptions and free school meals), but had asked the Social Security Advisory Committee to investigate this and to report in early 2012. Community Care Grants and Crisis Loans from the Social Fund will be abolished, with local authorities running replacement schemes, but with no ring-fenced funding and little central direction.[6]

The government has said that 2.7 million households will be better off, and poverty will be reduced by some 350,000 children and 600,000 adults, due to UC (DWP press release, 17 February 2011).[7] This, it argues, will result from both higher benefit levels for some claimants and the greater likelihood that people will take up their entitlements when all elements of benefit are claimed together. The government also says that UC will increase the numbers in jobs – even without using the 'dynamic' modelling, based on predictions of behavioural change, that was deployed by the CSJ to claim significant increases in employment as an outcome of its own single working-age benefit scheme, the inspiration for UC.

Responses to the reform proposals

The central goals advanced by the government – to simplify the social security system and to improve work incentives – were generally welcomed; indeed, it is hard to see how to dissent from these laudable aims. The overall response to UC itself was also largely positive. Many 'stakeholders' agree with the integration of benefits, as demonstrated by the range of recent proposals for a 'single working-age benefit', noted earlier. There has also been a welcome for the government's determination to tackle the administrative hiatus caused by the disjuncture between 'non-work' and 'work' and to eliminate 'cliff edges' (where entitlement to a benefit is abruptly terminated as a claimant's status shifts), and its promise to make all work pay.

Public attitudes became (even) less sympathetic towards unemployed claimants over the New Labour years (Sefton, 2009; see also Park et al, 2011). The government also claims that the public is sympathetic to the controversial 'benefit cap', under which benefit entitlement for some 50,000 households on out-of-work benefits will be limited to the average weekly wage earned by 'working households', regardless of the number of children they have (DWP, 2011d, p 2).

However, there has also been a range of more critical responses, from academics, voluntary organisations and others.[8] First of all, as the government acknowledges, there will be losers as well as gainers from the introduction of UC; and, although transitional protection will mask losses temporarily, this will not compensate for any cuts to benefits introduced in the run-up to UC. The Institute for Fiscal Studies has found that the net direct effect of the Coalition government's tax and benefits changes will be to increase both absolute and relative poverty (Brewer et al, 2011b).

In addition, despite the consensus about the importance of the government's central welfare reform goals, there is some scepticism about whether they will be achieved. One key objective, simplification, has been seen as more apparent than real – as noted, for example, by Gregg (2011) in oral evidence to the Public Bill Committee. UC does not radically simplify the benefits it brings together. Devolution of Council Tax Benefit, Community Care Grants and some Crisis Loans to local authority level will result in these becoming more discretionary and potentially susceptible to a 'postcode lottery', decreasing rather than increasing certainty for claimants.

Another key goal, as noted, is to improve incentives. This does not seem to include incentives to save, as the Income Support capital limit of £16,000 is being introduced into UC (rather than there being no capital rule, as with tax credits). But even in terms of incentives to work, the position is more complex than it may initially appear. Ministerial pronouncements sometimes seem to confuse the unemployment trap (the relationship between benefits out of work and income in work) and the poverty trap (the rate of withdrawal of tax, contributions and benefits for people already earning as they earn more). Also, as explored later, childcare costs are often not factored into the discussion.

Another set of arguments has concerned process issues – such as reliance on complex computer systems on the one hand, and low digital literacy among those on low incomes on the other (PAC, 2011). Some technology experts are predicting costly failure (see Seddon, 2011). There is scepticism about the ability of HM Revenue and Customs to come up with its 'real-time' information system for employers on time for the introduction of UC. In addition, many major issues have yet to be resolved, including how help with mortgage interest will be paid and what will be done about passported benefits.

Gender analysis: introduction

From the initial consultation document onwards, concerns were expressed about the gender implications of the government's proposals. A response from Oxfam (Veitch, 2010) suggested that the gender impact assessment should go further than just comparing the number of women and men affected by benefits/tax credit changes and calculating the resources that would be transferred from women to men (and vice versa) by any changes. Such an assessment should also examine the make-up and labelling of any transfer of resources between women and men and the impact of any such transfers on gender roles and relationships, and consider the effects on the degree of financial security and autonomy enjoyed by women and men, on their caring responsibilities, and on inequalities within the household, at the point of any change and over the life course.[9] These principles were cited by the government in its equality impact assessment of the welfare reform White Paper (DWP, 2010c), but not followed through.

Those concerned about the gender implications of the Welfare Reform Bill – including, in particular, the Women's Budget Group (WBG) – agreed that benefit simplification and improving work incentives were laudable aims, but had concerns about the design of UC and other aspects of the Welfare Reform Bill, which they believed could work against the government's duty to promote gender equality. They were concerned in particular about access to income – both earnings and benefits – for individuals living in couples[10] because of its potential impact on women's financial autonomy. But they also believed that the reform proposals took insufficient account of the nature of modern families and the lives of those on low incomes, and so might undermine some of the government's other policy goals – including encouraging committed couple relationships and tackling child poverty. The WBG, which has been involved in gender analysis of Budgets and spending plans in the UK since the early 1990s, has consistently argued that taking full account of gender implications not only facilitates progress towards gender equality, but also makes it more likely that policies will achieve their own objectives more comprehensively. Much of the detailed gender analysis of the Bill emanated from the WBG (eg, WBG, 2011a, 2011b), although it was echoed by many other organisations interested in welfare reform (eg FPI, 2011; see also MacLeavy, 2011).

Access to independent income: earnings and non-means-tested benefits

The government's focus on getting one person in each household into work as a priority should be helpful to lone parents, especially those trying out 'mini-jobs'. But the WBG argued that more couples in the UK now have two earners; and research shows that (potential) 'second earners' (often women) in couples, especially those with young children, are particularly sensitive to incentives.[11] Under UC, however, benefit withdrawal as incomes rise will be much faster for many prospective or actual 'second earners' than it is now – even leaving aside childcare costs (see later). In part, this is because couples will only get one 'disregard' (income ignored before it counts against benefit) between them; so if the 'first earner' has used that up, the 'second earner's' earnings will reduce UC from the first pound. This is the situation now with tax credits. But under UC, the withdrawal rate will be higher than the current tax credits taper for many.[12]

Support for childcare costs has already been reduced under the government's expenditure cuts, so that instead of Working Tax Credit meeting 80% of childcare costs up to certain ceilings, it now meets only 70%; this will continue under UC. The government has agreed to additional resources to extend assistance to those in 'mini-jobs' of a few hours per week (although this money is being taken from elsewhere in the budget for implementation of the reforms). And the 'poverty trap' as income rises is likely to become more visible under UC because 'real-time' information from employers will be used to reduce benefit more quickly in line with any additional income (see also Brewer et al, 2011a; Hirsch and Beckhelling, 2011). To date, the potential effect of this development seems to have been insufficiently recognised.

If these facets of UC result in fewer 'second earners' in couples, this would not only mean fewer women (and men) with access to an income of their own, it would also work against the aims of the sharing of parenting roles supported by the government (HMG, 2011). Personalised conditionality for UC will encourage both individuals in couples, where appropriate, into the labour market, but the message given by the higher withdrawal rate will contradict this for many potential 'second earners'. And while the government boasts of taking low-paid earners out of tax by raising the tax threshold in real terms, many 'second earners' will lose some two thirds or more of each pound under UC.

The government seems relaxed about the likelihood of fewer dual-earner couples, saying that increased income for the main earner will help families achieve their preferred work–life balance (DWP, 2010c). (Analysis by the Institute for Fiscal Studies [Brewer et al, 2011a] demonstrated that one-earner couples would be particular gainers under UC.) But choices exercised by couples 'together' are not the same as individual choices, and may not have an equal impact on these individuals' opportunities and outcomes (Bennett et al, 2012). This proposal has been described as tilting the 'architecture of choice' (Lister, 2011a) against dual-earner families, while the government fails to problematise diverging gender roles; and the rules will apply to couples without any caring responsibilities as well as those who have them. The various versions of tax credits introduced by previous Labour governments have been criticised in similar ways (see, eg, Bennett, 2010). But under UC, withdrawal of benefit will be more marked – and more immediate in its impact – for many; what is not yet clear is whether this will be outweighed by the impact of (stricter) conditionality being applied to potential 'second earners' in couples on UC.

The government also argues that its main priority is to help at least one person into work in order to reduce the number of workless households. But it is important to take a dynamic perspective here. The impact on the income profile and gender roles of those dissuaded from returning to the labour market could be long-lasting. And lone parents who were in employment as partners in intact couples are less likely to be jobless after family breakdown (Marsh et al, 2001); ensuring that 'second earners' have adequate incentives to enter paid work is, therefore, also relevant to achieving this key government aim.

An alternative route to an independent income for individuals is via non-means-tested benefits. The government decided to retain Carers' Allowance, which at one time seemed in danger of being swallowed up in UC. This was an important decision for many women, because Carers' Allowance is both non-contributory and non-means-tested, and gives an (albeit low) income to carers looking after a disabled/elderly person if they provide a regular and substantial amount of care and the person being cared for qualifies for the medium/higher rate of Disability Living Allowance; in February 2010, according to government statistics, 360,400 women received it, compared with 139,500 men.[13] There are concerns about the knock-on effects on Carers' Allowance of the introduction of Personal Independence Payments, as this will incorporate cuts in entitlement for disabled people, and therefore potentially their carers. To date, no official impact assessment has been produced of the (gendered) effects on carers.

In addition, there is great concern about time-limiting contributory Employment and Support Allowance to a year for the work-related activity group (those expected to return to work at some point). Employment and Support Allowance is replacing Incapacity Benefit and Income Support for those who are too ill or disabled to work, and has both contributory and means-tested elements. It is paid after an assessment period at a lower level for people in the work-related activity group, and at a higher level for those in the support group (those not expected to work again). Time-limiting will affect more men than women, according to the equality impact assessment, but where the woman is the claimant, means-tested compensation will be less likely (DWP, 2011c, para 16); a partner's earnings would be likely to take the couple above the means-tested benefit limit. For both men and women in couples, this cut means that they will become dependent on their partners after a year just because they still cannot work. This is also likely to result in more in-work poverty (Bennett and Sutherland, 2011).

With these proposals and the impact of UC on potential 'second earners', a clear theme emerges: while the government is keen to attack 'welfare dependency', it seems much less concerned about economic dependence within the family, and appears to hark back to a previous model of a single breadwinner family that many argue is no longer appropriate today (Esping-Andersen, 2009; FPI, 2011; Lister, 2011a).

How should Universal Credit be paid for couples?

As with current means-tested benefits/tax credits, whoever UC is paid to, it will not constitute an *independent* income in the same sense as earnings or non-means-tested benefits. This is because, for couples, it involves joint assessment of needs and resources. Couples are being treated as one unit, with sharing of resources assumed, as with all UK means-tested benefits. So an individual's income is affected by her/his partner's presence, actions and resources; and if one partner's income and/or assets are high enough for the couple to be ineligible, the other partner will get no UC. It is therefore also important to consider wider issues about access to an independent income for individuals, whether via earnings or non-means-tested benefits, as discussed earlier.

UC also involves joint claiming, ownership and liability for couples. This suggests a view of joint responsibility as unproblematic. However, debate has taken place recently in the UK about the recipient of means-tested benefits/tax credits in couples, in particular in relation to in-work support and help with the costs of children. Several arguments have been made. One is that the partner with the main responsibility for looking after the children's day-to-day needs (often, though not always, the mother) should receive the benefit for that purpose – which should also be labelled if possible. Recent government research (Hall and Pettigrew, 2008) showed claimants of Child Tax Credit identifying it as money for children and spending it accordingly. The 'main carer' is also more likely to be the partner with lower, or no, other income, reinforcing the case for paying her/him this money. More generally, a case can be made that relationships are likely to be more equal and balanced if both members of the couple have some income of their own; and cohabiting couples have been shown to be less likely to split up if they have more equal incomes (Brines and Joyner, 1999) (though, as noted earlier, independent income is not the same as means-tested income). There is clear evidence that economic abuse is frequently a component of domestic violence

(Sharp, 2008).The principle of a welfare contract, which the Coalition government has promoted, also suggests that individual conditionality under UC should be matched by a more individualised right to benefit (as in Australia) (Ingold, 2011; see also Sainsbury and Weston, 2010).

A leaked paper (*The Guardian*, 14 September 2011) suggested that the government should consider paying UC for couples to women (though it is probable that this would not be allowed under equality legislation). But the government is proposing that couples must have a single payment of UC in the majority of cases, nominating a partner to receive it, with regulations allowing (as now) for the splitting of benefit in certain exceptional circumstances only. In practice, for most couples, this means the decision they must make is about which account UC should be paid into; and the government (DWP, 2011b) notes that this could be a joint account. So the question is perhaps not 'Who should be paid UC in couples?' but 'How should UC be paid in couples?'. It is unclear as yet what will happen if the couple cannot agree. And though many couples may be stable, others may be breaking up, or getting together, or may contain children from previous relationships. How best to deliver welfare to *all* individuals within the household should be a key question for policymakers (Price, 2011); it is not clear that this is currently a prominent concern for the government (eg, see HMT, 2010b).

This is not (as often described) a delivery issue, but one that goes to the heart of UC design.The government justifies a single payment to couples in three ways.[14] First, such an arrangement would resemble wages. But, as noted, many couples now have two earners and UC is jointly claimed, owned and assessed; none of these is true of wages. The government argues that 'interference' would undermine couples' responsibility in managing their affairs. But the government is 'interfering' in any case, by making couples choose one partner to receive the payment. It also says that decisions over the allocation of resources are best made by households themselves.[15] But whoever UC is paid to, or even if it is split, couples can decide how to spend it – it is just that 'nudges' (such as labelling payments for children, and paying them to the main carer) seem to work in terms of maximising welfare for individuals within the household.And logically, if the government thinks choice is important, it should also allow couples to choose to split the payment between them, in the proportions they prefer. (Further, the process of making an informed choice about how to split UC could be valuable in terms of both partners considering what costs it is intended to cover, the elements that make it up and how it should be spent.[16])

Giving couples choice is clearly preferable to automatic payment of UC to the 'main earner'. But 'choice' takes place in a context of gender inequalities, within as well as outside the household. A recent House of Commons Written Answer notes that 'particularly in low-income households ... men sometimes benefit at the expense of women from shared household income'.[17] The Millennium Cohort Study showed that one in four mothers do not even have a small amount to spend on themselves, rising to one in two in households on under 60% of median income (Hansen et al, 2010).

The inclusion of help with housing costs in UC – and the government's determination to pay Housing Benefit direct to more tenants, rather than direct to landlords – means that payment could be made to the partner who is not the tenant (or mortgage-payer). This can happen sometimes now with Housing Benefit (though not with support for mortgage interest, which is paid to the lender). But this is currently not part of one big payment for virtually all the household's needs, paid monthly to one partner, as it will be with UC.

Alternatives to the government's preferred option of requiring couples to choose one payee for UC have been proposed. One argument that should be persuasive is that the government's own aim of encouraging committed coupledom may be undermined by this arrangement, as it could act as a financial disincentive to single people considering moving in with a new partner. Arrangements for UC must be flexible enough to work for all kinds of families, not just long-term stable married couples. In addition, if only one person is dealing with most of the money coming into the household, this does not encourage the financial capability that the government believes all individuals should acquire; indeed, if this arrangement is pursued, at retirement age – when the state pension is paid to each individual, rather than jointly – one partner may have had little experience of dealing with payments in and out of their own account.

However, splitting the UC payment is not a straightforward option from a gender perspective either. Lewis and Bennett (2004) discuss the broad concept of 'individualisation' in relation to gender. When it comes to the social security system, as already noted, paying half of a jointly assessed benefit to one partner in a couple is not the same as facilitating access to an independent income for both individuals. In addition, what little research has been done in the UK suggests the possibility of men in particular seeing their half of the joint benefit as personal spending money and using it accordingly, based on the finding that men are more likely to be seen as having a right to personal spending, whereas women's spending on home and children is seen (by men and women) as their personal spending (see Goode et al, 1998).[18]

Payment of the whole of UC could be made to the 'main carer'. The government has not suggested this, despite the proposal that couples nominate a 'lead carer' for the purposes of conditionality, mentioned earlier. It is possible that, if pursued, this option could result in a backlash from those (mainly men) who would thus be deprived of any income for themselves but who would be likely to have to fulfil more onerous conditions. And this proposal would of course not apply to those couples who were childless.

Frequency of payment

Currently, payment periods for different benefits/tax credits vary. Claimants of tax credits can choose whether to receive them weekly or four-weekly. Many major means-tested benefits are paid fortnightly. The government proposes to pay UC monthly. This, it says, is the 'modern' way, and resembles the way wages are paid. But at least one in five, if not more, employees is in fact still paid weekly or fortnightly,[19] and the government itself cites evidence that only about half those earning under £10,000 a year are currently paid monthly (DWP, 2011b). Moreover, monthly payment does not fit well with many low-income families' current patterns of managing their money.

The government says that those who find the transition to monthly budgeting difficult could be given help with budgeting, including financial advice and interim and bridging loans. But this would be costly and labour-intensive – and presumably it would mean having to apply, thus admitting that you were failing. Nearly 40% of families with children in the bottom fifth of the income distribution already run out of money at the end of the week/month (always, most often or more often than not) (Maplethorpe et al, 2010); so this is not just a problem for a small minority unable to budget. Concerns have been expressed that moving to monthly payment is likely to hit women in particular, because they are often responsible for managing the overall budget in low-income families and/or the more frequent spending on daily/weekly items that can be cut back in quality and quantity (unlike monthly direct debits). When the budget is tight, we know that mothers are often the 'shock absorbers' who bear the cost (Lister, 2006).

In this and other ways, the Coalition government's desire to help claimants towards paid work seems to be blinding it to the realities of everyday life on a low income. And the common division of labour in many low-income couples with children in particular means that the costs of less frequent payments are more likely to fall on women – and cause increased stress for families trying to stay together in difficult times (Bennett, 2011).

Conclusion

As the Family and Parenting Institute (FPI, 2011) has said:

> It is arguable that the cumulative effect of cuts to child benefit ..., the abolition of the health in pregnancy grant, restrictions to the Sure Start maternity grant, reductions in the childcare element of working tax credit, along with the design of Universal Credit, could all serve to undermine the financial independence of women in families. When considered in tandem with the cuts to public services and reductions in the numbers of employees in the public sector ... the impact of the emergency Budget and spending review could be regarded as biased against women.

And it asks: 'How can policy be recalibrated to ensure gender equality is also at the heart of welfare reform and family policy?'.

Facilitating individual access to income should not be seen as a threat to family stability, but as having the potential to strengthen it; financial security for both partners can be seen as a more secure basis for achieving flourishing relationships, and more flexible gender roles are more likely to result in stability and equality in couples in the UK today. But some provisions of the Welfare Reform Bill 2011, as this chapter has shown, may instead result in greater economic dependence within the family. These include changes to non-means-tested benefits, as well as the potential impact of decreased incentives for 'second earners' and payment provisions for UC. Moreover, as the FPI sets out (above), this sits alongside the gendered impact of the expenditure cuts (TUC, 2010), which the minister for equalities had reportedly foreshadowed in a letter to fellow ministers (*The Guardian*, 3 August 2010). The equality impact assessment of UC (DWP, 2011a) implies that the government is prioritising other social goals (such as incentivising a 'first earner' in families, and making benefit as much like wages as possible in order to prefigure the experience of being in work) over its duties on gender equality and other broader social goals. It is not surprising, perhaps, that in autumn 2011 polling by the government showed its support falling among women in particular (see, eg, *The Guardian*, 5 October 2011).

Notes

[1] This chapter draws (with permission) on an article, 'Universal credit: the gender impact', written by the author in a personal capacity for *Poverty* (issue 140, October 2011), the journal of the Child Poverty Action Group, as well as on submissions and briefings by/for the Women's Budget Group (WBG) on universal credit and the Welfare Reform Bill (available at: http://www.wbg.org.uk/RRB_Briefings. htm) and a paper by the author for the 2011 Social Policy Association conference, 'Money matters in low/moderate income families and the gender implications of welfare reform in the UK'. The author's work on this policy area has benefited from input from other WBG members, in particular Ruth Lister and Susan Himmelweit; she alone is responsible for any errors. The WBG is an independent voluntary organisation of individuals from academia, non-governmental organisations and trades unions that scrutinises the gender implications of government budgets and spending plans.

[2] The term 'holy grail' is from Baroness Lister of Burtersett during the Second Reading of the Welfare Reform Bill 2011, House of Lords *Hansard*, 13 September 2011, col 726.

[3] See, for example, the reports of a speech in Madrid by Iain Duncan Smith MP, Secretary of State for Work and Pensions, on 1 July 2011.

[4] The government has recently announced increases in the disregards to try to take account of the impact of localising Council Tax Benefit.

[5] For a discussion of 'rights and responsibilities' in the social security system, including in particular conditionality in relation to paid employment, see Griggs and Bennett (2009).

[6] A series of policy briefing notes issued by the DWP sets out more detail in certain areas (see: http://services.parliament.uk/bills/2010-11/welfarereform/documents.html).

[7] The Institute for Fiscal Studies suggests that 450,000 children will be lifted out of relative poverty in 2020–21 as a result of the introduction of UC (see Brewer et al, 2011b).

[8] Much of this has appeared in discussion or in briefings sent to MPs (by organisations in the Welfare Reform Consortium and others) for debates on the Welfare Reform Bill, and so is not yet published in academic sources.

[9] These principles were adapted from those discussed in Daly and Rake (2003).

[10] This chapter focuses on male–female couples. However, UC will also affect same-sex couples.

[11] For example, the presentation by Richard Blundell, Institute for Fiscal Studies, to HM Treasury on 25 January 2011 highlights women whose youngest child is of school age as a group that responds strongly to the structure of, and changes in, taxes and benefits.

[12] The government highlights the 96% withdrawal rate for some people; but this group (on Housing and Council Tax Benefit as well as tax credits) is relatively small, especially among couples. See the 'notes on second earners', written by Susan Himmelweit (available at: http://www.wbg.org.uk/RRB_Briefings.htm).

[13] Data from DWP benefits statistics, available at: http://statistics.dwp.gov.uk/asd/index.php?page=tabtool (accessed 1 October 2010); DWP 5% sample statistics, available at: http://83.244.183.180/5pc/tabtool.html (accessed 4 March 2011).

[14] The government's arguments were discussed by Baroness Lister (2011b) during the Grand Committee stage of the Welfare Reform Bill in the House of Lords.

[15] These two justifications may in fact refer to the desire to minimise payments to third parties (such as landlords).

[16] As Professor Susan Himmelweit of the Open University, a member of the WBG, has argued.

[17] House of Commons *Hansard*, Written Answers, 14 March 2011, col 126W.

[18] This question was also explored in semi-structured interviews with men and women conducted by the author and Dr Sirin Sung as part of the Within Household Inequalities and Public Policy research project (project 5 of the Gender Equality Network, see: www.genet.ac.uk), funded by the Economic and Social Research Council.

[19] Figures of 18.1% from the Office for National Statistics (Table G89.1, *Annual Survey of Hours and Earnings* [2010], based on employee jobs in the UK for workers on adult rates whose pay was unaffected by absence), supported by figures of one in five from the *Labour Force Survey* for October–December 2010, and the *Family Resources Survey* (personal correspondence from labour market researchers, September 2011).

References

Bell, K., Brewer, M. and Phillips, D. (2007) *Lone parents and 'mini-jobs'*, York: York Publishing Services for Joseph Rowntree Foundation.

Bennett, F. (2010) 'Gender analysis of transfer policies: unpicking the household', in V. Uberoi, A. Coutts, D. Halpern and I. Mclean (eds) *Options for Britain II: cross cutting policy issues – changes and challenges*, Oxford: Wiley/Blackwell and Political Quarterly, pp 100–16.

Bennett, F. (for Women's Budget Group) (2011) 'Universal Credit: frequency of payment'. Available at: http://wbg.org.uk/pdfs/Universal-credit-frequency-of-payment-Sept-2011.pdf

Bennett, F. and Sutherland, H. (2011) *The importance of independent income: understanding the role of non-means-tested earnings replacement benefits*, ISER Working Paper Series 2011-09, Colchester: Institute of Social and Economic Research, University of Essex; also published as Barnett Papers in Social Research 2011-1, Oxford: Department of Social Policy and Intervention, University of Oxford.

Bennett, F., Brewer, M. and Shaw, J. (2009) *Understanding the costs of compliance of benefits and tax credits*, London: Institute for Fiscal Studies. Available at: www.ifs.org.uk/publications/4558

Bennett, F., De Henau, J., Himmelweit, S. and Sung, S. (2012) 'Financial togetherness and autonomy within couples', in J. Scott, S. Dex and A.C. Plagnol (eds) *Gendered lives: gender inequalities in production and reproduction*, Cheltenham: Edward Elgar.

Brewer, M., Saez, E. and Shephard, A. (2008) *Means-testing and tax rates on earnings*, London: Institute for Fiscal Studies (for Mirrlees review of taxation).

Brewer, M., Browne, J. and Jin, W. (2011a) *Universal Credit: a preliminary analysis*, Briefing Note 116, London: Institute for Fiscal Studies.

Brewer, M., Browne, J. and Joyce, R. (2011b) *Child and working-age poverty from 2010 to 2020*, London: Institute for Fiscal Studies.

Brines, J. and Joyner, K. (1999) 'The ties that bind: principles of cohesion in cohabitation and marriage', *American Sociological Review* 64(3): 333–56.

CSJ (Centre for Social Justice) (2009) *Dynamic benefits: towards welfare that works*, London: CSJ.

Community Links, Low Income Tax Reform Group and Child Poverty Action Group (2007) *Interact: benefits, tax credits and moving into work*, London: Community Links, LITRG and CPAG.

Daly, M. and Rake, K. (2003) *Gender and the welfare state: care, work and welfare in Europe and the USA*, Cambridge: Polity Press.

Duncan Smith, I. (2011) 'Welfare reform: the wider context', Keith Joseph memorial lecture, 15 March. Available at: www.conservativehome. blogs.com/files/ids-speech.pdf (accessed 10 December 2011).

DWP (Department for Work and Pensions) (2010a) *21st century welfare*, Cm 7913, London: The Stationery Office.

DWP (2010b) *Universal Credit: welfare that works*, White Paper, Cm 7957, London: The Stationery Office.

DWP (2010c) *Equality impact assessment for 'Universal Credit: welfare that works' (Cm 7957)*, London: DWP.

DWP (2011a) *Welfare Reform Bill: Universal Credit – equality impact assessment*, November, London: DWP.

DWP (2011b) *Universal Credit policy briefing note 2: the payment proposal*, London: DWP.

DWP (2011c) *Time limiting contributory employment and support allowance to one year for those in the work related activity group: equality impact assessment*, London: DWP.

DWP (2011d) *Household Benefit cap: equality impact assessment*, London: DWP.

Esping-Andersen, G. (2009) *The incomplete revolution: adapting to women's new roles*, Cambridge: Polity Press.

FPI (Family and Parenting Institute) (2011) *Families in an age of austerity: how tax and benefit reform will affect UK families*, London: FPI.

Freud, D. (2007) *Reducing dependency, increasing opportunity: options for the future of welfare reform*, London: Department for Work and Pensions.

Goode, J., Callender, C. and Lister, R. (1998) *Purse or wallet? Gender inequalities and income distribution within families on benefit*, London: Policy Studies Institute.

Gregg, P. (2011) Oral evidence to Public Bill Committee on Welfare Reform Bill, 24 March.

Griggs, J. and Bennett, F. (2009) *Rights and responsibilities in the social security system*, Occasional Paper 6, London: Social Security Advisory Committee.

Hall, S. and Pettigrew, N. (Ipsos Mori) (2008) *Exploring the key influences on the tax credits claimant population*, HM Revenue and Customs Research Report 49, London: HMRC.

Hansen, K., Jones, E., Joshi, H. and Budge, D. (eds) (2010) *Millennium Cohort Study fourth survey: a user's guide to initial findings – 2nd edition, December 2010*, London: Centre for Longitudinal Studies, Institute of Education, University of London.

Hirsch, D. and Beckhelling, J. (2011) *Tackling the adequacy trap: earnings, incomes and work incentives under the Universal Credit*, London: Resolution Foundation.

HMG (HM Government) (2011) *Consultation on modern workplaces*, London: HMG.

HMT (HM Treasury) (2010a) *Spending Review 2010*, Cm 7942, London: The Stationery Office.

HMT (2010b) *Overview of the impact of Spending Review 2010 on equalities*, London: HMT.

Ingold, J. (2011) *An international comparison of assisting partnered women into work*, Working Paper 101, London: Department for Work and Pensions.

IFS (Institute for Fiscal Studies) (2010) Presentation following spending review, 21 October.

Kay, L. (2010) *Escaping the poverty trap: how to help people on benefits into work*, London: Policy Exchange.

Lewis, J. and Bennett, F. (2004) 'Introduction', *Social Policy and Society* 3(1): 43–6.

Lister, R. (2006) 'The links between women's and children's poverty', in Women's Budget Group (ed) *Women's and children's poverty: making the links*, London: WBG, pp 1-15.

Lister, R. (2011a) Oral evidence to House of Commons Work and Pensions Select Committee inquiry into Universal Credit (unpublished).

Lister, R. (2011b) House of Lords Grand Committees, 23 November, cols 433–6.

Lister, R. and Bennett, F. (2010) 'The new "champion of progressive ideals"? Cameron's Conservative Party: poverty, family policy and welfare reform', *Renewal* 18(1): 84–109.

Macleavy, J. (2011) 'A "new politics" of austerity, workfare and gender? The UK Coalition government's welfare reform proposals', *Cambridge Journal of Regions, Economy and Society* 4(3): 355–67.

Maplethorpe, N., Chanfreau, J., Philo, D. and Tait, C. (2010) *Families with children in Britain: findings from the 2008 Families and Children Study (FACS)*, Department for Work and Pensions Research Report 656, Leeds: Corporate Document Services.

Marsh, A., McKay, S., Smith, A. and Stephenson, A. (2001) *Low-income families in Britain: work, welfare and social security in 1999*, Department of Social Security Research Report 138, Leeds: Corporate Document Services.

Martin, D. (2009) *Benefit simplification: how, and why, it must be done*, London: Centre for Policy Studies.

PAC (Public Accounts Select Committee) (2011) *Reducing costs in the Department for Work and Pensions*, HC 1351, 47th Report (Session 2010-12), London: The Stationery Office.

Park, A., Clery, E., Curtice, J., Phillips, M. and Utting, D. (eds) (2011) *British social attitudes 28: 2011–2012*, London: Sage Publications.

Price, D. (2011) 'Key findings from the project "Behind closed doors: older couples and the management of household money" (ESRC research grant RES-061-25-0090)', London: Institute of Gerontology, Kings College London.

Sainsbury, R. and Stanley, K. (2007) 'One for all: active welfare and the single working-age benefit', in J. Bennett and G. Cooke (eds) *It's all about you: citizen-centred welfare*, London: Institute for Public Policy Research, pp 43–56.

Sainsbury, R. and Weston, K. (2010) *Exploratory qualitative research on the 'single working age benefit'*, Department for Work and Pensions Research Report 659, Leeds: Corporate Document Services.

Seddon, J. (2011) 'Universal credit: guaranteed to fail?', 29 September. Available at: http://www.guardian.co.uk/public-leaders-network/blog/2011/sep/29/universal-credit-fail?commentpage=last#end-of-comments

Sefton, T. (2009) 'Moving in the right direction? Public attitudes to poverty, inequality and redistribution', in J. Hills, T. Sefton and K. Stewart (eds) *Towards a more equal society? Poverty, inequality and policy since 1997*, Bristol: The Policy Press, pp 223–44.

Sharp, N. (2008) *'What's yours is mine': the different forms of economic abuse and its impact on women and children experiencing domestic violence*, London: Refuge.

Taylor, C., Denham, M., Baron, R. and Allum, A. (2010) *Welfare reform in tough fiscal times: creating a better and cheaper benefits system*, London: Taxpayers' Alliance.

TUC (Trades Union Congress) (2010) *The gender impact of the cuts*, London: TUC.

Veitch, J., with Bennett, F. (2010) *A gender perspective on 21st century welfare reform*, Oxford: Oxfam GB.

Women's Budget Group (2011a) 'Welfare Reform Bill: Evidence to the Public Bill Committee'. Available at: http://www.wbg.org.uk/RRB_Reports_15_4261226591.pdf

Women's Budget Group (2011b) 'Universal Credit: payment issues'. Available at: http://wbg.org.uk/pdfs/Universal-Credit-payment-issues-Sept-2011-revised.pdf

TWO

Family support and the Coalition: retrenchment, refocusing and restructuring

Harriet Churchill

Introduction

The scope and make-up of welfare state support for families with children are controversial social policy issues in the British context. However, under the former Labour government, concerns about childhood disadvantage and family functioning moved up the policy agenda. In turn, Labour invested in more universal and targeted family support provision and extended state intervention in childhood and child-rearing. Economic austerity measures, though, and the establishment of the Conservative–Liberal Democrat Coalition government in May 2010 constitute new policy contexts. After 18 months of Coalition government, this chapter examines the implications for, and recent developments in, family support and child well-being policies.

The chapter employs the concept 'family support' as a short-hand term to refer to a broad range of social policies and provisions that seek to assist families in caring for and raising children. These include financial support measures, parental leaves, childcare services, child welfare services, parent education and parenting support initiatives, childhood and family social interventions, and specialist family support services. Beyond this broad definition, there is a need to recognise the significance of informal family support and distinguish between different types of support and services for parents, children and families. Further, the analysis takes on board critical perspectives about 'care and control' dynamics in family support and problems with notions of 'family' (Frost et al, 2003). It examines the scope of family policies and the way child and family policies pursue wider socio-economic objectives and seek to uphold and enforce family responsibilities for children, social care and social reproduction.

The chapter considers the Coalition's evolving approach and early policies in three stages. First, the discussion reflects on the Coalition's inheritance from the Labour years. Second, the chapter considers the Coalition's founding *Programme for government* published in late May 2010 (HM Government, 2010). This combined elements of the Conservative Party's 'smaller state, bigger society' 2010 election campaign and the Liberal Democrat's criticisms of Labour's record on civil liberties, public service reform and social mobility (Conservative Party, 2010; Liberal Democrat Party, 2010). The Coalition's *Programme for government* set out a radical programme of public expenditure cutbacks and a new era of welfare state restructuring (HM Government, 2010). In spite of this, the Coalition claimed a 'progressive agenda', to address 'the root causes' of childhood disadvantage and to seek 'a more family-friendly Britain' (HM Government, 2010). Third, the chapter examines policy developments in the first 18 months of Coalition government.

The analysis discusses four major aspects of policy developments: (1) reductions in financial support for families; (2) cutbacks in children's services; (3) refocusing on the 'root causes of childhood disadvantage'; and (4) refocusing on the 'social crisis'. In respect of the devolved areas of policy, such as children's services, the analysis focuses on developments in England and notes the influence of the Coalition's broader programme for public services reform and restructuring. While recognising the scope for positive outcomes for service users, the chapter highlights critical issues about the Coalition's early family support and children's services reforms. In particular, the chapter raises social welfare and social justice concerns about the retreat in state support for families and children, which is accompanied by more emphasis on family responsibilities for children and childhood disadvantage.

The Coalition's inheritance: Labour's social investment approach and record

Labour's child and family policies sought to reduce child poverty, promote child well-being and promote 'the adult worker' family (Lister, 2003). Central was its emphasis on promoting employment opportunities as a Third Way anti-poverty and economic policy strategy (Blair, 1998). In the context of economic and social change, and rising demands on the welfare state, prosperity and opportunity were thought to critically depend on full employment and investments in an adaptable, flexible, skilled and educated workforce (Blair, 1998). This led to an emphasis on 'active social policies', which promoted economic activity (Blair, 1998). Moreover, concerns about human capital deficits and 'intergenerational cycles of social exclusion' led to a raft of policies targeted at children and families. However, children's rights and feminist critiques of what was termed the 'social investment state' (Lister, 2003) highlighted the way that children were primarily positioned as 'future adult worker citizens' rather than citizens with rights during childhood. There was also much criticism of the degree to which policies addressed gender inequalities in the family or sources of discrimination in the labour market (Churchill, 2011).

Nevertheless, there were major developments in family support. Universal and means-tested forms of financial support for families were substantially increased. An increasingly generous system of tax credits was introduced. The Working Tax Credit (WTC) sought to provide financial support for lower- and middle-earning employed parents while the Child Tax Credit (CTC) was provided to families with children irrespective of parental working status. Welfare-to-work reforms developed targeted support for welfare-reliant lone parents; a National Childcare Strategy sought more 'affordable, higher-quality and accessible childcare'; and working parents gained new entitlements to access childcare services to take up paid work and to request flexible working arrangements. Parents gained rights to subsidised part-time pre-school places (for 12.5 hours a week) for all four- and then three-year-olds. Moreover, entitlements to maternity leave and pay were increased and new paternity leave and pay rights were introduced for fathers.

'Investing in children' led to new forms of direct financial support for children and young people, such as Child Trust Funds (CTFs) and the Educational Maintenance Allowance (EMA). Labour invested in new Sure Start Children's Centres (providing a range of health, childcare, family support and early learning services to families with pre-school children) and an array of programmes for children and young people at risk of poor outcomes and social exclusion. Education and health reforms sought to reduce educational and health inequalities. Schools took on an extended role, providing wrap-around childcare (ie available from 8am to 6pm on weekdays) and parenting support. The Children Act 2004 promoted five key outcomes for young people aged 0–19: economic well-being, being healthy, staying safe, making a positive contribution to society and enjoying and achieving at school – which in turn led to a string of reforms and initiatives in England and Wales, including the establishment of a Children's Commissioner in England.

Children's services reforms sought to invest in 'a continuum of family support services' for families and better coordinate and join-up services and sectors to better meet children's and families' needs.

Concerns about child well-being led to a focus on 'parental responsibilities' and 'responsible parenting' (Churchill, 2011). Legislative developments sought to clarify and extend parental responsibilities for children's and young people's attendance at school, educational progress, social behaviour, economic well-being, contact post-divorce and parental separation, and health and well-being (Churchill, 2011). Interest in parent education and support initiatives blossomed, as 'good parenting' was viewed as critical to improving outcomes for children. Labour invested in authoritative parenting advice and support for all, emphasising parent–state partnerships for child well-being. Moreover, youth criminal justice policies laid emphasis on the role of parents, famously introducing Parenting Orders (statutory powers to compel parents to attend parenting classes or other services) and Parenting Contracts (more voluntary 'behaviour change' agreements to engage with family interventions with parents) for parents of youth at risk.

In the latter Labour years, youth crime prevention policies refocused on 'a small minority of high cost/high risk problem families' (Home Office, 2006). Family Intervention Projects were introduced whereby professionals took an assertive and intensive approach to working with these 'dysfunctional families' to prevent child protection procedures, housing eviction and/or criminal convictions (Home Office, 2006). Adult's and children's services were required to become more family-focused and assess both adults' and children's needs and risks. These developments mirrored other shifts towards more family-centred explanations for social problems. Informed by an evidence-based ethos, investment increased for cost-effective 'proven' parenting programmes and family interventions that enhanced children's development, behaviour and health. For example, from 2006, Labour invested in US-style Nurse–Family Partnerships whereby trained health practitioners provided intensive home-based support for vulnerable first-time mothers during pregnancy and the first two years of a child's life. Further, under Gordon Brown, from 2007, child well-being policies broadened in scope as did the responsibilities of the Department for Education and Skills, renamed the Department for Children, Schools and Families (DCSF) in 2007. More investment in recreational activities for youth and youth services were particular themes, as was more interest in couple relationship support to reduce the detrimental effects on children from parental conflict and separation (DCSF, 2010).

Labour's reforms contributed to significant reductions in child poverty, especially between 1998/99–2003/04 and substantial improvements in educational attainment rates (especially among primary schools), children's health and maternal levels of employment (Churchill, 2011). However, parents with few qualifications, disabled people and young people aged 16–24 years saw their employment prospects improve little and even get worse (Churchill, 2011). Overall, levels of economic inactivity increased slightly from 1997 to 2010 and household income among the poorest families fell further behind median levels (Churchill, 2011). Further, income inequalities and socio-economic disparities between the more affluent and deprived regions, areas and neighbourhoods remained stark (Churchill, 2011). In addition, research indicated that the vision of integrated needs-led children's services was far from realised on the ground and, in particular, there remained severe gaps in provision in specialist and targeted services for higher-need children, young people and families (Churchill, 2011).

Towards the Coalition's *Programme for government*

In several ways, the 2010 election campaigns of the three major Westminster parties were informed by similar Third Way and social investment ideological perspectives. Both David Cameron, Leader of the Conservative Party, and Nick Clegg, Leader of the Liberal Democrats, had become party leaders a few years earlier as self-proclaimed party modernisers. David Cameron described himself as a 'modern compassionate conservative' (Daniels, 2011). Compassionate conservatism was more supportive of early intervention initiatives, family-friendly employment policies and early education and childcare programmes, as these policies reduced child disadvantage, promoted equality of opportunity, boosted economic productivity and reduced the demand for costly welfare interventions (Daniels, 2011). This progressive agenda, however, jarred somewhat with the Conservatives' 'Broken Britain' campaign, which raised longer-standing traditional Conservative and Thatcherite concerns about declining rates of marriage and an emerging social underclass. In the Liberal Democrat Party, Nick Clegg had supported neo-liberal public service reform policies and promoted a 'liberal agenda to enable every child to reach their potential', illustrating commitment to social investment state principles (Webb and Holland, 2004, p 236). In contrast to the Conservatives, the Liberals' synopsis of childhood disadvantage, though, paid more attention to the pressures on families arising from long working hours, in-work poverty, lack of family-friendly employment opportunities, and poor-quality childcare (Webb and Holland, 2004). However, policies supported parenting and family interventions to address parenting deficits in children's early years and the detrimental effects on children from parental relationship problems, divorce and lone motherhood (Webb and Holland, 2004).

The 2010 election campaigns more immediately responded to the economic, political and social crises surrounding Gordon Brown's term in office. Following the 2008/09 financial crisis and bailout for the banking system, and subsequent rise in the public deficit and period of economic recession, all political parties set out fiscal containment measures. Of direct influence to the Coalition's *Programme for government* were the Conservatives' 'big government to Big Society' campaign and the Liberal Democrats' 'fairness' policies (Conservative Party, 2010; Liberal Democrat Party, 2010).

The Conservatives' 'big government' critique of Labour was short-hand rhetoric for 'excessive levels of public spending, borrowing and debt'; 'too much state intrusion into people's lives'; 'threats to civil liberties'; 'the micro-management of public services'; and 'top-down central state solutions' (Conservative Party, 2010). Labour was criticised for generating 'Britain's main economic problem – the record size of the public deficit' (Conservative Party, 2010). Conservatives sought to reduce 'the bulk of the structural deficit' in one parliamentary period from 2010 to 2014/15 (Conservative Party, 2010). They set out 'a new economic model' based on low levels of public borrowing, pro-business tax regimes and productive investments, which would promote private-sector-led economic growth and invest in a more 'educated and flexible' workforce (Conservative Party, 2010). The Conservatives would reduce the 'size and scope of the welfare state' (Conservative Party, 2010, p 8). Further 'the role of the state' would be revised with less 'top-down rules and regulations' and 'micro-managing' of public services and more private finance initiatives, outsourcing, 'payment by results', citizen involvement, use of volunteers and third-sector initiatives (Conservative Party, 2010). Overall, the Conservatives' approach was framed in terms of a shift from 'big government to Big Society' (Conservative Party, 2010). Proposals included reductions in financial support for families and a refocusing of initiatives such as Sure Start and Extended Schools on more targeted support for disadvantaged children and families. The Conservatives' election campaign echoed sentiments of the 'Broken Britain' campaign with 'welfare dependency' and 'problem families' cast as urgent social problems (Conservative Party, 2010). The Conservatives pledged to promote pro-marriage policies, 'end the couple penalty' in the benefits system, review family justice law, introduce 'a new approach to problem families' and support couple relationship services.

Labour and the Liberal Democrats sought delayed and less severe public spending cuts, pledging to half the public deficit by 2014/15. The Liberal Democrats criticised prior Conservative and Labour governments for overseeing widening inequalities in the UK and infringements to civil liberties (Liberal Democrats, 2010). They advocated tax reforms to reduce the burden of taxation on lower-paid workers and increase tax on wealthy individuals and 'big business' (Liberal Democrats, 2010). However, reductions in tax credits for higher-income families and government contributions to CTFs were proposed as necessary public spending containment measures (Liberal Democrats, 2010). To 'restore civil liberties', initiatives such as Labour's ContactPoint children's information database would be scrapped. More investment in youth services was proposed (Liberal Democrats, 2010, p 33). Compared to Labour and the Conservatives, the Liberal Democrats set out more generous and detailed plans for a 'Pupil Premium' to provide additional funds to schools to provide support for underachieving disadvantaged pupils (Liberal Democrats, 2010). More extensive, free part-time pre-school provision and family-friendly employment measures were proposed. Sure Start Children's Centres and Extended Schools were to retain their commitment to progressive universalism. Similar to the Conservatives, proposals included incremental reforms to Labour's parenting and family intervention policies.

Following the establishment of the Conservative–Liberal Democrat Coalition, the Coalition published its *Programme for government* (HM Government, 2010). This programme combined the Conservatives' 'smaller state, bigger society' proposals and the Liberal Democrats' 'fairness and civil liberties' policies. Spending cuts were to begin earlier, with £6 billion worth of cuts to be made in 2010/11 set out more extensively in an Emergency Budget in June 2010 (HM Government, 2010). Reforms to public services, tax credits, the benefit system, early years services, health, education, couple relationship support and family interventions were on the cards. The Coalition pledged commitments to meet the 2010 child poverty targets, make Britain more family-friendly, protect children more from 'commercialisation and corporate marketing' and review family law. The Conservatives' 'pro-marriage' reforms were dampened down, as were the Liberal Democrats' 'taxing the rich' plans and youth policy measures.

Recent policy developments

Soon after the Coalition published its *Programme for government*, Deputy Prime Minster Nick Clegg announced the 'Childhood and Families Taskforce'. The Taskforce involved leading Conservative ministers with interests in family policy reform – PM David Cameron, David Willetts and Iain Duncan Smith. The Taskforce had a broad remit to 'look at the barriers to a happy childhood and successful family life', but policy recommendations were limited to targeted 'policy proposals which will make the most difference to children and families' (Clegg, 2010). By late 2011, however, the Taskforce had yet to produce any reports. Nevertheless, there were significant developments in family support policies and children's services in the first 18 months of the Coalition. These were driven by austerity measures, social mobility initiatives, public service reforms and the governmental response to the 2011 August 'riots'.

Austerity measures and reductions in financial support for families

The June 2010 Emergency Budget set out a radical programme of public expenditure cuts. As previously indicated, £6.2 billion worth of savings were to be realised in 2010–11. Public expenditure overall was to be reduced by 19%, £95 billion, by 2015 (HM Treasury, 2010a, p 16; 2011). Further cuts were announced in the 2010 Spending Review (HM Treasury, 2010b) and 2011 Budget (HM Treasury, 2011). The majority of departmental budgets are to be cut by around 25% by 2014/15. The Treasury pointed to the support from the Organisation for Economic Co-operation and Development (OECD) for the scale of its fiscal containment measures. The OECD had argued that levels of household, business and public debt in the UK were unsustainable, limiting the scope of the government to protect the economy from global economic problems or boost demand and growth in the economy (OECD, 2011). In line with the Conservatives' 'new economic model', austerity measures were part of broader macro-economic policies that sought private-sector-led growth (ie via low business and labour taxes) and a focus on 'productive investments', including investing in 'an educated flexible workforce' (HM Treasury, 2011). However, repeated downward revisions to estimates economic growth, crisis in the Eurozone area and rising levels of unemployment, particularly among young people, led to persistent criticism of the Coalition's strategy for economic growth.

Public spending cutbacks prioritised major reductions in welfare spending. These included reductions in tax credit payments for family households introduced from April 2011. CTC entitlements were entirely withdrawn for middle-income families earning over £40,000 a year, adding up to a loss of at least £492 a year for previously eligible families. Other changes reduced the generosity of tax credit awards and revised eligibility criteria. At least one parent in couple-headed family households had to work 24 hours a week for the household to qualify for WTC (instead of 16 hours a week). Additional payments for having children aged 0–1 were withdrawn. The percentage of childcare costs that parents can claim through the childcare element of the WTC was reduced back down to a maximum of 70% of costs for one child and less for other children. Further announcements were for less generous tax credits as household incomes rise, and, from 2012/13, a freeze on the couple and lone-parent elements of WTC. The 2010 Emergency Budget confirmed a freeze of Child Benefit (CB) payments from 2010 to 2013. The Coalition then announced that CB entitlements would be withdrawn completely for family households earning over £43,875 a year from April 2013, adding up to a loss in benefit of £1,055 a year for a one-child family household, £1,752 for a two-child household and £2,500 for a three-child household. This announcement appeared to surprise many Coalition politicians in both parties and was widely criticised inside and outside the Coalition.

Welfare benefit cuts and reforms further reconfigured financial support for families. Cutbacks included the abolition of the Health in Pregnancy Grant (worth £190) from April 2011 and more restricted Sure Start Maternity Grant payments (worth £500 per child) so that eligible mothers only received one payment, for their first child. Changes to Housing Benefit (HB) were introduced from April 2011 (see Chapter Three in this volume). The introduction of caps in HB sought to restrict housing choices among claimants and limit HB awards. However, due in part to much opposition to these plans, particularly in terms of affordability issues in private rental markets in London, the government announced a discretionary support fund for local authorities to help support families at risk of homelessness. Stricter eligibility and medical assessments for disability benefits are to be introduced from 2013/14 (which have implications for families in receipt of such benefits and affected by disability and long-term health problems).

Benefit cuts were accompanied by broader welfare reforms. The Work Programme introduced from April 2011 replaced Labour's New Deal programmes. The design of the programme took forward Freud's (2007) model of contracted-out 'payment by results' employability programmes, which also informed Labour's welfare reforms. All Jobseeker's Allowance

(JSA) and Employment Support Allowance claimants can volunteer for the Work Programme, but young people aged 18–24 years in receipt of JSA for six months and all those in receipt of JSA for 12 months are compelled to take part or face benefit penalties. The reforms included reductions in targeted 'back-to-work' incentives such as those for lone parents to help with childcare costs. The 2011 Welfare Reform Bill then proposed the Universal Credit (UC), taking forward campaigns for a single working-age benefit system (see Chapter One in this volume). It proposed that UC replace all means-tested welfare benefits and tax credits for working-age people. The UC system will incorporate stricter work conditions and punishments for benefit fraud. The government states that the administrative savings made in simplifying the benefit system will allow for the UC system to incorporate a more generous system of in-work financial support and, hence, increase work incentives and reduce benefit traps (HM Government, 2011).

These changes have reduced financial support for families. The tax credit system no longer operates in line with 'progressive universalism' but provides more targeted support for lower-income working parents. With many working lone parents in receipt of tax credits and more mothers than fathers working part time, these changes particularly impact on women's employment decisions and household income in lone-parent families. The plans abolish social rights to universal CB and reduce state responsibilities to contribute to the cost of raising children irrespective of family income, which have stood for over 30 years. The withdrawal of CB for higher earners goes against Liberal Democrat policies and was not included in the Conservatives' 2010 election manifesto or the Coalition's *Programme for government* (HM Government, 2010). Welfare benefit cuts resurrect the notion of a safety net welfare system for those in most need and discretionary forms of crisis support. In addition, benefit reforms have included the abolition of direct financial support for children and young people, namely CTFs and EMA. Both schemes will be replaced with highly targeted discretionary support schemes. These changes reinstate personal responsibilities for economic well-being and post-16 education opportunities, and emphasise family responsibilities for children as well as personal responsibility for financing post-16 education among young people.

The Coalition, however, claims that benefit reforms and targeted initiatives (such as targeted increases in CTCs) will prevent increases in child poverty in 2010–15 (HM Treasury, 2011). However, anti-poverty campaigners claim that families with children will be worse off overall under the new UC system due to lower awards for childcare costs, having children, housing costs, having a disability or being in poor health compared to entitlements in 2009/10 (CPAG, 2011). The Institute for Fiscal Studies (IFS) criticised the Treasury's child poverty predictions for not taking account of all the relevant tax and benefit changes and acknowledging increases in absolute child poverty (Brewer and Joyce, 2010). Further, post-2012 child poverty data, according to the IFS, will start to show the detrimental effects of welfare reforms if economic growth remains stagnant. Brewer, Browne and Joyce (2011, pp 12–13) predicted a rise in the number of children in absolute poverty of 600,000 children and a rise in the number in relative child poverty of 300,000 from 2010 to 2013.

Cutbacks in children's services

The DCSF was renamed the Department for Education (DfE) once the Coalition took office – symbolising a return to education as the core business of the department. Although the schools and National Health Service (NHS) budget have received additional resources for major reforms, the 2010 Spending Review announced broader departmental cuts of around 10–20% in the DfE budget by 2014/15 and plans to make £20 billion worth of savings to the overall Department of Health (DH) budget by 2014 (HM Treasury, 2010b). Local Authorities (LAs) in England and Wales faced a reduction in their total annual budget of around 10% in 2010/11 (HM Treasury, 2011). These cutbacks led to major reductions in local children's services funding in 2010/11.

The National Society for the Prevention of Cruelty to Children (NSPCC) has undertaken an analysis of changes in local children's social care funding during 2010/11 (NSPCC, 2011). This survey defined children's social care funding as all funding for statutory children's social services and funding for early years services, youth services, prevention initiatives and family support services that is not part of mainstream education and health budgets. They found local children's social care services on average faced a reduction in annual budgets of around 13% in 2010/11. LAs varied in where and to what degree they cut children's social care funding, but the NSPCC found that cutbacks were disproportionately leading to less funding for prevention initiatives, Sure Start services, youth services and family support services (NSPCC, 2011). It warned that these cutbacks were likely to reduce the scope of local services to provide early support for vulnerable children and families and increase the number of registered children in need or at risk, placing more demand on social services (NSPCC, 2011). Voluntary agencies in receipt of relatively small local grants seemed disproportionately at risk of funding cutbacks (NSPCC, 2011). The report further raised concerns about cutbacks in staff numbers, training, quality assurance and service monitoring (NSPCC, 2011).

Another recent survey asked 72 major voluntary agencies in children's services about their financial situation (Mahadevan, 2011). Of these, 71% were experiencing funding cuts, with 25% experiencing more than a 25% cut in funding in 2011/12. This survey found that cutbacks particularly affected prevention initiatives, children's centres, play services, youth services and family support services (Mahadevan, 2011).

In addition, a number of cost-effectiveness reviews have been completed or are under way, such as those on Sure Start services and the Children's Commissioner's office. The ContactPoint database has been closed down and the national IT system which allows practitioners to record details following Common Assessment Framework (CAF) assessment is to be abolished. These closures seek to reduce administrative burdens on practitioners but may also be a backwards move for information-sharing and multi-agency working in children's services.

Refocusing on the 'root causes of social disadvantage'

As required by the Child Poverty Act 2010, the Coalition published its four-year plan to reduce child poverty in April 2011 (HM Government, 2011). The plan set out 'a new approach' to child poverty focused on the 'root causes of childhood disadvantage' rather than relative income poverty (HM Government, 2011). Drawing on the Conservatives' 'family breakdown' discourses and the Liberal Democrats' social mobility policies, these 'root causes' were framed as: worklessness, educational failure, parenting and early child development deficiencies, family breakdown, and health inequalities (HM Government, 2011). Looked-after children (LACs), teenage parent families and children with Special Educational Needs (SENs) and disabilities were also identified as particularly disadvantaged (HM Government, 2011). The welfare reforms discussed earlier sought to address long-term welfare reliance, benefit traps and 'worklessness', while reforms in health were concerned with reducing health inequalities. To address the other 'root causes', the strategy sought to refocus resources from welfare spending to investments in 'education and other services, particularly for young children, to help disadvantaged families improve their prospects' (HM Treasury, 2011, p 26). The Coalition's *Child Poverty Strategy*, therefore, took forward 'social investment state' perspectives. However, it emphasised highly targeted social investments and sought a shift from the 'social investment state' to the 'social investment market'.

The development of the Coalition's *Child poverty strategy* was strongly influenced by two government-commissioned reports – Frank Field's (2010) *Independent Review of Poverty and Life Chances* and Graham Allen's (2011) *Early intervention: the next steps*. Both reports stressed the 'fundamental importance of the early years in determining a child's life chances' (HM Government, 2011, p 43). Field argued that children's learning, emotional and physical abilities were largely determined by the age of five. He referred to influential longitudinal research that illustrated the wide gap in average terms in cognitive development among advantaged and disadvantaged children by school age, and the beneficial intellectual, social and emotional outcomes for young children associated with high-quality pre-school opportunities. Field called for the government to invest in more pre-school opportunities for disadvantaged young children as well as other early years initiatives such as family learning schemes and parenting programmes. He argued for the establishment of the 'Foundation Years' early education and family services. Field further argued that the income poverty measures in the Child Poverty Act 2010 should be supplemented by life chances, family context and child development indicators. These included indicators to monitor children's physical, emotional and cognitive development at ages three and five.

Allen's report was a review of early intervention approaches and initiatives. Drawing on early brain development research, Allen (2011) stressed that the first three years of a child's life are the most critical for human development and influence subsequent emotional and academic development. He emphasised that investment in early intervention programmes could in the long run lead to major savings in public spending (Allen, 2011). The evidence-based approaches were found to improve children's development, educational and health outcomes, and social behaviour; and, although there is much less research about longer-term outcomes, Allen (2011) argued that, in the long run, early intervention programmes would therefore lead to large public savings due to reduced welfare and criminal justice expenditures, higher employment rates and higher tax revenues. Developing the notion of the 'social investment market', Allen (2011) went on to develop proposals for more private finance for early years and family welfare initiatives, whereby investors received profitable returns when programmes effectively met service-user needs.

Both Field and Allen pointed to the critical role of parents and families in promoting early child development. Field (2010) set out several proposals to promote 'good parenting'. Allen called for a 'National Parenting Campaign', which would 'educate people on the basics of parenting' and 'the importance of the first 3 years of child development', again with an emphasis on poorer parents. Both reports advocated more extensive use of evidence-based parenting programmes in Sure Start Centres, better parent education for young people in schools, a national public health parenting campaign and targeted parent education initiatives for low-income groups.

The Coalition's *Child poverty strategy* then set out new life chances indicators of childhood disadvantage and confirmed plans to introduce the early years reforms already proposed, such as revising Sure Start funding and investing in more Health Visitors (HVs) (HM Government, 2011). The *Strategy* emphasised the following family-level explanations for childhood disadvantage: parental separation and divorce, parental conflict and relationship problems, growing up in a lone-parent family or step-parent family, growing up in a family with multiple problems, and poor parenting (HM Government, 2011). More recent announcements, though, have indicated that the Coalition's early years policies are to include the introduction of a flexible system of parental leave and more flexibility in the free pre-school places scheme.

From April 2011, funding for Sure Start and other early intervention and prevention initiatives (such as programmes concerned with health promotion, parenting support, youth crime prevention and family intervention developed under Labour) was repackaged as the new 'Early Intervention Grant'. This grant was for LAs to fund early intervention programmes for disadvantaged children, young people and families. Compared to the previous sources of funding, LAs had more freedom to allocate the funds according to local decisions and needs. However, the grant constituted an overall 11% cut in local children's services funding in 2011/12, placing the sustainability of existing provision at risk (NSPCC, 2011). Further, LAs were encouraged to use more evidence-based early years interventions (such as family learning schemes and maternal and child health programmes), sustain universal services via service-user charges and increase the involvement of voluntary and private organisations in the commissioning and delivery of Sure Start services. The government also wants parents and communities to be more involved in the running of Sure Start services.

In addition, the Coalition provided £60 million of funding for 2011–13 to support 'trusted voluntary organisations' to continue to provide various forms of parenting advice and family support services (HM Government, 2011). The Coalition further announced additional funding for the health budget to train and employ 4,200 more HVs in Sure Start centres by 2015. This initiative sought to increase local numbers of HVs, driving down caseloads and supporting an extended role for HVs in early child and family welfare. Particular concerns have further been raised about children growing up in teenage-parent families. This led to the pledge to double the number of Nurse–Family Partnership programmes in England to 100 by 2015 (HM Government, 2011).

In addition to these early years and parenting initiatives, concern about the detrimental effects on children from parental marriage and relationship problems and parental separations led to the Family Justice Review. Developments, in many ways, reflected incremental changes to Labour's reforms of 'therapeutic' couple mediation and dispute resolution approaches, which seek to avoid court-based resolutions to marital and divorce disputes. The Coalition pledged to increase the amount spent on relationship support for couples provided mainly by the voluntary sector to £7.5 million each year in 2011–15 (HM Government, 2011).

Where these service developments uphold good practice principles, they are likely to lead to beneficial outcomes for children, parents and families. However, in the context of public expenditure cuts, few reforms constitute additional resources for specialist family support services. Rather, funding streams appear to provide limited recompense for previous cutbacks. Children's services also face major challenges in responding to restructuring reforms in the context of funding uncertainty and cutbacks. Children's services will be faced with transaction costs from setting up new commissioning arrangements and training staff in evidence-based programmes. The refocusing on specific targeted reforms needs to ensure that the sustainability of established multi-agency arrangements is not threatened. For early intervention initiatives to effectively support children and families, it will be important that services do not return to 'silo' ways of thinking and for services to develop ways of appropriately identifying additional needs and problems at an early stage. To improve children's early development, for example, early intervention programmes need to effectively identify and respond to a range of problems that place young children at risk, such as parental health, substance misuse, domestic violence, poor housing, social isolation and parental depression. While parenting, family context and the early years are critical to children's everyday well-being and influence their future life chances, the Coalition's policies to reduce childhood disadvantage make dubious assumptions about parenting deficits in poor families and pay insufficient attention to rising living costs, material pressures and disproportionate challenges parents and families in socio-economic disadvantage face (Churchill, 2011). Further, the significance of gender, disability, place and ethnic background in relation to the dynamics of poverty and social mobility are not sufficiently addressed.

Refocusing on the 'social crisis'

The 2010 Spending Review set out more details of the Coalition's plans to establish local community budgets to fund family interventions for families with multiple problems (HM Treasury, 2010b). This approach was characterised by new forms of financing multi-agency interventions. Families with multiple problems are a diverse group of families defined, by the Coalition, as families suffering from five or more of the following problems: no adult in paid work; family living in poor-quality or overcrowded housing; no adult with any qualifications; mother having mental health problems; one adult or child with a limiting illness, disability or infirmity; relative household poverty; family not able to afford a number of food and clothing items; or at least one child in the family involved in the youth justice system or having a clinical behavioural problem. In September 2011, the DfE estimated that there were 117,000 such families in England. These, families, it is argued, are often involved with a number of adult and children's services. In the discussion earlier, it was noted that Labour developed 'family intervention projects and services' for these families – multi-agency responses coordinated by specialist lead professionals who worked 'intensively and assertively' with families and addressed multiple needs and problems in the family. Following impressive evaluation findings, the Coalition partners also supported investment in multi-agency intensive family services. However, the Coalition has set up 'Community Budget' pilots in 16 areas covering 28 LAs in England as a new approach to financing these types of services. Community Budgets provide LAs with considerable autonomy to decide on the model and type of approach to take, and to fund different types of help and support for families. The Coalition plans to roll out this approach nationwide from 2013/14. Further, taking forward proposals for the 'social investment market', the Coalition is looking into ways in which local businesses can contribute to Community Budgets and help fund projects for 'troubled families' via Social Impact Bonds, whereby businesses would secure an additional return on their 'investment' when projects meet their targets and objectives.

The August 2011 'riots' then led to much debate about 'problem families'. Starting in London after a local protest about a fatality following a police shooting, there was a week of social unrest in many English cities. The unrest saw retail outlets looted and vandalised, street violence, many arrests and several fatalities. With many young people and young adults involved, politicians and the media emphasised issues of youth gang involvement, lone motherhood, poor parenting and family breakdown as much as issues of social disadvantage and 'pure criminality'. In a speech about the riots in mid-August, Prime Minister David Cameron stated that the riots reflected 'the social crisis' facing the UK (Cameron, 2011). Cameron (2011) argued that the riots were caused by problem families and stated: 'we've got to get out there and make a positive difference to the way families work, the way people bring up their children'. Quicker policy action on parent education initiatives was announced. Cameron (2011) further announced a 'family test', which would assess policy impacts on families, although rhetorically the emphasis was on impacts on family structures.

In October 2011, Louise Casey, a prominent figure in Labour's 'Respect' agenda, was appointed to head up a new 'Troubled Families Unit' to ensure 'rapid' progress in the Coalition's work with 'troubled families'. In December 2011, more funding was announced to support this work. In October 2011, a pilot programme offering parenting classes to all parents with children under five in deprived areas in Middlesbrough, Derbyshire and London was announced. Parents will receive vouchers to pay for the parenting courses but it is unclear if one or two parents will be funded per family, an important factor if couples and fathers are to take part. It is hoped that these programmes will reach over 50,000 parents.

However, analysis of those arrested for taking part in the summer 'riots' found that 26% were aged 10–17 years (DfE, 2011). A further 27% were aged 18–20 years. Poverty and neighbourhood deprivation were prominent factors in these young people's lives. The Ministry of Justice figures found that a disproportionate number of young people taking part in the unrest lived in highly deprived neighbourhoods with high and rising levels of youth unemployment (DfE, 2011). Further, 66% were classified as having special education needs (DfE, 2011). These trends suggest the need for a range of issues to be addressed and a vital role for anti-poverty, youth, educational, neighbourhood and employment initiatives.

Conclusion

This chapter has examined the Coalition's evolving family support agenda and recent policy developments. It argued that the Coalition's economic austerity and welfare reform programmes reinstate a deficit-based approach to family support and child well-being policies. Some developments appeared more evidence-based, building on campaigns for more effective family support, for example, via effective engagement with high-need families and more investment in HVs and early intervention initiatives. However, these developments are threatened by cutbacks in benefits and services. Alongside this, poor parenting, family breakdown and poor early child development have become more strongly emphasised as 'the root causes' of childhood disadvantage and subsequent adult social exclusion. This takes forward social investment approaches to 'investing in human capital deficits' to promote economic activity and well-being. However, the Coalition's policies rely on highly targeted initiatives and seek to enhance family investments in child-rearing. In addition, reforms seek a greater role for the private sector in 'social investment', and, for citizens, the voluntary sector and the private sector in public services. Such agendas seek to promote more social responsibility for welfare, but private sector inputs are rewarded via the social investment market.

References

Allen, G. (2011) *Early intervention: the next steps*, London: DfE.

Blair, T. (1998) *The third way: New politics for the new century*, London: Fabian Society.

Brewer, M. and Joyce, R. (2010) *Child and working age poverty from 2010 to 2013*, IFS Briefing Note 115, London: IFS.

Brewer, M., Browne, J. and Joyce, R. (2011) *Child and working age poverty from 2010 to 2020*, London: Institute for Fiscal Studies.

Cameron, D. (2011) 'We are all in this together', speech on the August riots. Available at: http://www.conservatives.com/News/News_stories/2011/08/Cameron_Fightback_after_the_riots.aspx (accessed 25 September 2011).

Churchill, H. (2011) *Parental rights and responsibilities: analysing social policy and lived experiences*, Bristol: The Policy Press.

Clegg, N. (2010) 'Nick Clegg's speech on supporting families and children'. Available at: http://www.libdems.org.uk/ (accessed 17 September 2011).

Conservative Party (2010) *Invitation to join the government of Britain, Conservative Party Manifesto 2010*, London: Conservative Party.

CPAG (Child Poverty Action Group) (2011) *Response to the Welfare Reform Bill consultation*, London: CPAG.

Daniels, P. (2011) 'Conservative policy and the family', in H. Bochel (ed) *The Conservative Party and social policy*, Bristol: The Policy Press.

DCSF (Department for Children, Schools and Families) (2010) *Support for all: the Families and Relationships Green Paper*, Cm 7787, London: DCSF.

DfE (Department of Education) (2011) *Ministry of Justice: statistical bulletin on the public disorder August 6–9: October update*, London: DfES/DWP.

Field, F. (2010) *The foundation years: preventing poor children becoming poor adults: the report of the Independent Review on Poverty and Life Chances*, London: HM Government.

Freud, D. (2007) *Reducing dependency, increasing opportunity: options for the future of welfare to work*, Leeds: Corporate Document Services.

Frost, N., Lloyd, A. and Jeffrey, L. (eds) (2003) *The RHP companion to family support*, Lyme Regis: Russell House Publishing.

HM Government (2010) *The Coalition: our programme of government*, London: HM Government.

HM Government (2011) *A new approach to child poverty: tackling the causes of disadvantage and transforming family lives*, Cm 8061, London: Crown Copyright.

HM Treasury (2010a) *Budget 2010*, HC 61, London: Crown Copyright.

HM Treasury (2010b) *Spending Review 2010*, Cm 7942, London: Crown Copyright.

HM Treasury (2011) *Budget 2011*, HC 836, London: HM Treasury.

Home Office (2006) *Respect action plan*, London: Home Office.

Liberal Democrat Party (2010) *Change that works for you: building a fairer Britain*, Liberal Democrat Manifesto, London: Liberal Democrat Party.

Lister, R. (2003) 'Investing in the citizen-workers of the future: transformations in citizenship and the state under Labour', *Social Policy and Administration*, vol 37, no 5, pp 427–43.

Mahadevan, J. (2011) 'Preventive work hardest hit by cuts', *Children and Young People Now*. Available at: http://www.cypnow.co.uk/news/1064067/Preventive-work-hardest-hit-cuts/?DCMP=ILC-SEARCH (accessed 7 October 2011).

NSPCC (National Society for the Prevention of Cruelty to Children) (2011) *Smart cuts? Public spending on children's social care*, London: NSPCC.

OECD (Organisation for Economic Co-operation and Development) (2011) *Economic surveys: United Kingdom 2011*, Paris: OECD.

Webb, S. and Holland, J. (2004) 'Children, the family and the state: a liberal agenda', in P. Marshall and D. Laws (eds) *The orange book: reclaiming liberalism*, London: Profile Books.

THREE

Housing, the welfare state and the Coalition government

Alan Murie

Introduction

Housing policy in Britain has had a precarious relationship with social policy and the welfare state. At times, governments have appeared to believe that housing the population can be left to the market; and, at times, housing has been part of economic rather than social policy. But throughout, housing has had an unavoidable relationship with the modern welfare state. Housing directly relates to two of Beveridge's five giant evils – Want and Squalor – and indirectly impacts on the remaining three, because action to address Idleness, Disease and Ignorance is more successful where there is effective housing provision. Housing costs also form key elements in household budgets and social insurance and assistance schemes have to take these costs into account.

The approach to housing announced by the Coalition government in the 18 months following its election in 2010 draws attention to the position of housing in the wider welfare state. Although the immediate context was the credit crunch and economic recession, the proposals represented an attempt to realign housing in the welfare state. The Coalition initially focused on reducing government borrowing and embarked on a familiar round of housing expenditure cuts, with consequences for house-building and housing costs. Nevertheless, the housing strategy published in November 2011 declared that boosting housing construction was critical for the economy as well as housing opportunities. It boldly and categorically declared that 'Previous housing policies have failed' (HMG, 2011, p 1), but then set out an agenda that marked continuity with previous policy more than innovation. The reform of Housing Benefit, revival of private renting, the Right to Buy (RTB) and private development, and higher rents involved more of the same. The Coalition's proposals were designed to reduce social security spending, increase local control over housing and affect behaviour in seeking work and in housing and mobility. Under longer-term plans, Housing Benefit would be incorporated into a new Universal Credit (UC) (see Chapter One in this volume). Taken together, these proposals break the established pattern of tenants' rights and security in social rented housing and could force relocation for some lower-income households, especially in the private rented sector.

This chapter discusses the Coalition government's proposals relating to housing in a historical context. It goes on to argue that if the Coalition's proposals follow failed housing policies, the similarities of approach mean that they build on such failed policies. The approach involves further support and reliance on market processes without resolving underlying problems of housing shortages, stress and inequality. The consequence will continue to include increasing costs for the social security budget. Reduced rights and security will undermine self-sufficiency and independence for some households while doing little to remove barriers to mobility or improve choice and efficient use of housing.

The housing challenge

Adequate housing is essential for the operation of modern economies and social life. Insanitary and overcrowded housing undermines the health and welfare of the labour force and affects the functioning of the economy. Lack of security and high levels of forced residential mobility undermine capacity to take advantage of educational and work opportunities, to build what is now labelled as social capital, and to develop and use supportive services and networks including those associated with the family. In Britain, the political and economic case for state intervention to improve people's homes was shared across political divides before the end of the 19th century. Nevertheless, some commentators continued to argue that the state's role in housing should be restricted to establishing a basic legal and public health framework, leaving the unfettered market to respond to need and demand. This theoretical argument that markets would ensure sufficient supply is difficult to test but runs against experience and evidence. Housing shortages generate higher rents, prices and profits and, in contrast, making profits by housing people with limited capacity to pay is difficult except by reducing standards. Speculative investment is unlikely to be aimed at the poorest households and filtering mechanisms are unreliable or deliver substandard housing for the poorest households. Public health measures requiring closure of insanitary dwellings and investment to raise and maintain dwelling standards made the financial calculation more difficult for developers or landlords. Where it is necessary to establish minimum standards of housing, for social and economic reasons, market processes prove insufficient. In periods of economic downturn and political turmoil, including wars, the market has been further disrupted.

These realities have tempered theoretical models. Some form of subsidy is necessary if adequate housing is to reach all sections of society. The evidence in Britain is that housing supply was maximised when local authorities as well as private developers were most active in building houses and that allocation of housing according to need was the most effective way of channelling good-quality housing to households in greatest need. This reality was accepted for much of the period after 1945 whether as a transitional emergency measure to deal with the aftermath of war, to address general needs or to deal with slums. However, since the mid-1970s, policymakers channelled fiscal and policy support towards home-ownership and dismantled council housing. After a period of improving house conditions, housing stress and inequality increased.

The story of housing policy in Britain is one of struggling to build housing effectively into the welfare state. This is not just about assistance with housing costs. If housing supply and standards are not also addressed, housing costs are likely to rise more rapidly. The different dimensions of housing – supply, condition, cost, access, security – present a complex mix. Interventions designed to address one dimension have wider and difficult to predict impacts on others.

The historical legacy

The Coalition government elected in 2010 inherited a legacy shaped over a long period. Their proposals related to Housing Benefit represent another attempt to deal with unfinished business and failing policy, and are best considered in a context going back to the Beveridge Report in 1942 (Beveridge, 1942). This had proposed radical new approaches for social security, health and other services; but housing would play its role within the modernised welfare state without dramatic reorganisation. State intervention in housing was already well established through regulation, subsidy, local authority activity and rent control. Legislation had empowered local authorities to pursue distinctive strategies based variously on new building, slum clearance or reconditioning (Yelling, 1992). By 1939, local government dominated the politics and administration of housing and left distinctive local legacies in building activity, tenure structure, rent levels, differential rents and rent rebates (Malpass, 1990). After 1945, housing policy was not subject to a universal, uniform, national approach and remained part of a local welfare state requiring integration with the new national welfare system.

The immediate challenge arose from the much greater variation in rents and house prices than in the costs of food, clothing, energy or any of the elements in household budgets that social insurance needed to finance. The Beveridge Report argued against a variable rate of benefit to take account of rent variations but recognised that allowing for only an average rent would mean that benefits would be more generous where that allowance exceeded actual rents. In other cases, especially in London, the benefit rate would, on average, be too low. The decision to allow for an average rent was understandable in view of the complexity of any alternative. Two other considerations were important. First, the housing market was a managed market with some 10% of dwellings in the public sector and 60% in a private rented sector subject to rent controls. Second, Beveridge expressed the hope that there would be a successful effort to deal with urban congestion and housing shortage. In this event, differences in rents arising from housing shortages would be removed and people paying higher rents would do so by choice: 'a high rent will then represent a free choice by the householder and it will become indefensible to favour that form of expenditure over other forms of expenditure in fixing scales of benefit' (Beveridge, 1942, para 213). This argument is persuasive and has recurred subsequently, although shortages have been a permanent feature of British housing.

Subsequent decisions and changes in housing tenure undermined the compromise. In particular, Beveridge (1953) referred to 'a deal with the Treasury' that set the level of benefits close to the subsistence minimum. The consequence of this was that many of those who qualified for national insurance benefits also qualified for means–tested assistance benefits. This particularly applied where rents were higher than allowed for in calculating social insurance benefit rates. If insurance benefit rates had been higher, there would have been less dependency on means testing and on discretionary or rent additions.

High levels of investment in housing were achieved after 1946 and local policies improved housing standards and supply: housing unfitness, sharing, overcrowding and absence of basic amenities declined dramatically along with private renting. Housing investment, however, did not eliminate shortages, which fuelled housing cost differentiation. As in later years, the greater capacity to borrow and greater effective demand from higher-income households pushed up housing costs in parts of the home-ownership and deregulated private rented sectors and generated an affordability gap for lower-income households. Much good-quality, market-priced housing was unaffordable for lower-income groups. At the same time, decontrol associated with vacant possession speeded decline in the private rented sector and exposed more households to market prices. The government's misconceived attempts to revive private renting through decontrol (particularly through legislation in 1954 and 1957) failed to have the desired effect and speeded transfers to home-ownership (Donnison, 1967). As private renting declined, and slum clearance progressed, lower-income households had fewer choices beyond council housing.

The foundations for the Beveridge compromise had shifted and placed profound strain on the housing system. Problems of access to different tenures and of homelessness increased. The variation in rents was greater than under the managed system of the 1940s. Fewer of the poorest households had secure housing in a low-rent, low-standard private rented sector. Council housing, with higher rents than in private controlled tenancies, housed an increasing proportion of low-income households; consequently, more council tenants required assistance with their rent.

By the 1970s, the tensions associated with housing costs were chronic. The system of housing finance was partitioned between tenures, with different systems of housing finance, subsidy and arrangements for assistance with housing costs. Rent rebate schemes for council tenants had been more widely adopted but operated (alongside general assistance subsidies for council dwellings) with differences in local administration (Malpass, 1990). Private tenants and owner-occupiers only received additional assistance with housing costs where they qualified for national assistance and their rent or mortgage interest payments affected their benefit entitlement. The dominant view supported a move to reduce general assistance subsidies for council housing and provide means-tested benefits for all tenants to protect them from high rents. What this involved was a nationalisation of policy in order to integrate housing more effectively within the welfare state.

The Housing Finance Act 1972 introduced a national formula for rent increases in the public sector and a mandatory system of local rent and rate rebates that survived subsequent legislation. It also speeded decontrol of the private rented sector and introduced a mandatory rent allowance scheme for private tenants. But the formula left two systems operating in parallel. Before 1972, hardly any rent rebate schemes included households receiving Supplementary Benefit (SB) but the new rules required their inclusion. The assessment of what SB recipients would have received in rebates involved considerable administrative duplication. Local authorities made block payments to the Department of Health and Social Security (DHSS) to cover what recipients would have received from rebates. Rent rebate costs increased enormously because of rising rents, but also because the national scheme was more generous than most of the schemes it superseded (Holmans, 1987, p 359).

A comprehensive review of SB was embarked upon in 1976, partly because of these changes to the treatment of housing costs. The aim was to simplify a system 'having to play a role for which it was neither originally designed nor subsequently adapted' (DHSS, 1978, p 3). What had been designed as a subsidiary method of income support, which would diminish in importance, had expanded over 30 years into a service supporting nearly 10% of the population. Housing costs were one of the main elements of the scheme and a major source of complexity, high staff costs and duplication of effort with local authorities. The introduction of specialised assistance for housing through rent and rate rebates and allowances had added substantially to problems (DHSS, 1978, p 58). The operation of SB rent additions alongside rent rebates and allowances formed a system that was incomprehensible to claimants and staff and costly and inefficient to administer. Housing costs and subsidies 'lay at the heart of some of the most chaotic tangles of that chaotically tangled system' and even where it worked properly, the arrangements were often unfair, and widely resented (Donnison, 1982, p 185).

The Housing Benefit system, introduced in 1982, stripped housing costs out of the new Income Support system. A single, comprehensive Housing Benefit administered by local government was adopted because it enabled savings of staffing in SB rather than because it resolved the issues involved. Home-owners were still dealt with through Income Support, while Housing Benefit was administered through local authorities. Under the system, 100% of rent could be eligible for benefit. This did not itself provide an incentive for households to reduce housing costs and, because housing benefits existed, policymakers could regard any move to market prices as unproblematic. The conventional wisdom about the merits of markets and subject subsidies could be applied. Whatever rents emerged, there was a safety net and housing benefits could take the strain. This was exactly the position taken by governments encouraging private rented provision and the private financing of social housing from the mid-1980s onwards. The encouragement of private renting through deregulation would increase choice and higher rents would be managed through Housing Benefit. Housing associations could build with a lower government grant if the rents they charged were higher – government could generate more social rented housing from any given level of capital expenditure and housing benefits would assist with housing costs. If the rents of council housing went up, the need for subsidy to meet the deficit on the Housing Revenue Account would decline. The government's housing public expenditure could be reduced and any growth in Housing Benefit costs represented the improved targeting of subsidy. Inevitably, Housing Benefit costs exploded and it was not long before the system that had been seen as a solution became part of the problem. The debate shifted to actions to address 'abuse', cap rent payments and reduce the rate of growth of expenditure.

The period after 1979 was one of deregulation and privatisation. After 60 years of steady growth, the numbers of council dwellings declined with measures to restrict new construction, sell council housing and transfer stock to housing associations. By 2010, housing associations had overtaken local authorities as providers of social rented housing. Home-ownership had ceased to expand but private renting was growing (see Table 3.1).

Table 3.1: Tenure of dwellings: England, 1914–2010 (percentages)

	Owner-occupied	Rented from		
		Local authority	**Housing association**	**Private landlords**
1914	10	< 1	90	
1939	32	10	58	
1953	32	18	51	
1971	53	28	1	18
1981	60	27	2	11
2001	70	13	7	10
2010 est	69	8	10	13

Note: Figures before 1971 are for England and Wales.
Source: Holmans (1987) and DCLG.

The government increasingly regarded property ownership as a mechanism for not just meeting housing needs: it identified the advantages of investment in property as security in older age and encouraged access and trading up in owner-occupation and the buy-to-let market. In the 1980s, this encouragement operated alongside reduced ambitions for state pensions. The government encouraged private pensions systems and the transfer from the state earnings-related pensions scheme, and chose not to upgrade benefit levels in line with wages. Housing was more centrally placed in the welfare state because it involved individual asset ownership, financial security and independence. The combination of residual public provision and asset-based welfare represented a significant shift. The new approach aimed at universal coverage but not at uniformity or universal or high-quality public provision. It was a stratified system that encouraged people to regard the inequalities associated with the market as presenting opportunities to take responsibility for planning and meeting household needs. It shifted risk and responsibility to the individual and took advantage of the view that investment in housing provided opportunities for increasing wealth and storing it in a secure place. The view that tenants had no asset generated support for discounted sale of public housing to sitting tenants and stimulated plausible plans for other ways of providing tenants with equity stakes. This conveniently ignored the limited asset stakes associated with low-value properties and ignored the reality that security of tenure in a property subject to a rent below market levels represented an asset.

By 2007, the Labour government was identified with a residual/asset-based welfare model, but concerns about housing affordability and shortage generated reviews of housing supply (Barker, 2003, 2004, 2006), social housing (Hills, 2007) and its regulation (Cave, 2007). The Labour government rediscovered housing policy and especially the need to increase house-building. It restructured housing regulation, increased capital expenditure and developed higher regional house-building targets (Murie, 2009). However, Labour's belated ambition to increase housing supply was frustrated by the credit crunch and recession after 2007. The credit crunch was mainly caused by banks lending for house purchase in the sub-prime market in the US rather than in the UK. British banks exposed by their reliance on wholesale borrowing and their bulk purchase of mortgage-based securities and other investments were unable to continue to make loans. Even after cash injections from the state came to their rescue, their ability to finance new lending was enormously reduced. Rising unemployment, economic recession and shortages of credit sent the housing market and house-building into crisis.

The Labour government responded by increasing spending on construction and cajoling lenders to lend. While the former had some impact, the latter failed. The outcome was that lenders were not lending enough, buyers could not buy and builders were not investing (HMG,

2011). New private house-building collapsed to its lowest peacetime level since 1923/24, mortgage loans by banks and building societies fell by over 50% and negative equity re-emerged with falling house prices.

Credit and Coalition crunch

The Coalition government in 2010 faced long-term issues relating to the integration of housing within the welfare state, overlaid by the crisis that had emerged since 2007. Housing shortages had never been overcome and were complicated by uneven economic development and migration. An extended period of low rates of house-building, following the reduction in local authority activity after 1979, left greater problems of housing shortage that impacted adversely on housing costs and standards, including overcrowding. Higher unemployment and widening income inequality increased differentials in purchasing power and the size of loans that could be negotiated and contributed to housing cost inflation. The gap in incomes generated an unprecedented affordability problem for lower-income households. The demand for social rented housing had grown, with some 4.5 million people registered on social housing waiting lists. The variations in local rents and housing costs, which Beveridge and subsequent reform had struggled with, had increased, although rents in the social rented sector generally remained below market levels. Housing allocations throughout the social rented sector were based on housing need (and not income) and, once a tenancy was granted, tenants' rights were not conditional on any continuing test of need, income or capacity to access alternative housing. This continued to generate neighbourhood and tenure social mix as when tenants' circumstances changed, they stayed put.

Although the government had moderated Housing Benefit costs (especially by limiting benefit to regional average rents rather than meeting 100% of rents charged), the combined costs of rent rebates and allowances in Great Britain had increased from £3.4 billion in 1986/87 to £12.9 billion in 2006/07. In March 2011, almost 5 million households received Housing Benefit: 1,844,680 housing association tenants, 1,545,860 private tenants and 1,475,670 council tenants. A lower proportion of private tenants received benefit but their average benefit was higher.

The Conservative–Liberal Democrat Coalition government elected in May 2010 adopted an approach affected by the credit crunch, economic recession and the level of government debt, but also by long-standing ambitions to reduce the role of the state in housing. The focus was on cutting expenditure and dealing with the assumed effects of social security and tenancy rights on distorting housing decisions. Parts of the housing policy package emerged shortly after the formation of the new government, but the final element, the Housing Strategy, emerged in November 2011. The first steps included cuts in capital expenditure: Homes and Communities Agency (HCA) funding for affordable housing in England was reduced from £3.7 billion in 2009/10 to £2.7 billion in 2010/11 and £4.5 billion for the period 2011/15 (HCA, 2010). This effectively terminated continuing funding for existing Housing Market Renewal and some other regeneration schemes. Proposals envisaged rents for new social housing lettings rising to 80% of the market level. This could improve the finances of social landlords and increase their capacity to develop new housing without government grants. It would not have a massive immediate impact but a cumulative effect as more properties became subject to higher rents. The Tenant Services Authority (TSA), only created in 2008 when the regulatory and funding roles of the Housing Corporation were split between the TSA and HCA, would be abolished. Its remaining functions would transfer to an independent committee within the HCA. It was claimed that this would generate efficiency savings in back-office functions and exploit synergies across investment and regulation; but it weakened the division between funder and regulator that had previously been presented as essential (Murie, 2008).

Although cutting capital expenditure would reduce construction, the government declared itself concerned about house-building:

> For decades house building has failed to keep pace with people's needs. And recently, a combination of the recession, divisive top-down targets and a public subsidy-driven approach has led to a catastrophic decline in the number of new homes....
>
> We need to make building homes a motor for growth again – creating new jobs and great places to live and work. (DCLG, 2011, p 4)

The budget of 2011 introduced a first-time buyers scheme to demonstrate commitment to home-ownership and new building. It was claimed that this FirstBuy scheme should help 10,000 families after September 2011. The government also tuned to a familiar refrain under Labour and the Barker reviews of housing supply (see earlier): that the planning system was holding back housing supply. The evidence related to land banking and development had left this view contested and it was difficult to see how planning was responsible for the collapse of activity after 2007. Nevertheless, the government dismissed existing regional house-building targets and Regional Spatial Strategies and embarked on a populist attack on planning under the banner of 'localism'. A New Homes Bonus was designed to stimulate local encouragement for new house-building. This Bonus, provided for each additional property, and paid for the following six years as a non-ring-fenced grant, would be equal to the national average for the council tax band the property fell within. Proposals for a more development-friendly and local approach to planning and the repeated reference to planning as an important mechanism in promoting economic growth were not always welcomed despite assurances given by ministers over protecting the countryside and the green belt.

The budget of 2010 included proposals for reform of Housing Benefit from April 2011 as part of larger welfare reforms to make the system fairer and more affordable. Housing benefit expenditure would be reduced (by '£1.8 billion a year by the end of the Parliament') (Budget Statement, 2010) and tenancy and benefit arrangements would change. The maximum benefit available to tenants in the private sector would be capped at the average rent for the lowest 30% of the local market. Rules related to the appropriate size of property for households would limit benefit eligibility across the rented sectors and particularly affect young single-person households. Proposals included restricting Housing Benefit for working-age claimants in the social rented sector who were living in a larger property than their household size warranted, and adjusting Support for Mortgage Interest (SMI) payments, which would be paid at the Bank of England's published Average Mortgage Rate instead of the previous higher rate. From April 2011, Housing Benefit would be set in line with the Consumer Prices Index (CPI) instead of the Retail Prices Index (RPI) and this was expected to reduce the rate of growth of benefit. The budget had also proposed to time-limit the receipt of full Housing Benefit for claimants who could be expected to look for work, but this was not included in the Welfare Reform Bill 2011; and the budget of 2011 confirmed that the government would not take forward the planned 10% reduction in Housing Benefit for long-term Jobseeker's Allowance claimants. However, the possibility of an overall benefit cap (a new wage stop) that would prevent total benefits including those related to housing from exceeding average income would have more profound impacts on larger households and on those paying higher rents.

These changes immediately challenged the assumption that tenants could regard their dwelling as their home. Security and continuing occupancy would be put at risk if tenants needed benefit and this applied however long they had lived in their dwelling and whatever previous policies and undertakings had been given relating to security and continuing occupancy. Their rent might not be paid in full because it was above the 30% threshold, or was deemed to relate to a property that was larger than they needed. Tenants determined to keep their home would have to absorb the rent with lower benefits. The alternative of giving up their home and moving on could disrupt schooling, work and various networks that are important in the distinction between a house and a home.

Long-term proposals for housing emerged from the Department for Work and Pensions (DWP, 2010) rather than the department with housing responsibility (the Department for Communities and Local Government). They formed part of proposals to replace a number of benefits with the UC to be introduced in 2013/14 for new claims and 2014–17 for existing cases. Housing Benefit would form part of the UC but be paid for actual housing costs. Responsibility for housing costs within the UC would move from local authorities to a new national agency. The expressed aim of UC was to simplify the welfare benefits system, increase incentives to work and introduce conditionality (encouraging individuals to seek work) to the payment of benefits (see Chapter One in this volume). While Housing Benefit costs would be reduced by measures to limit entitlement, higher affordable rents could progressively have the opposite effect.

The government emphasised the enormous importance of social housing but declared: 'It is time to change the social housing system' to ensure 'that good, affordable housing is available for those who genuinely need it; and that we get the best from our four million rented homes'. There was to be a change of approach: 'Margaret Thatcher introduced statutory lifetime tenure for social housing in 1981. Times have changed, and it is no longer right that the Government should require every social tenancy to be for life, regardless of the particular circumstances' (DCLG, 2010, p 5).

The proposals for social housing used the rhetoric of localism and flexibility. They referred to 'a broken, centrally-controlled system in need of urgent reform' and asserted that:

Stable and secure social housing should provide a firm basis on which people can build a successful future. But far too often, the security and subsidised rent that social housing provides do not appear to help tenants to independence and self-sufficiency. (DCLG, 2010, p 12)

The Hills review of social housing (see earlier), and Labour's reaction to it, had introduced discussion of the high levels of worklessness and low mobility in social housing. Inflexible tenancy arrangements took no account of ability to pay or of changing household circumstances and contributed to imbalances between the size of households and the properties they lived in. In social housing, around 250,000 households were overcrowded but over 400,000 households were 'under-occupying' by two bedrooms or more (DCLG, 2010, p 13). The government proposed changes in how people accessed social housing and in the security and affordability of social rented tenancies. A new, more flexible 'affordable rent' tenancy would be introduced in the housing association sector from 2011 onwards to recognise households' differing ability to meet housing costs. Rents would be set at less than 80% of the market rent or at the Local Housing Allowance level and be eligible for housing benefit. The extra income generated would reduce the level of government grant needed to support new provision. The additional resources would be greatest where market rents were highest and be most effective in high-cost and high-demand areas. In some circumstances, social rented properties could be let on fixed-term tenancies: affordable rent tenancies would be for a minimum of two years with the maximum set by local policies. The details of a new flexible tenancy with longer tenancies for some groups would emerge following consultation.

The Localism Bill, published in 2010, included changes to the legislation governing local authorities' housing allocations, the types of tenancies social housing tenancies granted and duties related to homelessness. Local authorities would decide who should be considered for social housing, 'while continuing to ensure that priority for social housing goes to those most in need' (DCLG, 2010, para 1.28, p 16). Existing tenants trapped in unsuitable housing would be given greater priority, enabling social landlords to find 'creative solutions', helping tenants move to properties better suited to their needs, making better use of the stock and improving arrangements for mutual exchanges. Local authorities would be able to fully discharge the main homelessness duty by arranging offers of suitable accommodation in the private rented sector without requiring consent, subject to certain safeguards. Those owed the duty would no longer be able to insist on being offered social housing. This 'will give local authorities the scope to arrange appropriate housing solutions promptly, avoiding the need for long periods in temporary accommodation and freeing up social lets for others in housing need on the waiting list' (DCLG, 2010, para 1.31, p 16). The existing annual centralised Housing Revenue Account subsidy system for council housing was also to be abolished and replaced by 'a locally-run system where councils can keep their rental income and use it locally to maintain homes for current and future tenants' (DCLG, 2010, para 1.22, p 15).

The emphasis throughout the government's discussion was on flexibility, meeting housing need, making better use of the social housing stock, targeting support where it was needed most and getting more value for the money invested. Except where changes in Housing Benefit affected them, the individual rights and security of existing tenants in their homes were recognised, with new tenants and applicants treated differently. The impact on families, neighbourhoods and communities were referred to and were, no doubt, expected to be among the things taken into account when local decision-makers decided how to apply new policy options.

The riots in parts of London and other English cities in August 2011 further encouraged ministers to alter tenants' rights in the social rented sector. An updated version of the outstanding consultation document proposed a new mandatory power of possession for anti-social behaviour to make it easier to evict people whose criminal or anti-social behaviour had been committed away from their home. The housing minister stated: 'It cannot be right for the sanction [eviction] to apply only to criminal behaviour towards neighbours or in the locality of the property as it does at the moment' (Shapps, 2011).

By the time the DCLG launched its housing strategy in November 2011, the previous year's cuts were having an effect. In spite of the rhetoric, new construction had fallen even further with private housing starts continuing at a low level and the affordable housing programme, supported by government subsidy, in collapse. New completions had fallen by 6,500 in 2010/11 alongside falling net completions (see Table 3.2).

The housing strategy was presented as a plan to increase housing construction, help local economies and create jobs. The Prime Minister also referred to home-ownership as something that should be achievable for everyone. An extra £400 million was allocated to kick-start stalled private sector house-building and create new jobs. Although the stamp duty holiday for first-time buyers was not extended, a scheme developed between the House Builders Federation, Council of Mortgage Lenders

(CML) and government would provide cash for an extra 100,000 purchasers frozen out by the lack of finance. This mortgage indemnity scheme involved the government as backstop guarantor on new 95% loans on newly built dwellings. House-builders would contribute up to 3.5% of the dwelling value in the indemnity pot and would share the risk with lenders and the government. Scepticism about the impact of this and whether any dwellings sold under the scheme would be additional was strengthened as the CML forecast for lending involved a reduction from 2011 to 2012 and lenders outside the CML expressed little enthusiasm. Other measures would help councils take over empty properties, release public sector land and develop it on a 'build now, pay later' basis, and to reduce the obligations placed on developers in granting planning permissions. All of this represented a reduction in obligations or active government support for private development. The market needed state assistance to revive.

Table 3.2: Annual net additional dwellings: England, 2000/01–2010/11

	Net additional dwellings	**% change from previous year**
2000/01	132,000	–
2001/02	130,510	7%
2002/03	143,680	10%
2003/04	154,770	8%
2004/05	169,450	9%
2005/06	186,380	10%
2006/07	198,770	7%
2007/08	207,370	4%
2008/09	166,570	–20%
2009/10	128,680	–23%
2010/11	121,200	–6%

Source: DCLG.

The housing strategy also saw the resurrection of the RTB with reference to discounts of up to 50% of value. The detail surrounding this emerged later (DCLG, 2012). Labour's regional maximum discounts and the lower maximum discounts in localities with housing stress would be removed and a new maximum discount of £75,000 would apply throughout England. In the past, the RTB provided massive capital receipts for the Treasury and no doubt there were hopes that this would happen again. The new strategy referred to using receipts from sales to support funding for new affordable housing (on a one-for-one basis), but the income would also be applied to reducing local debt and it was unclear whether the new housing involved was additional – or how this was to be judged. The history of RTB (Jones and Murie, 2006) suggests that there would be some demand to buy – some households unable to buy in the past would have increased capacity while larger discounts, higher rents and uncertainties about the security of their tenancy might affect decisions. The questions about this policy would be about whether discounts represented good value for money; how they fitted alongside policies to reduce under-occupation and encourage mobility; and whether the approach was strategic or would further residualise the social rented sector and leave the dwelling size, type and location out of step with expressed need. Any replacement housing would also have higher rents. The dwellings sold in earlier phases of the RTB have not all remained in home-ownership but were subsequently transferred into private renting. The Coalition housing strategy offered no response to concerns expressed about the failings of management in parts of the private rented sector or the consequences of lack of security for tenants and continued to promote its growth. New measures were designed to be attractive to institutional investors. The package as a whole seemed more likely to result in the continuing decline of social rented and owner-occupied housing with the only growth in a private rented sector with rents inflated by housing shortage and few protections for tenants, and supported by a growing social security budget.

These proposals represent another redesign of housing in the welfare state. As in earlier compromises, simplification and saving money was important. Under the Coalition, direct measures affecting tenants' rights and the indirect impact of benefit changes reduced the security and bargaining power of tenants. Better-off tenants might escape by exercising rights under a revived RTB. Others would be subject to a more 'efficient' and judgemental regime in a more profoundly residual sector. Concerns that caps on benefits and measures to address under-occupation and reduce security of tenure would impact most heavily on poorer households and force mobility and ghettoisation were expressed by the Conservative London mayor, trade associations and charities. Poor people would be less likely to be forced to move if they lived in smaller properties and in poorer neighbourhoods. While policymakers referred to under-occupying social tenants, this was not a term driving policy in other tenures. The more that some households have to move as the size of their permanently resident family changes, the more there will be a difference in rights, living practices and what the family home represents between different tenures. The outcome is likely to be a closer fit between what a household's income and employment is and what housing it lives in. Less affluent households will live at higher occupancy levels and be less likely to have spare rooms. Private landlords operating in a continuing environment of shortage will raise rents or subdivide properties and trigger changes for their tenants. The inertia promoted by the old regime and sustaining some degree of social mix even in more affluent areas would be countered. The new rules could force tenants with long- or short-term dependency on housing benefits to move to lower rent areas or properties – so reducing social and income mix at the street level.

Flexible tenure and the increased role of private tenancies without security of tenure increase the risk that poorer families will be repeatedly forced to move as their household circumstances change or at the behest of their landlord. Such increased mobility will increase social and spatial differentiation, disrupt schooling and reduce opportunities in training and the labour market and the prospect of achieving self-sufficiency. The New Homes Bonus formula may provide an incentive for local authorities to approve new development but it is also plausible that it will fail to change the long history of urban containment in England. There is an open invitation to adopt strategies for territorial defence, to contain lower-income groups in their existing areas and to ensure that most new development in affluent urban and peri-urban areas is for affluent households. The implication of this is that, where social segregation has been increasing in England, it is likely to further increase. The proposals do not altogether remove factors that have induced inertia or moderated the market processes sorting households geographically according to class, occupation and income, and households will continue to identify good reasons not to adjust their housing every time their circumstances change. Nevertheless, if the factors encouraging social mix and moderating segregation weaken, such segregation will increase – with some rapid short-term changes and some over a longer period.

Conclusions

This chapter has outlined the latest in a succession of attempts to integrate housing within the British welfare state. The Beveridge welfare judgement fudged the problem posed by highly variable rents but, in retrospect, and if nothing else had changed, it offered a basis for muddling through. The housing system was, however, undergoing structural change and this was further affected by new housing, taxation and social security policies, and changes in incomes and income inequality. The government has pursued various strategies designed to reduce expenditure in a context of continuing housing shortage and movement towards market prices and processes. These have increased housing costs and the costs of assistance with them. Reductions in housing capital expenditure and the generation of capital receipts from the sale of housing assets provided short-term budgetary relief but left an increasing long-term commitment associated with rising housing costs. The continued failure to deal with housing shortage and the move away from a managed to a market system had consequences for government expenditure. Having chosen to dismantle council housing and shift to subject subsidies, the latter became a problem. The costs involved have been used to justify new approaches to housing rights, security and stability. Not only does this seem inconsistent with previous undertakings, but it also appears to take no account of the costs to households, communities and future governments of insecurity, inequality and segregation.

More recent approaches to housing in the welfare state have sought solutions in national control, greater reliance on the market and various hybrid neo-liberal approaches. But local differences have increased and challenge this approach. Housing policy in Britain has periodically been informed by hunch, plausible theories and accepted orthodoxies rather than robust evidence. New blueprints have often been associated with incoming governments seeking to remedy the failures of previous unsatisfactory settlements made worse by rapid changes in the market. The Coalition government has made scant reference to recent evidence related to the performance, efficiency and costs of private renting and appear to have accepted selective versions of how housing tenure affects worklessness and mobility. The Coalition's approach to housing in the welfare state emerged bit by bit over 18 months. Powerful rhetoric about housing construction backed with attacks on planning, worklessness and aspects of tenants' rights was reminiscent of Labour's last years but higher public expenditure, the next phase of decent homes and regeneration were missing. There was no strategy for the worst estates or for areas marked by instability and high turnover with adverse effects on families, education, communities and employability. There were no new ambitions for the social rented sector and the priority given to empty homes and first-time buyers had been asserted before. The revival of private renting was emphasised without admitting that it was likely to conflict with ambitions to extend home-ownership or to improve the quality and management of rented housing.

National policy changes are interpreted and implemented differently at a local level and affected by dynamic market and political contexts. Local outcomes are difficult to predict from national policy changes. Questions remain about how different households and groups of households that comprise neighbourhoods will respond to and be affected by change. Particular focus will be placed on how housing and the welfare state perform for lower-income and vulnerable households. Such households are present in all of the major tenures in Britain and all of them are affected by changes in benefits and employment that affect their incomes. Older owners with small or zero mortgages are best able to absorb any changes, although neglect of repair and maintenance and high energy bills remain issues. Younger owners may have been helped by low interest rates and the low levels of repossessions attest to this. They may nevertheless face difficulties in moving and be exposed if interest rates rise. Unemployment and relationship breakdown also affect security. The greatest concentration of poorest households is in parts of the private rented sector and in social renting. It is these parts of the system that are most affected by rising rents and changes in benefit related to household composition, under-occupation, rent caps and any wage stop. And it is consequently households from these tenures that are most likely to be forced to adjust household budgets to absorb changes, or forced to move. Households affected by changes that mean that Working Tax Credit, Child Tax Credit or other benefits do not retain their value or keep pace with inflation are less likely to be able to absorb other changes and more likely to accumulate debts. It is hard to dispute that these groups are more likely to see living standards eroded. The lack of security of tenure in the private rented sector adds to this but the next generation in the social rented sector may be in the same position as their rights and wealth is eroded. One possibility is that the consolidation of a more residual and market policy approach will increase stratification and social and spatial divisions that will frustrate other agendas relating to social cohesion, health, education, employment and even the 'Big Society'. The Coalition blueprint is unlikely to resolve long-standing challenges and failures but is likely to introduce new problems for housing policy and tensions affecting the wider welfare state in the next generation.

References

Barker, K. (2003) *Review of housing supply: interim report*, London: HMSO.

Barker, K. (2004) *Review of housing supply, delivering stability: securing our future housing needs, final report – recommendations*, London: HMSO.

Barker, K. (2006) *Barker review of land use planning: final report*, London: HMSO.

Beveridge,W. (1942) *Social insurance and allied services*, Cmd 6404, London: HMSO.

Beveridge, W. (1953) *Power and influence*, London: George Allen and Unwin.

Budget Statement (2010) *Statement of the Chancellor of the Exchequer*, Rt Hon George Osborne, 22 June, www.hm-treasury.gov.uk/junebudget_speech.html

Cave, M. (2007) *Every tenant matters: a review of social housing regulation*, Wetherby: Communities and Local Government.

DCLG (Department for Communities and Local Government) (2010) 'Local decisions: a fairer future for social housing', November.

DCLG (2011) 'New homes bonus: final scheme design', February.

DCLG (2012) *Reinvigorating Right to Buy and one for one replacement*, March, London: DCLG.

DHSS (Department of Health and Social Security) (1978) *Social assistance: a review of the supplementary benefits scheme in Great Britain*, London: DHSS.

Donnison, D. (1967) *The government of housing*, Harmondsworth: Penguin.

Donnison, D.V. (1982) *The politics of poverty*, Oxford: Martin Robertson.

DWP (Department for Work and Pensions) (2010) *Universal Credit: welfare that works*, Cm 7957, London: Department for Work and Pensions.

Hills, J. (2007) *Ends and means: the future roles of social housing in England*, London: Centre for Analysis of Social Exclusion, London School of Economics and Political Science.

HMG (HM Government) (2011) *Laying the foundations: a housing strategy for England*, London: DCLG.

Holmans, A.E. (1987) *Housing policy in Britain*, London: Croom Helm.

Homes and Communities Agency (2010) *Affordable housing programme* www.homesandcommunities.co.uk

Jones, C. and Murie, A. (2006) *The Right to Buy: analysis and evaluation of a housing policy*, Oxford: Blackwell.

Malpass, P. (1990) *Reshaping housing policy: subsidies, rents and residualisation*, London: Routledge.

Murie, A. (2008) *Moving homes: the Housing Corporation 1964–2008*, London: Politico's.

Murie, A. (2009) 'Rediscovering housing policy', in P. Malpass and R.O. Rowlands (eds) *Housing, markets and policy*, London: Routledge, pp 224–44.

Shapps, G. (2011) 'A new mandatory power of possession for anti-social behaviour', 15 August, DCLG.

Yelling, J.A. (1992) *Slums and redevelopment*, London: UCL Press.

FOUR

The 2012/13 reforms of higher education in England: changing student finances and funding

Claire Callender

Introduction

The expansion and growing importance of higher education (HE) in England since the 1980s have prompted numerous reforms aimed at reshaping and restructuring HE and its funding, reflecting the changing ideological, economic and social functions of HE. The proposed reforms to be introduced in 2012/13 in England are by far the most radical and those concerning HE funding and student finances the most far-reaching. This chapter aims to unpack the drivers for these reforms, locating them in a broader historical and policy context. It describes the proposed 2012/13 HE changes and analyses their potential impact against their stated aims.

It is argued that the reforms herald a fundamental change in the role of the state in HE provision and in the balance of public and private contributions towards its costs, in line with broader shifts in responsibility and risk for welfare from the state to the individual. In turn, they reflect changes in beliefs about HE, its purpose and role in society, and who should have access to it and pay for it. The reforms are both driven and shaped by ideological, political and economic factors that together are leading to deleterious policy change. The new policies are untested. They represent a big experiment with unknown consequences and unforeseen unintended consequences. It is unclear, therefore, whether the reforms will meet their stated aims, or whether they will stand the test of time. We will not know for sure, for several years to come. However, they are likely to have a destabilising effect on the HE sector in the short term, and to polarise HE in the longer term, exacerbating existing social divisions and inequalities within and across the sector.

The chapter starts by examining the changing nature of undergraduate student finances in England, as the legacy of earlier policies are key to understanding the proposed 2012/13 reforms. Next, it explores the lead-up to the 2012/13 reforms and the recommendations of the 2010 Independent Review of Higher Education Funding and Student Finance – chaired by Lord Browne of Madingley – which informed the Coalition's proposals. Then, the government's response to Browne, encapsulated in their November 2010 announcement and their subsequent 2011 White Paper *Higher education: students at the heart of the system*, will be discussed. Finally, the changes will be critiqued and assessed against the stated aims of the White Paper. The discussion throughout focuses on England[1] and primarily on UK-domiciled full-time undergraduates.

The context for the reforms of financial support

To understand the precise nature of the 2012/13 student funding reforms, it is imperative to locate them within a historical context, particularly earlier changes to student finances. Three major shifts in student funding policies in England can be identified. First, government-funded student loans were established by the Education (Student Loans) Act 1990 as a new form of student financial assistance with mortgage-style loan repayments that depended on student earnings on graduation. Second, the Teaching and Higher Education Act 1998 introduced means-tested tuition fees of £1,000 paid up front, signalling that students as well as taxpayers should contribute towards the costs of HE. Finally, the Higher Education Act 2004, which came into force in 2006, launched variable tuition fees of up to £3,000 repaid by graduates via income-contingent student loans alongside student support funded by HE institutions (HEIs). These changes meant that all students, even the poorest, had to pay tuition fees. They also promoted a more marketised system of HE through both variable tuition fees and bursaries. Thus, they abandoned the general principle that all students, irrespective of where and what they studied, should be treated the same, pay the same tuition fees and receive the same types and amount of financial support if they met universal and fixed government-set national eligibility criteria. The 2004 Act also established the idea that universities should provide students with financial support but that universities, not the state, should select the beneficiaries and what they receive; for the first time, therefore, discretionary rather than universal financial support became widespread (Callender, 2010).

These changes in student financial support and finances reflect gradual transformations in beliefs about HE, its role in society, who benefits from it and so who should pay for it. Central to this is the balance of private and public contributions towards the costs of HE, and what proportion of these costs should be borne by: students and/or their families; employers; and the government or taxpayer. Since 1990, all the reforms to HE student funding in England have adopted a 'cost-sharing agenda' (Johnstone and Marcucci, 2010). They have attempted both to reduce public expenditure and to shift the costs of HE away from government and taxpayers so that more of these costs are borne by students and/or their families. The 2012/13 reforms will continue this trend and encourage another form of cost-sharing – private providers who will bear most of the costs of provision rather than the state.

This 'cost-sharing agenda' is a global policy, not restricted to England. According to Johnstone and Marcucci (2010), HE needs a more robust stream of non-governmental revenue because of: the growing importance of, and demand for, HE; the increasing costs of HE driven by HE expansion and rising per-student costs; the inability of governments to meet these costs; and the inadequacy of cost-side solutions to solve these problems. Their answer is more money from tuition fees paid for by students and/or their families alongside financial assistance in the form of student loans, grants and other public subsidies. Johnstone and Marcucci (2010, p 283) insist that cost-sharing for 'almost all countries ... is an imperative for the financial health of their colleges and universities' but warn that cost-sharing must 'always ... supplement and augment government revenue, never replace it'.

Review of Higher Education Funding and Student Finance, 2009

The Independent Review of Higher Education Funding and Student Finance, chaired by Lord Browne, was launched on 9 November 2009 with all political parties' support. It arose from the previous Labour government's commitment to review the operation of variable tuition fees for full-time students after three years – not because of a need for reform. It was 'tasked with making recommendations to Government on the future of fees policy and financial support for full and part-time undergraduate and postgraduate students' (BIS, 2009a) and report after the May 2010 general election. So, the highly contentious (and vote-losing) issue of resolving student finances was wiped off the election agenda, and left to the incoming government – the Conservative–Liberal Democrat Coalition.

The economic context within which the Review operated was one of the global recession and unprecedented cuts in public expenditure (HM Treasury, 2010). This is paramount for understanding the Review's recommendations, and the Coalition's response to them. So too is the political context, and the Coalition's ideology. This political environment was not exceptional. As Johnstone and Marcucci (2010, p 102) in their global review of funding remind us, tuition fees are the 'political and ideological flashpoint for debates over the need for, and the propriety of, cost-sharing in all its forms'. They continue, 'tuition fees are almost everywhere contested' (2010, p 123), reflecting the cultural and historical acceptability of tuition fees as well as the prevailing political ideologies.

Consequently, to understand tuition fee and financial support policies in England and elsewhere, we have to acknowledge the political and ideological context in which they are formulated and implemented, and how these shape the nature of the provision. Hence, whatever way forward economic or cost-sharing theory, or research evidence, may suggest, that direction will be both determined and compromised by political considerations. This is true of earlier student funding reforms in England,[2] and of Browne's recommendations and the government's response to them.

'The case for reform'

The Browne Review's final report – Independent Review of Higher Education Funding and Student Finance (IRHEFSF) – was published on 12 October 2010. The Report's case for reform focuses on three issues (IRHEFSF, 2010, p 23). First, increasing HE participation because demand exceeds supply; low-income students and under-represented groups are not going to the most prestigious universities, so 'fair access' has not been achieved; and access to part-time study is hampered by a lack of government financial support. Second, improving quality because students lack the skills employers want to improve productivity; HEIs need more money to upgrade their courses; and HEIs lack incentives to enhance the 'student experience'. Third, creating a sustainable system of HE funding because the balance of private and public contributions to the HE sector remains unchanged since 2006. Tuition fees of £3,000 had generated more income for HEIs, but the government was spending more on student financial support. Consequently, HE remained overly reliant on public funding, and if subject to public expenditure cuts, the HE sector would be unable to attract additional funds.

Browne's diagnosis of HE's problems are contestable. The report is devoid of research evidence. Unlike previous inquiries into HE funding, Browne commissioned no research to inform its deliberations, bar an opinion poll. At the Committee's public hearings, only nine of the 31 witnesses were academic specialists – the rest were HE stakeholder representatives. Undoubtedly, Browne's recommendations were driven by the Coalition's desire to reduce both the costs of student support and HE public expenditure, in line with their broader strategy to cut the fiscal deficit and stimulate economic growth. By 2010/11 (before any cuts) over half the Department for Business, Innovation and Skills' (BIS's) total HE annual expenditure was to be devoted to financing student aid, compared with 38% in 2003/04. Such costs arose from the 2006 reforms, particularly the large government subsidy on student loans. For every £100 a student borrows, it costs the government £28. This is because the interest rate on these loans is linked to inflation, which is lower than the government's costs of borrowing, and some graduates never repay their loans in full because repayments depend on graduates' earnings. These high costs limited the number of students who could receive loans, and restricted the number of student places. Since 2009/10, HEIs were prohibited from expanding to meet increasing demand. Money spent on student support also diverted funding from universities' other activities, yet they wanted more money to compete in an international, globalised, HE market.

The Report's key recommendations were as follows:

1. Most of the money HEIs receive from the government for teaching undergraduate courses should be withdrawn, but government subsidies for science, technology, engineering and mathematics courses should continue at a reduced level. This lost income would be replaced by higher tuition fees. Consequently, there would be no, or limited, taxpayer support for teaching, with these costs being met by students paying higher fees with the help of student loans. Government financial support for undergraduates, therefore, would shift from teaching grants to student loans.

2. The government-set cap of £3,375 on undergraduate tuition fees should be removed.

3. HEIs charging tuition fees over £6,000 should be subject to a levy. HEIs would keep a diminishing proportion of any fees charged

above £6,000, and the levy would be returned to government to help fund the national student financial support system.

4. All full-time students would continue to receive student loans to pay all their tuition fees, including those attending private HE institutions and, for the first time, part-time students should also be eligible for fee loans.

5. All full-time students would still get student loans for maintenance but these should not be means-tested. Full-time, low-income students would also still receive maintenance grants, which would be increased to compensate for the proposed abolition of statutory bursaries.

6. The terms and conditions of student loans repayment should change. The point at which graduates start to repay their loans should increase from £15,000 to £21,000, and all outstanding debt should be forgiven after 30 years – previously 25 years. Consequently, graduates would pay 9% (unchanged) of their income above £21,000 until they had repaid all their student loan debt with any outstanding debt written off after 30 years.

7. The interest paid on the loans for graduates earning above £21,000 should be equal to the government's cost of borrowing (inflation plus 2.2%), and no longer rise in line with inflation.

8. Potential students should be provided, primarily by HEIs, with more information and careers advice about courses and their outcomes, so that they can make informed HE choices.

Browne's recommendations are an attempt to develop a quasi-market in HE. As Le Grand reminds us in relation to other public services, markets are considered a means for delivering 'high-quality services efficiently, equitably and in a responsive fashion' (Le Grand, 2007, p 38). For choice and competition to operate effectively, 'competition must be real', whereby the money must follow users' choices; there must be a variety of types of provision and providers, with new providers entering the market and failing ones exiting; and 'users must be properly informed' (Le Grand, 2007, pp 76–7).

One of the six principles guiding Browne's report is increasing student choice by putting 'students at the heart of the system' and 'relying on student choice to drive up quality' (IRHEFSF, 2010, pp 25, 29). Other recommendations aim to increase competition between HEIs by abolishing the cap on tuition fees so that universities charge different fees, and by giving students loans that, in effect, are like an educational voucher that students redeem at the HEI of their choice. Consequently, the bulk of universities' money will follow students' choices while, theoretically, consumer demand will determine what HEIs offer. To survive, HEIs will have to become more responsive to student needs. Those with high student demand will be able to charge higher fees and expand, while those that cannot recruit enough students will fail and potentially close down.

Browne's proposals also seek to provide greater student choice and provider competition by enabling the development of a more diverse and flexible HE sector with more variety in the range and nature of HE provision, including part-time study. Essential to this is allowing new providers, including private universities and Further Education Colleges (FECs), to enter the HE market and encouraging HE providers to compete by driving up teaching quality and driving down price through efficiency gains.

The promotion of a market in public services, characterised by user choice and provider competition, is not new. It was central to Labour's modernisation agenda and public services reforms, with the consumer at its heart (Clarke et al, 2007). This steered Labour's HE policies too, and was most pronounced in their final HE document – *Higher ambitions: the future of universities in a knowledge economy* (BIS, 2009b). But it was crucial to Labour's introduction of variable tuition fees and bursaries in 2006, which together would establish price differentials among providers. Yet, by 2010/11, all HEIs were charging the maximum tuition fee for bachelor's degrees. Any competitive advantage of charging lower fees was outweighed by the benefits of higher fee income. Consequently, contrary to Labour's intentions, the new maximum fee had become a new flat rate. So the Browne Report, and the Coalition government's response to it, could be seen as an attempt to complete Labour's unfinished HE agenda.

The Coalition government's response to the Browne Report

The Coalition government's formal response to the Browne Report came in two stages: first, in a statement by David Willetts, Minister for Universities and Science, in the House of Commons on 3 November 2010 (Willetts, 2010); and, second, in their publication on 28 June 2011 of the White Paper *Higher education: students at the heart of the system* (BIS, 2011a), which reiterated the November 2010 announcement. Unsurprisingly, the government accepted some of Browne's proposals while rejecting others, and introduced some new mechanisms in the

White Paper while supporting the notion of an HE market and students as consumers.

Announcement by David Willetts in the House of Commons on 3 November 2010

All the changes Willetts pronounced on 3 November 2010 will come into force in 2012/13 for new HE entrants. First, the government endorsed Browne's recommendation to withdraw most of HEIs' teaching funds (see recommendation 1 earlier), representing a cut of 80% in HE's teaching budget. Second, the Coalition rejected Bowne's suggestion that the tuition fees cap should be abolished (2). Instead, the existing cap of £3,375 per annum will rise to a maximum of £9,000. Third, they abandoned the idea of a fees levy (3), but HEIs charging more than £6,000 will be subject to 'a tougher regime' to ensure that they meet their widening participation and fair access responsibilities. Fourth, the government agreed that tuition fee loans should be extended to part-time undergraduates (4), but maintenance loans for full-time students will continue to be partially means-tested, as they are now (5). Fifth, maintenance grants for low-income students will be increased (5), but eligibility to partial grants will be limited to students whose annual family income is between £25,000 and £42,000, down from the present £50,000. Sixth, the government agreed with Browne's earnings threshold for loan repayments and the extended period of debt forgiveness (6). However, the government will charge higher interest rates on loans (7). Both graduates from part-time and full-time study will not start repaying their loans until earning £21,000 a year, when the interest on their loan will be limited to inflation. Graduates earning between £21,000 and £41,000 will be charged interest on a sliding scale up to a maximum of inflation plus 3% when annual earnings exceed £41,000. The government also supported more information for students (8). Finally, the government announced a National Scholarship Programme (NSP), co-funded by the government and HEIs, as a sop to the Liberal Democrats in the Coalition. This support for low-income students, worth at least £3,000, is not an entitlement. HEIs will determine who receives help and what they get. The NSP is a lottery of the worst kind. Alongside this aid, HEIs will continue to give these and other students discretionary bursaries, scholarships and fee waivers.

Significantly, both Browne and the government recognise the importance of a comprehensive student support system to safeguard HE participation. Without it, fee increases would lead to substantial falls in participation (Dearden et al, 2010), and still may. The overall structure and type of student financial support for full-time students remain largely unchanged compared with provisions introduced in 2006. However, students will graduate with much higher student loan debt and it will take graduates far longer to pay this off.

For these announcements to be implemented by 2012/13, HEIs had to respond rapidly. HEIs had to set their tuition fees, fee waivers and other financial support offered to students *before* some changes outlined by Willetts had reached the statute book, and *before* the publication of the White Paper in June 2011. In July 2011, the average tuition fee HEIs and FECs planned to charge in 2012/13 was £8,393 (£8,161 after fee waivers).[3] Most (59%) were charging the maximum fee of £9,000 for at least one of their courses, while a third were charging this for all their courses (OFFA, 2011). These fee levels were well above the average of £7,500 anticipated by the Treasury.

2011 White Paper: Higher education: students at the heart of the system

The 2011 White Paper (BIS, 2011a), unlike previous HE White Papers, is very narrowly drawn. It focuses exclusively on the undergraduate economy, especially student funding, while failing to locate HE within a broader context or addressing other HE concerns. It primarily repeats, in more detail, Willetts' November 2010 statement but also seeks to deal with HEIs' responses to that announcement, especially the higher-than-expected fees HEIs planned to charge.

The White Paper mirrors the Browne Report's case for reform:

> Our reforms tackle three challenges. First, putting higher education on a sustainable footing. We inherited the largest budget deficit in post-war history, requiring spending cuts across government. By shifting public spending away from teaching grants and towards repayable tuition loans, we have ensured that higher education receives the funding it needs even as substantial savings are made to public expenditure. Second, institutions must deliver a better student experience; improving teaching, assessment, feedback and preparation for the world of work. Third, they must take more responsibility for increasing social mobility. (BIS, 2011a, p 4)

The White Paper establishes mechanisms to reduce HEIs' tuition fees (and the government's student loan bill), and to create more competition between providers in an environment of constrained student numbers by 'liberating student number controls' (BIS, 2011a, p 48). It introduces 'core and margin' student places. HEIs will be allowed to recruit as many students as they like scoring the equivalent of AAB or above at A level,[4] while 20,000 places will be reserved for higher education providers whose average tuition fee (after fee waivers) is £7,500 or below. These places will be removed from the national pot of government-allocated student places, and a HEI's core allocation. This will lead to an estimated 9% reduction in core allocations in 2012/13, but over time the number of 'core' places will decline while the number of competitive 'margin' places will increase. With no increase in total student numbers, there will be winners and losers: HEIs with few AAB students charging fees over £7,500 will be particularly badly affected.

An assessment of the 2012/13 reforms

The rest of the chapter assesses the government's reforms against the White Paper's three stated aims regarding HE funding, the 'student experience' and social mobility. The reforms are untested, and, at the time of writing, there was no hard evidence about their impact. Some argue that the changes are so radical that we cannot even learn from earlier funding reforms, or from other countries' experiences, to gauge their effects.

'Putting higher education on a sustainable financial footing'

The 2012/13 reforms aim to reduce public expenditure on HE while maintaining the sector's income. The most costly component is student financial support, specifically the government subsidy on student loans – the part of loans written off by the government that will never be recovered fully from graduate loan repayments. Significantly, *only* this subsidy counts as public spending (as measured by the Public Sector Borrowing Requirement) and is a cost to the taxpayer. The money raised to provide student loans is not. However, any part of a loan not repaid by graduates appears in BIS's budget as current spending. Will the reforms reduce this level of subsidy and, hence, public expenditure?

The simple answer is no, certainly not in the short to medium term. The proposed rise in student loan interest rates will eradicate one element of the government subsidy on student loans. But other changes planned for 2012/13 mean that loans will continue to be highly subsidised because of increasing proportions of graduates who never fully repay their loans. First, the high level of average tuition fees means larger average tuition fee loans. The face value of loans increases and, therefore, their total value increases. Larger loans mean graduates are less likely to pay them off in full. The combined effect is that public spending becomes a bigger share of a larger total loan amount. Arguably, if the government had withdrawn a smaller proportion of HEIs' teaching funds, rather than all of them for some courses (see recommendation 1 earlier), HEIs would not need to charge such high tuition fees.

The second reason for the continued government subsidy on loans relates to the rise in the loan repayment threshold (see recommendation 6 earlier), which will be uprated annually. This is expensive because it reduces the monthly repayments of all graduates (not just low-earning graduates); takes a large number out of repayments; and makes it more likely that graduates will not repay their loan fully. Barr and Shephard (2010) argue that this threshold acts as an incentive for all HEIs to charge higher fees because the cost of non-repayment falls on the taxpayer, not HEIs.

The net result is that under the new system, an estimated 50–60% of graduates will have some, or all, of their student loan written off compared with around 15% under the current system (Bolton, 2012, p 7). The government estimates that the student loan subsidy will rise to £32 for every £100 a student borrows, up from the current £28 (BIS, 2011b, p 57). This could increase public spending by around £300 million in steady-state (OFFA, 2011). Others believe that the subsidy will be higher, which would increase government spending and reduce any savings (Thompson and Berkhradnia, 2011). The exact costs are unknown, and arguably will not be fully known until 2046 at the end of the 30-year loan period for the first cohort of students graduating under the 2012/13 funding regime. HEIs may reduce their fees in the light of the White Paper, students may opt for less expensive courses, student numbers may fall and previous patterns in graduate earnings may change – all of which will impact on these costs. As David Willetts, Minister for Universities and Science, admitted: 'No one can be certain. This is a set of big changes. I am not claiming that we can be absolutely certain' (House of Commons, 2011, p 19, para 72).

Will other elements of the 2012/13 reforms reduce public expenditure and public sector debt? The shift in funding away from direct public support for teaching undergraduate courses (see recommendation 1 earlier) to student loans means that public expenditure on HE will fall. The money the government currently provides HEIs for teaching is counted as public expenditure but most spending on student loans, which will replace these teaching funds, is not – apart from the loan subsidy. As Barr (2011, para 2) observes:

> Though little has changed in cash terms (since the government has to finance the upfront cost of loans), there is an apparent reduction in the BIS budget; it is not unfair to say that an accounting trick is driving deleterious policy change.

The cash needed to provide loans will add to the stock of public sector debt. Government spending on HE could increase by around 10% between 2010/11 and 2014/15, so the net impact of the changes in funding could increase public sector debt in the short to medium term, possibly by around £1 billion in 2014/15. In the longer term, the loan repayments are expected to reduce the size of the debt. With a £7,500-fee loan from 2012/13, the addition to national debt from student loans will peak in around 2030 at 3.4% of GDP or around £50 billion in current prices (OBR, 2011).

Delivering 'a better student experience'

The main driver in the 2012/13 reforms for improving the 'student experience' (whatever this term really means[5]) is the development of an HE market that, in theory, will lead to better-quality provision, drive down prices and put 'students at the heart of the system'. It is debatable whether a market in HE will lead to falling costs. The US has a well-established market, but tuition fees there have consistently grown at a much faster pace than inflation or average earnings (College Board, 2011).[6] It is questionable how much of a market will actually develop in England. First, there will be no free HE market because fees are capped, and, most importantly, so are student numbers because of the continuing high costs of student financial support. Consequently, admissions are a zero-sum game. If some universities expand, others must contract. If the number of institutions increases with new entrants, the average size of each must fall (Barr, 2011, para 5). Without an increase in student numbers, participation is unlikely to increase even if more providers enter the market, or new types of more flexible and diverse provision are offered. HE providers will be unable to respond to a growth in demand. In a competitive market, if a university's quality dropped, we would expect reduced demand and a downward pressure on price, but excess demand largely negates these pressures. Without more student numbers, demand will continue to outstrip supply, which will constrain competition on quality and limit student choice. Where demand exceeds supply, HEIs select students and there will be little incentive to invest in an improved 'student experience'.

Second, currently universities' income from teaching depends on student preferences and universities' success in recruiting students. Students have always been able to choose where and what to study, but, to date, their choices have rarely followed the logic of economic orthodoxy; and it is not clear that they will in the future, especially if there are limited price differences in tuition fees to signal variations in quality. A myriad of social, economic and cultural factors influence student HE decision-making and choices (Reay et al, 2005; Bates et al, 2009). Financial concerns and material constraints play a major role, but costs and finances are just one set of factors that explain patterns of HE participation and why students select a particular HEI (Usher et al, 2010). Indeed, US research (Baum et al, 2008) shows that price has a greater impact on low-income students' decision to enter HE than on their choice of HEI.

Third, quality at some HEIs may fall rather than improve because not all HEIs will charge fees high enough to replace their lost income from government-funded teaching grants. This has become more likely since the publication of the 2011 White Paper. It aims to put a downward pressure on tuition fees by reserving 20,000 student places for HEIs charging less than £7,500, but Browne estimated that HEIs need to charge £7,000 to replace their lost teaching funds. Consequently, some HEIs are unlikely to have the additional funds to improve the 'student experience' while efficiency savings are likely to be at the expense of 'the student experience' and an investment in teaching. HEIs with extra income may not invest it in students – the additional fee income they gained since 2006 has gone into improving their surpluses and on academic staff rather than on students (Universities UK, 2011).

Finally, as the 2011 White Paper acknowledges, 'wider availability and better use of information for potential students is fundamental to the new system' (BIS, 2011a, p 32). It is argued that students currently have inadequate access to information to make informed HE decisions, which disproportionately affects disadvantaged students, impacting on social mobility. Consequently, in future, HEIs will have to provide prospective students with standardised and comparable 'Key Information Sets' about undergraduate courses, including data on: student satisfaction; employment and salary outcomes; and costs and fees. Such developments are welcome, but it is debatable how far more information will address the market failure in information asymmetry whereby students, especially those from poorer backgrounds, will be able to judge in *advance* the quality of courses and whether they will lead to 'graduate' jobs. Students will not know this until they actually take their course and enter the labour market. The information required is simplistic, can be manipulated and is difficult to present in an accurate and meaningful way, so without help in interpreting the information, it could be misleading. The provision of information alone will not lead to improvements in the quality of the 'student experience'.

'Increasing social mobility'

Just as constraints on student places will limit improvements in the 'student experience', so too will they undermine efforts to increase social mobility and widen participation. The prospective students least likely to get a university place are those from the most disadvantaged backgrounds, who up till now have benefited, albeit to a limited extent, from the expansion of HE (HEFCE, 2010). Yet there is little in the 2011 White Paper to help eradicate the large social class inequalities in HE access and participation, which widening participation aims to tackle. The Coalition abandoned Labour's target to increase HE participation to 50% and their student funding reforms alongside other policy changes might exacerbate these inequalities.

First, the White Paper subtly redefines both the parameter and scope of debate, and its policy focus. Gone is the notion of widening participation and improving HE access to under-represented groups – of opening up the doors to HE. Widening participation is trumped by 'relative social mobility' defined in terms of fairness: 'For any given level of skill and ambition, regardless of an individual's background, everyone should have a fair chance of getting the job they want or reaching a higher income bracket' (BIS, 2011a, p 54). So fairness rather than disadvantage is to steer policy. Hence the White Paper's focus on the fair access agenda – of trying to get more disadvantaged students into the most selective universities rather than opening university doors to a wider cross-section of students.

Second, in an environment of limited university places, there is a tension in the White Paper between the 'core and margin' places and widening participation. The AAB policy potentially undermines the fair access agenda because universities offering bright disadvantaged students, with potential, lower A level entry grades may be reluctant to offer places below AAB. Furthermore, under-represented students are the least likely to benefit from the unlimited AAB places because of the strong links between high A level grades and socio-economic advantage.

Disadvantaged students are also less likely to have the qualifications to access the reduced number of 'core' university places, especially at universities with a low proportion of AAB students. According to the government, a squeeze on places at these universities:

> will impact disproportionately on opportunities for widening participation students, many of whom apply to ... [these] universities.... A shift in the availability of sub-AAB places from ... [these] universities towards FE colleges will not necessarily provide greater social mobility or better returns for any widening participation students displaced from HEIs to HE in FE. (BIS, 2011b, p 71)

Third, responsibility for driving social mobility has shifted away from the state to the efforts of individual HEIs and students, as evidenced by the Coalition's other post-compulsory education reforms and their reinforcement of the hollowing out of the welfare state. First, the Coalition abolished Educational Maintenance Allowances, designed to incentivise low-income pupils to stay on in post-compulsory education to gain the qualifications needed to enter HE. Second, they withdrew funding from Aimhigher, which, albeit through a deficit discourse of under-represented groups who lacked certain skills, competences or appropriate attitudes and aspirations, did encourage them to apply to university, and to the most prestigious ones. Third, the government, in effect, has curtailed important routes into higher education for many adults, especially women, wanting to improve their qualifications and skills to get on the higher education ladder by withdrawing funding from Level 3 courses (equivalent to A levels) for those over 24 years old and from access courses. In future, adults will have to pay much higher fees themselves and take out student loans. Given these students' backgrounds, and the way the education system has failed many of them, will they be willing to take the risk and make the financial commitment demanded of loans and to speculate financially on an uncertain future – especially given the limited financial returns to these qualifications? And will they be willing to accumulate at least four years' worth of student loan debt to progress to a full-time degree?

Finally, tuition fees will triple for most students come 2012/13, as will student loan debt. It is impossible, at this stage, to predict the impact of the reforms and increases in tuition fees and debt on individuals' HE aspirations, their participation rates and HE choices in the medium and long term. The 2006 HE finance reforms did not lead to a sustained fall in HE participation but their full effects are unknown because we do not know what would have happened to participation in the absence of the reforms (Crawford and Dearden, 2010). Yet, the 2012/13 reforms are more extreme. Early data on university applications for 2012/13 show a fall, especially among older students (UCAS, 2012). Nor is it clear if the new student financial support will adequately offset rising HE costs, and concerns about them and escalating student loan debt – modelling suggests not (Dearden et al, 2010). Research shows that those most likely to be affected will be low-income students who are more price-sensitive, less price-inelastic (Baum et al, 2008) and more debt-averse (Callender and Jackson, 2005) than their wealthier peers – the very target of social mobility. Taken together, all these government policies are likely to reduce rather than enhance the chances of those from disadvantaged backgrounds being able to enter HE to improve their job prospects and earning capacity. It is hard to imagine how these students are at the heart of any of these changes.

Conclusion

As the 2011 White Paper acknowledges, the proposals represent a radical reform of the HE system. They herald a retreat of the state's financial responsibility for HE with a shift towards individual HEIs and especially students carrying most of this responsibility and the risks. Implicit in this strategy is a fundamental ideological revision about the purpose of HE. HE is no longer seen by the government as a public good, of value to society as a whole beyond those who receive it, and so worthy of public funding, but instead as a private good with private economic returns from individual investment. HE's private-good functions are pitted against its public-good functions and reveal a policy mindset and political ideology where the public and private benefits of HE are a zero-sum game.

The proposed policies are unproven, with unknown consequences and unforeseen unintended consequences. It is highly questionable whether the reforms will meet their stated aims of putting HE on a sustainable financial footing, improving the 'student experience' and increasing social mobility, or whether they will stand the test of time. We will not know for sure, for several years to come.

In the short term, the changes will have a destabilising effect on the HE sector. There may be some fiscal savings but will these be at the expense of the longer-term effects on quality, social equity and universities as public, civic and cultural institutions? The concern is that the reforms will entrench elitism in HE and perpetuate existing inequalities within and across the HE sector whereby universities revert to one of Castells' (2001) key functions, as mechanisms for selecting and socialising elites and for establishing these elites from the rest of the society, and at the expense of HE's other functions. There is a danger that HE will become more elitist and polarised with bright and wealthy students being concentrated in a few 'traditional' well-resourced universities while other financially constrained students are confined to poorly resourced low-cost alternatives. Privileged students who populate the top universities will pay more but get a high-quality education and highly valued degrees. Low-income students who populate HE providers at the bottom of the hierarchy will pay less and get less, but still have large student loan debts. Others may be excluded completely. Will these divisions between institutions and between students reinforce both social class and disadvantage whereby HE becomes more socially and ethnically differentiated and polarised than ever before, rather than cherished centres of teaching, learning and knowledge creation for all to benefit?

Notes

[1] Higher education policy within the UK is devolved. The reforms discussed relate only to England-domiciled students studying in England but do have implications for other UK students. However, it is beyond the scope of this chapter to discuss these complicated cross-border arrangements.

[2] It will be recalled that Prime Minister Tony Blair staked his career on the successful passage of the Higher Education Act 2004, which passed by just five votes.

[3] These figures rise to £8,509 and £8,267 if FECs are excluded. These averages may well change as a result of the White Paper.

[4] A levels are a national General Certificate of Education qualification usually taken in the optional final two years of secondary schooling and are traditionally a prerequisite for university entry.

[5] Given the diversity of the student population, it is highly questionable if we can really talk about a monolithic 'student experience'.

[6] Over the decade from 2001/02 to 2011/12, published tuition fees for students attending public four-year colleges and universities in their state increased by an average rate of 5.6% per year above the rate of general inflation. This rate of increase compares to 4.5% per year in the 1980s and 3.2% per year in the 1990s (College Board, 2011).

References

Barr, N. (2011) 'Assessing the White Paper on Higher Education', Evidence Ev 185–188, in House of Commons (ed) *Government reform of higher education, twelfth report of session 2010–12*, Business, Innovation and Skills Committee, HC 885, London: Stationery Office.

Barr, N. and Shephard, N. (2010) 'Towards setting student numbers free'. Available at: http://econ.lse.ac.uk/staff/nb/Barr_Setting_numbers_free_101217.pdf (accessed 29 October 2011).

Bates, P., Pollard, E., Usher, T. and Oakley, J. (2009) *Who is heading for HE? Young people's perceptions of, and decisions about, higher education*, BIS Research Paper 3, London: Department for Business, Innovation and Skills.

Baum, S., McPherson, M. and Steele, P. (eds) (2008) *The effectiveness of student aid policies: what the research tells us*, New York, NY: The College Board.

BIS (Department for Business, Innovation and Skills) (2009a) 'Press release'. Available at: http://hereview.independent.gov.uk/hereview/press-release-9-november-2009/ (accessed 9 September 2009).

BIS (2009b) *Higher ambitions: the future of universities in a knowledge economy*, London: Stationery Office.

BIS (2011a) *Higher education: students at the heart of the system*, Cm 8122, London: Stationery Office.

BIS (2011b) *Impact assessment higher education: student at the heart of the system*, London: BIS.

Bolton, P. (2012) *Changes to higher education funding and student support in England from 2012/13*, House of Commons Library, SN/SG/5753, www.parliament.uk/briefing-papers/SN05753 (accessed 10 February 2012).

Callender, C. (2010) 'Bursaries and institutional aid in higher education in England: do they safeguard access and promote fair access?', *Oxford Review of Education*, vol 36, no 1, pp 45–62.

Callender, C. and Jackson, J. (2005) 'Does fear of debt deter students from higher education?', *Journal of Social Policy*, vol 34, no 4, pp 509–40.

Castells, M. (2001) 'Universities as dynamic systems of contradictory functions', in J. Müller, N. Cloete and S. Badat (eds) *Challenges of globalisation: South African debates with Manuel Castells*, Cape Town: Maskew Miller Longman.

Clarke, J., Newman, J., Smith, N., Vindler, E. and Westerland, L. (2007) *Creating citizen-consumers: changing publics and changing public services*, London: Paul Chapman Publishing.

College Board (2011) *Trends in college pricing 2011*, New York, NY: College Board.

Crawford, C. and Dearden, L. (2010) *The impact of the 2006–07 HE finance reforms on HE participation*, Research Paper Number 13, London: Department for Business, Innovation and Skills.

Dearden, L., Fitzsimons, E. and Wyness, G. (2010) *The impact of higher education finance on university participation in the UK*, Research Paper Number 11, London: Department for Business, Innovation and Skills.

HEFCE (Higher Education Funding Council for England) (2010) *Trends in young participation in higher education: core results for England*, Bristol: Higher Education Funding Council for England.

HM Treasury (2010) *Spending review*, Cm 7942, London: Stationery Office.

House of Commons (2011) *Government reform of higher education, twelfth report of session 2010–12*, Business, Innovation and Skills Committee, HC 885, London: Stationery Office.

IRHEFSF (Independent Review of Higher Education Funding and Student Finance) (2010) 'Securing a sustainable future for higher education: an independent review of higher education funding and student finance'. Available at: http://webarchive.nationalarchives. gov.uk/+/reviews.independent.gov.uk/reviews/report/ (accessed 26 March 2012).

Johnstone, D.B. and Marcucci, P. (2010) *Financing higher education worldwide: who pays? Who should pay?* Baltimore, MD: Johns Hopkins University Press.

Le Grand, J. (2007) *The other invisible hand: delivering public services through choice and competition*, Princeton, NJ: Princeton University Press.

OBR (Office for Budget Responsibility) (2011) *Fiscal sustainability report*, London: Stationery Office.

OFFA (Office for Fair Access) (2011) *Access agreement data tables for 2012–13*, July, Bristol: Office for Fair Access. Available at: http://www. offa.org.uk/publications/

Reay, D., David, M. and Ball, S.J. (2005) *Degrees of choice: social class, race and gender in higher education*, Stoke-on-Trent: Trentham Books.

Thompson, J. and Berkhradnia, B. (2011) *'Higher education: students at the heart of the system' – an analysis of the Higher Education White Paper*, Oxford: HEPI.

UCAS (Universities and Colleges Admissions Service) (2012) '2012 application figures – January'. Available at: http://www.ucas.ac.uk/ about_us/media_enquiries/media_releases/2012/20120130/ (accessed 26 March 2012).

Universities UK (2011) *Patterns and trends in UK higher education 2011*, London: Universities UK.

Usher, T., Baldwin, S., Munro, M., Pollard, E. and Sumption, F. (2010) *The role of finance in the decision-making of HE applicants and students*, Research Paper No 9, London: Department for Business, Innovation and Skills.

Willets, D. (2010) Higher Education Funding, *Hansard*, vol 517, no 64, cols 924-46, 3 November.

FIVE

Division and opposition: the Health and Social Care Bill 2011

Sally Ruane

Introduction

In mid-July 2010, a few weeks after the creation of the Coalition government, Andrew Lansley, Secretary of State for Health, issued a heavily leaked White Paper called *Equity and excellence: liberating the NHS* (DH, 2010). Despite the fact that its package of proposals had featured in neither the Conservative Party nor Liberal Democrat general election manifestos, the White Paper contained a radical programme of reform for the National Health Service (NHS), contradicting the Conservative Party's repeated reassurances before the general election that there would be no imposed top-down reorganisation of the NHS as well as an explicit statement to that effect in the post-election Coalition agreement (HM Government, 2010). Although Lansley insisted that the proposals should have come as no surprise to anyone following the development of Conservative health policy during their years in opposition, some organisations claimed that the government did not have a democratic mandate for its proposals.

From the outset, the proposals were controversial. The trade union, UNISON, which represents 400,000 workers in the NHS, described the reforms as heralding 'the end of the NHS as we know it' (UNISON, 2010); the then shadow health spokesman, Andy Burnham declared that they 'represent the break-up of the NHS' (Ramesh, 2010); the influential King's Fund think tank described them as 'the most radical restructuring of the NHS since its inception' (cited by Peedell, 2011); and Kinglsey Manning of Tribal (a private company providing health services) claimed that the proposals could lead to 'the denationalisation of healthcare services in England' (Quinn, 2010). Numerous organisations regarded the proposals as 'accelerating the trend to privatisation' (Quinn, 2010).

In these circumstances, it is perhaps unsurprising that the passage of the proposals into law has proven tortuous and troublesome. The Health and Social Care Bill was introduced into Parliament in January 2011 but the parliamentary process had to be 'paused' the following April for a two-month 'listening exercise' under the auspices of a new, specially mandated quango, the Future Forum, when Liberal Democrat MPs signalled that they would not support the Bill in its original form. A revised version of the Bill was eventually passed to the House of Lords where, at the time of writing (December 2011), it faced further amendment, at the least. Although they had their supporters, the White Paper and Bill faced sustained extra-parliamentary criticism from July 2010.

The 'NHS reform process' (meaning that series of actions and developments relating to the launch and progress of the government's health reform package before and during the formal legislative process) offers an opportunity for tentative reflections on the character of opposition against a controversial policy initiative in a specific political context in which the official opposition has just lost power after a lengthy period in office and in which the first peacetime coalition government since the 1930s is in office. Inevitably a selective approach must be adopted and this chapter focuses on the opposition proffered by three key institutions.

The first institution is the Liberal Democrat Party. The votes of Liberal Democrat MPs are essential to the successful passage of Coalition government legislative proposals. The junior party in a coalition government can expect to find itself in politically uncomfortable and compromising situations but this difficulty has been exacerbated by the perception of the Liberal Democrat Party as a left-leaning party in a coalition with a party of the Right. In fact, the party is itself a mix of more right-wing 'Orange Book' supporters and more left-wing 'social liberals'.

The second is the British Medical Association (BMA), whose members are among those most obviously and directly affected by the proposed reforms. The BMA is the 'doctors' trade union' and was historically the most influential interest group in policymaking, extracting significant concessions from Aneurin Bevan at the founding of the NHS. It is some decades since it enjoyed the intimate 'politics of the double bed' (Klein, 1990), however, and its influence has declined in recent decades in the context of a strengthened policy arm in the Department of Health and more formalised policy process, stronger management, the more effective organisation of other health care workers and a rising 'consumer' voice (Alaszewski and Brown, 2011).

The third institution is the Labour Party. As Her Majesty's loyal opposition and as the party that established the NHS over 60 years ago, it can be expected to have a special role in spearheading opposition to the proposals. Both its historic identity as 'the party of the NHS' and its need to re-engage with the public after a poor showing in the 2010 general election suggest that vigour could be added to conviction. However, the post-defeat period for a political party is often characterised by an absence of policy definition and coherence.

This chapter examines the nature of opposition to the government's health proposals within these institutions and what this reveals about the contemporary politics of health.

The proposals

Lansley's proposals entailed a complex reorganisation of the health service, including the abolition of the principal regional and local planning and commissioning bodies, respectively Strategic Health Authorities and Primary Care Trusts (PCTs). Instead, several hundred new organisations, GP Commissioning Consortia, would be established to take on most commissioning of health services and to which all GP practices would be required to sign up. They would be required to commission health care from a wide range of licensed organisations, including commercial and not-for-profit organisations. The new health system would assume the character of a regulated market such as that found in the utilities sector and would function according to competition law as enforced by a new economic regulator. Although NHS services would remain free to patients, all NHS providers would assume autonomous Foundation Trust status, effectively operating as independent businesses, and would be free to generate as much income as they could from treating patients privately. None of these organisations would be accountable to the Secretary of State but a new national quango would be 'mandated' to run the NHS on his/her behalf. Local authorities would establish new committees to promote integrated commissioning. Furthermore, the entire reorganisation was to be undertaken in a context of severe management cutbacks and financial constraints.

These proposals can be seen in the context of the government's wider public service reform agenda as set out in a White Paper entitled *Open public services* (Cabinet Office, 2011) in July 2011, the publication of which was reportedly delayed by Liberal Democrat opposition. This emphasises a purchaser–provider split with a diversity of providers working on a 'level playing field', mainstreaming commercial and not-for-profit provision, service user choice within a consumerist model and the decentralisation of decision-making.

Despite the far-reaching content, a formal consultation exercise asked not *whether*, but *how*, to implement the proposals and a reported 6,000 responses were received. The government's response to the consultation made no major concessions to the concerns expressed and this was reflected in the subsequent Bill. Mounting opposition and a growing sense of crisis prompted the announcement of the legislative 'pause', which coincided with the local elections and alternative vote referendum. The Future Forum published its recommendations for modifications to the Bill in mid-June and the listening exercise was hailed by both David Cameron and Nick Clegg as a triumph. The recommendations were immediately adopted and after a brief, guillotined, discussion in the Public Bill Committee, the revised Bill was submitted for third reading immediately following the summer recess in September 2011 and made its passage to the House of Lords.

The Liberal Democrats

As a co-signatory to the White Paper's Foreword in July 2010, Clegg himself did not appear to regard the content of the health reforms as problematic and he barely mentioned the NHS in his 2010 autumn party conference speech. This changed in the run-up to the party's spring conference in March 2011 when it became evident that discontent among party members threatened to defeat a health motion, sponsored by the Liberal Democrat Minister for Care, supporting government policy. Substantial amendments to the motion had been tabled.

Those behind the amendments included members of the Social Liberal Forum, on the left of the party, former MP and hospital doctor Evan Harris and practising GP Charles West, and the amendments were strongly supported by the popular and influential Baroness Shirley Williams. The amendments to the motion, which in the event were so strongly supported that they were conceded by the movers of the motion without a vote, noted that provisions within the Bill fell outside Liberal Democrat policy as set out in the 2010 general election manifesto and even contradicted the Coalition agreement in several respects (Harris, 2011; Liberal Democrat Party, 2011). The motion implied specific alterations that would be required of the Bill in relation to governance, the role of private companies and rules of competition.

In subsequent interviews, Williams, who sought a more circumscribed role for the private sector, emphasised the importance of rejecting the 'mixed system' or mixed economy approach to the NHS, saying that the 'level playing field' implied by this would 'destroy the NHS'. She pointed out that while EU competition law excluded public services based on social solidarity, it did not exclude mixed systems. She went further to suggest that the cherry-picking of easy, profitable services favoured by private companies could not be prevented except by 'enormous bureaucracy' (Williams, 2011).

This stance, and Harris's similar position, was deeply at odds with the provisions of the Bill and the stated intention of Lansley to prioritise competition and 'any willing provider'. Harris's analysis specified precisely which amendments to the Bill would be necessary to make it consistent with the amended conference motion (Harris, 2011). The views of Harris and Williams, going to the heart of the character and consequences of open competition, were a long way from the view expressed by Clegg.

After months of support for the Secretary of State's proposals, that is, his own government's proposals, Clegg was forced to alter his stance following the Liberal Democrat conference and to signal to his Conservative colleagues in cabinet that the Bill could proceed no further in its parliamentary journey without significant change. Following the announcement of the 'pause', he promised substantial changes to the Bill to strengthen accountability and governance arrangements, minimise the financial risks of the commissioning consortia and set some limits on the 'types of provider' that could provide NHS-funded services (Mulholland et al, 2011).

Clegg's close ally and senior parliamentary advisor, Norman Lamb, insisted that unless specific changes to the Bill were made, Liberal Democrat MPs would not vote for it. These included a more evolutionary approach to establishing commissioning consortia over a longer timescale and retaining PCT clusters to observe the performance management of consortia. Lamb's proposed minimum amendments to the Bill focused on the commissioning consortia, a policy with which he agreed in principle (Lamb, 2011). This was a far narrower focus of required change to the Bill than either that expressed through the Liberal Democrat conference motion or that articulated by Harris and Williams. However, since Lamb represented the Liberal Democrats in negotiating changes to the legislation, his statement confirmed that the Bill would not survive the 'pause' intact.

There was clearly, then, no single Liberal Democrat position on the Bill. Paul Burstow, a Liberal Democrat minister in the Department of Health, fully supported the Bill and so apparently had other Liberal

Democrat members of the government, although *The Guardian* reported in mid-February that some cabinet members were privately expressing 'doubts' about the Coalition's reforms (Wintour and Curtis, 2011). Certainly, no Liberal Democrat MPs voted against the Bill at second reading. One of the most significant differences lay between those who believed a 'level playing field' among providers was possible (and these would include Clegg) and those, like Williams, who believed that it was incompatible with an equitable, integrated public service. The Liberal Democrat manifesto included a commitment to a 'patient guarantee', which entitled patients to have health care from a non-NHS provider paid for by the NHS where the patient had not been diagnosed and treated 'on time' and to 'level playing fields in any competitive tendering' (Liberal Democrat Party, 2010).

This was a commitment to stick with a market system already introduced by Labour but ending higher tariffs and payment guarantees for private providers. 'Clarifying' the party's position on the role of private providers in public services, Clegg used a speech at a public services 'summit' in February 2011 (ahead of the crisis surrounding the Bill) to denounce the preferential treatment of private providers in Labour's 'rigged' NHS market and to underline his belief that public monopolies should be replaced by a diversity of providers (Clegg, 2011). So the Liberal Democrat Party policy, as articulated by Clegg, favoured the level playing field Williams explicitly warned would 'destroy the NHS'.

During the course of the Future Forum's listening exercise, the amendments sought by the Liberal Democrat part of the Coalition as a price for supporting the Bill were progressively widened and deepened. This reflected the growing awareness by the parliamentary party of its precarious political position. If its own grassroots had fired warning shots during the spring conference, the electoral drubbing it suffered at the hands of voters in the May local elections and alternative vote referendum confirmed the deep unpopularity into which it had sunk during its time in government. Clegg's language became increasingly bullish and the final list of demands, including changes to the economic regulator, the place of competition and the role of local democratic safeguards, went far beyond those articulated in Clegg's and Lamb's earlier statements.

Both Harris and Williams expressed concerns that some Liberal Democrat objections had not been translated into amendments to the Bill, for instance, in relation to the retention of the Secretary of State's duty to provide a comprehensive health service. However, some cleverly choreographed and tightly managed political manoeuvring in both the policy and the parliamentary processes around the time of the publication of the Future Forum report permitted the Liberal Democrat leader to present the rebellion as successful in saving the NHS and evidence of the difference that the Liberal Democrats could make in government.

This seemed to be enough. Despite ongoing criticism of the Bill by professionals and the public, the Bill completed its third reading safely with just four Liberal Democrat MPs voting against it. An amendment in the Lords to refer lengthy passages of the Bill to committee for detailed scrutiny, thereby endangering the parliamentary timetable and thus the success of the Bill, was rejected by almost all voting Liberal Democrat peers. Finally, an attempt by social liberals to resurrect the Bill for discussion at the Liberal Democrat autumn conference failed to secure the necessary votes.

The British Medical Association

The lead organisation in pursuing the interests and demands of doctors throughout the reform process was the BMA. Royal Colleges, particularly the Royal College of General Practitioners (RCGP), also played a role but by far the greatest organised medical engagement with the process has been conducted via the BMA. The BMA represents all elements of the profession, including GPs and hospital doctors for which there are specialist committees. It is overseen by a 25-person Council, whose chair is Dr Hamish Meldrum and has around 140,000 members, some 70% of UK practising doctors. The chairman of the GP committee is Dr Laurence Buckman.

The BMA gave a guarded welcome to the White Paper, indicating its willingness to discuss the proposals while signalling certain conditions for implementing them. Meldrum pointed out that doctors were ideally placed to determine the needs of local populations through commissioning and stressed the importance of consultation. Buckman indicated that the involvement of doctors in commissioning must be voluntary and in a context of adequate resourcing (BMA, 2010a; Campbell, 2010).

Within a week, a letter was sent by Buckman to all GP members, reporting that BMA leaders had already met with the Secretary of State and were engaged in a critical dialogue to shape and improve the government's proposals (Buckman, 2010). This signalled that the BMA was not going to mount a campaign against the government's plans, thereby significantly weakening any wider political movement of opposition. To place this decision in context, plans to implement the proposals *had already begun on the ground* under the instructions of NHS Chief Executive David Nicholson, and the BMA leadership clearly considered a rapid response essential. They were, however, stung by the concerns of some of their members into defending their stance just a few days later:

> The BMA believes that it is absolutely vital that we critically engage with the consultation process. Government has clearly indicated its overall direction of travel and non-engagement in the consultation period would greatly increase the risk of bringing about the adverse outcomes that many of you fear. (Meldrum, 2010)

The first detailed BMA assessment of the proposals was published in early October 2010 following the online canvassing of members' views. It characterised the proposals as a 'large curate's egg'. The response welcomed some proposals, including clinician commissioning, but claimed that the proposals could undermine doctor–patient trust, threaten the terms and conditions of NHS employees, and destabilise the NHS through the operation of market practices (BMA, 2010b). In mid-December 2010, the government's response to the consultation exercise was published, making little concession to the concerns expressed by the BMA. Meanwhile, poll evidence suggested that doctors were unconvinced that the proposals would improve patient care despite this being the government's main justification for them.

The leadership affirmed its commitment to critical engagement but its stance became embattled as splits among its own members became more perceptible. Some GPs formed shadow commissioning consortia, which entered into contracts with commercial organisations, despite the BMA's opposition to further commercialisation in the NHS and advice to its members not to enter into financial arrangements while the outcome of the NHS reform process remained subject to change. At the same time, grassroots pressure was building from those who believed the BMA should adopt an oppositional rather than reformist stance. This boiled over in January 2011 into an open letter to Meldrum and Buckman published in the *British Medical Journal* (Peedell, 2011). The letter was organised by Clive Peedell, a member of the BMA Council, and attracted around 120 signatories; it received over 100 online rapid responses, the vast majority supporting the wishes expressed in the letter. The letter criticised the policy of critical engagement as a failure and not based on a survey of members' views and called on the leadership to abandon it and instead mobilise the professions to oppose the reforms, which, it claimed, would destroy the NHS.

The leadership was forced to concede a Special Representative Meeting (SRM) to take place in March, over three months ahead of the usual Annual Representative Meeting (ARM), and the first such emergency meeting since 1992 when the then Conservative government's 'internal market' was first introduced. An Ipsos Mori poll indicated that, if anything, medical opposition to the Bill was growing (Laja, 2011) and the political temperature rose as a series of regional BMA meetings agreed strongly worded motions highly critical of the Bill to take to the SRM. By mid-February, Meldrum's leadership was considered at risk (Campbell, 2011).

The SRM was attended by around 400 doctors. Meldrum's illuminating opening address stressed that neither he nor the BMA supported the Bill but emphasised that the question was how in practical terms to influence the course of policy. He pointed out that it was highly unlikely that the government would withdraw the Bill entirely given its prioritisation of NHS reform. He noted that, as policies of both Coalition and Labour governments, market and private sector involvement were 'here to stay' and that threats to terms and conditions remained regardless of what happened with the Bill. If the BMA did not remain engaged, therefore, the medical profession could be left facing the worst of both worlds: increased privatisation but reduced medical influence. He reminded his audience that a survey of members' opinions suggested mixed views and warned of the dangers of professional division in an increasingly difficult health policy environment (Meldrum, 2011).

The decision to be made by the BMA was between outright opposition to the whole Bill and selective opposition to parts of the Bill. It stopped short of a vote of no confidence in the Health Secretary, of censuring Hamish Meldrum and of calling on the leadership to abandon the policy of critical engagement. It did, however, call for the immediate withdrawal of the Bill by Lansley and a halt to the top-down reorganisation of the NHS. The meeting was covered widely in the media and, coming just four days after the tumultuous events at the Liberal Democrat spring conference, contributed significantly to irresistible political pressure on Lansley and his increasingly unpopular Bill.

By the time the 'pause' was announced, the BMA had established the principal amendments it wished to see *if* the 'ideal scenario' (the withdrawal of the Bill) failed to materialise (BMA, 2011b). Some of these were incorporated into the government's response to the Future Forum report. However, the ARM in June resurrected further problems for the leadership when a motion was passed calling for the withdrawal of the Bill (disregarding, unusually, the advice of the chairman who claimed that the competition element had been taken out of the Bill), although a motion calling on the BMA to oppose the Bill in its entirety was narrowly lost.

By the time of the third reading in September 2011, the next occasion when the legislative progress of the Bill could be halted, the BMA found itself in the curious position of having voted three times not to abandon its stance of critical engagement but also twice to campaign for the withdrawal of the Bill. In fact, no public campaign was launched but instead Meldrum and other clinician bodies co-signed a letter to *The Times* seeking further amendments to the Bill on the eve of the vote. This 'acceptance' of the Bill's passage helped defuse the political tension that greeted the third reading and arguably helped it through. It was not until late November when the publication of official guidance confirmed that the real power and influence in commissioning would be exercised by commercial 'support bodies' rather than the clinicians themselves that the BMA finally announced that it opposed the Bill *in toto*, following a 12:8 vote in the Council.

The Labour Party

The Labour Party's initial response to the White Paper was rather muted, possibly because shadow Health Secretary Burnham was distracted by the Labour leadership contest, which continued through the summer. Burnham refocused for the Labour Party conference in late September. His strategy consisted of, first, challenging the Secretary of State with a defined set of proposals as the basis of Labour's engagement with the government's plans. These included piloting GP commissioning consortia, retaining PCTs for at least the medium term and turning the White Paper into a Green Paper – that is, as a consultation document, thereby restoring, he claimed, the proper democratic policy process. Second, he attempted to forge common cause with the medical profession, which had published its consultation response. Third, he declared that Labour would 'launch a major campaign in every city' to defend the NHS (Burnham, 2010).

In the event, this did not happen. The following week, Burnham was replaced by John Healey as spokesman for health. Healey said relatively little on the Coalition proposals for the remainder of 2010 and any momentum that Burnham might have developed by the autumn was dissipated. Instead, Healey's approach was to get to grips with his brief first; his interventions became more consistent and confident after the New Year. Healey's strengths as shadow Health Secretary were his grasp of the detail – necessary given the complexity of the proposals and Lansley's depth of knowledge – and his ability to make political capital out of the criticism or reservations expressed by the principal organisations involved such as the BMA, RCGP, the NHS Confederation and the Royal College of Nursing. However, Labour's opposition was severely hampered by four factors: first, an overly technical approach; second, a largely parliamentary strategy with virtually no engagement with a wider popular base; third, the Labour Party's own record of marketisation and privatisation in government; and, fourth, the current Labour Party policy stance.

While Healey's strength was his ability to master the technical specifics of the Health and Social Care Bill, the other side of this coin was an overly detailed and insufficiently populist approach to opposition to which it would be very difficult for anyone other than those with specialist knowledge to relate. A letter to the Secretary of State in late February asked for clarification on the latter's plans to turn the NHS into a 'genuine market', which raised questions of price competition, EU competition law and commercial insolvency regimes. These focuses for opposition had their own merit and echoed concerns being expressed by NHS organisations and think tanks but did not in any way engage with the popular hostility to and suspicion of the government's plans or with that apparent majority among the public who continued to have little awareness or comprehension of the contents of the Bill. The themes identified by Healey as threads of opposition, such as risks to the stability of the service and patient care and the opening up of the NHS to EU competition law, informed and shaped the opposition expressed by Ed Miliband in Prime Minister's Questions (PMQs).

Healey successfully drew upon the concerns and criticisms expressed by the principal players in the drama. In the middle of March, he was able to make political capital out of Liberal Democrat and BMA opposition, claiming that the government's plans were 'descending into chaos'. Healey also attempted to build a relationship with the Liberal Democrat Parliamentary Party, going so far as to attend the health debate at the Liberal Democrat spring conference. Labour's strategy, according to a former chair of the Health Select Committee, was to open up the arguments to enable Liberal Democrat MPs to see the problems inherent in the Bill and to engage with key external organisations (personal communication).

However, Labour MPs did not in any strategic way use the menace of 'privatisation' or 'break-up' of the NHS as a basis for re-engaging with voters through public meetings or mass rallies. In fact, although Healey's critique of the Bill encompassed these observations, his public statements, at least as reported in the generalist press, emphasised the 'risky', 'costly', 'rushed' and 'ill-timed' character of the government's plans rather than invoking the more emotionally and politically rousing condemnation of the plans as privatisation.

The third difficulty in Labour's opposition was its vulnerability in terms of its own record in government. The open, competitive market had been created by Labour; the commodification of health care and the associated pricing regime had been created by Labour; the mainstreaming of private providers in this market (such as the Extended Choice Network comprising 149 non-NHS providers) had been established by Labour; even the involvement of private companies in the commissioning process had been a Labour government policy. This created two problems for any Labour MP, but especially the Party leader and shadow Health Secretary. First, Coalition MPs responded to criticism by repeatedly pointing out that many of its policies were the same as or more moderate than the former Labour government's policies. This occurred on numerous occasions both at PMQs and in broadcast 'question and answer' programmes involving members of the public. For instance, at PMQs in mid-March, the day after the BMA's SRM and just a few days after the Liberal Democrat conference, when Labour's opposition enjoyed significant political advantages, Miliband's attack was severely undermined by an effective counter-offensive by Cameron who pointed out that the Labour Party 2010 general election manifesto, which had been written by Miliband himself, had favoured competition in the NHS. Cameron was also able to point out, as Lansley did on numerous occasions, that Labour had created *more* favourable conditions for the private sector in health than the Coalition proposals: in other words, the suggestion was made that Labour's position was inconsistent, that Labour was pro-market and that it had a more pro-private policy than did the Coalition.

The second difficulty Labour's record created was the need to pick and choose carefully the basis for its opposition to the Bill. Healey did articulate a coherent stance in his speech at the King's Fund in January 2011, which might have shielded Labour from some of the charges of blatant hypocrisy (Healey, 2011). However, Labour's willingness to engage with both the market and private companies created enormous difficulties in establishing clear red water between the proposals of the government and Labour's own position and Healey never succeeded in communicating Labour's precise policy stance effectively to the public. This added further delays to the sharpening up of Labour's opposition so that for many months it was difficult for any but the most committed followers of politics to discern Labour's position on the government's plans for the NHS. This was exacerbated by the fourth factor hampering Labour's opposition: Miliband's insistence that all Labour policy be put under review.

The need for Healey as a new health spokesman to acquire a detailed knowledge of his brief, the need to pick out safe ground on which to oppose and the absence of a firm alternative policy stance, all delayed the emergence of a clear 'narrative' against the Bill. This hampered the building of political momentum and the possibility of Labour's 'leading' any coordinated movement of opposition to the Bill. Labour's opposition was cleverly argued but at the expense of a wider political campaign.

Discussion

In considering what this tells us about the contemporary politics of health, we focus on four interwoven themes: the character and implications of institutional divisions and tensions; the influence of the medical profession in the policy process; the further contraction of between-party differences and the tightening of the neo-liberal grip on policy; and the absence of the public.

The three organisations studied have each had to engage with internal contradictions, which have shaped their evolving stance. BMA members' views are politically diverse, with some welcoming or indifferent to growing entrepreneurial opportunities and commercial penetration but others deeply hostile. Divisions emerged within branches rather than between them and, while partly ideological in character, expressed themselves through conflict over the leadership's strategy, with a significant gap opening up between it and an increasingly organised portion of its membership. Underpinning the conflict lay different assessments as to how likely it was that the government could be dissuaded from the main thrust of its proposals. The leadership believed that outright opposition would forfeit current and future medical influence in a hopeless fight; the grassroots rebels (along with some Council members) believed that medical influence could best be exercised through risking the fight.

The Liberal Democrat leadership faced two aspects of division: first, the social liberals within the party had articulated a strong critique of the proposals that their own (generally more right-wing) leadership was advocating; and, second, the social liberals were able to use the spring party conference to demonstrate that a chasm had opened up between the leadership and the grassroots and that the leadership were out of touch. This was enough to persuade a critical number of MPs not to support the Bill in its original draft. The poor showing of the Liberal Democrats in the May elections and the personal unpopularity of Clegg following his support of tuition fee rises ensured that both the recovery of the Liberal Democrats and the survival of Clegg as their leader became embroiled in the urgency of striking out distinctively on health. By the same token, however, compromising enough to remain in government and avoid a disastrous general election secured their eventual support for the third reading, justified on the grounds that the dangers contained in the original drafting had been corrected.

The Labour Party did not face internal political divisions – differences existed but these did not become critical. Rather, the party was hamstrung by another kind of contradiction: the tensions that inevitably come into play in trying to oppose a set of reforms that could easily be presented as extensions of its own previous policy. The absence of intra-party splits may itself be significant. The radical proposals for the NHS did not set the Labour Party on fire, although at another time or in other circumstances they might have done. This might be because party members had cohered around a consensus regarding the desirability of market competition in public services; or because the party was absorbed in its own recovery following the 2010 general election defeat; or because developments in higher education and the economy had absorbed Labour's energies. Thus, the absence of a fight over the party's position on health reform may reflect a weakness rather than a strength.

Paradoxically, it was precisely the emerging splits within the Liberal Democrats and the BMA that enabled them to have a dramatic impact on the policymaking process. The 'impact' of the BMA, though, and with it our understanding of the influence of the medical profession in policymaking, should be carefully understood. The NHS reform process confirms continuing government determination to delimit the collective influence of the profession on policy. The BMA's impact was felt in two ways: one was through its lobbying for specific amendments to the Bill, some of which were incorporated; the second was through its contribution to the political crisis surrounding the Bill in March. It was this latter impact, arising from conflict within the BMA reflecting ideological and strategic differences, that became critical, opening up the political space for the more politics-as-usual lobbying to bear some fruit. The stance of the leadership can be interpreted as an attempt to prevent a repeat of their experience during the formulation of the first 'internal market' policy in the late 1980s when the medical profession, excluded, was reduced to outsider status. Insider status confers access to ministers and inclusion in early consultation processes and, thereby, an ability to influence policy directly. However, the perceived need to break open the political space implies *outsider* frustration and not only suggests a decline in confidence among some within the medical profession in the traditional means of insider pressure group lobbying to secure its policy objectives, but also differences as to whether it occupies an insider status at all. This is consistent with the varying perceptions of doctors as to the extent of their influence on policy (Baggott, 2007), notwithstanding the apparent increase in influence enjoyed by the Royal Colleges.

The risks inherent in coalition government – the need to find consensus with another party and the need to secure sufficient public support to win the subsequent election – suggest, excepting 'red line' issues, a more moderate or cautious policy programme overall than a single party majority government might have pursued (see Quinn et al, 2011). In addition, the Conservatives had seen their own 'detoxification' on the NHS as essential to secure electoral success. Despite this, a highly risky strategy was pursued by Cameron's cabinet. To some extent, this reflected a wish to learn from Tony Blair's 'mistake' of being too timid during his first term in office, but might also reflect a calculated strategy in terms of both the politics of health reform and the politics of managing a coalition. Conservative confidence in taking risks with the NHS reflects perhaps an assessment that no force would or could defeat the policy: the medical profession could be either convinced (through GP commissioning) or split; the Labour Party would be too compromised and too weak; and the public could be sidelined. In terms of managing the politics of a coalition, the Conservatives retained their health proposals largely intact despite the rebellion and, while this wrong-footed the social liberals within the Liberal Democrat camp, it sat easily with the Conservative–right-wing–Liberal alliance, which formed the bedrock of the consensus. The highly controversial Bill was ironically *more*, not less, likely to pass successfully through the House of Lords than it would have been under a single party government, since the Liberal Democrat peers would vote for rather than against it (Thornton, 2011). In these conditions, the special status of the NHS and sensitivities surrounding the politics of health care could be neutralised.

With no majority government, political leaders have greater leeway than usual in deviating from the policies they advertised before the election (see Hilder, 2005). The Coalition agreement was already a highly attenuated expression of the 'public will', which returned a hung parliament. However, even this was not respected in the drawing up of the White Paper and nor did the Liberal Democrat amendments roll back the Bill sufficiently to reflect the provisions of the Coalition agreement. Public debate on the Liberal Democrats as the minor party in government has focused on its discomfits and uneasy compromises but, arguably, these have also created the political space for the leadership to pursue a much more radical agenda than its grassroots would otherwise have endorsed. The partial restoration of discipline within the parliamentary party (with 12 Liberal Democrat MPs still refusing to back the Bill at third reading) may point to an unresolved split and the marginalisation of the old social democrat elements in the face of a strengthened liberal mass. This helps consolidate a neo-liberal consensus dominating the formal political scene in England's NHS.

The traditional Conservative–Labour Party differences on health that pre-dated New Labour, and which were to a great extent dissolved during the New Labour years, have not re-emerged even in the context of a radical and highly controversial reform and this contributes to the further consolidation of the neo-liberal grip on health policy. The party decided not to return to a clear-cut anti-privatisation, anti-marketisation agenda and there appears no clear ideological water between the two parties in either substance or rhetoric. Moreover, the absence of any struggle over this within the party contributed to its near-irrelevance in the policy process. Overall, then, although the focus here has been on conflict and opposition, the case of health points to a more explicit convergence within the political class of policy and ideology and in the policy domain most socialised in the 'new society' created by Labour in the 1945–50 period, there is no force strong enough to resist this neo-liberal advance.

All of this points to a very weak citizenry. This chapter has not focused on the public or on popular campaigns and yet it is evident from the analysis of the three chosen institutions that the public has been considered largely irrelevant. None of the institutions examined here engaged extensively with the public, although the Liberal Democrat leadership was forced to engage with its own grassroots. Labour did not use instinctive public hostility towards privatisation or the opportunity afforded by the listening exercise to reconnect with the public even though this might have worked to Labour's electoral advantage.

If Labour pursued their programme of NHS marketisation significantly by subterfuge (Leys and Player, 2011), the Conservatives have confronted their opponents in the open. This suggests greater confidence that, in the field of health, interest groups can be managed and the public's consent is not required.

References

Alaszewski, A. and Brown, P. (2011) *Making health policy*, Cambridge: Polity.

Baggott, R. (2007) *Understanding health policy*, Bristol: The Policy Press.

BMA (British Medical Association) (2010a) *Press release: BMA response to the health White Paper*, 12 July, London: BMA.

BMA (2010b) *Press release: potential benefits of health White Paper could be undermined by increased competition*, 1 October, London: BMA.

BMA (2011) *BMA submission to the NHS Future Forum*, London: BMA.

Buckman, L. (2010) *Letter from the GPC chairman to all GPs in England regarding the NHS White Paper*, 18 July, London: BMA.

Burnham, A. (2010) *Letter to Andrew Lansley*, 10 October. Available at: http://conservativehome.blogs.com/files/650059-andy-burnham

Cabinet Office (2011) *Open public services*, Cm 8145, London: The Cabinet Office.

Campbell, D. (2010) 'NHS shakeup: private companies see potential to expand their role', *The Guardian*, 12 July.

Campbell, D. (2011) 'BMA leader could be toppled in revolt by doctors against NHS reforms', *The Guardian*, 15 February.

Clegg, N. (2011) *Speech to public services summit*, St Albans, 10 February.

DH (Department of Health) (2010) *Equity and excellence: liberating the NHS*, Cm 7881, London: Department of Health.

Harris, E. (2011) Analysis of Coalition Programme Social Liberal Forum, Available at: http://socialliberal.net/wp-content/uploads/2011/04/CoalitionAgreement.pdf

Healey, J. (2011) *The truth behind the Tory plans*, Speech to the King's Fund, London, 21 January.

Hilder, P. (2005) 'Open parties? A map of 21st century democracy'. Available at: www.opendemocracy.net/democracy-open-politics_2312.jsp

HM Government (2010) *The Coalition: our programme for government.* London: Crown.

Klein, R. (1990) 'The state and the profession: the politics of the double-bed', *British Medical Journal*, vol 301, pp 700–2.

Laja, S. (2011) 'Doctors fear private sector will damage NHS', *The Guardian*, 3 March.

Lamb, N. (2011) 'Interview', *The Politics Show*, BBC News, 10 April.

Leys, C. and Player, S. (2011) *The plot against the NHS*, London: Merlin.

Liberal Democrat Party (2010) *Liberal Democrat manifesto 2010*, London: Liberal Democrat Party.

Liberal Democrat Party (2011) *Conference daily*, 12 March.

Meldrum, H. (2010) *Letter to the profession*, 29 July, London: BMA.

Meldrum, H. (2011) 'Opening address to the SRM', London, 15 March.

Mulholland, H., Watt, N. and Curtis, P. (2011) 'NHS reforms: We will address "legitimate" concerns, says Nick Clegg', *The Guardian*, 5 April.

Peedell, C. (2011) 'Open letter to the BMA about the health white paper', *British Medical Journal*, vol 342, 4 January.

Quinn, I. (2010) 'Private firms prepare major initiative on GP commissioning', *Pulse*, 14 July.

Quinn, T., Bara, J. and Bartle, J. (2011) 'The UK Coalition agreement of 2010: who won?', *Journal of Elections, Public Opinion and Parties*, vol 21, no 2, pp 295–312.

Ramesh, R. (2010) 'Andy Burnham calls on Lib Dem MPs to oppose Tory NHS "break-up"', *The Guardian*, 30 August.

Thornton, Baroness G. (2011) 'Personal communication', 28 October.

UNISON (2010) *UNISON puts government in court*, Press release, London: UNISON.

Williams, S. (2011) 'Interview', *The World at One*, BBC Radio 4, 4 April.

Wintour, P. and Curtis, P. (2011) 'Liberal Democrat cracks appear over NHS reform plans', *The Guardian*, 14 April.

Part Two

Social policy in the developed and developing worlds

Immigrant-targeted activation policies: a comparison of the approaches in the Scandinavian welfare states

Karen Nielsen Breidahl

Introduction

Is there a fundamental contradiction between inclusive welfare policies and immigration? And can universal welfare states accommodate the increasing diversity characterising contemporary societies (Freeman, 1986; Alesine and Glaeser, 2004; Banting and Kymlicka, 2006)? These questions are much disputed in academic and public debate. Some argue that ethnic diversity poses no problem for liberal welfare states, but that it represents a dramatic challenge to social democratic welfare state types, as the latter have historically been rooted in uniform, homogeneous and collective class identities (Necef, 2001). However, a number of studies have been conducted to elucidate this presumed negative relationship, and the results are rather contradictory; 'no smoking gun' has been found (Larsen, 2010, p 3).

When examining the recent developments in European welfare states, we see that instead of a general downscaling of the welfare state, there have been tendencies towards 'welfare chauvinism', which means that immigrants are entitled to welfare services to a lesser degree than natives (Sainsbury, 2006; Breidahl, 2011a). It is therefore important to distinguish between: (1) the impact of immigration on the welfare state in general; and (2) the impact of immigration on the part of the welfare state that immigrants are entitled to and confronted with. This chapter focuses on the latter by analysing and comparing the development of activation policies for immigrants in Norway, Sweden and Denmark from the early 1990s until 2010 in order to shed light on the following overall question: *are the features of the Scandinavian welfare states, such as redistributive income security, reflected in the activation policies introduced in order to promote and ease the integration of immigrants into the labour market?*

By immigrants, this chapter refers to persons born outside of Scandinavia who have gained entry to a Scandinavian country to live there permanently and attained legal resident status. More specifically, the group in focus is newly arrived immigrants and the long-term recipients of social assistance with an immigrant background. There are many similarities in the history of migration to the three countries; however, the percentage of foreign-born residents in Sweden is almost twice as high as in Denmark and Norway: 13.9% of the Swedish population in 2008 had been born outside of the country, whereas the corresponding figure for Denmark was 7.3% and 10.3% for Norway (OECD, 2010, p 299).

The Scandinavian welfare states are generally interesting cases to explore when it comes to the interplay between welfare state policies and immigrants as a target group given that these cases illustrate the importance of going beyond traditional comparative welfare state typologies (Esping-Andersen, 1990) in order to capture the specific features of labour market and social policy reforms aimed at immigrants, and take into account the 'interplay between welfare regimes, forms of immigration, and immigration policy regimes in producing distinctive patterns of immigrants' social rights across countries' (Sainsbury, 2006, p 229).

Hence, when it comes to welfare policies and the institutional and political structure of the three Scandinavian welfare states in general, the existence of a distinct 'Scandinavian welfare model' is widely acknowledged. All three countries are generally seen as very ambitious in terms of living up to their ideals concerning solidarity, universalism, equality and redistribution (Brochmann and Hagelund, 2010). These goals have been pursued by providing: relatively high social protection and generous benefits; high minimum wages and a compressed wage structure; universal, predominantly tax-financed welfare state arrangements; a high degree of government intervention; strong labour union involvement; and comprehensive work–family policies (Greve, 2007; Breidahl, 2011a). Finally, these welfare states are also internationally renowned for their comparatively high levels of redistribution, comparatively high employment rates among men and women, and high degrees of gender equality (Siim and Borchorst, 2008). Conversely, it is commonly held that the Scandinavian countries differ on a number of counts when it comes to immigration and integration policies. Hence,

Sweden is especially renowned for upholding 'multicultural' principles and limited barriers and conditions for naturalisation, whereas Denmark is renowned for its '*assimilistic* principles' and strict immigration control; for example, Denmark requires a pass mark on a language test before a residence permit is granted (see Jørgensen, 2006; Brochmann and Hagelund, 2011). By examining the interplay between activation reforms and immigrants as a target group, the chapter contributes to the overall discussion about the link between immigration, integration and welfare states, which was a rather neglected topic in comparative welfare state research until recently (Morissens and Sainsbury, 2005; Sainsbury, 2006; Brochmann and Hagelund, 2010).

Activation policies are the main instruments for (re)integrating persons depending on social insurance or social assistance into the labour market (Johansson and Hvinden, 2007; Djuve, 2011), and they have also been introduced specifically in order to promote and ease the integration of immigrants into the labour market during recent years. In the public as well as the academic debate, the Scandinavian countries have been highlighted as some of the countries facing the greatest challenges in terms of integrating immigrants into the labour market (Tranæs and Zimmermann, 2004). The rationale here relates to the perception that the incentives embedded in the social security system not only prevent immigrants from entering the labour market, but also tend to attract disadvantaged, marginally skilled immigrants. Whether these assumptions hold true is debatable, and the employment rates for immigrants in all three Scandinavian countries have generally increased considerably since the mid-1990s (Breidahl, 2011b). Nevertheless, compared to the native population (which has some of the world's highest labour market participation rates), the employment rate among immigrants – men and women alike – remains relatively low. In all three countries, labour market integration has therefore been emphasised as one of the most pressing challenges related to the integration of new members of society.

Scholars have commonly held that the specific institutional and normative features of the Nordic countries, such as redistributive income security, are also reflected in their activation policies (Esping-Andersen, 2002; Ferrera and Hemerijck, 2003). Whether or not this is the case is disputed (Johansson and Hvinden, 2007), and the chapter will illustrate how it is particularly questionable when we are dealing with immigrants as the target group and the elements of activation reforms concerning income security. Hence, at some points, harsher policies have been introduced and implemented more eagerly when the target group for activation reforms has been immigrants. Despite the traditions regarding the welfare state being common in the three countries, Denmark, Norway and Sweden appear quite different on some points when immigrants as a target group are taken into account.

Furthermore, the chapter argues that a combination of conditions and explanations can explain these trends. On the one hand, the country-specific party political constellations are important to take into account in order to understand the differences on some points between the countries in the activation policies for immigrants. However, on the other hand, national and transnational policy-learning mechanisms on some other points also seem to have played a crucial role.

The rest of the chapter is structured in four sections. The next section clarifies the conceptualisation of activation policies, while the second section outlines and analyses similarities and differences in the activation policies introduced and implemented over the last 20 years (from the early 1990s until 2010) in order to (re)integrate immigrants into the labour market in Norway, Sweden and Denmark, respectively. In the third section, underlying factors behind the trends outlined in the second section are assessed, and the implications of these activation reforms for the features of the Scandinavian welfare states and immigrants as a target group are discussed. The final section sums up the findings.

Conceptualising activation policies

The literature addressing the shift from passive to active labour market policies in most Western countries since the late 1980s has been extensive. This change, meaning that the unemployed must participate in activation programmes in return for unemployment benefits or social assistance, has received many different labels, such as workfare, active line and welfare to work. One of the common conclusions in the literature is that remarkable cross-national differences persist and that countries have applied different 'activation approaches' (Lødemel and Trickey, 2001; Barbier, 2004).

Activation policies concerning income security are the focus of this chapter. Immigrants have long been over-represented among social assistance recipients in Denmark, Norway and Sweden, partly because many often do not qualify for unemployment insurance benefits due to inadequate work experience in the receiving country (Johansson and Hvinden, 2007, p 56). Before special arrangements were introduced for newly arrived immigrants in the form of the so-called introduction programmes, many of these people (often refugees) depended on social assistance from day one in the absence of work (which was often the case). Reforms targeting newly arrived immigrants have been implemented in the three countries and a new kind of social provision – introduction allowance – specifically targeting newly arrived immigrants for the first two or three years has been introduced: in Denmark in 1999, in Norway in 2004 and in Sweden in 1993 (reformed in 2010). This benefit replaced the ordinary social assistance benefit in the introduction period, which varies between 24 and 36 months in the three countries. The target group for the introductory programme is defined differently in the three countries; in Sweden and Norway, the programme only applies to humanitarian immigrants (refugees who have received residence permits on humanitarian grounds), whereas the target group in Denmark is broader (by also including some immigrants resulting from family reunification).

In order to combat the over-representation of immigrants in the social assistance schemes, extraordinary measures targeting the long-term recipients of social assistance with an immigrant background who have lived in the respective countries for a number of years have also recently been introduced in Denmark (in 2002 and 2006) and Norway (2005).

In tracing the development of these activation policies in Denmark, Norway and Sweden since the early 1990s, it is important to consider how income security reforms in several ways are used as a strategy to promote the (re)integration of the unemployed into the labour market, including: (1) strengthening the financial incentive to find employment by reducing the income benefit level and to 'make work pay' by preventing social protection schemes from creating disincentives to work; and (2) placing a greater emphasis on conditionality by redefining the relationship between rights and duties through the introduction of a closer link between income-maintenance schemes and employment-promoting measures.

These two approaches concern the content of activation policies (formal reforms) and are the main focus of the chapter. However, a third approach concerning reforms of the governance of employment policies (operational reforms), which can transform employment policies towards 'work first' via steps such as standardising or de-standardising payment rates, reducing or increasing the local autonomy or granting discretion to front-line workers in the municipalities, is also taken into account (Larsen, 2009).

Activation reforms targeted at immigrants

Norway: from local discretion to standardised rates for payment

The over-representation of immigrants among social assistance recipients and the risk of welfare dependency became a central topic in the 1990s, and it became obvious at the political level that the existing social assistance system was unable to handle these problems. The Labour government of the day, therefore, granted these problems serious consideration (St. Meld., 1996/97: 17). In response to these concerns, the Norwegian government decided that a special introduction allowance for newly arrived immigrants was necessary, which should figure as an alternative to social assistance (St. Meld., 1998/99: 50). In order to review and submit proposals for new legislation concerning economic support for newly arrived immigrants, a so-called Introduction Act Commission was set up (NOU, 2001: 20) and in 2004, a new Introduction Act and a universal introduction allowance for newly arrived immigrants, which lasts up to two years, were introduced.

The ambition was, first, to get people out of the social assistance system and, more specifically, to stimulate and motivate the target group to remain in the programme while at the same time promoting the transition to active participation in the labour market (Ot. prp., 2002/03: 28). In order to fulfil these ambitions, conditionality was put forward by introducing a closer link between income-maintenance schemes and employment-promoting measures. The introduction allowance introduced in 2004 was a fixed-rate benefit with standardised rates for payment with the character of a universal benefit, whereas the social assistance in Norway was (and still is) largely means-tested and the degree of local autonomy high. Furthermore, the introduction allowance was equal for everyone, regardless of their place of residence, and depended on active participation in activities such as language training and employment-promoting measures. In the event of absence not due to illness or other compelling reasons for which permission has not been given, the benefit was thus reduced correspondingly.

The introduction allowance was set to be the equivalent of twice the basic amount from the National Insurance Scheme (for full participation in a programme) and was estimated as being neither considerably lower nor higher than the benefit level newly arrived immigrants were hitherto entitled to (before 2004).[1] The 'make work pay' approach whereby the income benefit level is reduced was not applied; rather, it was at least as generous as ordinary social benefits, and in some cases (if both spouses participate in the programme) substantially higher (Djuve, 2011). This reform not only concerned the content of activation policies, but also to a large degree the governance of activation policies. The administrative framework related to the introduction allowance did break with the administrative framework related to social assistance in general, concerning local autonomy and local variations relating to the content, scope and quality of activation policies that had previously applied to newly arrived immigrants.

The standardised fixed-rated payment of the introduction allowance has given rise to new initiatives in the general social assistance system in Norway together with new income-maintenance measures targeting the long-term receivers of social assistance with an immigrant background. Hence, in 2005, a pilot project was introduced, *New Chance* (*Ny Sjanse*), which was a programme targeting immigrants who have been in the country for two years or more without gaining a foothold in the labour market.

Sweden: from rights to duties

Like in Norway, the over-representation of immigrants among social assistance recipients and the risk of welfare dependency became a central topic in Sweden in the 1990s. A Swedish version of the introduction allowance was launched in 1993, meaning that the municipalities were encouraged (and therefore not forced) to grant individuals participating in an introduction programme an introduction allowance rather than social assistance. The objective of the introduction allowance was to emphasise the special character of the allowance granted upon first coming to Sweden. The Swedish introduction programmes were voluntary for the municipalities and the newcomers alike, and the introduction allowance only served as an alternative to social assistance therefore, not as a replacement. The amount of the introduction allowance and whether absence from active participation was to be punished were also up to the municipal authorities. As a consequence, the implementation of the introduction allowance varied from municipality to municipality: in some municipalities the amount was the same as regular social assistance, while the level of the introduction allowance in other municipalities was actually higher than the social assistance level (Integrationsverket, 2007). Until 2010, therefore, the administrative framework for paying the introduction allowance to newly arrived immigrants did not stand out much from the regular social assistance system and the rights for newcomers remained substantially more important than the duties (Djuve and Kavli, 2007).

After a Liberal–Conservative government came to power in 2006, however, the question about the effort and income sources provided for newly arrived immigrants was again put on the agenda. In 2007, a commission was set up with the remit to review and submit proposals concerning the responsibility for and design and financing of refugee reception and other initiatives for newly arrived refugees and others requiring protection and their relatives (SOU, 2008: 58). Later, in November 2009, the Swedish government presented a proposition (Prop., 2009/10: 60) based on many of the proposals that the commission submitted in 2008, and a government reform entitled 'Labour market introduction of newly arrived immigrants – individual responsibility with professional support' was implemented in December 2010.

The introduction allowance launched as part of this reform in many ways follows some of the same lines and considerations as the Norwegian introduction allowance from 2004, and an important consideration was how it could serve as an alternative to regular social assistance and that the benefit level was, therefore, neither too high nor too low compared to general social assistance. As in Norway, the introduction allowance was universal and fixed-rate, whereas social assistance in Sweden was (and still is) largely means-tested and the degree of local autonomy high (although to a lesser degree than in Norway), which meant that it differed from the administrative framework related to the social assistance scheme. What was at stake in 2010 was not to 'make work pay' by reducing the benefit level but rather to put greater emphasis on conditionality by introducing a closer link between income-maintenance schemes and employment-promoting measures.

Denmark: a shift away from income security and equal social rights

The activation reforms targeting immigrants in Norway and Sweden have particularly focused on conditionality by introducing a closer link between income-maintenance schemes and employment-promoting measures and operational reforms concerning the governance of employment policies. Conversely, the activation reforms targeted at immigrants in Denmark have mainly focused on a strengthening of the financial incentive to work by reducing the benefits and, compared with the active line in general in Denmark, economic sanctions and incentives particularly targeting immigrants have become substantially more important in the period from 2001 to 2010.

The first national integration legislation was implemented under the Social Democratic government in 1999. This legislation included the introduction of an introductory programme and an introduction allowance targeted at newly arrived immigrants. At that time, the degree of conditionality was strengthened through the introduction of a closer link between income-maintenance schemes and employment-promoting measures. This was also the case a year earlier in 1998, where a reform of ordinary social assistance was carried out in Denmark. At that point, the two reforms more or less followed the same lines and considerations therefore. However, contrary to Norway and Sweden and to the general reform of social assistance in 1998, the introduction allowance introduced in 1999 was considerably lower than the ordinary social assistance level, although in 2000 the benefit level was raised up to the level of ordinary social assistance because, among other things, the UN Refugee Agency, UNHCR, criticised the new introduction allowance as being discriminatory (Breidahl, 2011a).

In 2002, a so-called 'start assistance' or 'introduction allowance' (paid amount is the same) was introduced once more, which was to replace the social assistance for newly arrived immigrants. The introduction allowance was paid for the first three years after a person had arrived in Denmark and obtained a resident permit if they participated in an introduction programme. Afterwards, they were eligible to receive 'start assistance' for a four-year period. The benefit level was the same for the entire seven-year period.[2] These benefits were also – like in 1999 – considerably lower than the ordinary social assistance level but this time it was not subjected to the same criticism because it was also aimed at citizens with Danish roots who had been outside the country for seven years or more and had returned. Start assistance/introduction allowance was some 35–50% lower than ordinary social assistance, depending on the family situation (reductions being lower for families with children) (Andersen, 2007). While Danish social assistance was comparatively generous, the start assistance and introduction allowance schemes were among the *least* generous schemes in north-western Europe (Hansen, 2006). As in Sweden and Norway, in the event of absence not due to illness or other compelling reasons for which permission has not been given, the benefit was reduced correspondingly.

The formal political argument for introducing lower benefits was to reinforce the financial incentive to find employment and, like in 1999, greater emphasis on conditionality was put forward, which meant that active participation in activities such as language training and employment-promoting measures was crucial. In the event of absence not due to illness or other compelling reasons for which permission has not been given, the benefit was thus reduced correspondingly.

In 2002, the 'More people to work' reform reduced social assistance in a number of situations for persons receiving social assistance for six consecutive months. More specifically, families where both spouses received social assistance had their benefits reduced by €135 per month after six months. A maximum for supplementary support (mainly for families with children) was introduced at the same time (reductions of up to €350/month in some cases). If a spouse was considered a homemaker, social assistance was replaced with a homemaker supplement (which was abolished entirely in 2006). The initiative was a general social policy element but, in reality, the majority of those affected were immigrants (Andersen, 2007).

Finally, a reform aimed at immigrants, *A new chance for everyone*, was introduced in 2005. The most controversial aspect of this reform was the so-called '300-hour rule' (which later became the 450-hour rule), formally introduced in 2006 and in effect as of April 2007. The rule applied to everybody, regardless of citizenship or ethnicity; however, it primarily was targeted at immigrants, especially immigrant women. This was underscored in the official reform documents issued by the Minister of Employment (The Danish Government, 2005). The reform meant that married couples receiving welfare benefits would lose their right to social welfare if they work less than 300 hours over a two-year period.[3] Before losing their benefits, the legislation requires that the person in question receives a warning six months beforehand so that they have the opportunity to find work in the meantime. The rule was very controversial due to the fact that it contained considerable work requirements and economic sanctions and that it was used for testing whether immigrant women were actually available to the labour market. The rule was formally implemented in April 2007. In 2008, the work requirement was increased to 450 hours and the legislation was modified so as also to include the married recipients of social assistance, regardless of whether one of them was employed. The rule applied to four out of five 'match groups'[4] – excluding those where 'no job functions are possible at all'.

The administrative framework for the introduction allowance (and start assistance), the 300-hour rule and the reduced 'social assistance in a number of situations' did not differ much from the administrative framework of the Danish social assistance scheme. For example, we are dealing with standardised rates for payment, where the exact rate depends on factors such as marital status, number of children, property and the like as opposed to local discretion in the municipalities.

Underlying factors and implications

The analysis gives the impression that we are dealing with an interesting pattern whereby institutional preconditions occasionally prevail when new measures targeting immigrants are introduced (as in Sweden in the early 1990s), while countries break with existing institutions, practices and principles at other times (as with the benefit reductions in Denmark and the introduction allowance in Norway in 2004). Furthermore, the period studied includes a number of common tendencies towards convergence (greater emphasis on conditionality by introducing a closer link between income-maintenance schemes and employment-promoting measures), but we also see that the three countries are going in opposite directions on other points, with Denmark being the only country that has introduced 'make work pay' activation policies for immigrants.

In order to assess the underlying factors behind these trends, it is not enough, therefore, to rely on historical institutionalist accounts referring to how the 'past influences present-day politics through a variety of mechanisms, ranging from concrete political institutions to patterns of interests associations to broadly accepted definitions of justice or even mundane ideas about the accepted way of doing things' (Immergut, 2005, p 289).

Instead, a combination of conditions and explanations are at stake, whereby different policy dynamics were identified depending on which of the activation approaches (the greater emphasis on conditionality or the 'make work pay' approach) we are focusing on. It is not possible to fully unfold the underlying factors here, however, due to limited space (see instead Breidahl, 2012).

One of the key factors to understanding the benefit reductions in Denmark in the period from 2001 to 2010, which have not been practised in Sweden and Norway, is the influence of the country-specific party political constellations in this period, in particular the influence of right-wing populist parties. On this point, the three Scandinavian countries have very different experiences (Green-Pedersen and Krogstrup, 2008). Hence, national elections in November 2001 resulted in a Liberal–Conservative minority coalition government relying on the support of the right-wing populist Danish People's Party. One of the key issues – if not *the* key issue – for the latter was immigration and the perceived threat immigration poses to Danish culture. Furthermore, Denmark is the only Scandinavian country where a right-wing populist party has been a formal coalition partner. And it was in this period that benefit reductions and 'make work pay' strategies targeted at immigrants were introduced (Brochmann and Hagelund, 2011). Analysis of the actual policy processes also substantiates the influence of this factor (Breidahl, 2012).

What, then, explains the tendencies towards convergence, where we have seen greater emphasis on conditionality in all three countries in the period from the early 1990s until 2010? Once again, it is not possible in this case to rely on historical institutionalist accounts due to the important differences in the respective institutional frameworks related to the social assistance schemes in the three countries, including the scope for local and professional discretion, which varies considerably. Hence, while the social assistance scheme in Denmark is the most centralised, and the government has created standard payment rates and specified in detail when and how municipalities must apply sanctions towards social assistance recipients in the event of illegal absence, this is not the case in Norway and Sweden, where the incentives and sanctions towards social assistance recipients are more open to local and professional discretion (Johansson and Hvinden, 2007, pp 61–3). As examination of the development of these rather new activation policies targeting immigrants in Denmark, Norway and Sweden illustrates, these differences are not reflected in the administrative framework related to the introduction allowance for newly arrived immigrants.

Instead, this chapter argues that the driving forces behind these changes have been policy learning, consisting of national as well as transnational policy-learning mechanisms (Heclo, 1974; Dolowitz and Marsh, 2000). From this theoretical point of view, policy change is not seen as a reflection of political power and 'powering', but policies are rather 'shaped directly by civil administrators and experts who puzzle over new problems on the basis of, and in reaction to, previously institutionalized governmental policies' (Amenta et al, 1987, p 147).

As mentioned, Denmark had already introduced an introduction allowance with a strong emphasis on conditionality in 1999. When Norway was going to reform their introduction effort, civil administrators and experts in the Introduction Act Commission were – according to their own statements – looking to their neighbouring countries in order to learn from their policy experiences; in particular, experiences from the reform in Denmark in 1999. According to a civil servant in the Norwegian Ministry of Labour and a member of the

Introduction Act Commission, the prevailing notion at the time was that the existing ordinary social assistance system was not sufficient and that it was necessary to go one step further in order to handle the problems immigrants were facing to enter the labour market, which was why they were examining the new reform in Denmark from 1999, and afterwards learned from it. Even though this mechanism cannot stand alone, it can contribute to the explanation of why the introduction programme and allowance introduced in Norway in 2004 in many ways followed the same line as the Danish variant when it came to the emphasis on conditionality. The reason why Sweden also introduced a very similar introduction allowance some years later, in 2010, can also be attributed to policy learning, but not transnational policy-learning mechanisms. Instead, much of the content of the reform – the introduction allowance in particular – was shaped by experts who were puzzling over 'policy failure' in the past (Breidahl, 2012).

When referring to the 'implications' of these activation reforms for immigrants, we can distinguish between two topics: (1) the implications for the basic principles related to the Scandinavian welfare states concerning solidarity, universalism, equality and redistribution; and (2) the implications for the target group (the immigrant population) in the three countries affected by these reforms.

We start by considering the latter topic. In the period from 2001 to 2010, where Denmark in particular stood out as the only Scandinavian country in which immigrant-targeted measures were introduced in order to strengthen the financial incentive to work by reducing social security benefits, the number of persons generally facing poverty in Denmark increased considerably – an increase of around 50% from 2001 to 2007 (students living under the poverty line are not included) (AE, 2010) – and an increasingly disproportionate number of immigrants (and their Danish-born descendants) figured in the Danish poverty statistics. It is tempting to draw the conclusion that poverty among immigrants remains much higher in Denmark than in Sweden and Norway. Unfortunately, however, no comparative studies concerning this issue have been conducted in recent years. However, it is well documented that poverty among immigrants was higher in Denmark than in Sweden in the 1980s and 1990s (Blume et al, 2005).

What are the implications of these activation reforms for the basic principles related to the Scandinavian welfare states? As mentioned earlier, scholars have commonly held that the specific institutional and normative features of the Nordic countries, such as redistributive income security, are also reflected in their activation policies. As the former analysis illustrates, it is questionable whether this is the case when we are dealing with immigrants. However, Denmark is the only Scandinavian country that has moved away from some of the basic principles of the Scandinavian welfare state, such as income security and generous benefits. Hence, even though harsher policies – compared to activation policies in general – have also been introduced in Sweden and Norway, these policies do not break with the basic principles, and there is no evidence that we will see any change there in the future.

The September 2011 election resulted in a new coalition government in Denmark consisting of the Social Democrats, Socialist People's Party and the Danish Social Liberal Party. In the course of the election campaign, the parties forming the coalition government had proclaimed that they would remove the start assistance, the reduced social assistance in a number of situations as well as the 300–450-hour rule. Moreover, it was announced in November 2011 that these benefit reductions will be abolished, that the benefit level for the introduction allowance will be the same as for regular social assistance and that the start assistance as well as the 300–450-hour rule and reduced social assistance in a number of situations will be abolished. However, what will be introduced instead and what will happen to the introduction allowance remains an open question at the time of writing.

Conclusion

The examination of the trends in activation reforms from the early 1990s until 2010 in Norway, Sweden and Denmark shows that there are not clear-cut answers to the overall question about whether the features of the Scandinavian welfare states, such as redistributive income security, are reflected in the activation policies introduced in order to promote and ease the integration of immigrants into the labour market. Instead, the chapter argues that the relatively harmonic image of a unified group of generous Scandinavian welfare states falls apart at some point when the link between immigration, integration and welfare states is taken into account and the examination of recent trends clearly illustrates that when we are dealing with immigrants, harsher policies have been introduced and implemented more eagerly in all three countries. These policies seem to rest on the assumption that an 'extraordinary' effort was required and that the regular social assistance scheme was unable to handle the problems newly arrived immigrants were facing to enter the labour market.

Hence, the approaches applied in the three Scandinavian welfare states from the early 1990s until 2010 have at some point been different, with Denmark in particular standing out as the only Scandinavian country where the social rights and specific status of social citizenship of immigrants have been the object of activation reforms and the only Scandinavian country that has moved away from some of the basic principles of the Scandinavian welfare state, such as income security and generous benefits. As a consequence of these changes, immigrants (and their descendants) in Denmark became highly over-represented among those in enduring poverty as well as long-term poverty. However, in the autumn of 2011, these benefit reductions were abolished.

Nonetheless, in the period studied, we also see common trends in the activation policies targeting newly arrived immigrants, with conditionality being strengthened and implemented in all three countries. These reforms have been controversial in Sweden and Norway in particular, because the administrative framework related to the introduction allowance did break with the administrative framework related to social assistance in general, concerning local autonomy and local variations concerning the content, scope and quality of activation policies that had previously applied to newly arrived immigrants. However, these policies do not break with the basic principles of the Scandinavian welfare state, such as income security and generous benefits.

In order to assess the underlying factors behind these trends, a combination of conditions and explanations were identified. On the one hand, the country-specific party political constellations in Denmark in the period from 2001 to 2010 – and the influence of the Danish right-wing populist party in particular – was one of the key factors to understanding the emphasis on 'making work pay' in the activation policies for immigrants in Denmark. On the other hand, what might explain the common turn in the three countries towards a greater emphasis on conditionality is a rather alternative driving force. Hence, national and transnational policy-learning mechanisms seem to have played a crucial role in this turn, with Norway, in particular, being open towards learning from the experiences of others.

Notes

[1] Due to the means-tested character of the social assistance benefit, however, it is not possible to make an exact and direct comparison of the benefits levels before and after 2004.

[2] For immigrants coming to Denmark after 1 July 2006, the transition from start assistance to social assistance after seven years required that

the recipients had had ordinary, full-time employment for at least two and a half of the last eight years.
[3] In the first year, from 1 April 2007 to 1 April 2008, the requirement was 150 hours of ordinary work within the last year.
[4] Match groups are as follows: (1) good match with the labour market; (2) good match, a few qualifications missing; (3) partial match, some relevant qualifications; (4) low match, only very limited job functions are available; and (5) no match, no job functions.

References

Alesine, A. and Glaeser, E.L. (2004) *Fighting poverty in the US and Europe: a world of difference*, Oxford: Oxford University Press.

Amenta, E., Clemens, E.S., Olsen, J., Parikh, S. and Skocpol, T. (1987) 'The political origins of unemployment insurance in five American states', *Studies in American Political Development*, vol 2, pp 137–82.

Andersen, J.G. (2007) 'Restricting access to social protection for immigrants in the Danish welfare state', *Benefit*, vol 15, no 3, pp 257–69.

AE (Arbejderbevægelsens Erhvervsråd) (2010) *Det opdelte Danmark [Denmark divided]*, Fordeling og levevilkår.

Banting, K. and Kymlicka, W. (eds) (2006) *Multiculturalism and the welfare state: recognition and redistribution in contemporary democracies*, Oxford: Oxford University Press.

Barbier, J.C. (2004) 'Systems of social protection in Europe: two contrasted paths to activation, and maybe a third', in J. Lind, H. Knudsen and H. Jørgensen (eds) *Labour and employment regulations in Europe*, Brussels: Peter Lang Publishing.

Blume, K., Gustafsson, B., Pedersen, P.J. and Verner, M. (2005) 'At the lower end of the table: determinants of poverty among immigrants to Denmark and Sweden', IZA Discussion Papers. Available at: http://ftp.iza.org/dp1551.pdf

Breidahl, K.N. (2011a) 'Social security provision targeted at immigrants – a forerunner for the general change of Scandinavian equal citizenship? A Danish case study', in S. Betzelt and S. Bothfelt (eds) *Activation and labour market reforms in Europe: challenges to social citizenship*, Palgrave Macmillan.

Breidahl, K.N. (2011b) 'The incorporation of the 'immigrant dimension' into the Scandinavian welfare states: a stable pioneering model?', Discussion Papers des Harriet-Taylor-Mill Instituts. Available at: http://www.harriet-taylor-mill.de/pdfs/discuss/DiscPap16.pdf

Breidahl, K.N. (2012) 'Labour market policies towards immigrants in the Scandinavian countries in the period from 1970–2011: changes and driving forces', PhD thesis, Aalborg University.

Brochmann, G. and Hagelund, A. (eds) (2010) *Velferdensgrenser: Innvandringspolitikk og velferdsstat i Skandinavia 1945–2010* [*The limits of welfare: immigration policy and the welfare state in Scandinavia 1945–2010*], Oslo: Universitetsforlaget.

Brochmann, G. and Hagelund, A. (2011) 'Migrants in the Scandinavian welfare state: the emergence of a social policy problem', *Nordic Journal of Migration Research*, vol 1, no 1, pp 13–24.

Djuve, A.B. (2011) 'Introduksjonsordningen for nyankomne innvandrere. Et integreringspolitisk paradigmeskifte?' ['The introduction programmes for newly arrived immigrants. An integration policy paradigm shift'], PhD thesis, *Fafo-rapport 2011: 19*.

Djuve, A.B. and Kavli, H.C. (2007) 'Integrering i Danmark, Sverige og Norge. Felles utfordringer – like løsninger?' ['Integration in Denmark, Sweden and Norway. Common challenges – not solutions?'], *TemaNord 2007: 575,* Copenhagen.

Dolowitz, D. and Marsh, D. (2000) 'Learning from abroad: the role of policy transfer in contemporary policy-making', *Governance*, vol 13, no 1, pp 5–24.

Esping-Andersen, G. (1990) *The three worlds of welfare capitalism*, Cambridge: Polity Press.

Esping-Andersen, G. (2002) 'Towards the good society once again?', in G. Esping-Andersen, D. Gallie, A. Hemerijck and J. Myles (eds) *Why we need a new welfare state*, New York, NY: Oxford University Press.

Ferrera, M. and Hemerijck, A. (2003) 'Recalibrating Europe's welfare regimes', in J. Zeitlin and D.M. Trubek (eds) *Governing work and welfare in the new economy: European and American experiments*, Oxford: Oxford University Press.

Freeman, G.P. (1986) 'Migration and the political economy of the welfare state', *The Annals of the American Academy of Political and Social Science*, vol 485, no 1, pp 51–63.

Green-Pedersen, C. and Krogstrup, J. (2008) 'Immigration as a political issue in Denmark and Sweden', *European Journal of Political Research*, vol 47, no 5, pp 610–35.

Greve, B. (2007) 'What characterise the Nordic welfare state model', *Journal of Social Sciences*, vol 3, no 2, pp 43–51.

Hansen, H. (2006) *From asylum seeker to refugee to family reunification: welfare payments in these situations in various Western countries*, Copenhagen: The Rockwool Foundation Research Unit.

Heclo, H. (1974) *Modern social politics in Britain and Sweden*, New Haven, CT: Yale University Press.

Immergut, E.M. (2005) 'Historical-institutionalism in political science and the problem of change', in A. Wimmer and R. Kössler (eds) *Understanding change: models, methodologies, and metaphors*, Basingstoke: Palgrave.

Integrationsverket (2007) 'Ett förlorad år. En studie och analys av innsatser och resultat under introductionens första 12 månader' ['A lost year. A study and analysis of measures and results during the first 12 months of the introduction'], *Integrationsverkets stancilserie 2007: 05*, Stockholm.

Johansson, H. and Hvinden, B. (2007) 'Nordic activation reforms in a European context: a distinct universalistic model?', in B. Hvinden and H. Johansson (eds) *Citizenship in Nordic welfare states: dynamics of choice, duties and participation in a changing Europe*, London/New York: Routledge.

Jørgensen, M.B. (2006) 'Dansk realisme og svensk naivitet? En analyse af den danske og svenske integrationspolitik' ['Danish realism and Swedish naiveté? An analysis of the Danish and Swedish integration policy'], in *Bortom stereotyperna? Invandrare och integration i Danmark och Sverige [Beyond stereotypes? Immigrants and integration in Denmark and Sweden]*, Makadam förlag.

Larsen, F. (2009) 'Operationelle reformer som drivkraft for forandring: Kommunale jobcentre som det gode eksempel?' ['Operational reforms as the driver for change: municipal job centres as the good example?'], *Samfundsøkonomen*, no 5, pp 23–31.

Larsen, C.A. (2010) 'Ethnic heterogeneity and public support for welfare policies: is the "black" American experience resembled in Britain, Sweden, and Denmark?', CCWS Working Paper No 2010–68,. Available at: www.epa.aau.dk/fileadmin/user_upload/ime/CCWS/workingpapers/2010-68-CAL.pdf

Lødemel, I. and Trickey, H. (2001) *An offer you can't refuse – workfare in a international perspective*, Bristol: The Policy Press.

Morissens, A. and Sainsbury, D. (2005) 'Migrants' social rights, ethnicity and welfare regimes', *Journal of Social Policy*, vol 34, no 4, pp 637–60.

Necef, M.Û. (2001) 'Indvandring, den nationale stat og velfærdsstaten' ['Immigration, the national state and the welfare state'], in P. Seeberg (ed) *Ubekvemme udfordringer [Uncomfortable challenges]*, Odense: University Press of Southern Denmark.

OECD (Organisation for Economic Co-operation and Development) (2010) *International Migration Outlook*.

Sainsbury, D. (2006) 'Immigrants' social rights in comparative perspective: welfare regimes, forms of immigration and immigration policy regimes', *Journal of European Social Policy*, vol 16, no 3, pp 229–44.

Siim, B. and Borchorst, A. (2008) 'The multicultural challenge to the Danish welfare state – social politics, equality and regulating families', FREIA's Working Paper Series No 65. Available at: http://vbn.aau. dk/files/13982679/FREIA_wp_65.pdf.

Tranæs, T. and Zimmermann, K.F. (2004) *Migrants, work, and the welfare state*, Odense: University Press of Southern Denmark.

Norway

St. Meld. (1996/97: 17) *Om innvandring og det flerkulturelle Norge* [*On immigration and the multicultural Norway*], Kommunal og Arbeidsdepartementet.

St. Meld. (1998/99: 50) *Utjamningsmeldinga: Om fordeling av inntekt og levekår i Norge* [*The distribution of income and living conditions in Norway*], Sosial- og helsedepartementet.

NOU (2001: 20) *Lov om introduksjonsordning for nyankomne innvandrere* (Introduksjonsloven) [*The Introductory Programme for Newly Arrived Immigrants Act (The Introduction Act)*].

Ot.prp (2002/03: 28) *Om lov om introduksjonsordning for nyankomne innvandrere* (introduksjonsloven) [*On the Introductory Programme for Newly Arrived Immigrants Act (The Introduction Act)*].

Sweden

Prop. (2009/10: 60) *Nyanlända invandrares arbetsmarknadsetablering – egenansvar med professionellt stöd* [*The establishment of newly arrived immigrants in the labour market – own responsibility with professional support*].

SOU (2008: 58) *Egenansvar – med professionellt stöd: Betänkande av Utredningen om nyanländas arbetsmarknadsetablering* [*Own responsibility – with professional support: report of the inquiry on new arrivals' integration into the labour market*].

Denmark

The Danish Government (2005) *En ny chance til alle: Regeringens integrationsoplæg* [*A new chance for everyone: the government's integration presentation*], Copenhagen.

SEVEN

Welfare retrenchment under Left and Right government leadership: towards a consolidated framework of analysis?

Stefan Kühner

Introduction

Over the course of the last two decades, comparative welfare research has dealt with two puzzles. Initially, it was commonplace that Western European welfare states remained remarkably 'resilient' despite major fiscal and socio-economic pressures, globalisation, and frontal assaults by austerity governments (see, eg, Castles, 2004). To explain this first puzzle, the 'new politics' of the welfare state became synonymous with the politics of 'blame avoidance' (Green-Pedersen and Haverland, 2002; Starke, 2006): the persistent popularity of welfare programmes was said to trigger coalitions of welfare defenders, making downward adjustments of post-war welfare settlements, that is, welfare retrenchment, electorally highly risky for office-seeking policymakers (Pierson, 1994, 1996, 2001b). In addition, path dependency theory pointed towards 'lock-in' and 'feedback effects' of past policy decisions (Weaver, 1986; Pierson, 2000; Swank, 2001) while defenders of the welfare state made use of constitutional constraints to hinder welfare retrenchment (Swank, 2001; Kühner, 2010). The 'new politics' thesis views 'retrenchment politics [as] a distinctive enterprise' from the politics of welfare expansion – not least because it argues that 'the centrality of left party and union confederation strength to welfare outcomes has declined' (Pierson, 1996, p 151, cited in Scarbrough, 2000). More recently, however, numerous Western European governments were identified as having engaged in welfare retrenchment during the three decades since the 1970s' oil and stagflation crises (Ferrera and Rhodes, 2000; Scharpf and Schmidt, 2000; Palier, 2010). What is more, rather than losing their 'centrality', several scholars have argued that Left parties played a critical role in the politics of welfare retrenchment across Western Europe. Contrary to mainstream partisan theory, which has traditionally viewed Left parties as representatives of blue-collar interests (Hibbs, 1977; Castles, 1982; Shalev, 1983; Korpi, 1989; Hicks and Swank, 1992), the capacity of Left parties to facilitate or even spearhead welfare retrenchment has been emphasised (Levy, 1999; Ross, 2000; Armingeon et al, 2001). Simultaneously, it was pointed out that trade unions continued to assert their influence (Ebbinghaus and Hassel, 2000; Trampusch, 2006, 2007).

As a consequence of these contrasting accounts, comparative welfare research has attempted to answer 'why', 'when' and 'how' policymakers, particularly on the left of the political spectrum, engage in 'treacherous' (Pierson, 1994, p 18) welfare state retrenchment. First, rather than assuming the effect of fiscal and socio-economic problem pressures, recent contributions outline precarious economic and political situations – so-called 'losses domains' – as the 'cause' for welfare retrenchment (Vis and Van Kersbergen, 2007). Second, rather than adding multi-party systems to the list of constitutional constraints that create a barrier to welfare retrenchment (Schmidt, 1996; Tsebelis, 2002), electoral competition between Left and Right parties is considered a key mechanism facilitating welfare retrenchment (Kitschelt, 2001). Finally, rather than focusing on policy stability caused by 'lock-in' and 'feedback' effects, the role of consensus-seeking as a tool to break policy gridlock gained more attention (Levy, 1999; Ross, 2000; Kitschelt, 2001; Vis and Van Kersbergen, 2007).

While typically discussed separately, this chapter aims to assess the potential of consolidating these three conceptual perspectives into one framework of analysis. Although interrelated, each of the answers to the 'why', 'when' and 'how' questions tackles distinct aspects of the dynamics of welfare retrenchment. This chapter hopes to show that combining causes, mechanisms and tools of welfare retrenchment presents a valuable move forward for the comparative analysis of social policies, which will hopefully facilitate a more holistic understanding of related policy processes. This chapter tests the potential of the suggested consolidated approach against comparative historical evidence for four Western European democracies, namely Denmark, France, Germany and the Netherlands. These countries were chosen because they all feature either state corporatist or encompassing welfare systems, multiple constitutional barriers, and comparatively strong trade union movements (Hicks and Kenworthy, 1998; Schmidt, 2000; Armingeon, 2002; Korpi and Palme, 2003) – a combination that should render welfare retrenchment particularly difficult and electorally costly.

The chapter is structured as follows. First, it briefly reviews the three theoretical perspectives on 'why', 'when' and 'how' policymakers choose to engage in welfare retrenchment and suggests how these can be consolidated into one framework of analysis. Second, the conceptualisation of 'welfare retrenchment' employed to explore the four cases is briefly introduced. This is followed by more detailed discussions of welfare retrenchment in each of the four Western European democracies between 1980 and 2002.[1] Third, the main findings of the analysis are drawn together. This section highlights some of the key findings, but also includes suggestions for further inquiry. Finally, the conclusion assumes a broader outlook, stressing the need for more systematic explorations of welfare retrenchment along the lines suggested in this chapter and putting these into the context of more current debates in the post-2008 financial crisis environment.

'Why', 'when' and 'how' do policymakers engage in welfare retrenchment?

Post-industrial 'problem pressures' typically describe overlapping social transformations that affect the dynamics of welfare retrenchment in a loose sense (Pierson, 2001c; Bonoli, 2006). Vis and Van Kersbergen (2007) also try to answer the question of 'why' exactly office-seeking policymakers engage in unpopular welfare retrenchment. Based on prospect theoretical experiments on how people choose risky options (Kahneman and Tversky, 1979), they argue that governments in a strong economic and political position, that is, governments in a so-called 'gains domain', are generally unwilling to engage in welfare retrenchment. In contrast, governments in a precarious economic or political position, that is, governments in a 'losses domain', 'are more willing to accept the risks of reform' (Vis and Van Kersbergen, 2007, p 159). In other words, policymakers generally choose unpopular and risky policy changes only if the status quo is 'unacceptable' (Vis and Van Kersbergen, 2007, p 153). Therefore, the motivation to pursue a risky policy strategy depends on whether the electorate considers the status quo 'acceptable or tolerable' or not (Vis and Van Kersbergen, 2007). They conclude that risk-seeking governments do not have to fear electoral conflict if voters favour a change to the status quo. It is risk-averse voters who see themselves in a 'gains domain' that will prefer the status quo to any suggested welfare retrenchment (Vis and Van Kersbergen, 2007). In this latter scenario, 'blame avoidance' strategies become unavoidable to minimise potential electoral punishment and to diffuse oppositional coalitions (Weaver, 1986).

In a widely cited empirical test of these hypotheses, Vis (2009a, 2009b; see also Vis, 2010) demonstrates that Right government leadership in conjunction with a precarious socio-economic situation – operationalised as the level and change of economic growth and unemployment together with electorates' perceptions as to whether these are problematic – is a sufficient condition for unpopular social policy reform. In contrast, Left governments engage in unpopular social policy reform only if a precarious socio-economic position is present in combination with a precarious political position – operationalised as unfavourable opinion polls, unfavourable results in federal and municipal elections, intra-party conflicts, as well as marginal parliamentary majorities (Vis, 2009a, pp 17–18). Crucially, however, Vis (2009a, pp 17-18) points out that not all Right governments in her study follow this general pattern: at least two (Right Danish) governments should have engaged in unpopular social policy reform but failed to do so. She speculates that this was 'at least partly related to the relatively short duration of an average Danish government (two years) and the usual type of government (multiparty minority)', both of which create a 'road block in the paths that hinders reform from coming about'. This finding is indicative of an important caveat: although a considerable step forward, emphasising the 'causes' of welfare retrenchment by means of 'losses domains' cannot fully account for the mediating impact of party politics and constitutional constraints on policy outputs.

Kitschelt (2001, p 274) focuses on specific features of party systems in Western democracies in an attempt to tackle the question of 'when' policymakers engage in welfare retrenchment. He argues that the existence of Centre/Right parties that force the issue is crucial to explain the dynamics of welfare retrenchment. Yet, Centre/Right governments are more likely to argue in favour of welfare retrenchment if they face 'weak' Left parties. Left parties become 'weak' if they lose economic credibility or if they are in a position too far to the Left to be attractive for the median voter. According to Kitschelt (2001, p 276), policymakers are more likely to engage in unpopular welfare reform if a low electoral trade-off between office- and vote-seeking exists. This trade-off increases if Centre/Right governments operate in party systems with 'moderate Social Democratic parties [that] support the welfare state in credible ways'. Armingeon et al (2001, p 3) add that Left parties 'have an electoral incentive to criticise retrenchment policies of Centre governments, [even] knowing that the reorientation of the welfare state cannot be avoided'. They come to the conclusion that 'Centre parties are much less suited for the task of retrenching [welfare programmes]' – a view that is shared by Kitschelt (2001, p 269), who stresses that 'in an environment of fiscal and economic crisis, it is not the … Left that display the greatest propensity to defend existing welfare states and resist retrenchment'.

Indeed, the so-called 'Nixon-in-China' logic suggests a strategic advantage for Left parties seeking to re-establish voter confidence in the context of fiscal austerity and a precarious socio-economic situation. Ross (2000, pp 164–5) also argues that welfare retrenchment carries the most risk for Right governments, but she attributes this to the fact that 'voters do not trust [them] to reform the welfare state whereas they assume Left parties will engage in genuine reform rather than indiscriminate and harsh retrenchment'. She continues that 'cuts imposed by the Left may be viewed as trade-offs for increased spending in other policy areas, absolute essentials, strategic necessity, or, at a minimum, lower than those that would be experienced under parties of the Right'. Not least, 'the Left may even be viewed as fiscally prudent and economically responsible' (Ross, 2000, pp 164–5) and choosing the reduction of further welfare expansion merely 'in order to avoid its erosion' (Armingeon et al, 2001, p 3). Levy (1999) demonstrates how progressive Left governments were able to turn policies of 'vice' into policies of 'virtue' by 'targeting inequities within welfare systems that [were] a source of either economic inefficiency or substantial public spending' (Levy, 1999, p 240). Rather than having to 'avoid blame', the 'Nixon-in-China' logic postulates that Left parties were able to 'claim credit' when restructuring the welfare state.

While all of the above entertains the adversarial nature of welfare retrenchment processes, several contributions highlight a more consensual approach to achieving envisaged policy outputs. There is much evidence to suggest that policy deliberation is key to fully comprehending the very tools of welfare retrenchment – that is, 'how' policymakers engage in such processes. This is true for the 'old' politics of welfare expansion (Baldwin, 1990; Manow, 2009; Manow and Van Kersbergen, 2009), it is also true for the 'new' politics' of welfare retrenchment. Including the main parliamentary opposition in negotiations about welfare retrenchment is a useful 'blame avoidance' strategy as it diffuses responsibilities across the political system (Weaver, 1986; Pierson, 1996; Clayton and Pontusson, 1998; Vis and Van Kersbergen, 2007). As cross-party consensus on welfare retrenchment makes it difficult for voters to concentrate their anger on one single political player, Hering (2003, p 9) suggests that 'governments are more likely to initiate welfare reforms if they command a large [cross-party] majority in parliament'. Similarly, Vis and Van Kersbergen (2007, p 167) conclude that 'in systems with multiple veto points ... all major reforms necessarily are the result of system-wide bargains such as a grand coalition'.

Negotiating compromise with trade unions is also seen as much easier for Left parties because of their 'close proximity' to these political forces: 'veto points ... only limit the scope of retrenchment where they encourage veto players to mobilize on the Left' (Ross, 2000, p 169). In other words, while multiple constitutional constraints, and particularly Left veto players, have a retarding effect on the pursuit of Right governments to retrench welfare programmes (Schmidt, 1996; Kühner, 2010), counter-majoritarian and corporatist structures in Western European democracies can become conducive to welfare retrenchment under Left government leadership (Armingeon, 2002). Finally, Left parties are more likely to oppose welfare retrenchment by Centre/Right governments when in opposition: once incumbent 'Left parties are in favour of retrenchment measures there is little electoral incentive for parties on the Centre and the Right to criticise these policies' (Armingeon et al, 2001, p 3). In short, party competition and consensus-seeking strategies are clearly interrelated and should be considered jointly.

Together, the above boil down to a set of central arguments describing the dynamics of welfare retrenchment. Following Vis and Van Kersbergen (2007) and Vis (2009a), we should expect an intolerable status quo created by a precarious socio-economic position to cause engagement in welfare retrenchment – but not policy outputs per se. It is also fair to assume, in line with Kitschelt (2001), that these attempts are initially led by Centre/Right governments and are more likely to succeed in the absence of credible Left opposition both within and outside of parliament. Left parties come under pressure if their last stint in office is remembered as unsuccessful and if their promoted policies are perceived to divert too far from the middle ground (Kitschelt, 2001), but also if the electorate views the status quo as a 'losses domain'. The same is broadly true for trade unions opposed to welfare retrenchment. The latter is crucial only if the socio-economic *and* political position is skewed in favour of the status quo and only if the Left poses a credible alternative in the eyes of voters should they be able to mobilise resistance to welfare retrenchment led by Centre/Right governments. In this context, the ability of Centre/Right governments to establish cross-party consensus with oppositional forces is instrumental and yet unlikely, as Left parties and trade unions should have little incentive to compromise. Only if Left parties lack credibility (for instance, subsequent to an unsuccessful stint in office) can Centre/Right governments hope to neutralise the strategic advantage of the Left and their power to veto welfare retrenchment.

Table 7.1: Towards a consolidated framework of welfare retrenchment?

Policymakers engage in unpopular and electorally risky welfare reform:	Cause		Mechanisms/tools	
	'Why'?		**'When'?**	**'How'?**
	Precarious socio-economic situation?	**Weak political situation?**	**Credible Left opposition?**	**Consensus-seeking?**
	Sluggish economic performance, structural unemployment, fiscal austerity and so on.	*Public perception, intra-party conflicts, election defeats and so on.*	*Economic credibility, proximity to median voter, effective trade union mobilisation and so on.*	*Large parliamentary majorities, tripartite agreements, side payments and so on.*
Right government leadership	Yes	No	No	
			Yes	
Left government leadership	Yes	Yes	No	

In contrast, once Left policymakers accept that they are in a 'losses domain', embrace ideational reframing of their own party strategies (Levy, 1999) and communicate these changes to trade unions and the electorate via the 'Nixon-in-China' logic (Ross, 2000), they should find it easier, in relative terms, to claim credit for engaging in welfare retrenchment. Left governments should also find it easier to gain support from Centre/Right parliamentary opposition. The need to establish consensus with the parliamentary opposition should still be important in the sense that it diffuses responsibility for welfare retrenchment, but is much less likely to restrain changes of the status quo under Left government leadership. There are, then, distinct paths to welfare retrenchment if the three theoretical perspectives and their respective answers to the 'why', 'when' and 'how' questions of welfare retrenchment are considered jointly and depending on whether Left or Right governments are incumbent. Table 7.1 attempts to summarise these in a simplified framework of analysis. The potential of this framework will be subsequently assessed against the empirical evidence in the four chosen Western European democracies.

Case evidence

There is no shortage of answers to the question of what qualifies as welfare retrenchment (Pierson, 2001a). In order to ensure a systematic analytical approach and to enable readers to compare findings across different studies, it is important to briefly summarise the underlying operationalisation of 'welfare retrenchment' in this chapter. There is no scope here to do justice to important debates around the so-called 'dependent variable problem' within the comparative analysis of social policy (Clasen and Siegel, 2008; Howlett and Cashore, 2011). Suffice it to say that, albeit using slightly different terminologies, scholars are typically interested in delineations of paradigmatic change that go against the dominating welfare logic of more incremental policy reform (see, eg, Hall, 1993; Pierson, 1994; Daly, 1997). In regards to the latter, Kvist (1999, p 249) distinguishes 'visible, immediate, painful and easily trackable (to responsible policymakers)' welfare cuts and more 'technical [welfare cuts that] are invisible to the layperson, have little immediate impact and are time-consuming to explain'. The fact that policies that cut or freeze replacement rates are 'immediately painful' is uncontroversial. Policies that tighten eligibility rules with immediate effect, introduce means/income tests and/or otherwise increase targeting fall in the same category. Technical forms of welfare retrenchment typically include the longer-term tightening of eligibility rules, such as the lengthening of qualifying periods. Typically considered in this category are policies that raise retirement ages or change the indexation rules of benefits, although such initiatives often result in replacement rate cuts. Transferring state responsibilities to the private sector or introducing new private tiers of pension provision are labelled 'radical' in some contributions (see, eg, Weaver, 1988; Pierson, 1996); others treat such initiatives more conservatively (Hudson et al, 2008). Shifts towards earnings-related elements in formerly universal benefits, negative income tax-style policies as well as activation policies to 'make work pay' are slightly harder to categorise as they often combine policy 'carrots *and* sticks' in various ways. Despite a degree of controversy, most contributions classify these policies as belonging to more technical types of welfare retrenchment (see, eg, Clasen, 2000; Holden, 2003).

Table 7.2: Left and Right government leadership and welfare retrenchment, 1980–2002

	Resilience	Retrenchment	
		Technical, obfuscated, time-lagged	**Visible, immediate, painful**
Denmark	Jørgensen IV 1979, Jørgensen V 1981, Schlüter II 1984, Schlüter IV 1988, Schlüter V 1990	Schlüter I 1982, **Rasmussen I 1993, Rasmussen IV 1998**	**Rasmussen II/ III 1994**
France	**Mauroy II 1981, Fabius 1984,** Chirac II 1986, **Rocard II1988, Cresson 1991, Bérégovoy 1992**	Juppé 1995, **Jospin 1997**	Balladur 1993
Germany	Kohl I 1983, Kohl II 1987, Kohl III 1990	Kohl IV 1994, **Schröder I 1998**	**Schröder II 2002**
Netherlands	Van Agt I/II/III 1977, **Kok II 1998**	Lubbers II 1986, Lubbers III 1989	Lubbers I 1982, **Kok I 1994**

Note: Governments led by Socialist/Social Democratic/Labour Prime Ministers in boldface, adapted from Kühner (2012).

The description of cases in this chapter is based on an ongoing data collection of historical case study evidence that is combined in the *Comparative historical welfare reform data set* (Kühner, 2012).[2] Table 7.2 provides a summary of incidences of welfare retrenchment in the four observed countries following the earlier delineation of 'technical, obfuscated, time-lagged' and 'visible, immediate, painful' policy change (see also Kühner, 2011). Welfare programmes have remained resilient under a number of Centre/Right governments. There are also numerous Left governments that did not engage in welfare retrenchment – the majority of which were in power during the 1980s and early 1990s. These findings are in line with mainstream partisan and institutional hypotheses described in the introduction (Schmidt, 1996; Kühner, 2010). But there are also some Right governments that managed to retrench welfare programmes despite operating in political systems with mature welfare states, multiple constitutional constraints and strong trade unions. More interestingly still are the numerous Left governments responsible for important welfare retrenchments. Indeed, the majority of Left governments during the 1990s and early 2000s did not excel as defenders of post-war welfare settlements – far from it! It is the latter Left and Right governments that the subsequent case descriptions will focus on. The leading questions of the following sections are whether case descriptions are broadly in line with the earlier framework of analysis and, ultimately, whether they indicate that more systematic exploration along those lines is warranted.

Denmark

Schlüter I came to power after the resignation of the last Jørgensen government in 1982 (Schwartz, 1994, p 550) in what is described as a 'generally optimistic and favourable mood towards the coalition' (Vis, 2010, p 196). Yet unemployment in Denmark had steadily increased from a relatively low 4.9% in 1975 to a peak of 11.6% in 1983 (OECD, 2011). Despite the fact that Danish Social Democrats together with the trade union movement consistently and strongly opposed welfare cutbacks (Green-Pedersen, 2001b, p 975), Schlüter I was able to implement a freeze of benefits for three years – a significant change considering the high level of inflation at the time (Green-Pedersen, 2001b). The Left struggled to mobilise resistance against these welfare retrenchments because they were not unpopular within the electorate (Vis, 2010, p 183). Shortly after another decisive victory in the general election of 1984, Schlüter II proposed to shorten the duration of unemployment benefits. This time, the pressures from the Left paid more dividends: indexation of benefits was reinstated and old-age pensions improved; the proposed cuts in unemployment were first postponed and later given up altogether; and, in 1987, the Conservative–Liberal coalition government and Social Democrats jointly increased unemployment benefits and early-retirement benefits. Unemployment started to rise again in the early 1990s, this time paired with several years of sluggish economic growth. Although the Conservatives (Schlüter III, IV and V) remained keen to cut unemployment benefits in light of a worsening socio-economic position, it oversaw the implementation of several improvements of social security, including unemployment, disability and early-retirement compensation, as the Left continued to assert pressure (Clasen, 2000, p 94; Green-Pedersen, 2001b, p 976; Green-Pedersen and Lindbom, 2006, p 254; Vis, 2010, p 184).

N. Rasmussen I pledged to continue the course of the late Conservative–Liberal coalition (Schwartz, 1994, p 551). N. Rasmussen I controlled a parliamentary majority and the largest cabinet in the history of Denmark after both Centre and Christian Democrats joined his government. Opposition from Liberals and Conservatives was muted (Vis, 2010, p 198). At the same time, economic growth figures improved significantly, which had a favourable effect on employment figures (Clasen, 2000, p 94). Nevertheless, N. Rasmussen I strove to implement the recommendations of a series of White Papers on welfare reform published in the early 1990s: the means-tested part of old-age pensions was increased immediately in 1993, while a comprehensive labour market reform emphasising activation was passed in parliament. These activation measures presented 'a precursor for a plethora of policies introduced by the Social Democratic government in successive labour market reforms after 1993' (Clasen, 2000, p 94). Against the backdrop of favourable economic and labour market figures, N. Rasmussen II (and III) and IV retrenched unemployment benefits twice in 1995 and 1998 by cutting benefit levels for the young unemployed and by reducing its maximum duration (Torfing, 1999, pp 15–16). Activation was the centrepiece of the 1998 'Act on Active Social Policy'. While the parliamentary opposition agreed to the majority of these measures, they caused dismay within parts of the trade union movement, the Social Democratic Party itself and the electorate (Green-Pedersen, 2001b, p 976). Still, after six years of negotiating, N. Rasmussen IV passed comprehensive early-retirement pension reform, including an equalisation of early-retirement pensions and unemployment pensions (Bertelsmann Foundation, 2000). These reforms proved politically costly: the number of members in the Social Democratic Party decreased rapidly, together with trade union donations and levels of support in opinion polls (Vis, 2010, p 199).

Germany

Welfare retrenchment initiatives also led to divisions on the left of the political spectrum in Germany. Internal debates partly explain the lack of major labour market reform during Schröder I, despite a clear mandate for the newly elected Red–Green coalition (Zohlnhöfer, 2003). Although major in several respects (Hinrichs, 2010), the 2001 old-age pension reform was less far-reaching than initially intended. Fierce pressure from trade unions, traditionalists within the Social Democratic Party as well as from Christian Democrats meant that the initially envisaged compulsory character of private savings had to be given up, and generous subsidies to stimulate private savings had to be provided (Zohlnhöfer, 2003). The trade union movement and the different wings within the Social Democratic Party were even more opposed to Schröder II's *Agenda 2010*, which had not been part of the Chancellor's 2002 election platform. Trade unions cancelled talks with the leadership of the Social Democrats in protest against proposed welfare cuts, particularly the integration of social and unemployment assistance into one benefit (Fleckenstein, 2008, p 179). Resistance within the Social Democratic Party remained strong and eventually triggered a secession of parts of Left traditionalists into a new Leftist party. Schröder II found a new majority in the upper house through an alliance with Christian Democrats (Zohlnhöfer, 2004). Nevertheless, Schröder II and the Social Democrats did very badly in opinion polls and lost a host of federal elections – the last Red–Green coalition at the federal level was defeated in 2005. Schröder himself had by then been forced to step down from the party leadership.

The implementation of Schröder II's *Agenda 2010* illustrates the significance of consensus-seeking, especially if compared with the experience of the last Kohl government (Kohl IV). The adversarial style of German policymaking in this period is well documented (Hudson and Kühner, 2011): in 1996, trade unions left summit talks initiated by the Christian Democratic–Liberal government in protest against proposals to cut sick pay from 100% to 80% (Ebbinghaus and Hassel, 2000). The Social Democrats refused to cooperate with the Kohl government and started to oppose government proposals in the upper house in which they had held a majority since 1991. The implementation of far-reaching reform had been difficult for some time, but on several occasions the respective Kohl I, II and III cabinets managed to secure the support of Social Democrats in the upper house (Zohlnhöfer, 2003) – although the welfare retrenchment efforts remained comparatively limited during this period (Vis, 2010, pp 189–90). Kohl IV was no longer able to break the resistance of Social Democrats decisively: as non-wage labour costs and unemployment increased in tandem and discussions about Germany as a business location dominated public debates (Hudson and Kühner, 2011), the 1999 pension reform entered German history books as the first significant change of old-age pensions that failed to be implemented with the support of the major parliamentary opposition (Hinrichs, 2010). The accelerated increase in the retirement age and introduction of a demographic factor that this reform entailed were hugely unpopular within the electorate; additional reforms that deregulated and reformed the labour market were also implemented against the resistance of the Left. Together, they constituted the basis of a pledge by the Social Democratic Party to reverse unpopular reforms, which they did immediately after winning the 1998 general election (Hudson and Kühner, 2011).

France

The experience of the Schröder and Kohl governments reverberate in the experience of the 1993 Balladur and 1995 Juppé governments in France. The Centre-Right Balladur government came to power with a substantial parliamentary majority (Palier, 2000), and after a decade dominated by a series of relatively short-lived Socialist governments. Governments during this period largely dealt with persisting social security deficits through increasing social contribution rates; yet unemployment rates remained on a steady upward trajectory (Palier, 2000). Early government plans to cut the minimum wage for the young unemployed were dropped after trade union protest (Palier, 2000). Nevertheless, the Balladur government managed to pass a private-sector pension reform that extended the number of contributory years needed to qualify for a full pension and shifted pension indexation from gross wages to prices (Bonoli, 1997). These changes were negotiated in tripartite consultations and contained a key concession to trade unions: an old-age solidarity fund financed through general taxation was introduced in order to bolster means-tested minimum pensions. This was a key demand of trade unions as these benefits were previously financed by employer contributions (Ebbinghaus and Hassel, 2000).

When the Juppé government tried to extend the same measures to public pensions two years later without consulting social partners prior to the publication of reform plans, it triggered some of the most severe demonstrations and rail strikes in recent French history and ultimately led to the plans being abandoned (Bonoli and Palier, 1998). Public pension reform was part of the so-called Juppé Plan, which also changed claiming principles for health care, introduced means-tests for family allowances, altered the composition of the management boards of social security funds and enhanced the use of taxation in financing social security (Vail, 1999). The social partners were invited to a 'social summit' to discuss solutions to the unemployment problem, but more strike action continued throughout 1996 and 1997 (Scarbrough, 2000, p 242). Trade unions were more divided than the mass protest of the winter of 1995/96 would have indicated. A number of less radical unions agreed to the majority of proposed measures (Bonoli and Palier, 1998).

The same can be said about the biggest parliamentary opposition, the Socialists, as some of the proposals in the Juppé Plan were introduced by the Socialists only a few years previously. Also, despite arguing against the Juppé Plan while in opposition, it was a Socialist government that continued to implement its key measures after Jospin won the 1997 election (Bouget, 1998, p 164). Nevertheless, further pension reform remained extremely difficult and was postponed as trade unions opposed proposals to increase eligibility criteria (Palier, 2000). The Jospin government managed to pass several labour market reforms to intensify job search, subsidise employers and increase financial incentives to work (Erhel and Zajdela, 2004), including the introduction of a new unemployment insurance scheme, which emphasised individual support and obligations for unemployed persons (Bertelsmann Foundation, 2000). It was only with these changes that unemployment decreased slightly from levels in excess of 10% during the majority of the 1990s.

Netherlands

When Lubbers I came to power in 1982, this Christian Democratic–Liberal coalition followed a 'no-nonsense' platform for economic profitability and fiscal consolidation. Part of this programme was an attempt to alleviate the severe unemployment problem at the time – unemployment in the Netherlands increased from just over 2% around 1970 to a peak of 12% in the early 1980s (OECD, 2011) – by freezing social security benefits initially from 1983 through 1989, and again from 1993 through 1995; eligibility criteria for social assistance were tightened, old-age pensions were indexed and unemployment and disability retrenched (Green-Pedersen, 2001a, 2001b). The Dutch Labour Party strongly opposed these changes, but the Lubbers government helped its social image by introducing a special benefit for poor single-earner families, the so-called 'real social minima', which gave the Left a smaller target to aim its opposition against (Cox, 1998). In preparation for upcoming elections, the Dutch Labour Party released its own ideas on social policy reform, including its own welfare retrenchments and a refusal to guarantee to abolish the benefit freeze (Green-Pedersen, 2001a, 2001b). Welfare retrenchment continued under Lubbers II, albeit at reduced stealth in light of improving economic and labour market figures.

After the break-up of the Christian Democratic–Liberal coalition and another general election in 1989, the Dutch Labour Party found itself as the junior partner in a grand coalition with the Christian

Democrats (Lubbers III). It was to support implementation of a series of contentious welfare retrenchments. The generosity of old-age pensions and unemployment benefits was retrenched, and activation measures concentrated on the young unemployed (Vis, 2010, p 187). Social Democrats increasingly struggled in opinion polls on the back of these measures and performed poorly in some municipal elections. In a general election of discontent triggered by government plans to freeze Dutch old-age pensions for a four-year period in 1994 (Green-Pedersen, 2001a, p 138), the Dutch Labour Party ended up being the strongest party despite suffering significant losses. Although pledging not to tamper further with welfare benefits, Kok I oversaw several considerable welfare retrenchments: unemployment insurance became a minimum benefit for those with short or disrupted work histories, while eligibility for disability pensions and sickness benefits were privatised. These retrenchments caused mass protest in the streets in Den Haag (Becker, 2000) and nearly forced the leadership of the Dutch Labour Party to step down as its popularity plummeted in opinion polls (Hemerijck and Visser, 2000). Kok II followed a more expansionary approach to welfare reform. It privatised job-placement services and deregulated the Dutch law on protection against dismissal. At the same time, the public sector created permanent jobs for the long-term unemployed and unemployed youths, and the legal right to more flexible work patterns was introduced alongside several other measures to support families (Bertelsmann Foundation, 2001).

Discussion

The central objective of this chapter was to assess the potential of three theoretical perspectives and the distinct paths to welfare retrenchment that emerge once they are considered jointly. Indeed, the case descriptions suggest the different dynamics of welfare retrenchment across four Western European democracies can be accounted for by the developed framework of analysis. The case evidence suggests a series of key lessons.

1. It was suggested that both Centre/Right and Left governments should be more willing to engage in welfare retrenchment under precarious socio-economic circumstances – an assumption that rings true in the majority of observed cases across the four countries.
2. It was also suggested that Right governments should be more likely to achieve welfare retrenchment if they compete against Left parties

that suffered from a loss in electoral credibility or are too far away from the median voter (see Schlüter I).

3. In cases where Left parties were more credible and united with trade unions, Right governments relied on consensus-seeking strategies such as side payments (see Balladur, Lubbers I) or formal coalitions with Left parties (see Lubbers III); those Centre/Right governments that pushed through welfare retrenchments against the Left had to sacrifice components of their welfare retrenchment agenda (see Juppé) and/or pay dearly in subsequent general elections (see Kohl IV).

4. In contrast, once Left governments found themselves in a precarious socio-economic and political situation, it was suggested that they should have been better able to reframe welfare retrenchments into virtuous and progressive welfare restructuring and, to a certain extent, to negotiate welfare retrenchment with trade unions. Several Left governments engaged in welfare retrenchment once they found themselves in a precarious political situation (see Rasmussen II [and III], Schröder II).

5. The 'Nixon-to-China' logic clearly has some purchase. Yet, despite their 'close proximity' to Left veto players, Left governments were only successful in retrenching welfare programmes to the extent to which they managed to negotiate welfare retrenchment with trade unions and traditionalists in their own ranks (see Schröder I) or, in cases where these negotiations were unsuccessful, to the extent to which they were able to establish parliamentary majorities with Centre/Right parties (see N. Rasmussen II [and III], N. Rasmussen IV, Schröder II).

These suggested linkages between causes and mechanisms are naturally far from deterministic. Some governments meet theoretical expectations much more unambiguously than others. Clearly, more systematic investigation is needed to dispose of the white noise surrounding the above classifications. This chapter does not pretend to test 'hypotheses' in the true sense of the word. Still, much suggests that the conceptual framework developed in this chapter deserves further scrutiny and has the potential to lead to more holistic findings than currently offered in the existing literature. We want to end by suggesting possible starting points for further investigation.

First, in regards to the causes of policymakers engaging in welfare retrenchment, a precarious socio-economic situation has played a key role. At first glance, this provides ammunition for Vis's (2009a, 2009b) argument that the identification of socio-economic 'losses domains' is a crucial starting point for any serious exploration of welfare retrenchment dynamics. At the same time, measuring and operationalising precarious socio-economic positions is not always straightforward. What is more, some governments engaged in welfare retrenchment in reaction to improvements in economic performance, which suggests that causal linkages may in fact not be unidirectional in every case. Considering broader discussions on the process sequencing of policy dynamics may prove to be a useful resource to develop hypotheses further (Howlett, 2009). It would also be fruitful to explore the interplay between precarious socio-economic positions, policy discourse (Schmidt, 2002), imperatives (Cox, 2001) and the framing of social citizenship (Taylor-Gooby, 2010) to gain a fuller understanding of 'losses domains' and their impact on political decision-making.

Second, the picture is also complicated when it comes to establishing a link between a precarious political situation and the engagement of Left governments in unpopular welfare retrenchment. Left governments engaged in welfare retrenchment not only when they were in a precarious political situation, but also when they were relatively strong (see, eg, N. Rasmussen I, N. Rasmussen IV, Schröder I, Jospin, Kok I). There is some evidence that declining approval ratings, intra-party conflicts and lost majorities in upper houses have led to more risky behaviour by some Left governments. At the same time, it was exactly these circumstances that created a stumbling block for the implementation of far-reaching changes of the status quo, in some instances creating friction between the causes and mechanisms of welfare retrenchment. This points to the previous argument in this chapter that 'losses domains' alone cannot fully account for policy outputs due to the mediating effect of party competition and constitutional constraints. It presents a confirmation of the need to consider institutional contexts at the meso-level when analysing the dynamics of welfare retrenchment (Hudson and Lowe, 2009).

Third, the case for party competition is probably the most well rehearsed: in the Netherlands, the existence of a pivotal Centre Party led the moderate Left to accept tough retrenchment measures in order to regain credibility within the electorate. This in turn helped the Centre/Right to diffuse responsibility and argue that there was no workable alternative to welfare retrenchment (Green-Pedersen, 2001b). Left parties in Denmark had the strategic capacity to be more consistently opposed to welfare retrenchment measures (Cox, 2001). In Germany, once Social Democrats decided to cease cooperation, Kohl IV found it extremely difficult to implement welfare retrenchment. Party competition was also crucial in France, but in slightly different ways. Socialist governments often relied on external support during the 1990s, but the Communist Party was not willing to back retrenchment of pension entitlements, and the Right-of-Centre parties were opposed to assisting its political opponents. This meant that no significant reform could be negotiated, despite official debates that clearly stressed the need for reform (Bonoli, 1997, pp 115–16). The latter suggests that the politics of welfare retrenchment may be more complicated than allowed for in this chapter. Not unlike Centre/Right governments, Left parties were less vulnerable to electoral discontent if no significant competition to their Left existed (Kitschelt, 2001).

Fourth, the 'Nixon-in-China' logic does not go far enough. Despite their closer proximity to trade unions and favourable issue associations among the electorate, Left governments in each country were limited in regards to their ability to negotiate welfare retrenchment with Left veto players – in this sense, differences between Left and Right government leadership may in fact be less pronounced than typically suggested. Inner-party and trade union discontent, while somewhat variable across cases, consistently proved a stumbling block for Left governments and sparked the search for alternative coalitions with bourgeois parties to enable welfare retrenchment. There is much to suggest that consensus-seeking deserves much more explicit attention in comparative welfare research.

Finally, whether the power of Western European trade unions has waned is hotly debated (Häusermann et al, 2010) – despite Pierson's (1994, p 165) suggestion that it is 'difficult to identify examples where unions took the lead role in mobilization against [welfare retrenchment]' such examples appear to be, in fact, abundant. The strategic strength of Left parties is apparent whether or not they were in government or a pressure on government: Left parties formed policy-specific coalitions with Right parties in parliament or upper houses; and they refrained from vetoing Right government initiatives in some instances, although they could have done so. Not least, there appears to be a good deal of cross-governmental consistency in some instances with major longer-term welfare retrenchment projects being seen through by Right and Left governments respectively once they are in power. In many ways, this presents the most unambiguous finding of this chapter: Scarbrough (2000, p 245) stresses that 'Left parties of Western Europe are not a spent force' – a statement that very much reverberates with the case descriptions in this chapter.

Conclusion

This chapter attempted to consolidate three different theoretical explanations of welfare retrenchment and aimed to assess the potential of an ensuing framework for further investigation. While each tackles a different aspect of the dynamics of welfare retrenchment, it was argued that answers to the questions of 'why', 'when' and 'how' policymakers engage in welfare retrenchment are best considered jointly. Looking at the 'why' question through 'losses domains' enables us to identify governments that are more likely to engage in 'treacherous' welfare retrenchment, but it falls short of telling us much about possible stumbling blocks in political systems with multiple constitutional constraints, corporatist structures and mature welfare programmes. Considering party competition and particularly the strength of Left parties helps us to understand much about 'when' policymakers are more likely to engage in unpopular policy retrenchment, but it fails to illuminate 'how' – or the mechanisms through which – many welfare retrenchments are achieved, namely consensus-seeking.

So where does all of the above leave us? The restriction to merely four Western European democracies featuring state corporatist or encompassing welfare systems, multiple constitutional barriers and comparatively strong trade union movements was dictated by the scope of this chapter. There are many more cases that one might want to explore. There are at least five additional Western European nations that would have met the criteria for inclusion: namely Austria, Belgium, Finland, Italy and Switzerland. Pluralist democracies outside of Western Europe, such as Australia, Canada and the United States, all differ slightly in their institutional and party political set-up, and have been studied at length (Pierson and Myles, 1997; Saunders, 1999; Schwartz, 2000; Shaver, 2002). Not least, some of the most prominent examples of welfare retrenchment, namely New Zealand, the United Kingdom and also Sweden, occurred in systems with comparatively lower numbers of constitutional constraints, broadly defined (Vis, 2009a; Kühner, 2011). Expanding the country sample seems inevitable to produce findings that are sensitive to different institutional contexts.

The discussions in this chapter have been overrun by developments in the wake of the 2008 global financial and current EU debt crises. Further welfare retrenchments are on the cards: as many governments have already engaged in new austerity measures more rounds are potentially on the way (Farnsworth and Irving, 2011). To what extent these crises constitute a critical juncture facilitating paradigmatic welfare retrenchment in the short and medium term remains to be seen. The direct relevance of the discussions in this chapter to these current processes appears self-evident. Yet it is advisable to use caution when transferring lessons from the pre- to the post-global financial crisis era. Similar to the way in which the end of the *trente glorieuses* after the Second World War gave birth to permanent austerity and the 'new politics' of the welfare state, the unmodified applicability of the central arguments in this chapter should not simply be assumed, but ought to be empirically tested and debated.

This chapter is meant as a step in the right direction rather than an end point of inquiry. More thorough and systematic analysis is not only desirable, it is inevitable. The politics of welfare retrenchment depends on a myriad of ideational, institutional and other strategic factors influencing Left and Right party behaviour that are incredibly difficult to conceptualise and measure. There is no shortage of opportunities to add to and improve the discussions in this chapter. Welfare retrenchment has captured the imagination of comparative welfare research for several decades. Efforts of generations of researchers were not in vain: our knowledge of the causes and mechanisms of welfare development and retrenchment has extended at great pace. It is certain that the number of studies devoted to the 'why', 'when' and 'how' questions of welfare retrenchment is bound to increase given the current position of most Western European democracies. If this chapter should end up influencing part of these future discussions, it will have humbly served its purpose.

Acknowledgements

I would like to express my gratitude to the editors of the *Social Policy Review* for their patience and many constructive suggestions during the process of finalising this chapter. Part of the data collection and research for this chapter was undertaken during a University of York Anniversary Lectureship – many thanks to Mary Maynard and John Hudson, who helped me to secure this award.

Notes

[1] The end point of inquiry, the year 2002, is admittedly arbitrary and driven primarily by the availability of key comparative historical (Esping-Andersen and Regini, 2000; Ferrera and Rhodes, 2000; Scharpf and Schmidt, 2000) and quantitative (Budge and Klingemann, 2001; Scruggs, 2004) data sources.

[2] Available at: http://www.stefankuehner.co.uk. This is an ongoing

data collection – comments and suggestions for improvement are very welcome. Please contact stefan.kuehner@york.ac.uk for correspondence.

References

Armingeon, K. (2002) 'Corporatism and consociational democracy', in H. Keman (ed) *Comparative politics. New directions in theory and method*, London: Sage.

Armingeon, K., Beyeler, M., and Binnema, H. (2001) *The changing politics of the welfare state – A comparative analysis of social security expenditures in 22 OECD countries, 1960–1998*, Unpublished manuscript, Berne: Institute of Political Science, University of Berne.

Baldwin, P. (1990) *The politics of social security. Class bases of the European welfare state 1875–1975*, Cambridge: Cambridge University Press.

Becker, U. (2000) 'Welfare state development and employment in the Netherlands in comparative perspective', *Journal of European Social Policy*, vol 10, no 3, pp 219–39.

Bertelsmann Foundation (2000) *International reform monitor*, Gütersloh: Bertelsmann Foundation Publishers.

Bertelsmann Foundation (2001) *International reform monitor*, Gütersloh: Bertelsmann Foundation Publishers.

Bonoli, G. (1997) 'Pension politics in France: patterns of co-operation and conflict in recent reforms', *West European Politics*, vol 20, no 4, pp 111–24.

Bonoli, G. (2006) 'New social risks and the politics of post-industrial social policies', in G. Bonoli (ed) *The politics of post-industrial welfare states*, London: Routledge/EUI Studies in the Political Economy of Welfare, pp 3–26.

Bonoli, G. and Palier, B. (1998) 'Changing the politics of social programmes: innovative change in British and French welfare reforms', *Journal of European Social Policy*, vol 8, no 4, pp 317–30.

Bouget, D. (1998) 'The Juppé plan and the future of the French social welfare system', *Journal of European Social Policy*, vol 8, no 2, pp 155–72.

Budge, I. and Klingemann, H.D. (2001) *Mapping preferences: parties, elections, and governments, 1945–1998*, Oxford: Oxford University Press.

Castles, F.G. (1982) *The impact of parties. Politics and policies in democratic capitalist states*, London/Beverly Hills, CA: Sage.

Castles, F.G. (2004) *The future of the welfare state. Crisis myths and crisis realities*, Oxford: Oxford University Press.

Clasen, J. (2000) 'Motives, means and opportunities: reforming unemployment compensation in the 1990s', *West European Politics*, vol 23, no 2, pp 89–112.

Clasen, J. and Siegel, N.A. (eds) (2008) *Investigating welfare state change: the 'dependent variable problem' in comparative analysis*, Cheltenham: Edward Elgar Publishing.

Clayton, R. and Pontusson, J. (1998) 'Welfare state retrenchment revisited. Entitlement cuts, public sector restructuring, and inegalitarian trends in advanced capitalist societies', *World Politics*, vol 51, no 1, pp 67–98.

Cox, R.H. (1998) 'From safety net to trampoline: labour market activation in the Netherlands and Denmark', *Governance*, vol 11, no 4, pp 397–414.

Cox, R.H. (2001) 'The social construction of an imperative. Why welfare reform happened in Denmark and the Netherlands but not in Germany', *World Politics*, vol 53, no 3, pp 463–98.

Daly, M. (1997) 'Welfare states under pressure: cash benefits in European welfare states over the last ten years', *Journal of European Social Policy*, vol 7, no 2, pp 129–46.

Ebbinghaus, B. and Hassel, A. (2000) 'Striking deals: concertation in the reform of continental European welfare states', *Journal of European Public Policy*, vol 7, no 1, pp 44–62.

Erhel, C. and Zajdela, H. (2004) 'Dynamics of social and labour market policies in France and the United Kingdom: between path dependence and convergence', *Journal of European Social Policy*, vol 14, no 2, pp 125–42.

Esping-Andersen, G. and Regini, M. (eds) (2000) *Why deregulate labour markets?*, Oxford: Oxford University Press.

Farnsworth, K. and Irving, Z. (eds) (2011) *Social policy in challenging times: economic crisis and welfare systems*, Bristol: The Policy Press.

Ferrera, M. and Rhodes, M. (eds) (2000) *Recasting European welfare states*, London: Frank Cass Publishers.

Fleckenstein, T. (2008) 'Restructuring welfare for the unemployed: the Hartz legislation in Germany', *Journal of European Social Policy*, vol 18, no 2, pp 177–88.

Green-Pedersen, C. (2001a) 'The puzzle of Dutch welfare state retrenchment', *West European Politics*, vol 24, no 3, pp 135–50.

Green-Pedersen, C. (2001b) 'Welfare-state retrenchment in Denmark and the Netherlands, 1982–1998: the role of party competition and party consensus', *Comparative Political Studies*, vol 34, no 9, pp 963–85.

Green-Pedersen, C. and Haverland, M. (2002) 'Review essay: the new politics and scholarship of the welfare state', *Journal of European Social Policy*, vol 12, no 1, pp 43–51.

Green-Pedersen, C. and Lindbom, A. (2006) 'Politics within paths: trajectories of Danish and Swedish earnings-related pensions', *Journal of European Social Policy*, vol 16, no 3, pp 245–58.

Hall, P.A. (1993) 'Policy paradigms, social-learning, and the state – the case of economic policy-making in Britain', *Comparative Politics*, vol 25, no 3, pp 275–96.

Häusermann, S., Picot, G. and Geering, D. (2010) 'Rethinking party politics and the welfare state: recent advances in the literature', Paper presented at the 17th International Conference of the Council for European Studies, 15–17 April, Montreal.

Hemerijck, A. and Visser, J. (2000) 'Change and immobility: three decades of policy adjustment in the Netherlands and Belgium', *West European Politics*, vol 23, no 2, pp 229–56.

Hering, M. (2003) 'The politics of institutional path-departure: a revised analytical framework for the reform of welfare states', Mannheim Centre for European Social Research, Working Paper No 65.1, Mannheim, Germany.

Hibbs, D.A. (1977) 'Political parties and macroeconomic policy', *American Political Science Review*, vol 71, no 4, pp 1467–87.

Hicks, A.M. and Kenworthy, L. (1998) 'Cooperation and political economic performance in affluent democratic capitalism', *American Journal of Sociology*, vol 103, no 6, pp 1631–72.

Hicks, A.M. and Swank, D.H. (1992) 'Politics, institutions, and welfare spending in industrialised democracies, 1960–82', *American Political Science Review*, vol 86, no 3, pp 658–74.

Hinrichs, K. (2010) 'A social insurance state withers away. Welfare state reforms in Germany – or: attempts to turn around in a cul-de-sac', in B. Palier (ed) *A long goodbye to Bismarck? The politics of welfare reform in continental Europe*, Amterdam: Amsterdam University Press, pp 45–72.

Holden, C. (2003) 'Decommodification and the workfare state', *Political Studies Review*, vol 1, no 2, pp 303–16.

Howlett, M. (2009) 'Process sequencing policy dynamics: beyond homeostasis and path dependency', *Journal of Public Policy*, vol 29, no 3, pp 241–62.

Howlett, M. and Cashore, B. (2011) 'The dependent variable problem in the study of policy change: understanding policy change as a methodological problem', *Journal of Comparative Policy Analysis: Research and Practice*, vol 11, no 1, pp 33–46.

Hudson, J. and Kühner, S. (2011) 'Tiptoeing through crisis? Re-evaluating the German social model in light of the global recession', in K. Farnsworth and Z.M. Irving (eds) *Social policy in challenging times: economic crisis and welfare systems*, Bristol: The Policy Press.

Hudson, J. and Lowe, S. (2009) *Understanding the policy process: analysing welfare policy and practice*, Bristol: The Policy Press.

Hudson, J., Hwang, G.J. and Kühner, S. (2008) 'Between ideas, institutions and interests: analysing third way welfare reform programmes in Germany and the United Kingdom', *Journal of Social Policy*, vol 37, no 2, pp 207–30.

Kahneman, D. and Tversky, A. (1979) 'Prospect theory: an analysis of decision and risk', *Econometrica*, vol 47, no 2, pp 263–92.

Kitschelt, H. (2001) 'Partisan competition and welfare state retrenchment: when do politicians choose unpopular policies?', in P. Pierson (ed) *The new politics of the welfare state*, Oxford: Oxford University Press.

Korpi, W. (1989) 'Power, politics and state autonomy in the development of social citizenship: social rights during sickness in eighteen OECD countries since 1930', *American Sociological Review*, vol 54, no 3, pp 309–28.

Korpi, W. and Palme, J. (2003) 'Class politics and "new politics" in the context of austerity and globalization: welfare state regress in 18 countries 1976–1995', *Sociologisk Forskning*, vol, no 4, pp 45–85.

Kühner, S. (2010) 'Do party governments matter after all? Executive ideology, constitutional structures and their combined effect on welfare state change', *Journal of Comparative Policy Analysis: Research and Practice*, vol 12, no 4, pp 395–415.

Kühner, S. (2011) 'When Nixon went to China: Government ideology, constitutional road-blocks and beyond. A fuzzy-set qualitative comparative analysis of welfare state retrenchment in 12 high-income nations', paper presented at the Social Policy Association Conference, 'Bigger Societies, Smaller Governments', University of Lincoln, Lincoln, UK.

Kühner, S. (2012) *Comparative historical welfare reform data set*, York: University of York.

Kvist, J. (1999) 'Welfare reform in the Nordic countries in the 1990s: using fuzzy-set theory to assess conformity to ideal types', *Journal of European Social Policy*, vol 9, no 3, pp 231–52.

Levy, J.D. (1999) 'Vice into virtue? Progressive politics and welfare reform in continental Europe', *Politics & Society*, vol 27, no 2, pp 239–72.

Manow, P. (2009) 'Electoral rules, class coalitions and welfare state regimes, or how to explain Esping-Andersen with Stein Rokkan', *Socio-Economic Review*, vol 7, no 1, pp 101–21.

Manow, P. and Van Kersbergen, K. (2009) *Religion, class coalitions and welfare states*, New York, NY: Cambridge University Press.

OECD (Organisation of Economic Co-operation and Development) (2011) *Annual labour force statistics*, Paris: OECD.

Palier, B. (2000) 'Defrosting the French welfare state', *West European Politics*, vol 23, no 2, pp 113–36.

Palier, B. (ed) (2010) *A long goodbye to Bismarck? The politics of welfare reform in continental Europe*, Amsterdam: Amsterdam University Press.

Pierson, P. (1994) *Dismantling the welfare state? Reagan, Thatcher and the politics of retrenchment*, Cambridge: Cambridge University Press.

Pierson, P. (1996) 'The new politics of the welfare state', *World Politics*, vol 48, no 2, pp 143–79.

Pierson, P. (2000) 'Increasing returns, path dependence, and the study of politics', *American Political Science Review*, vol 94, no 2, pp 251–67.

Pierson, P. (2001a) 'Coping with permanent austerity: welfare state restructuring in affluent democracies', in P. Pierson (ed) *The new politics of the welfare state*, Oxford: Oxford University Press, pp 410–56.

Pierson, P. (ed) (2001b) *The new politics of the welfare state*, Oxford: Oxford University Press.

Pierson, P. (2001c) 'Post-industrial pressures on the mature welfare state', in P. Pierson (ed) *The new politics of the welfare state*, Oxford: Oxford University Press, pp 80–106.

Pierson, P. and Myles, J. (1997) 'Friedman's revenge: the reform of "liberal" welfare states in Canada and the United States', *Politics & Society*, vol 25, no 4, pp 443–72.

Ross, F. (2000) '"Beyond left and right": the new partisan politics of welfare', *Governance*, vol 13, no 2, pp 155–83.

Saunders, P. (1999) 'Social security in Australia and New Zealand: means-tested or just mean?', *Social Policy & Administration*, vol 33, no 5, pp 493–515.

Scarbrough, E. (2000) 'West European welfare states: the old politics of retrenchment', *European Journal of Political Research*, vol 38, no 2, pp 225–59.

Scharpf, F.W. and Schmidt, V.A. (eds) (2000) *Welfare and work in the open economy. Volume II: diverse responses to common challenges*, Oxford: Oxford University Press.

Schmidt, M.G. (1996) 'When parties matter. A review of the possibilities and limits of partisan influence on public policy', *Journal of Political Research*, vol 30, no 2, pp 155–83.

Schmidt, M.G. (2000) *Demokratietheorien*, Opladen: Leske + Budrich.

Schmidt, V.A. (2002) 'Does discourse matter in the politics of welfare state adjustment?', *Comparative Political Studies*, vol 35, no 2, pp 168–93.

Schwartz, H. (1994) 'Small states in big trouble: state reorganization in Australia, Denmark, New Zealand and Sweden in the 1980s', *World Politics*, vol 46, no 4, pp 527–55.

Schwartz, H. (2000) 'Internationalization and two liberal welfare states: Australia and New Zealand', in F.W. Scharpf and V.A. Schmidt (eds) *Welfare and work in the open economy. Volume II: diverse responses to common challenges*, Oxford: Oxford University Press, pp 69–130.

Scruggs, L. (2004) 'Welfare state entitlements data set: a comparative institutional analysis of eighteen welfare states', version 1.1, University of Connecticut.

Shalev, M. (1983) 'The social democratic model and beyond: two "generations" of comparative research on the welfare state', *Comparative Social Research*, vol 6, pp 315–51.

Shaver, S. (2002) 'Australian welfare reform: from citizenship to supervision', *Social Policy & Administration*, vol 36, no 4, pp 331–45.

Starke, P. (2006) 'The politics of welfare state retrenchment: a literature review', *Social Policy & Administration*, vol 40, no 1, pp 104–20.

Swank, D.H. (2001) 'Political institutions and welfare state restructuring: the impact of institutions on social policy change in developed democracies', in P. Pierson (ed) *The new politics of the welfare state*, Oxford: Oxford University Press, pp 197–237.

Taylor-Gooby, P. (2010) *Reframing social citizenship*, Oxford: Oxford University Press.

Torfing, J. (1999) 'Workfare with welfare: recent reforms of the Danish welfare state', *Journal of European Social Policy*, vol 9, no 1, pp 5–28.

Trampusch, R. (2006) 'Industrial relations and welfare states: the different dynamics of retrenchment in Germany and the Netherlands', *Journal of European Social Policy*, vol 16, no 2, pp 121–33.

Trampusch, R. (2007) 'Industrial relations as a source of solidarity in times of welfare state retrenchment', *Journal of Social Policy*, vol 36, no 2, pp 197–215.

Tsebelis, G. (2002) *Veto players: how political institutions work*, Princeton, NJ: Princeton University Press.

Vail, M.I. (1999) 'The better part of valour: the politics of French welfare reform', *Journal of European Social Policy*, vol 9, no 4, pp 311–29.

Vis, B. (2009a) 'Governments and unpopular social policy reform: biting the bullet or steering clear?', *European Journal of Political Research*, vol 48, no 1, pp 31–57.

Vis, B. (2009b) 'The importance of socio-economic and political losses and gains in welfare state reform', *Journal of European Social Policy*, vol 19, no 5, pp 395–407.

Vis, B. (2010) *Politics of risk-taking: welfare state reform in advanced democracies*, Amsterdam: Amsterdam University Press.

Vis, B. and Van Kersbergen, K. (2007) 'Why and how do political actors pursue risky reforms', *Journal of Theoretical Politics*, vol 19, no 2, pp 53–172.

Weaver, K.R. (1986) 'The politics of blame avoidance', *Journal of Public Policy*, vol 6, no 4, pp 371–98.

Weaver, K.R. (1988) *Automatic government: the politics of indexation*, Washington, DC: The Brookings Institute.

Zohlnhöfer, R. (2003) 'Partisan politics, party competition and veto players: German economic policy in the Kohl era', *Journal of Public Policy*, vol 23, no 2, pp 123–56.

Zohlnhöfer, R. (2004) 'Destination anywhere? The German Red–Green government's inconclusive search for a third way in economic policy', *German Politics*, vol 13, no 1, pp 106–31.

EIGHT

From black hole to spring: the coming of age of social policy in the Arab countries?

Rana Jawad

Introduction

This chapter gives a broad overview discussion of social policy in the Arab region with the aim of arguing for its viability as a subject of academic study and its legitimacy as an arm of state policy and public intervention. The key units of analysis in the subject of social policy, such as social welfare, citizenship, equality, justice, poverty and rights, have never been more relevant than now, as mass political mobilisation grips Arab countries which have earned that region the bad reputation of being socially and politically backward (Jawad, 2009) – a situation captured figuratively by the image of a black hole (see also Jawad, 2009) where very little exists by way of coherent state social policy and any action towards social justice is thwarted by harsh political realities. Yet, regardless of the new wave of revolutions in the Arab countries and an apparent reawakening of government agencies to issues of social equality and justice across Arab countries where a popular uprising has not taken place, it is the fundamental egalitarian concerns of a politically engaged social policy research agenda that forms the basis of the arguments of this chapter. Indeed, research by the author spanning the last decade (Jawad, 2002, 2006, 2008, 2009) and others (Saeidi, 2004; Karshenas and Moghadam, 2006; Messkoub, 2006; Yakut-Cakar, 2007) attests to the validity of both a social policy analysis in the Arab region and to the question proposed in the title of this chapter, this being that we can now begin to speak of a coming of age of social policy studies and public interventions in the Arab countries.

But as the title also suggests, this issue is not couched in naive optimism. While it is already very plausible to study the mixed economy of welfare in the Arab countries and to examine the implications of state discourses for social development, it is important to remember that the Arab region is characterised by particular social and political structures that will no doubt influence the progression of political and social change that the region is seeing. For example, patrimonial, tribal, sectarian and clientelism structures have become deeply ingrained in this region, as have newer habits of modern consumerism. Together, the two have produced some of the least palatable forms of social inequity and elitism in the Arab region. This is not to mention the broader policymaking capacities of Arab governments and the need to create policy environments that can make government work in the interests of the people.

Moreover, as a series of United Nations Development Programme (UNDP) *Arab human development reports* (see for example the ones for 2002 and 2009) continue to show, social problems such as youth unemployment, illiteracy and a poor record of democratisation and human capital have plagued the Arab countries for decades and cannot be resolved overnight. Outward migration and the 'brain drain' continue to pose a real challenge for future prosperity and nation-building. Generations that have lived under police-state repression in countries where regimes are now toppling down, unable to voice an alternative social vision beyond discontent with the status quo, will nevertheless not be able to articulate discourses of social rights and social justice overnight.

Moreover, the rentier state paradigm, and its accompanying rentier state mentality, also shed a long shadow on the future of political and social reform. By definition, a rentier state is one where the primary source of revenue is from natural resources such as oil and natural gas (Beblawi, 1990). This is particularly the case for the oil-rich countries in the Gulf, as well as Iran, Iraq and Algeria. The over-reliance on oil revenue has meant that some states were able to provide social welfare and social insurance services to citizens during the oil boom era of the 1960s–1980s without having to tax citizens on the basis of their civic membership of the nation (Beblawi, 1990).

This rather grim situation does not, however, mean that Arab countries do not already have systems of welfare provision in place. Indeed, as this chapter will show, it has long been possible to examine the institutional and political discourses shaping social policy in the region, as well as to begin to think through the meaning of key concepts like social welfare and human well-being there. But the urgency and relevance of these matters is now being given impetus with the political changes happening in the Arab world.

In response to the issues highlighted earlier, this chapter will explore the following key themes. The first section offers a broad historical overview of social policies since the era of independence in the Arab countries. The second section complements this by considering the key role religious values institutions and actors have played in shaping social welfare provision in the Arab countries both in terms of shaping state social policies and society-based charitable initiatives and in acting as a driving force for political movements like Hizbullah and Hamas and their affiliated welfare agencies. The third section then explores what a potential regime classification might look like in this region. In the fourth section, various preliminary models of how social policy works in the Arab countries are presented. Much of this centres around the need to clearly delineate how social policy is different and complementary to the more dominant discourse of economic development and growth in the Arab countries. The conclusion summarises some of the key issues for this area of study and concludes with some comments on the social prospects of the current Arab spring. The chapter cautions against overly optimistic prospects for welfare state development in Arab countries, arguing that the future of social policy there is very much constrained by the historical and political forces that have so far led to the proliferation of social problems in the Arab countries.

A historical perspective on social policy in the Arab region

Social policy in the Arab region has been quite heavily influenced by international intervention, for example, opening up to the European-dominated economy since the 17th century through colonisation and mandate rule, which set particular political and economic structures in motion (El-Ghonemy, 1998; Karshenas and Moghadam, 2006), and, since the 1980s, economic reform under the pressure of globalisation and structural adjustment programmes led mainly by international development agencies such as the International Monetary Fund (IMF) and World Bank. In all these instances, the groups that have taken control of state social policy have been mainly local elites made up of tribal, religious or ethnic leaders and wealthy merchants whose privileged status during mandate rule and afterwards marginalised the interests of a primarily rural agricultural population (El-Ghonemy, 1998). The increasing market orientation of Arab economies and the privatisation programmes they underwent under the influence of globalisation and international development actors has further retrenched the role of the state as principle provider of social services and employer in the public sector.

Karshenas and Moghadam (2006), El-Ghonemy (1998), Henry and Springborg (2001) all describe how the states in Arab countries have failed or are failing to develop effective democratic institutions that can ensure representative government and political participation for all citizens. Whether oversized and coercive (such as Egypt and Saudi Arabia) or weak and dysfunctional (such as Sudan and Lebanon), states are rife with corruption. State social provisioning is especially hard hit because of several factors, such as: (1) the misallocation of resources and the prioritisation of military spending over key social sectors such as health and education; (2) the narrow economic focus of public policy, which hinges social progress on economic prosperity; (3) the dominance of minority factions in Arab countries dating back to the colonial era; (4) political insecurity and military conflict, with the protraction of the Arab–Israeli conflict; (5) high levels of state indebtedness, which have taken away funds from social welfare services; and (6) the introduction of structural adjustment programmes and the increasing privatisation programmes, which have reduced the role of the state further as provider of social services and public sector jobs (El-Ghonemy, 1998; Bayat, 2006; Karshenas and Moghadam, 2006). The resulting social ills of unemployment, wealth polarisation and even undernourishment need to be addressed through the reform of public policy and state legislation.

The most comprehensive employment-based insurance goes to urban public sector workers, particularly those who are unionised, with the best protection going to the army and security forces. At the heart of this residual social policy are key conceptual blockages, namely the overly economic focus of public policy and a corresponding lack of importance accorded to the social. A significant example of this residual or piecemeal approach to social policy is highlighted by the Egypt case study in Bayat (2006) where, since the 1990s, the state has not been able to cut back on key consumer subsidies, as it has wished, due to the outbreak of violent public protest. Related to this is the characterisation of Arab states as 'rentier'. The easy access to capital and the sudden overnight affluence brought about by the oil windfall in the region is depicted as a curse by El-Ghonemy (1998) since it has directly undermined the structures of social citizenship and the need to develop the productive capacity of the local population, due to the over-reliance on foreign labour. A further classification is of social policy as neo-patrimonial due to the persistence of gender discrimination (Bayat, 2006; Karshenas and Moghadam, 2006). Islamic family planning laws, female illiteracy and labour legislation impede women from free participation in the labour market and from equal political rights to men. The persistence of the family as a key social unit in society and the main locus of social care also impinges upon gender equality.

Another major factor hampering social policy has been the politicisation of welfare and the instrumental use of social policy by the state to gain power and political legitimacy (Jawad, 2009). Some authors argue that this is a historical factor as well, for example, the introduction of social benefits to workers and employment guarantees to university graduates in Iran and Egypt in the 1950s/60s were motivated by the need to win the support of the working classes in the postcolonial states, and were not based on a civic discourse of social citizenship (Bayat, 2006). Today, social benefits are channelled though clientelist networks, which link ruling governments to their supporters. Thus, social policy today in the Arab region lacks a sense of its own legitimacy (Jawad, 2009).

The major challenges facing the Arab countries in terms of social welfare provisioning are less about the long-term structures of democratic participation and a share in decision-making by society, and more about the urgent measures of wealth redistribution, income transfers, provision of basic needs and ensuring the basic support systems of survival (Karshenas and Moghadam, 2006). When measures of human well-being are discussed in some of the literature, it is in the developmental/survival terms of child mortality, female literacy, sanitation and housing.

At the heart of social policy, then, are the key challenges of basic economic and social development. This gives the desired purpose and definition of social policy by Arab governments old and new a particular focus on economic productivity, creating more employment opportunities, reducing indebtedness, reforming property rights and reforming the Islamic laws that dominate personal status law. This is not to say that social policies in the past did not bring about improvements in society in the Arab region: the immediate post-independence era in the 1940s and subsequently the oil-boom era, which lasted until the 1980s, saw rapid social transformation of the region with enormous improvements in education and health, as well as rapid urban transformation (El-Ghonemy, 1998; Karshenas and Moghadam, 2006). But these gains were rapidly lost as states became more authoritarian in character and failed to develop adequate economic policies. Indeed, the problem of the disjuncture between state and society interests has become a defining feature of Arab societies and partly explains the explosion in civil unrest that is now taking place.

Today, the region demonstrates diverse socio-economic profiles with per capita income levels ranging from over US$25,000 to below US$1,000. The first *Arab human development report* (UNDP, 2002) described the Arab region in particular as being 'richer than it is developed', with its oil-driven economic policies resulting in substantial social and economic volatility. There is also limited availability of poverty statistics. The region has made some progress in reducing absolute poverty levels in the last two decades. Extreme poverty is especially acute in the low-income Arab countries, affecting around a third of the population. A distinctive demographic feature with important social policy implications is the region's 'youth bulge' with around 60% of the population under the age of 25 years. But poverty is a multidimensional phenomenon (UNDP, 2009). There are, therefore, a variety of social problems that Arab countries are grappling with today, namely: unemployment, particularly among the youth; population growth; adult illiteracy; high school drop-out rates; lack of access to universal health care; and social, income and gender disparities (UNDP, 2009).

Thus, the key characterisation of the Arab region has therefore been one of a detachment between state and society (Henry and Springborg, 2001); indeed, relations between the two reach competition or violent hostility, as the Arab uprisings that began in 2010 have shown. The sense of social unrest is exacerbated further by the common notion within society that the state should take more responsibility for the welfare of citizens and that the latter have the right to be provided with state social services. A main area of contention is basic consumer subsidies, particularly food, where the local population has mounted riots to protest against their withdrawal, for example, in Egypt (Bayat, 2006). Competition between state and societal groups over the public sphere is most acutely expressed in the rise of Islamic groups in the Arab countries, which are providing vital public and social services, and thus challenging the state not only as a provider of welfare, but also as a modern secular institution of government (Jawad, 2009). Some of these groups are well-known political groups such as the Muslim Brotherhood (Egypt) and Hamas (Palestinian Territories) but others are more local and less political, such as the Islah Charitable Society in Yemen or the Mustafa Mahmood Health Clinic in Egypt (Clark, 2004).

Religion and social policy

Islam (like Judaism and Christianity) is an important cultural influence on social and political institutions in the Arab world and even makes its way directly into government social vision statements as in the cases of Qatar and Saudi Arabia. Islamic values and traditions greatly influence social welfare programmes, inheritance laws as well as family planning. In this sense, Islam is sometimes considered to perpetuate wealth and gender inequalities, although perspectives differ, with researchers arguing that women do have rights to property and to work or do have a say in family planning (Bowen, 2004).

Islamic doctrine makes specific provisions for welfare through the *waqf* (religious endowments) and *zakat* (an obligatory 2.5% tax levied on assets). *Zakat* has acted as a hugely important source of poverty alleviation for the poor and *waqf* played a key role in the socio-economic development of the Middle East in the last few centuries prior to colonisation (Heyneman, 2004). Islamic principles have also made their way into particular public policy areas such as health, finance and economy and human rights legislation (Heyneman, 2004). In the health sector, for example, some countries such as Iran have been able to make substantial improvements to primary care thanks to the influence of Islamic principles in Iran after the revolution (Underwood, 2004). As mentioned earlier, Islamic values are also important as an activating force for social groups and movements in society to engage in public and social service provisioning. In Egypt, Yemen and Jordan, for example, Islamic movements or Islamic charity organisations use social welfare to challenge the basis of the secular modern state and/or to protect the political status of the professional classes through the provision of employment opportunities and social networks (Wiktorowicz, 2003; Clark, 2004). In the case of political Islamic groups, the volume edited by Wiktorowicz (2003) depicts organisations such as Hamas in Palestine as social movements that have developed locally and are now supported by a comprehensive institutional basis of which the provision of social welfare and public services is a vital component. In these cases, Islam is depicted as the only remaining platform for political contestation and struggle for social justice in the Middle East (El-Ghonemy, 1998) and, indeed, as has been demonstrated so far in Tunisia, Morocco and Egypt, Islamic political parties are re-entering centre-stage in political life in Arabic societies.

Regime classifications and the production of social welfare

In order to discuss the classification of welfare regimes in Arab countries, it is apt that we begin with some notion of how social welfare is produced. As Van Kersbergen and Manow (2009) argue, there are two overarching accounts of the evolution of welfare states: one focusing on the role of industrialisation and the social needs it generates, particularly unemployment and poverty, which make the provision of state welfare inevitable; the other focusing on the role of political competition. This latter perspective highlights how new political groups such as industrial workers, feminists or minority ethnic groups emerge and seek to have their interests represented in government and thus their needs met through the welfare state. It is the industrialisation thesis that has tended to dominate accounts of social policy due to the close association of these social processes to Northern Europe (Van Kersbergen and Manow, 2009).

This split in perspective parallels two opposing approaches in the study of social policy, both of which rest upon the tension between state and market in the provision of social welfare services. The first approach considers social policy as subsidiary to capitalist development, a tool for serving the needs of the capitalist market and for alleviating the social problems that market forces cause. At the opposite end is a view of social policy as a central pillar of progressive social change, actively employed to achieve a more equitable and just society. In practice, whichever stance is adopted, the key dynamics underpinning the nature and scope of social policy in any particular national setting are affected by the interplay between the main institutions of society: the state, the market and the family/community.

For this reason, it may be more plausible for the purposes of analysing social policy in the Middle East to speak of the 'mixed economy of welfare' or the 'welfare mix', which refers to the varying configurations of state, market and family/community in the provision of social protection. This means that different elements (of welfare) are delivered in different measure by different means. The Middle East social welfare mix is dominated by: a strong role for the nuclear and extended family; tribal, sectarian and religious communities; market-based social welfare, such as private medical insurance and paid-for domestic help to assist with social care needs; and basic state provision in health and education.

The underlying philosophy behind the welfare regime approach as developed by Esping-Andersen (1990) is to avoid normative statements about the 'best' kind of welfare arrangement and to include a political analysis of welfare systems. In particular, Esping-Andersen followed a long tradition in Western social policy analysis that linked the political strength of labour movements to the development of the welfare state, against a relatively uniform level of economic growth in Western countries. A key feature of the welfare regime approach is to compare states that have generous welfare provision with those that do not. This consists of two key elements that distinguish between different types of welfare state. These are de-commodification and stratification. Based on these two key features, Esping-Andersen identified three types, or 'regimes', of 'welfare capitalism', which focused on the welfare conditions of male waged workers.

Esping-Andersen's model has raised criticism on a number of counts, as discussed in detail in Arts and Gellison (2002): this has ranged from its lack of gender-sensitiveness, to its assumption of the homogeneity and internal coherency of policy regimes, to questioning of the accuracy of the clusters of nations. Where developing-country contexts are concerned, criticisms have been raised regarding the transferability of the model (Kabeer, 2004). Research led by Gough and Wood (2004) on the transferability of the welfare regime model to the non-Western world omits from its analysis the region of the Middle East (including North Africa) entirely. There is discussion of informal security regimes in Africa but this primarily focuses on the high risk of war and violence in agrarian peasant societies there, a situation that does not characterise the more urban societies of the Arab region. Discussion of the segmented public–private provision of welfare in Latin America in the Gough and Wood (2004) volume does, however, bear relevance for the Arab region, where the labour market and family are core providers of welfare.

Esping-Andersen's welfare regime approach has also been criticised for its assumption of the internal coherency of social policy formulation since this assumes a false level of stability in the era of globalisation and structural adjustment programmes (Arts and Gellison, 2002). Other critics note that the concept fails to highlight the importance of health, education and housing programmes, which play a more important role in poor countries than do income-maintenance schemes (Davis, 2001). This latter argument is quite relevant for the Arab region. Criticisms have also been raised about welfare outcomes in the approach (Davis, 2001). Needs satisfaction and self-sufficiency, it is argued, are more important in lower-income settings, whereas Esping-Andersen's typology is built on de-commodification. Furthermore, it is argued that stratification outcomes overemphasise class-based social structures at the expense of gender, religious, ethnic and clientelistic outcomes, which are more relevant to social settings in developing countries (Davis, 2001; Gough and Wood, 2004). Esping-Andersen's typology is also criticised for not giving enough attention to the critical role of international development institutions, without which policy analysis of social welfare in low-income settings would be very lacking (Davis, 2001; Gough and Wood,

2004). Finally, it is pointed out that there is a problem of terminology inherent in the concept of welfare, which in certain country contexts, such as the Far East, denotes charity and is contrasted with development, which implies more long-term notions of social investment (Davis, 2001). This latter argument also bears relevance for Arab countries, where development is the focus of government policy.

Towards new welfare regime classification(s) of the Arab countries?

The welfare regime approach offers both opportunities and challenges for the task at hand because it is possible to apply only some aspects of it, and to a certain extent. Moreover, the argument works the other way, in that the particular construction of the welfare regime approach may not capture the entire dynamics of social policy in the Middle East. This is because the welfare regime approach is underpinned by particular assumptions and values about society, which have been described earlier and which highlight the debate surrounding the transferability of the welfare regime approach to developing countries. Thus, by employing a process of elimination, it becomes clear what elements of the welfare regime classification we can use for the Middle East region. This also begins to draw a picture of the configuration of social policy in the region. For example, we do not have adequate comparable data on social welfare expenditure in the Arab countries; labour movements and class conflict have not had the same importance in the political life there as they did in the West; and social security schemes are partial and still in their infancy in most Arab countries and are confined in the large part to health and pension schemes with more marginal benefits for unemployment and maternity when these exist. As a result of incomplete data availability and problems of the definition of social security packages, it is difficult to accurately measure benefit levels and to be confident that rules of entitlement are being correctly applied.

Thus, in order to move this argument for the classification of the welfare regimes of the Middle East forward, it is possible to begin to classify the social contexts and social policies of the region as follows (for more detail, see also Gal and Jawad, 2012):

1. The oil-rich Arab Gulf countries and Iran: as well as Iran, countries such as Qatar, Bahrain, Oman, Kuwait, the United Arab Emirates and Saudi Arabia are primarily concerned with reaping and accelerating the benefits of economic prosperity and oil wealth, and

integrating their economies into the global market where possible. With the exceptions of Iran and increasingly so Saudi Arabia, these countries have tended to be much less concerned with problems of social inequalities and deprivation.

2. (Post-)Conflict countries: countries such as Lebanon, Iraq, Sudan, the Palestinian Territories and now Libya and Yemen are struggling to cope with major issues of political impasse, debt, weak economic development, unemployment and rising costs of living leading to significant flows of out-migration and brain drain. These countries demonstrate residual welfare regimes whereby family- and market-based social welfare more clearly supersedes state provision as can be found in the other two classifications presented here.

3. Non-oil producing countries with strong state control over social and economic policy: countries such as Egypt, Syria and Jordan that have or have had strong socialist tendencies and state intervention in economic activity though not necessarily a more expansive social welfare system.

Arab countries have income-transfer policies that are primarily employment-based and particularly generous towards military, security and public sector workers. There is also a lack of adequate public provision of social care for vulnerable children and adults, though orphans tend to be well covered and groups of this nature rely on family support. A key challenge of social policies in the region is their urban bias, which means that unionised workers in industry, construction and trade tend to be among the best protected (Jawad, 2009). As a result, social concerns in government policy have tended to be less important.

In the absence of such comprehensive and concrete social policy, it is more accurate to argue that Arab countries have social strategies or social policies. These seek to alleviate the negative effects of economic growth by offering various social safety net schemes. The emphasis on private sector investment and employment-based social insurance in the Arab countries is also evident from the types of social security cover that exist in the region, as illustrated in Table 8.1.

Thus, the main social policy approach of Arab countries is one where the levels of protection offered to the population are weak and more likely to deal with the symptoms of poverty. This social policy approach is a residual one where government policies remain closely attached to private sector-led economic growth supported by state-sponsored social safety nets and a contributions-based social security system that mainly caters for pensions and health coverage. The role of major development institutions such as the World Bank or the European Union is also funding and, indeed, instigating the state-sponsored systems of social safety nets. In Lebanon, for example, an unconditional cash transfer programme overseen by the World Bank is being introduced.

Table 8.1: Formal contribution-based social security schemes for Arab countries (2010)

Country	*Scheme						
	Old age	Disability and survivors	Work injury	Unemploy-ment	Sickness	Maternity	Family
Bahrain	X	X	X	X			
Jordan	X	X	X				
Kuwait	X	X	X				
Lebanon	X	X	X			X	X
Oman	X	X	X				
Saudi Arabia	X	X	X		X	X	
Syria	X	X	X				
Yemen	X	X	X		X*	X*	

Note: * Public sector employees only.

Source: International Social Security Association country profiles. Available at: www.issa.int/Observatory/Country-Profiles

Arab countries, therefore, demonstrate features of both residual and corporatist models of welfare, as discussed in Esping-Andersen's (1990) welfare regime typologies. Most countries are now going with the flow of global economic marketisation and emphasising the role of the private sector and international finance as the main drivers of social and economic progress. In this sense, the state provides social safety nets for inadequately defined categories of poor or vulnerable people, supplemented by the family (both nuclear and extended) and religious or secular charities. In the Arab and Persian Gulf states, social welfare provision is primarily funded by oil revenues and is detached from taxation or citizenship. Some Gulf states are seeking to diversify their economies in order to reduce their dependency on oil revenue and are investing heavily in their knowledge economies, as is the case in Qatar for example; but in Iran, no quick alternative has as yet been found. It should also be noted that the development of future social policy in the Arab region will also rely on the availability of better data on poverty and human deprivation. Thus, Arab countries have yet to fully conceptualise notions of social rights and citizenship, which are more typical of the Western context.

In conclusion, Arab governments have two overarching tendencies in social policy: (1) employment-based social security whereby employed private and public sector workers receive cover for basic contingencies such as retirement and sickness; and (2) prioritisation of economic growth, contracting out of social welfare services and provision of subsidies for basic commodities or social safety nets that merely alleviate the problem of poverty. Social policy in Arab countries thus distinguish between able-bodied men who are in employment and able to be covered within the formal social security system for pensions and sickness, and vulnerable groups such as children, the disabled, the elderly and female-headed households who are left in the care of their families or non-state welfare providers.

Conclusion: the coming of age of social policy for the Arab world?

This chapter has sought to provide a basic analytical map of how social policy works in the Arab countries. Based on a historically and theoretically sensitive approach, it has shown that although the academic study of social policy in the Arab region has been somewhat of a 'black hole', a variety of social welfare initiatives at both state and non-state levels have existed in the region and further research is required to provide a more comprehensive picture of what kind of welfare regime(s) may be said to exist in the Arab countries. The timeliness of this subject academically is given further impetus by the Arab spring, which started in 2010, and while this chapter has not focused as much on the social welfare dimensions of the Arab spring, elements of it remain relevant for the discussion at hand.

Thus, it has been argued that social policy is coming of age in the Middle East, both as a field of study and also as a legitimate arm of state action – though the process is by no means clear-cut. It is an especially important time for the Arab countries as they finally wake up to the need for democratic political reform. The riots and populist uprisings that began in Tunisia in late 2010 and spread very fast to other countries have unified secular and religious sentiments and seen both men and women from all classes, sects and generations take to the streets in mass protest against political repression, poverty and corruption. The vociferous calls and sometimes violent confrontations for political reform that continue at the time of writing emphasise how important the issues of social justice and human rights have become for the region, especially for the Arab countries. As some of these stage historic elections and begin to rewrite their constitutions, the key emerging issues for social policy in the region are: how will social rights be defined, if at all recognised, and how will they be accessed in the new era of more accountable government?

Many governments in the region had already begun to produce social policy vision statements from the early 2000s, which have attempted to set out fairer and wealthier societies. Though modest, and in all cases favouring a private sector-led economic development path, these vision statements will need to take serious account of the needs of the popular masses even in countries where there has not been serious social unrest. In Jordan, Syria and Saudi Arabia, for example, governments rushed to bring in political reform or to give out one-off cash payments or social assistance services as a way of allaying public unrest. These are proving to be insufficient, as the case of Syria clearly shows, and the government of Jordan seeks a political overhaul to include the opposition.

Thus, government policy discourses will need to address the significant socio-economic problems and inequalities their societies face – youth unemployment being key among these. Moreover, political instability always looms on the horizon of this region and has stood in the way of social policy: countries such as Lebanon and Iraq are in the throes of economic reconstruction; and emergency relief often impedes social policy development. Religious political parties are beginning to spring up, such as the Al-Nahda in Tunisia who have just won the elections at the time of writing, and other long-standing groups such as the Nour Party and the Muslim Brotherhood in Egypt are poised for greater political power in government.

Of paramount importance is how countries move beyond oil revenue to finance social services for the future. The Gulf countries are keen to find alternative ways of diversifying their economic bases further. But the lack of reliable data needs to be dealt with. It is, therefore, important to conduct further quantitative and qualitative research on the institutional configurations of social welfare in the Arab and wider Arab world and to devise measures of social welfare there that are more culturally sensitive.

Political rights will dominate the reform agenda in the Arab countries of the region for the near future. However, the surviving and new Arab governments post-2011 will need to realise that subsidies and one-off cash assistance do not feed the people's demands for social justice, which requires deeper social-structural changes and an overhaul of the residual welfare mentality that has long subsisted in most countries of the Middle East. As expressed by a leader of the Al-Nahda Party, now taking over the government of Tunisia (October 2011), the key objective of the new government will be to secure the 'conditions for a dignified life' – is this the new language of social policy in the Arab world? Politically engaged academic research in this area has never been so sorely missed as now.

Acknowledgements

Acknowledgements are due to the ESRC for providing grants to the author that funded much of the empirical research on which this chapter is based, as well as to research colleagues in Lebanon, Iran, Turkey, Egypt and other countries without whom the ESRC research would not have been possible. Research in this area is ongoing and interested readers are invited to contact the author for further information. Email: R.Jawad@bath.ac.uk

References

Arts, W. and Gellison, J. (2002) 'Three worlds of welfare capitalism or more? A state-of-the-art report', *Journal of European Social Policy*, vol 12, no 2, pp 137–58.

Bayat, A. (2006) 'The political economy of social policy in Egypt', in M. Karshenas and V. Moghadam (eds) *Social policy in the Middle East*, UNRISD Social Policy in a Development Context Series, New York: Palgrave Macmillan, pp 135–55.

Beblawi, H. (1990) 'The rentier state in the Arab world', in G. Luciani (ed) *The Arab State*, London: Routledge.

Bowen, D.L. (2004) 'Islamic law & the position of women', in S.P. Heyneman (ed) *Islam and social policy*, Nashville, TN: Vanderbilt University Press, pp 44–117.

Clark, J.A. (2004) *Islam, charity and activism: Middle class networks and social welfare in Egypt, Jordan and Yemen*, Bloomington, IN: Indiana University Press.

Davis, P. (2001) 'Rethinking the welfare regime approach: the case of Bangladesh', in *Global Social Policy*, vol 1, no 1, pp 79–107.

El-Ghonemy, R. (1998) *Affluence and poverty in the Middle East*, London: Routledge.

Esping-Andersen, G. (1990) *The three worlds of welfare capitalism*, Cambridge: Polity Press.

Gal, J. and Jawad, R. (2012) 'The Middle East', in B. Greve (ed) *The international handbook of the welfare state*, London: Routledge.

Gough, I. and Wood, G (eds) (2004) with A. Barrientos, P. Beval, P. Davis and G. Room 'Welfare regimes in a development context: A global and regional analysis', in *Insecurity and welfare regimes in Asia, Africa and Latin America: Social policy in a development context*, Cambridge: Cambridge University Press.

Henry, C.M. and Springborg, R. (2001) *Globalization and the politics of development in the Middle East*, Cambridge: Cambridge University Press.

Heyneman, S. (2004) 'Introduction', in S.P. Heyneman (ed) *Islam and social policy*, Nashville, TN: Vanderbilt University Press.

Jawad, R. (2002) 'A profile of social welfare in Lebanon: assessing the implications for social development policy', *Global Social Policy*, vol 2, no 3, pp 319–42.

Jawad, R. (2006) 'Lebanon', in T. Fitzpatrick, H.-J. Kwon, N. Manning, J. Midgley and G. Pascall (eds) *International encyclopedia of social policy*, Volume 2 G–P, Oxford: Routledge.

Jawad, R. (2008) 'Possibilities of positive social action in the Middle East: a re reading of the history of social policy in the region', *Global Social Policy*, vol 8, no 2, pp 267–80.

Jawad, R. (2009) *Social welfare and religion in the Middle East: a Lebanese perspective*, Bristol: The Policy Press.

Kabeer, N. (2004) 'Re-visioning "the social": Towards a citizen-centred social policy for the poor in poor countries', IDS working paper, Brighton, accessed on 23 February 2004 at http://server.ntd.co.uk/ids/bookshop/details.asp?id=791

Karshenas, M. and Moghadam, V. (eds) (2006) *Social policy in the Middle East*, UNRISD Social Policy in a Development Context Series, New York: Palgrave Macmillan.

Messkoub, M. (2006) 'Constitutionalism, modernization and Islamization: the political economy of social policy in Iran', in M. Karshenas and V.M. Moghadam (eds) *Social policy in the Middle East: economic, political and gender dynamics*, Basingstoke: United Nations Research Institute for Social Development and Palgrave Macmillan, pp 190–220.

Saeidi, A.A. (2004) 'The accountability of para-governmental organizations (Bonyads): the case of Iranian foundations', *Iranian Studies*, vol 37, no 3, pp 479–98.

Underwood, C. (2004) 'Islam and health policy: a study of the Islamic Republic of Iran', in S.P. Heyneman (ed) *Islam and social policy*, Nashville, TN: Vanderbilt University Press, pp 181–206.

UNDP (United Nations Development Programme) (2002) *Arab human development report*, New York: United Nations Publications. Available at: www.arab-hdr.org/publications/other/ahdr/ahdr2002e.pdf (accessed 23 March 2012).

UNDP (2009) *Arab human development report*, New York: United Nations Publications. Available at: http://www.arab-hdr.org/publications/other/ahdr/ahdr2009e.pdf (accessed 12 July 2002).

Van Kersbergen, K. and Manow, P. (2009) 'Religion and the Western welfare state – the theoretical context', in P. Manow and K. Van Kersbergen (eds) *Religion, class coalitions and welfare states*, Cambridge: Cambridge University Press, pp 1–38.

Wiktorowicz, Q. (ed) (2003) *Islamic activism: A social movement theory approach*, Bloomington, IN: Indiana University Press.

Yakut-Cakar, B. (2007) 'Turkey', in B. Deacon and P. Stubbs (eds) *Social policy and international interventions in South East Europe*, Cheltenham: Edward Elgar, pp 103–29.

NINE

China's developmental model in Africa: a new era for global social policy?

Marian Urbina Ferretjans and Rebecca Surender

Introduction

Chinese engagement in the continent of Africa has grown exponentially in the last decade. Although, historically, China's trade and economic activities in the region have attracted most attention (Mohan and Power, 2008), it is increasingly recognised that Sino-African cooperation now also embraces development aid and social welfare assistance. However, there is awareness that Chinese assistance in Africa appears to be mediated under a different set of normative premises, institutional actors and policy mechanisms from traditional bilateral and intergovernmental institutions (Chin and Frolic, 2007; Alden et al, 2008; Brautigam, 2008; Davies et al, 2008; Brautigam, 2009) and interest in whether a new and distinctive Chinese approach to development in Africa is emerging.

In this context, the research presented in this chapter examines the Chinese 'model' of social development in Africa in terms of the instruments and mechanisms used to deliver it and the normative goals underpinning it, and compares it with current Western donor approaches. The focus is important since it has implications for social policy and welfare arrangements in developing countries. Although for advanced welfare economies, analysis has traditionally centred on the role of the nation state in explaining social policy dynamics, there is growing understanding that in a developing-country context, the influence of international development actors and institutions on social policies is paramount (Deacon, 1997; Hall and Midgley, 2004). Although policy models and prescriptions in developing countries have been traditionally influenced by European and North American institutions (Midgley, 2004;

Deacon, 2007; De Haan, 2007; Adésíná, 2008), the new phenomenon of 'South–South' interactions potentially changes this. Investigating the nature and processes of Chinese aid and social assistance in areas such as health and education in Africa thus provides new momentum to our understanding of the ways in which policy processes and outcomes in developing countries are shaped by transnational and globalisation processes (Yeates, 2008).

The chapter first briefly introduces the main social policy debates surrounding the relationship between the economic and social dimensions of development and the notion of a 'fourth world of productivist welfare capitalism' beyond the three Western ideal types characterised by Esping-Andersen's welfare regime typology. It then discusses to what extent China's approach to social development at home and in Africa is guided by this fourth welfare regime.

Economic growth and social protection

In order to assess whether China's development interventions in Africa represent a new social policy model, it is necessary to begin by examining existing frameworks. Esping-Andersen's (1990) seminal typology of welfare regimes provided a structure of ideal types to examine national experiences in the Organisation for Economic Co-operation and Development (OECD) context. His analysis, mainly guided by the dominant political movements in 20th-century Western Europe, demonstrated that there were different types of welfare systems within capitalist nations, each with different ideologies and principles. Crucially, it was these different normative goals and principles that explained why such different responses arose to common social pressures and needs. Despite its historic contribution, more recent analysis has highlighted the limitations of Esping-Andersen's typology in capturing the distinctive characteristics of welfare systems outside the Western world (Kwon, 1997; Gough and Wood, 2004). In particular, discussion has centred on the East Asian context, and the 'unearthing' of a 'fourth' developmental/ productivist welfare regime (Lee and Ku, 2007). It has now been argued that this developmental regime, conceptually positioned between a liberal open economy and a centrally planned model, better characterises East Asian welfare systems, including China, than any of the traditional welfare regime types (Bolesta, 2007).

While variation between systems exists and it is misleading to suggest that there is a homogeneous East Asian welfare 'type' (White and Goodman, 1998), there is some consensus that an 'East Asian welfare model' can be identified (Kwon, 1997; Holliday, 2000). Common features that have been detected in this 'fourth productivist model' include: 'a "productivist" social policy focused on economic growth; hostility to the idea of the welfare state; low public expenditure on social welfare; strong residualist elements in programmes; a central role for the family; a regulatory and enabling role for the state; piecemeal, pragmatic and ad hoc welfare development; use of welfare to build legitimacy, stability and support for the state; and limited commitment to the notion of welfare as a right of citizenship' (Wilding, 2000). However, despite resistance to the notion of a 'welfare state', the state is necessarily a strongly interventionist one in order to support a developmental approach (Bolesta, 2007).

Perhaps most importantly for social policy analysis, this 'fourth world' of developmental welfare[1] has been characterised by a social policy that is subordinated to the overriding economic policy objective of economic growth. So, while the model promotes public expenditure in some areas of social welfare, services and benefits tend to be linked to human capital formation, productive activity and state–market–family relationships directed towards growth (Holliday, 2000). The basic idea guiding East Asian developmental welfare states has been the discouragement of people from dependence on the state, while supporting those working in the productive sectors (Kwon, 1997). The state mainly exercises a regulatory role, rather than a role of provider of social services, and policies are aimed at achieving overall development and social well-being for society as a whole, rather than targeting more vulnerable groups or marginalised populations (Midgley, 2006). Although establishing a positive relationship between macroeconomic policy and social policy, social policy is typically introduced as an instrument to 'bolster' the market in achieving economic growth.

Debates about the optimal relationship between the economic and social spheres of policy are of course not new and have been extensively examined in both developed and developing contexts (Mkandawire, 2001). Those who argue that the social dimension is a crucial precondition and driver of economic development (since it contributes to, among other things, human capital investment) (Temple and Johnson, 1998; Atkinson, 1999; Sen, 1999) tend towards an 'institutional social policy' approach favouring extensive government intervention and social policies that provide universal and comprehensive long-term benefits and social services (Midgley, 2006). In contrast, those who see social expenditure as an obstacle for economic growth (because it reduces savings and investment and weakens labour market attachment) (Dornbusch and Edwards, 1990) tend towards a 'residual social policy' model, which favours a high degree of personal responsibility, limited state intervention and the maximum use of market mechanisms and non-profit organisations to meet social needs. In this latter scenario, the government's role should be limited to providing a safety net for that small proportion of the population that is not able to function effectively in the market. While some identify strong residual elements in the developmental social policy perspective (Wilding, 2000), nevertheless it is argued that the East Asian model is more complex and differs from both residual and institutional approaches because it promotes social welfare interventions that are 'productivist' and contribute to economic development (Midgley, 2006).

The Chinese productivist model?

Current debates about how much China conforms to this fourth developmental/productivist regime type are ongoing (Ngok, 2009). Certainly, China's social policy approach within its own borders in recent years shows some congruence with the classic developmental model (Ngok, 2009; Ngok and Zhu, 2010). The growing use of social instruments to achieve economic objectives, the government's support of education, entrepreneurship and employment programmes, and the State's mainly regulatory role rather than direct provider of social services, all seem indicative of a 'productivist investment' strategy. 'New Left' and other critics within China now also assert that, in traditional development style, this new orientation in the social policy arena is a strategy or a 'tool used by the new Chinese leadership to consolidate their authority and legitimacy' (Pei, 2006; Ngok and Zhu, 2010).

However, some key distinctive features differentiate China from the classic developmental model. China's political system and sheer size complicate the effective and consistent implementation of policies set at the centre: sub-national governments thus have greater autonomy in determining the terms of local development than in other East Asian systems (Tsai and Cook, 2005). Also, in contrast to classic developmental models, China's state bureaucracy is significantly developed and likely to become even more professionalised and independent (Bolesta, 2007).

Thus, debates continue about whether there exists a unique and distinctive 'Chinese model' of development or whether this is 'merely' a Chinese mode or variant of existing strong state models (Breslin, 2011). However, for the purposes of this analysis, the idea of a 'Chinese model' becomes important not so much for the specific characteristics that it might or might not have, but rather for becoming a metaphor of a distinctive alternative to the Western way of doing things (Breslin, 2011). Scrutiny of the Chinese 'model' is therefore gaining force in part because of the enormous achievements China has made in tackling poverty within its own borders and the imperative to understand 'what works'. Equally, however, in terms of China's emergence as a new global actor and an 'exporter' of its model to other developing countries, the debates also have significance for global social policy analysis. It is this latter set of issues that this chapter aims to examine.

Methodology

In order to gauge the extent to which China's social development approach diverges from current Western models, this chapter utilises Hall's framework of 'policy paradigms' in analysing public policymaking (Hall, 1993). It explores whether China's beliefs and practices in the provision of social sector aid to African countries constitutes a qualitative ('paradigm') alternative in relation to traditional donor models. Hall identifies three distinct levels of change in policy: changes to the *settings* of existing policy instruments, for example, the rate, amount or entitlement to something (first-order change); changes in the *instruments* used to attain policy goals, for example, a move from cash benefits to work programmes (second-order change); and, finally, changes in the *policy goals* themselves and the definition of the policy problem (third-order change). In order for a 'paradigm change' to occur (ie for one system or framework to be systematically different to another), difference has to be realised across all three levels but, most fundamentally, at the third-order level, since it represents a marked shift in the very conceptualisation of the problems that policies are meant to be addressing.[2] This analysis accordingly examines the settings, instruments and goals of Chinese development policies and Sino-African cooperation. It includes how welfare and social policy is conceptualised by the Chinese and how that conceptualisation has evolved over time, and the main actors involved and the strategies and mechanisms for the implementation of social interventions. The main interest of this chapter is therefore on the analysis of policy concepts and narratives rather than the implementation of policy. We now understand very well that how a social problem is defined will strongly affect how it is confronted and lays the foundations for the following stages of the policy process (Grindle and Thomas, 1991). Thus, in order to investigate China's social policy model in Africa, we examine how, as an emerging and influential development actor, China conceptualises 'the social'.

The study has two main components, which were both undertaken between 2009 and 2010. First, a comprehensive documentary analysis of over 50 key Sino-African, Chinese and Western policy documents was undertaken. The texts analysed include China's 2006 African policy, Organization for Economic Cooperation and Development – Development Assistance Committee (OECD–DAC) national aid policies and policy statements, and each political declaration and action plan produced in the four meetings of the Forum of China and Africa Cooperation (FOCAC) since its creation in 2000. The analysis stems from 2000 since it is then that cooperation between Beijing and African countries first became institutionalised. Since FOCAC's creation, further ministerial meetings have been held every three years: the 2003 FOCAC in Addis Ababa; the 2006 FOCAC in Beijing; and the 2009 FOCAC in Sharm el Sheik.

These meetings generated three Political Declarations and four Action Plans. The Political Declarations established the framework and guiding principles of cooperation between China and Africa and highlight the overall goals that China aims to achieve with its African partners. The Action Plans identify more practical instruments and mechanisms to operationalise cooperation across specific sectors (ie economic, political, social) and specific implementation strategies under each sector. Additionally, in 2006, Beijing developed its first 'China's African Policy', a White Paper that identifies the main principles and areas of cooperation between China and Africa. More recently, in April 2011, China adopted its Foreign Aid policy, which includes broad information on financial resources, forms, distribution and management of China's foreign aid. The Western documents comprise national aid policies and policy statements on China–Africa cooperation from OECD–DAC countries.

Following the documentary analysis, in-depth elite interviews were conducted with 12 senior Chinese officials, policy advisers and academics,[3] nine African Ambassadors and diplomats in Beijing, and 31 Western bilateral and multilateral donors (from OECD–DAC, the European Commission [EC], United Nations and international financial institutions [IFIs]), all involved in Sino-African cooperation. Interviews were carried out to investigate how these policy actors understood and assessed the social dimensions of Sino-African cooperation. In addition to Chinese stakeholders, the study also interviewed stakeholders from African countries (in receipt of Chinese aid) and Western donor agencies in order to triangulate across all three relevant 'data sources' and strengthen the analysis and conclusions that are generated.

This chapter mainly presents the findings and analysis from Sino-African documents and interviews with Chinese stakeholders. These findings form one component of a larger research project that includes analysis of the impact of the role of China on multilateral organisations and individual bilateral donor agencies and, most crucially, the views of African aid recipients to these new dynamics. In contrast to China as an emerging development aid actor, we refer to OECD–DAC and other bilateral and multilateral organisation interviewees as 'traditional donors' or 'the West' throughout the chapter.

China in Africa: a new paradigm for social development?

Settings

Although China's engagement with the developing world had previously largely prioritised trade and investment, it is evident that during the last decade, the substance of Chinese social development assistance has gone through a process of continuous transformation; significantly diversifying and expanding. FOCAC Action Plans divide the areas of cooperation between China and its African partners according to various groupings: political, multilateral/international, economic, social and, more recently, cultural and institutional.

Figure 9.1 shows how these official documents and plans classify the 'Social' grouping – the activities most analogous to social policy interventions. As can be seen, there has been a significant expansion in the prominence of social sector fields over the past decade, rising from three social fields in the second FOCAC Action Plan (2004–06) to nine in the last Action Plan (2010–12). To this extent, this expansion of social sector activity or settings has brought a convergence in the approaches of China and existing Western donors and, arguably, does not indicate a paradigm change from traditional donor models.

It is important to note that the documents demonstrate that 'science and technology', 'cultural exchanges', 'environmental protection', 'tourism' and 'climate change' are considered to be as equally 'social' as poverty reduction, education and health. It highlights both the broad definition of 'social' and the strong links between social interventions and economic development. The various documents illustrate the prevailing Chinese view that poverty reduction is necessarily addressed in conjunction with a dynamic process of economic activities. For instance, 'tourism' is acknowledged as 'an important activity which has the potential for generating financial resources that will help Africa's accelerated economic growth, the creation of employment opportunities and the alleviation of poverty' (2000–03 FOCAC Action Plan). Likewise, 'debt relief' is discussed as an important area of concern not only because it 'causes worsening social problems', but primarily because 'the heavy debt burden ... seriously hampers the economic growth of African countries' (2000–03 FOCAC Action Plan).

Figure 9.1: 'Social fields' in the Sino-African Action Plans

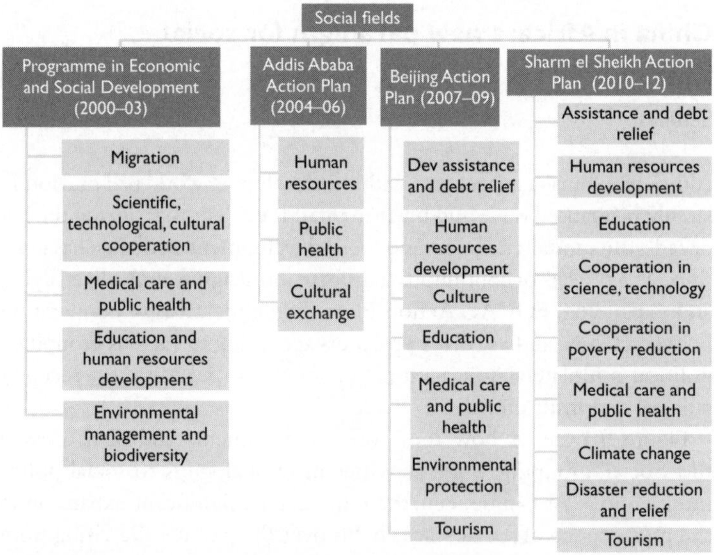

Note: The figure illustrates the social fields in the areas of 'social development' and 'development' (2010–12) exactly as described in the FOCAC Action Plans (official English version) with one exception. The 19 fields of cooperation in the 2000–03 Programme were not divided by sectors or areas. Therefore, the categories considered as 'social fields' have been established by the authors, guided by the classification undertaken in the FOCAC document.

However, even within the area of poverty reduction itself, we see an expansion of activities or 'settings'. Not only was poverty reduction explicitly included for the first time as a social field in the recent 2010–12 FOCAC Action Plan, but China's contribution provides a wider range of entitlements for African nations to benefit from poverty-reduction interventions: 'China will continue to share experience in poverty reduction with African countries through seminars and training sessions in order to jointly raise development capacity and make poverty alleviation efforts more effective' (2010–12 FOCAC Action Plan). The increase in the number of social fields is evident not only in absolute, but also in relative, terms. As demonstrated in Figure 9.2, social development cooperation (along with multilateral/international cooperation), has increased markedly compared to other areas during the period of analysis and especially in relation to economic areas of cooperation.

Figure 9.2: Evolution in the number and size of fields by area of cooperation

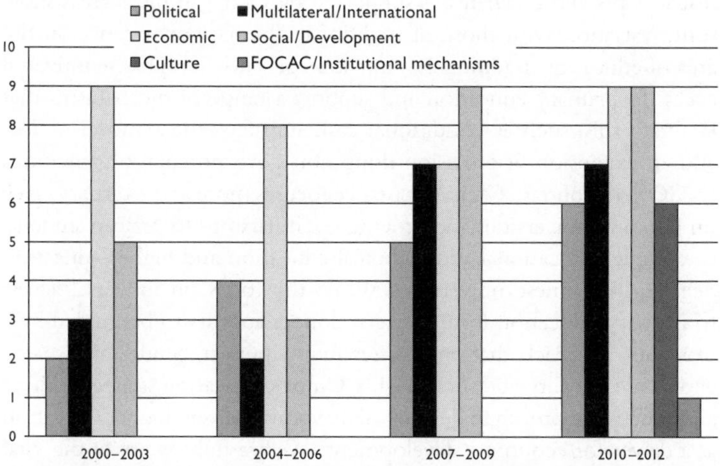

Note: The number of fields in the respective areas of cooperation is illustrated in the above figure as they appear in the FOCAC documents, with one exception. The 2000–03 Programme had not been divided by areas of cooperation in the official document. Therefore, the five fields included in this graph for the period 2000–03 have been identified as such by the authors (see note for Figure 9.1).

It is clear, then, that social development assistance has grown in importance in the last 10 years and, as part of this, greater efforts to optimise poverty reduction and social development strategies are more apparent. To this extent, however, while there has been a change in 'settings' – that is, from less social welfare to more – for the purposes of this analysis, the change in settings has produced convergence with the West rather than moved in the direction of a new approach.

Instruments and mechanisms

In contrast to the *settings* of existing social policy instruments, when we examine whether China has introduced changes in the range and type of *instruments* and *mechanisms* of social protection more generally, we do observe a divergence with traditional Western models. Our analysis shows that while China focuses on some of the same traditional social policy sectors (such as public health or education) prioritised by the Millennium Development Goal (MDG) framework, the specific instruments and mechanisms supported by China in these areas show some variation with those of traditional donors. For instance, in the area of education, traditional donor strategies now emphasise universal access to primary education and support a range of mechanisms that facilitate this, such as conditional cash transfers, the removal of fees and an expansion of provision using non-governmental organisations (NGOs). In contrast, China's assistance focuses more at the tertiary level; on building universities and providing scholarships to African students to complete vocational and technical education and higher education degrees in Chinese universities. While the focus on universal access to primary education from Western donors appears to be guided by a pro-poor approach that emphasises redistribution, gender and socio-economic equality, and social rights, China's education strategy reflects a productive approach to development: vocational and higher education as a driver for economic development: 'We are fully aware of the vital importance of [education] … talent training and capacity building to sustainable development in Africa' (Addis Ababa Action Plan 2004–06).

Likewise, in the area of health, traditional donors are increasingly focusing on the provision of technical assistance, capacity building and sector-wide policy dialogue rather than investing in public heath infrastructure or providing health services at the grassroots level. While some Western aid continues to be directed to NGOs to provide clinical services and public health interventions, there is now a distinct turn to more macro or systems-wide solutions for delivering health, most recently through market-based social insurance initiatives (WHO, 2010). In contrast, China directly provides services through building hospitals, health centres and sending medical teams to African countries to provide health services at the community level:

> "They are very strong in roads, buildings, clinics, etc. the hardware, and we do the software. I mean, they build the hospital, we have

the expertise, the tradition … to organize a health system." (Small central European OECD–DAC country)

"In the area of public health, I think … public health is our weakness. We have been focusing more on [direct] clinical work … China might not have a comparative advantage in this area." (Chinese government official)

Most noticeably, however, China does not actively endorse the sorts of targeted 'pro-poor' instruments – whether social insurance, social assistance, cash transfers or services – currently being promoted by Western multilateral, bilateral and NGO aid institutions. The emerging consensus among this community – that targeted social protection strategies provide a necessary and effective route out of poverty for the world's poorest – has resulted in a staggering increase in social protection measures being rolled out since the mid-1990s across the developing world (Barrientos and Hulme, 2008). Among them are: the 'Targeting the Ultra Poor' (TOP) and Employment Guarantee schemes of Bangladesh and India; the safety net cash transfer programmes of OXFAM/CARE/ Department for International Development (DfID) in Kenya, Zambia and Indonesia; the Conditional Cash Transfer programmes of Progressa and Bolsa Familia throughout Latin America; and the introduction of a myriad of social pension, micro insurance and credit schemes. In contrast, China gives little if any financial aid in the form of direct social protection transfers or services:

"the Chinese come along, and say 'You want a hospital that's fine, I make a design, this is the design, you like it, fine. I build you the hospital, I give you the keys.' So, there is absolutely no involvement of X [African country] or the X [people from African country] for any possibility of misappropriating the funds." (African Ambassador)

Finally, in terms of China's policy mechanisms, we see divergence with traditional donors concerning the role of state versus non-state actors and the institutional arrangements involved in delivering social interventions. While international donor organisations continue to conduct a large part of their work via NGOs and local community organisations, Sino-African cooperation appears to be mainly via government-to-government links, with the state as the main actor in both settings. Civil society has a limited role and is generally only mentioned under the 'cultural' area of cooperation for people-to-people exchanges rather than in the area of social development (2010–12 FOCAC). Also, while there has recently been a broadening of the intensive promotion of private sector organisations and market mechanisms prevalent in the 1980s among traditional donors, Chinese state-owned enterprises are defined as new and increasingly important players. The focus is on economic growth, and the use of market mechanisms and private sector organisations is accepted and promoted as part of the Chinese development effort in Africa: 'The Ministers note that China and African countries have made great efforts in recent years to explore new forms of cooperation, particularly between enterprises' (Programme for China–Africa Cooperation in Economic and Social Development, 2000).

Policy goals: social or economic?

The findings from this study support the view that China's engagement in Africa has introduced a different conceptualisation from current Western models in the way social development issues are framed and how social policies are justified. Documentary analysis shows that aid, trade and investment provided by China to Africa are intertwined in an integrated package and cannot be easily separated – firmly guided by an approach where the social dimensions of development are closely related to the economic dimensions. Thus, China does not follow the conventional guidelines of Official Development Assistance (ODA)[4] adopted by OECD countries, where trade and investment are explicitly excluded from development aid packages and social sector aid cannot be financially profitable for the donor country. Also, unlike most Western donor nations, which have separate ministries of 'overseas aid and development', aid, trade and investment are coordinated under one single ministry in China:

"Development assistance should be understood only as a part of economic cooperation. The West establishes boundaries between development assistance and businesses. However, the ultimate purpose of development assistance is that local businesses grow and don't need the assistance anymore." (Chinese policy adviser)

Several Chinese interviewees emphasised not only the idea that social and economic development are inextricably linked, but also that economic development precedes and is a prerequisite for achieving any social gains: "The first stage should be economic development and later social development. If not, you do not have credibility" (Chinese policy adviser). Chinese interviewees repeatedly asserted the idea that economic development should be the priority in the development process and that the other gains will follow; it is a stage in the development process that should be achieved after economic development:

> "So, priority, economic reform.... And then ... the social. After the financial crisis, you know, that is a driving force for our social reform.... So that is the sequence of our experience, sequence of the development.... Of course I don't mean if we focus on economic reform, just completely freeze those political reforms or social reforms – only mean [first] focus more energy on economic reform." (Chinese policy adviser)

Texts and interviews also reveal that the notion of welfare as an individual human right is absent from China's discourses on social development. Documents refer to the need to attain a more equitable international order rather than specific 'welfarist' interventions targeting vulnerable groups. Economic and social development interventions should aim to benefit all members of society and seek to enhance the social well-being of the whole population. Consequently, the emphasis on social development continues to revolve mainly around wider processes and structures rather than specific instruments for the provision of goods or services to individuals. Despite some traditional social protection interventions in health and education, most efforts of the Chinese government in Africa, as illustrated earlier, do not promote assistance directed at the income poverty and social exclusion of individuals, groups or communities. The mantra 'a rising tide lifts all boats' was frequently repeated.

Finally, in terms of the issue of 'conditionality', the Chinese approach to social development in Africa contains no prescriptive idea about what comprises 'good social policy' or how to achieve it. Most clearly spelled out in the Beijing Declaration (2000), but evident also in the other documents, diversity and respect for differences between nations is promoted, without statements about what African states are obliged to do: 'Each country has the right to choose, in its course of development, its own social system, development model and way of life in light of its national conditions.' Thus, Beijing does not require any specific policy responses or changes from recipient states, who are uninhibited in the conduct of their internal social policies: 'No country or group of countries, has the right to impose its will on others, to interfere, under whatever pretext, in other countries' internal affairs, or to impose unilateral coercive economic measures on others' (Beijing Declaration, 2000). This 'non-conditionality' is an overriding theme in Chinese engagement with Africa and has meant that China is open to working with any African country irrespective of its internal governance arrangements or political conditions. Documentary analysis suggests that the rationale for China's non-conditionality approach must be located in the context of a 'South–South' philosophy where developing countries assist each other in the achievement of common goals rather than engaging in 'one-way altruism'. The 2000 Declaration highlights the South–South nature of the cooperation and defines it 'as a new-type of long-term and stable partnership based on equality and mutual benefit'. In this context, China's close strategic integration of aid, trade and investment forms a reciprocal set of bonds rather than one based on paternalism or charity: 'The two sides will encourage and promote two-way trade and investment, diversify ways of cooperation and strengthen collaborative efforts in such priority areas as poverty relief' (Declaration of the Beijing Summit, 2006).

Discussion

During the past 10 years, the aid to Africa provided by OECD–DAC and other Western donors has been largely guided by the Millennium Development Goal (MDG) framework. It has focused on poverty alleviation and couched access to health or education in terms of the promotion of basic human rights (OECD, 2010). Social welfare interventions have concentrated on a pro-poor approach and on social protection measures involving means-tested targeted interventions to the poorest of the poor. Senior-level policy dialogue has also supported public expenditure allocations for social protection with set measures and specific budgetary items (OECD, 2009). There has been support for public finance for social protection at regional, national and local levels, and civil society and private actors have been encouraged to participate and complement government interventions.

However, in the last decade, China has also emerged onto the international development aid scene as an important player and appears to offer a different approach. Using Hall's classic framework to assess 'paradigm change', we see that despite arguably some convergence in terms of 'settings', China's understanding of the social dimensions of development differs from the Western approach across various dimensions. These include the instruments and mechanisms for the provision of social sector aid, the respective role of governmental and non-governmental actors, and, perhaps most importantly, in terms of the problem definition, normative underpinnings and goals for the provision of social aid.

According to the research presented here, China, like the 'West', aims to promote economic and social development and in turn contribute to poverty reduction in the countries that it is trying to assist. But Chinese development aid, while encompassing social protection measures, is not limited to it. Instead, China appears to be guided by a social development approach that establishes strong links between the economic and social dimensions of development. Thus, Beijing tends to prefer macro-economic interventions such as social infrastructure development, special economic zones or debt relief. This is guided by a rationale which posits that poverty reduction and social development are ultimately secured by productive activities that contribute to economic development and create employment opportunities. This strategy is significantly different from the pro-poor targeted interventions supported by Western donors, although the overall objectives might be the same. The state has a primary role, but other actors (state-owned companies) also contribute to generate economic growth and social development.

It is important of course not to overstate the situation, the reality of which is more complex and dynamic than can be captured by abstracted models. As illustrated earlier, social sector aid and the social dimensions of development are becoming increasingly important in China's policy agenda in Africa, as a parallel phenomenon to the social policy developments observed within China's own borders. Equally, policy models and prescriptions emanating from Western donor organisations are more heterogeneous and differentiated than the unified 'Western approach' presented here. There continue to be wide differences between the 'rights' perspective articulated by the ILO, the social risk management approach of the World Bank and the investment/needs approach of the UN (Deacon, 2007).

Nevertheless, despite these differences, there is evidence that Western multilateral governance and development institutions increasingly share a common view that a primary cause of poverty (and hence development and growth) is the economic and human capacity constraints faced by the poor. Targeted interventions to address immediate levels of consumption as well as longer-term investment in human resource capabilities are thus promoted and embedded in a transformative and pro-poor policy agenda. However, just when traditional donors appear to be embracing a 'post-Washington consensus' social policy agenda for developing nations (arguably moving from a 'liberal' model to a more 'social democratic' approach), China's ideas and activities appear to be located on a different trajectory, approximating more of a 'fourth' productivist regime approach. Whether the approach is indeed 'new', or merely a return to previously rehearsed ideas of 'economy first' and 'trickle down', is still to be assessed.

China's presence in Africa has many practical and substantive implications for global social welfare, including whether developing countries will favour this model, whether China will influence the policy prescription of Western multilateral or bilateral donors, and, perhaps most crucially, whether it will result in more effective outcomes for poverty alleviation and social development in the global South. However, these developments also have significant implications for the traditional analytical frameworks for understanding global welfare dynamics and many interesting questions emerge. The increasing importance of China and other emerging donors in the developing world and the revival of interest in the role of economic growth in development have precipitated a rethinking of the fundamental debate on the two-way influence of economic development and social policy. It also reopens theoretical debates on globalisation processes and the growing transnational nature of social policy.

The emergence of China and other powers as increasingly influential social actors in the South is undoubtedly changing the global social policy landscape and reopening past social policy debates in international development. As stated earlier, some of the debates are not new. In previous eras, traditional donors have also emphasised the importance of infrastructure, or the key role of economic growth for development. It is also true that other OECD–DAC members, most notably Japan and South Korea, similarly subscribe to a developmental model of social policy within their own borders. It is important to recognise that, in their capacity as OECD–DAC members, both explicitly support the organisation's principles and approach guiding Western aid to other developing countries. China, however, has not joined this 'donor group'. Thus, China's distinctiveness becomes significant not so much as a model in its own right, but as a 'model' of international development aid. For the first time ever, we see that global social policy debates and ideas are now increasingly influenced by non-Western players, and it is perhaps in this sense that the possibility of a new paradigm for global social policy analysis really emerges.

Notes

[1] Alternative conceptions of 'fourth models' include Castles and Mitchell's Antipodean model (Castles and Mitchell, 1993; Castles, 1996) and Ferrera's Southern European model (Ferrera, 1996). Here, we refer to Holliday's fourth world of productivist welfare capitalism.

[2] There are of course several alternative frameworks within the social policy literature for examining social policy streams, models and paradigms, among them: Kingdon (1995), Dolowitz and Marsh (2000), Sabatier (2007) and Béland (2005). Much of this literature, however, is concerned with examining the determinants and processes of policy change (eg rationalism versus incrementalism) or nationally/culturally specific modality comparisons. The broader paradigmatic framework of Hall is therefore utilised here.

[3] Senior representatives from the following organizations were interviewed: Ministry of Commerce (MOFCOM), Ministry of Health (MoH), National Development and Reform Commission (NDRC), China Exim Bank, International Poverty Reduction Center in China, China-Africa Business Council (CABC), Chinese Academy of Social Sciences (CASS), China Institute of Contemporary International Relations (CICIR), Peking University, and ChinAfrica Magazine.

[4] The definition of ODA on the OECD website (www.oecd.org) is as follows: 'Grants or Loans to countries and territories on Part I of the Development Assistance Committee (DAC) List of Aid Recipients (developing countries) which are: (a) undertaken by the official sector; (b) with promotion of economic development and welfare as the main objective; (c) at concessional financial terms [if a loan, having a Grant Element (q.v.) of at least 25%]. In addition to financial flows, Technical Co-operation (q.v.) is included in aid. Grants, Loans and credits for military purposes are excluded.... Transfer payments to private individuals (e.g. pensions, reparations or insurance payouts) are in general not counted.'

References

Adésínà, J. (2008) *Transformative social policy in a postneoliberal African context: Enhancing social citizenship*, Paper prepared for the RC19 Stockholm Annual Conference 4-6 September. Available at: www2.sofi.su.se/RC19/pdfpapers/Adesina_RC19_2008.pdf

Alden, C., Large, D. and Soares de Oliveira, R. (eds) (2008) *China returns to Africa. A rising power and a continent embrace*, London: Hurst & Company.

Atkinson, A.B. (1999) 'Macroeconomics and the social dimension', in Division for Social Policy and Development (ed) *Experts discuss some critical social development issues*, New York, NY: United Nations Department of Economic and Social Affairs.

Barrientos, A. and Hulme, D. (2008) *Social protection for the poor and poorest*, Basingstoke: Palgrave Macmillan.

Béland, D. (2005) 'Ideas and social policy: an institutionalist perspective', *Social Policy & Administration*, vol 39, no 1, pp 1–18.

Beijing Declaration (2000) *Forum on China-Africa cooperation (FOCAC)*, Beijing.

Bolesta, A. (2007) 'China as a developmental state', *Montenegrin Journal of Economics*, 5, pp 105–11.

Bräutigam, D. (2008) *China's African aid. Transatlantic challenges*, Washington: The German Marshall Fund of the United States.

Bräutigam, D. (2009) *The dragon's gift. The real story of China in Africa*, Oxford: Oxford University Press.

Breslin, S. (2011) 'The "China model" and the global crisis: from Friedrich List to a Chinese mode of governance', *International Affairs*, vol 87, no 6, pp 1323–43.

Castles, F.G. and Mitchell, D. (1993) 'Worlds of welfare and families of nations', in F.G. Castles (ed), *Families of nations*, Aldershot: Dartmouth, pp 93–128.

Castles, F. (1996) 'Needs-based strategies of social protection in Australia and New Zealand', in G. Esping-Andersen (ed) *Welfare state in transition: national adaptation in global economies*, London: Sage.

Chin, G.T. and Frolic, B.M. (2007) 'Emerging donors in international development assistance: the China case', Partnership and Business Development Division, IDRC.

Davies, M., with Edinger, H., Tay, N. and Naidu, S. (2008) 'How China delivers development assistance to Africa', University of Stellenbosch, Centre for Chinese Studies.

Deacon, B. (2007) *Global social policy and governance*, London: Sage.

Deacon, B., with Hulse, M. and Stubbs, P. (1997) *Global social policy. International organizations and the future of welfare*, London: Sage Publications.

De Haan, A. (2007) *Reclaiming social policy*, Palgrave.

Declaration of the Beijing Summit (2006) *Forum on China-Africa cooperation (FOCAC)*, Beijing.

Devereux, S. and Sabates-Wheeler, R. (2007) 'Debating social protection', *IDS Bulletin*, vol 38, no 3, Institute of Development Studies.

Dolowitz, D.P. and Marsh, D. (2000) 'Learning from abroad: the role of policy transfer in contemporary policy-making', *Governance; An International Journal of Policy and Administration*, vol 13, no 1, pp 5–24.

Dornbusch, R. and Edwards, S. (1990) 'Macroeconomic populism', *Journal of Development Economics*, vol 32, no 2, pp 247–77.

Esping-Andersen, G. (1990) *The three worlds of welfare capitalism*, Cambridge: Polity.

Ferrera, M. (1996) 'Southern model of welfare in social Europe', *Journal of European Social Policy*, vol 6, no 1, pp 17–37.

Gough, I. and Wood, G., with Barrientos, A., Bevan, P., Davis, P. and Room, G. (2004) *Insecurity and welfare regimes in Asia, Africa and Latin America*, Cambridge: Cambridge University Press.

Grindle, M.S. and Thomas, J.W. (1991) *Public choices and policy change. The political economy of reform in developing countries*, Baltimore, MD: The Johns Hopkins University Press.

Hall, A. and Midgley, J. (2004) *Social policy for development*, London: Sage Publications.

Hall, P.A. (1993) 'Policy paradigms, social learning, and the states: the case of economic policymaking in Britain', *Comparative Politics*, vol 25, no 3, pp 275–96.

Holliday, I. (2000) 'Productivist welfare capitalism: social policy in East Asia', *Political Studies*, vol 48, pp 706–23.

Kingdon, J.W. (1995) *Agendas, alternatives, and public policies*, New York, NY: Harper Collins College Publishers.

Kwon, H.-J. (1997) 'Beyond European welfare regimes: comparative perspectives on East Asian welfare systems', *Journal of Social Policy*, vol 26, pp 467–84.

Lee, Yih-Jiunn and Ku, Yeun-wen (2007) 'East Asian welfare regimes: testing the hypothesis of the developmental welfare state', *Social Policy and Administration*, vol 41, no 2, pp 197–212.

Midgley, J. (2004) 'Social development and social welfare: implications for social policy', in P. Kennett (ed) *A handbook on comparative social policy*, Cheltenham: Edward Elgar.

Midgley, J. (2006) 'Developmental social policy: theory and practice', *Asian Journal of Social Policy*, vol 2, no 1, pp 1–22.

Mkandawire, T. (2001) 'Social policy in a development context', *Social Policy and Development*, Programme Paper No 7, June, Geneva: United Nations Research Institute for Social Development.

Mohan, G. and Power, M. (2008) 'New African choices? The politics of Chinese engagement', *Review of African Political Economy*, no 115, pp 23–42.

Ngok, K. (2009) 'Redefining development in China: towards a new policy paradigm for the new century?', in K.H. Mok and R. Forrest (eds) *Changing governance and public policy in East Asia*, Oxon: Routledge.

Ngok, K. and Zhu, Y. (2010) 'In search of harmonious society in China: a social policy response', in K.H. Mok and Y.-W. Ku (eds) *Social cohesion in greater China. Challenges for social policy and governance*, Singapore: World Scientific Publishing.

OECD (Organisation for Economic Co-operation and Development) (2009) 'Promoting pro-poor growth: social protection', DAC Network on Poverty Reduction (POVNET).

OECD (2010) 'Active with Africa, Centre for Co-operation with Non-Members', Africa Partnership Forum Support Unit, Paris.

Pei, M. (2006) *China's trapped transition: the limits of developmental autocracy*, Cambridge, MA: Harvard University Press.

Sabatier, P.A. (ed) (2007) *Theories of the policy process*, Boulder, CO: Westview Press.

Sen, A. (1999) *Development as freedom*, New York, NY: Anchor Books.

Temple, J. and Johnson, P.A. (1998) 'Social capability and economic growth', *Quarterly Journal of Economics*, vol 113, no 3, pp 965–90.

Tsai, K. and Cook, S. (2005) 'Developmental dilemmas in China: socialist transition and late liberalization', in K. Tsai and S. Pekkannen (eds) *Japan and China in the world political economy*, London: Routledge.

White, G. and Goodman, R. (1998) 'Welfare orientalism and the search for an East Asian welfare model', in R. Goodman, G. White and H.-j. Kwon (eds) *The East Asian welfare model: welfare orientalism and the state*, London: Routledge.

Wilding, P. (2000) 'Review of Roger Goodman, Gordon White and Huck-ju Kwon (eds) *The East Asian welfare model: welfare orientalism and the state*', *Public Administration and Policy*, vol 9, no 2, pp 71–82.

WHO (World Health Organization) (2010) *The World Health Report - Health systems financing: The path to universal coverage*, Geneva: WHO.

Yeates, N. (ed) (2008) *Understanding global social policy*, Bristol: The Policy Press.

Part Three

Severe crisis: social policy in most challenging circumstances

The Greek welfare state in the age of austerity: anti-social policy and the politico-economic crisis

Theodoros Papadopoulos and Antonios Roumpakis

Introduction

Greece was the first of the countries in the EU periphery engulfed in the so-called sovereign debt crisis that followed the crisis in the financial and banking sectors. The sovereign debt crisis exposed the serious weaknesses of the politico-economic regime that shaped Greece's development after the end of the military dictatorship in 1974. It also revealed the unprecedented power of unaccountable international financial institutions, banks and agencies to shape the dynamics of government bond markets across the globe and, therefore, the trajectories of national and regional political economies. More fundamentally, the Greek crisis exposed the limits of EU solidarity, and accelerated changes in the future politico-economic governance of the EU: the institutional innovations pursued as a means for managing the sovereign debt crisis, especially within the Eurozone, undermine national economic sovereignty to an unprecedented degree and, thus, place under serious question the role of national democratic politics in the process of EU integration.

This chapter begins with a brief discussion of the background to the crisis and explores how multiple and mutually reinforcing causes created the 'perfect storm' conditions for its eruption. This is followed by a critical presentation of the key austerity and deregulatory measures adopted by the Greek government until the end of December 2011. Most of these measures were preconditions for the tranches of the 'bailout' loan agreed with the so-called 'troika' of lenders, the ad hoc body comprising representatives of the European Central Bank (ECB), the European

Commission (EC) and the International Monetary Fund (IMF). A discussion of the impact of austerity measures on the economy, welfare and society more generally, as well as our final reflections, conclude the chapter. It is argued that the austerity measures and the deregulatory, pro-market, policy reforms prescribed by the ECB/EC/IMF and pursued by consecutive Greek governments have culminated in an anti-social policy that has done nothing to alleviate the crisis. Instead, it has severely reduced socio-economic security, traumatised social cohesion and democratic governance, and sunk the Greek economy into the deepest and most prolonged recession in recent memory with detrimental effects for the state's finances and Greek society more generally.

Explaining the Greek crisis: historical legacies and politico-economic dynamics

The story so far

By the end of 2008, the global crisis in the financial and banking sectors was engulfing the majority of European economies. Despite the fact that Greek banks were not exposed to the so-called 'toxic assets', which had a particularly devastating impact in the US, the UK, Ireland and Iceland, the government at the time (led by the centre-right New Democracy Party) sought to take pre-emptive measures. Following similar actions in other EU member states, the government provided a €28bn package (11.8% of Greek GDP for 2008) to support the Greek banking sector in order to boost liquidity, revive inter-bank loans and sustain economic growth. This package came on top of an already burdened budget that included, among others, meeting the excessive costs of hosting the 2004 Olympic Games, continuing with the highest military expenditure in the EU (3% of GDP in 2008; see SIPRI, 2011), and servicing an already substantial public debt (approximately 110% of GDP in 2008; see IMF, 2011). With the economy in recession and amidst accusations of serious political mismanagement and economic scandals, the then Prime Minister Kostas Karamanlis called for elections in autumn 2009.

Widespread media reports about a looming Greek crisis began in October 2009 when the newly elected PASOK government was reportedly 'surprised' to discover that Greece's public budget deficit was much higher than previously calculated by the Greek statistical authorities. It accordingly revised the official estimate of the 2009 annual deficit from 6.7% to 12.7% of GDP. This figure was later revised again, upwards, to 15.4% of GDP (Nelson et al, 2011), a controversial act that, at the time of writing, was under judicial investigation (*The Economist*, 2011). These revisions – to be added to others before and since the country joined the Eurozone in 2001 – not only worsened the already damaged reputation of 'Greek statistics', but, more importantly, set off alarm bells in the EC and ECB as well as the international financial markets and credit-rating agencies. Subsequent and consecutive downgradings of Greece's creditworthiness increased the costs of borrowing and fuelled speculative attacks. With its credit ratings in free fall and its government bond *spreads* and sovereign *credit default swaps* (CDSs)[1] reaching all-time highs (Gibson et al, 2011), Greece became the first Eurozone member state to formally seek financial assistance from the IMF and the European Union. On 23 April 2010, the then Prime Minister George Papandreou announced the Greek government's request for activating an ad hoc support mechanism jointly supervised by the IMF/ECB/EC that was to provide a 'bailout' loan to Greece with lower-than-market interest rates.

On 3 May 2010, the so-called Memorandum of Understanding (Μνημόνιο) of the Loan Facility Agreement (LFA) was approved by the Greek parliament amidst massive demonstrations and street violence. Greece was promised €110 billion (€80 billion from Eurozone member states and €30 billion from the IMF) to be used solely to meet the liabilities to its debtors, that is, banks, financial institutions and states. The LFA involved a regime of very strict conditionality that was accompanied by what, by international standards, was an unprecedented loss of its national economic sovereignty. According to the LFA's Article (5) 'the Borrower [the Greek state] hereby irrevocably and unconditionally waives all immunity to which it is or may become entitled in respect of itself or its assets', which effectively means that the Greek government *voluntarily* surrendered national sovereignty to its lenders and placed the country under a type of economic surveillance that could lead to claims over its resources and territory if the terms of the agreement were not fulfilled (LFA, 2010). In fact, by October 2011, there were already calls by a number of Eurozone countries for the creation of a special task force by the EU to be given extra powers to oversee the sale of Greek state assets and the country's civil service, which some officials described as 'a form of colonialism' (Reuters, 2011). Further, while the vast majority of the Greek bonds prior to the LFA were issued under Greek law, the 'bailout' loan under the LFA was issued under English law, which substantially weakened the position of Greece as a borrower. Overall, as Dizard (2010) put it:

Greece is exchanging outstanding debt that is legally and logistically easy to restructure on favourable terms with debt that is difficult or impossible to restructure. It's as if they were borrowing from a Mafia loan shark to repay an advance from their grandmother.

By July 2011, only part of the loan (€65 billion) had been released to Greece (see Table 10.1). The next tranche, scheduled for October 2011, was postponed until December 2011 due to 'lack of progress' with reforms demanded by the ECB/EC/IMF. Subsequently, it was further postponed to March 2012 depending upon Greece fulfilling various old and new requirements of the loan to the satisfaction of its creditors (Reuters, 2012).

Table 10.1: Overview of disbursements, in billions of Euros, December 2011

Tranche	Disbursements	Euro-area	IMF	Total
1	May 2010	14.5	5.5	20
2	Sep 2010	6.5	2.5	9
3	Dec 2010/Jan 2011	6.5	2.5	9
4	March 2011	10.9	4.1	15
5	July 2011	8.7	3.3	12
6	Dec 2011*	5.8	2.2	8
	Total	52.9	20.1	73

Note: * Postponed until March 2012.
Source: European Commission (2011c).

By the middle of 2011, total Greek public debt was estimated to be approximately €360bn, comprising €285bn debt in bonds and €75bn in loans. Table 10.2 shows the distribution of holders of Greek government bonds and debt by the origin of financial institutions. The majority of the debt is owed to the ECB and the national banks (NBs) of the Eurozone countries, with the IMF holding a €15bn loan. Greek banks hold an estimated total of €57bn debt, while Greek pension funds hold an additional €30bn in bonds. French and German banks hold approximately €19bn and €15bn, respectively – several large private European banks, such as BNP Paribas, Société Générale and Generali hold significant amounts of these bonds – while other private investors hold approximately €94bn in bonds and €16bn in loans (see Barclays Capital, 2011).

Table 10.2: Holders of Greek government bonds and debt, 2011

	Bonds (€bn)	Loans (€bn)
Europe (ECB, NBs)	49.0	38.0
IMF	–	15.0
Greek banks	45.7	11.4
Greek public funds	30.0	–
Germany	15.2	–
France	19.1	–
Italy	4.7	–
United Kingdom	1.9	–
Rest of the World (Asia)	25.0	–
Others	94.4	16.0
Total	285.0	75.0

Source: Authors' calculations based on estimates from Barclays Capital (2011).

During the ad hoc talks of European leaders on 26 October 2011, a bond exchange was proposed with the overambitious aim of bringing the Greek public debt down to 120% of GDP by 2020, which, incidentally, was the level of debt in 2009, prior to the IMF/EC/ECB involvement. The proposed so-called 'haircut' involved the voluntary exchange of Greek government bonds with new bonds of up to 50% of the original value. However, it is to exclude the European and IMF parts of the Greek public debt, and concentrates mostly on domestic Greek bondholders (ie Greek banks and social security funds) as well as European banks and institutional investors. The announcements that followed this meeting were vague and many details were still to be decided at the time of writing, most important of which were the change of the legal framework regulating all bonds to be exchanged from Greek to English law and the level of interest rate, which was expected to be higher than the original bonds. Any agreed 'haircuts' and bond exchange will touch upon the profitability of major European private financial institutions as well as the solvency of the Greek banking sector while the viability of Greek pension and health insurance funds, and their capacity to meet their social policy obligations (eg occupational pensions, health coverage liabilities), would be under serious question.

Villains or victims: towards a synthesis of domestic and systemic explanations of the Greek crisis

Explanations of the causes of the Greek crisis oscillate between those that give emphasis to domestic causes and those that emphasise systemic reasons. For the former, the crisis is mainly attributable to the behaviour of a profligate society that 'consumed beyond its means', and its corrupt governments that ran large public debts and budget deficits. As a result, when the 2008 global financial crisis erupted, confidence in the capacity of the Greek state to service its debt plummeted and Greece was forced to seek the assistance of the IMF/EC/ECB. For the latter approach, the crisis was the outcome of chronic economic inadequacies and lack of policy options within the Euro, mostly outside the country's influence, with domestic factors acting as triggers rather than as causes of the crisis. Our view draws from both approaches and argues that the eruption of the crisis was the combined result of 'perfect storm' conditions, both domestic and external, but also argues that the continuation and deepening of the crisis is a product of the very measures that were taken, supposedly, to alleviate it.

First, the crisis has to be understood in a historical context. There is a legacy of reoccurring defaults of the Greek state, as well as direct and indirect foreign interventions in the Greek politico-economic life related to servicing foreign-owned public debt (Levandis, 1944; Kofas, 1989; Eliadakis, 2011). This legacy is also related to the emergence and position of Greece as a semi-peripheral economy in Southern Europe (Fotopoulos, 1985), highly dependent on capital from core lending countries and their economic trajectories. As Michael-Matsas (2010, p 171) put it, 'the history of Greek capitalism [and the Greek state] is the history of its bankruptcies', which follow global crises with remarkable regularity. Indeed, the Greek state was declared bankrupt at least twice before the current crisis, in 1893 and 1932, closely following respective global Great Depressions. This reoccurrence has been attributed to the so-called 'sudden stop' in lending, a rather familiar pattern in the history of emerging economies (Calvo, 1998; Catao, 2006; Lazaretou, 2010; Bordo et al, 2010), which also occurred recently in the Eurozone (Mansori, 2011). As Lazaretou (2010, p 10) summarised it: 'every time the economic and financial circumstances in the advanced lending countries changed leading to a cut off of cheap capital inflows to the emerging economies, the latter soon faced a balance of payments crisis and a debt crisis.' Against this background, it can be safely argued that the 2007/08 financial crisis was not a direct cause of the Greek crisis and, indeed, Greece did not immediately suffer the 'first-order' effects of the global crisis (see Farnsworth and Irving, 2011). Instead, the 'sudden stop' in lending that followed the global financial crisis operated as a catalyst to what was a disastrous combination of mutually reinforcing factors, of which the pivotal one, as we will demonstrate later, was Greece's economic and fiscal performance after the adoption of the Euro.

Focusing on the domestic factors, the politico-economic regime established after the collapse of dictatorship in 1974 used state resources and public borrowing not only as a means to legitimise the young democracy, but also to maintain the political reproduction of ruling elites (see Karamesini, 2008; Katsimi and Moutos, 2010; Kouvelakis, 2011) and facilitate their enrichment in the context of the semi-peripheral Greek political economy. This was particularly the case in the 1980s and early 1990s when the public debt ballooned due to excessive borrowing (see Figure 10.1), which was partly used to fund a substantial increase in public sector employment and a modest expansion of the welfare state, without increasing substantially the taxes on higher earners and businesses. In this respect, the current crisis in Greece is not purely economic or fiscal in nature, it is deeply politico-economic, signalling, among other things, the exhaustion of the politico-economic regime that emerged in Greece in the last 35 years. This regime, characterised by state patronage and clientelism, tolerated extensive tax evasion practices (especially of higher earners, businesses and powerful individuals) while privileging specific socio-professional groups via a fragmented and highly unequal social security system (Petmesidou, 1991, forthcoming; Venieris, 1997). Further, its corresponding semi-peripheral political economy was 'benefiting' from the functioning of a substantial underground economy, which utilised uninsured and precarious labour, keeping production costs low, while continuing with familistic welfare arrangements that 'externalised' the costs of social reproduction to Greek families (see Papadopoulos and Roumpakis, 2009). These costs continued to remain low, especially since the mid-1990s, due to the extensive use of migrant workers, most of whom where undocumented, especially in the agriculture, construction and domestic/care sectors.

Regarding the systemic factors, one of the key economic consequences of Greece's entry in the Eurozone in 2001 was the dramatic amplification of the already widening asymmetries in productivity and competitiveness between Greece's semi-peripheral economy and those of core EU countries, asymmetries that followed Greece's entry into the EEC in 1981 (see Fotopoulos, 1993). Following the adoption of the Euro, economic growth in the Greek economy was maintained primarily by boosting domestic demand through consumption and to a lesser extent

Figure 10.1: Historical evolution of public debt as percentage of GDP in Greece, 1960–2012

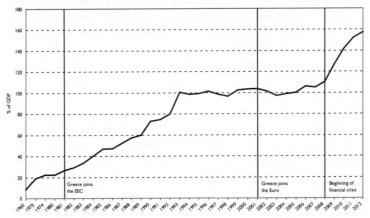

Note: Estimated data for 2012.
Source: IMF (2011).

investment in construction and real estate. While the supply of cheap credit from the ECB allowed the banking sector to expand rapidly, at the same time, the real economy did not yield enough streams of revenue to prevent the accumulation of high domestic debt while the trade deficit worsened. While advanced core EU countries, like Germany, were able to constrain wages, maintain higher productivity rates and create trade surpluses (Lapavitsas et al, 2010), the only option for productively weaker states with chronic trade deficits, like Greece, was to borrow in Euros from the markets, given that the Eurozone states cannot expand their money supply unilaterally. The combination of these systemic factors contributed towards the 'twin deficits' of Greece: on the government budget and on the current account balance (see Figure 10.2). The end result was that the negative tendencies prior to the entry into the Euro (trade deficits, dismantling of the structure of production, etc) were further amplified. The lack of the policy option to issue its currency meant that, within the Euro, Greece's semi-peripheral capitalism stood little chance of balanced endogenous growth (Lapavitsas, 2011; Polychroniou, 2011) similar to other semi-peripheral EU economies like Portugal and Ireland (Mansori, 2011).

Examining the composition of debt reveals another systemic trend that was a direct consequence of Greece's joining the Eurozone, namely the rise in private debt. At first glance, as Table 10.3 demonstrates, when we compare *private* debt, including household and business credit exposure,

Greece comes off relatively well with one of the lowest levels of private debt (122%) in comparison to other EU countries. This can at least partly explain why Greece did not suffer the first-order effects of the original global crisis in 2008: the latter was about servicing private debt and the risk of defaults from private debt. Sovereign debt became an issue after the 'sudden stop' in lending took place following the original crisis.

Figure 10.2: Greece's 'twin' deficits: budget and current account deficits, 1999–2009

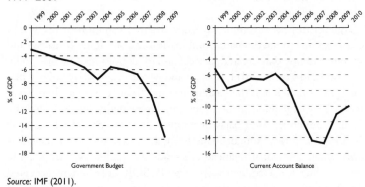

Government Budget   Current Account Balance

Source: IMF (2011).

Table 10.3: Public and private* debt as a percentage of GDP, 2007–10

	Net general government debt		Private sector debt*	
	2007	**2010**	**2007**	**2010**
France	60	77	142	160
Germany	50	58	131	135
Greece	105	143	105	122
Ireland	11	78	241	305
Italy	87	99	122	133
Netherlands	22	28	209	217
Portugal	64	89	225	249
Spain	27	49	215	224
UK	43	67**	216	232**

Notes: * Includes household debt and non-financial corporate debt but excludes financial sector debt. ** UK data for 2009.

Sources: Data for UK from PricewatehouseCoopers (2010), calculations based on data from Office for National Statistics (2010). Data for all other countries from Papadimitriou and Wray (2011).

Still, despite the fact that Greek private debt is significantly lower than other Eurozone countries and the UK, private debt and in particular household borrowing boomed with the coming of the Euro. In fact, it increased faster than the public debt (Lapavitsas et al, 2010) following a trend already set in the 1990s: since 1994 and up to 2006, the total increase of consumer credit touched upon the astronomic figure of 2,106% (Papadopoulos and Roumpakis, 2009). Sanctioned by the Greek banks, and helped by lower interest rates, this expansion of consumer credit was mainly concentrated on mortgages and consumer loans and left Greek households exposed to unprecedented levels of debt when the crisis erupted.

Against this background, we argue that the eruption of the Greek crisis was due to the dramatic combination of both domestic causes and systemic trends that created 'perfect storm' conditions (on this point, see also Featherstone, 2011; Katsimi and Moutos, 2011). By 2009, when the budget deficit and the current account balance were at their worst with a very large public debt, a substantial trade deficit and a chronically weak productive base (that worsen after its entry into the Euro), the Greek government sought loans from the international markets at a time when the global financial crisis was still under way and lending was heading for a 'sudden stop'. The PASOK government accepted the dramatic curtailment of national economic sovereignty as a price for the so-called 'bailout loan', and, under the strict supervision of the IMF/EC/ECB, began legislating and implementing austerity measures as preconditions of the loan's tranches.

Austerity measures: the internal devaluation of Greece

The austerity measures and reforms that accompanied the IMF/EC/ECB 'bailout' loan were unprecedented, in their scope, severity, volume and speed. Substantial income cuts and extraordinary increases in taxation, accompanied the extensive deregulation of Greek industrial relations, the abolition of many hard-won socio-economic rights of numerous professions both in the public and private sectors, as well as an ambitious programme of far-reaching privatisations of state enterprises and the selling-off of public property. A selected number of these are critically presented below.

Wages, unemployment benefits and conditions of labour

Even before the EU/IMF bailout, the period 1995–2010 was characterised by the expansion of precarious jobs in the formal labour market, both in the public and private sectors (Karantinos 2006; INE-GSEE, 2008). As a precondition for the 'bailout' loan, the government accepted further moves towards the 'flexibilisation' of the labour market and strengthening of the rights of employers to 'hire and fire'. Trade unions, meanwhile, would lose their right to refer to the Conciliation and Arbitration Service following disputes with employers over wage increases and collective agreements. Additionally, employers are no longer obliged to offer permanent contracts to employees on rolling temporary contracts. In June 2011, and in order to reduce government expenditure, 30,000 public servants, all aged over 60, were placed on an official 'labour reserve', with the number expected to reach 100,000 by the end of 2012. Public servants with the status of 'labour reserve' will receive 60% of their salary for 12 months and if they are unable to find a job in the private sector, they will receive early (and reduced) pensions.

This planned 'flexibilisation' of the labour market was accompanied by a stagnation or even reduction of real wages. Already in 2008, a substantial percentage of the workforce (22%) received very low salaries, with the average wage estimated at 83% of the European average (INE-GSEE, 2008). This situation changed for the worse after the PASOK government began adopting the new measures. The IMF recommendation for a 15% wage decrease in the public and private sector was accepted and the minimum wage was reduced by 20% for workers under 24 years old, setting a monthly minimum wage of €595 (Megas, 2010). Further, as part of the medium-term fiscal strategy and the pressures for additional structural reforms in 2011, the PASOK government introduced more cuts in wages that resulted in a 25% total wage cut in the public sector, while, at the time of writing, the government was discussing the possibility of further reducing the minimum wage in the private sector to €560 per month, applicable to the total workforce, with under-24-year-old workers receiving even less.

Back in May 2010, the government introduced new legislation that placed new employment contracts in the public sector under severe constraints, as five existing public servants have to be fired or retire for one new opening. In June 2011, the government further constrained new recruitments, as the 'one to five' rule was replaced for the 'one to 10' rule. It also curtailed by 50% the ability of the local governments and the so-called wider public sector (public utilities) to hire personnel in 2011, with an additional 10% reduction for each year up to 2015 (INE-GSEE, 2011). Further, in November 2011, and as a precondition for the next tranche of the IMF/EU loan, the PASOK government introduced an amendment in collective bargaining and labour law that removed the role of national collective bargaining agreements and prioritised negotiations at the firm level. Unions can be bypassed as workers can form 'voluntary' associations within the firm. If the minimum majority of workers in a firm accept the new wage agreement on wage and working conditions (eg three out of five workers) following individual meetings with their employer, then these become applicable to all workers at the firm. The existing sectoral agreements, which will apply until 2014 regardless of future negotiations between unions and employers, set a de facto maximum on wages and erode working conditions. Mr Panagopoulos, President of the General Confederation of Greek Workers (GSEE) and a PASOK syndicalist, summarised the mood of the trade unions as follows:

> the government's submissiveness has no end.... The government should not 'toil' to keep the country in Europe and in the Euro. With such decisions the government takes the Greek workers outside European protection, outside the European social acquis, outside the European civilization, i.e. outside what is the real Europe.... This final hour I urge the government not to legislate what the troika [IMF/EC/ECB] obliges, because it opens the door (more appropriately tearing down the walls) for wages and industrial relations of the type that exist in China, India and third world countries. (Panagopoulos, 2011)

Conditions for the unemployed have also deteriorated in recent years. Unemployment benefits in Greece have for decades remained very low in comparison to European averages with eligibility criteria strictly linked to previous employment records, thus excluding first entrants and the young unemployed or those with poor contribution records (Papadopoulos, 2006). While unemployment benefit (currently at €461.5 per month) is still well below the poverty line, lasts for a maximum of one year and has no follow-up benefits for the long-term unemployed, the government announced in April 2010 that state support towards the unemployed was to be reduced by €500 million (Kostarelou, 2010) at a time when unemployment was increasing rapidly.

Tax measures

As a desperate measure to increase the revenues to the state budget, the government decided to increase the standard rate of VAT to 23% (up from 19%) in July 2011, for medical services to 13% (up from 9.5%) and for books and newspapers to 6.5% (up from 4%). The increase of the standard rate was also accompanied with new listings of products that were previously taxed with the medium tax rate (eg restaurants, taverns). Additional increases applied to excise duties for petrol, gas, tobacco and alcohol. Thus, while wages and pensions are being curtailed, the cost of living is being increased. Further, the Greek government reduced the income tax threshold twice, first in May 2010 when it was set at €9,000 (from €12,000) and then in September 2011 when it was further reduced to €5,000.

Under the tax law of March 2011, a withholding tax of 25% shall be levied from 2012 on profits distributed by corporations, limited liability companies and cooperatives; for the year 2011, the withholding tax rate was 21%. Still, corporate taxation, which had already been reduced by 40% in 10 years (from 40% in 2000 to 24% in 2010), was to further drop to 20% under the new tax law. Also enacted were generous tax incentives for new enterprises, reaching up to five years of free taxes.

Finally, in September 2011, the government also introduced a controversial new property tax on top of existing ones for more than 5 million private houses and commercial properties, with the aim to achieve annual revenues of €2bn. The total bill for each household depends on the size of the property as well as the location but, crucially, it is not linked to any means testing or any ability-to-pay test. This tax hits at the core of the main pillar of socio-economic security of Greek families (Allen et al, 2004) – home ownership and small private property – and, in an unprecedented move, will be collected via electricity bills. In case of refusal to pay, electricity supply will be cut off from the property, a very controversial measure that met tough resistance by electricity workers' unions who declared that they will refuse to implement such orders.

Pensions

Already by 2008, the then Greek centre-right government had introduced a series of key changes in the basic parameters of the pension system. These changes strengthened the links between contributions and pension income, increased the statutory retirement ages and altered the calculation of pension benefits and included, among other measures, a

6% pension reduction penalty for each year of early retirement. However, the policy impetus towards further cutbacks accelerated following the eruption of the crisis. There have been two waves of pension reform: one as part of the first tranche of 'bailout' loan in May 2010 and one during the adoption of the 'medium-term fiscal strategy' that followed the fifth tranche in July 2011. The changes have touched upon stricter eligibility rules, lower replacement rates and lower contribution levels for employers. As it will be argued, the reforms not only curtail public spending, but also essentially question the 'social' and 'redistribution' principles of the system.

By May 2010, the PASOK government universally reduced pension incomes while the contribution years necessary for entitlement to a full pension increased from 35 to 40. For a full pension, the retirement age is set at 65 for both men and women, with early retirement at the age of 60 requiring 35 years of contributions. Previously, pension entitlement was calculated on the basis of the last five years of employment, but, since 2010, the formula includes all working years (GGG, 2010). Changes in eligibility were accompanied by curtailments in the pension replacement rates. Maxima on pension incomes were enacted (currently €2,500 per month) while a pension amount equal to two monthly payments (the so-called 13th and 14th month payments) was replaced by a fixed amount (€1,000), leading to further reductions. Substantial cuts to the so-called auxiliary pension supplements (which were financed solely by employer and employee contributions) were planned for 2012, which in some cases could reach 80%.

More important, however, was the regressive increases of replacement rates of future pensioners with higher wages and longer contribution records. According to new legislation, the pension system removes any redistribution from higher- to lower-income earners and, instead, uses contributions from low-income workers to finance higher pensions for high-wage earners. While the pension pot remains collective, the reward and the calculation of pension entitlement is divided among wage groups, with higher-income groups awarded pensions with higher replacement rates. The new average replacement rate for first-pillar pensions is to fall from 70% to 42.5%, while pensioners with disrupted and insufficient employment records are to be 'awarded' a pension with an, even lower, 30% replacement rate, a measure that will hit hard those in precarious employment and women. One can easily question why employees should continue to contribute with the same rates, only to receive substantially lower pensions.

In terms of financing, the Greek pension system is based on a tripartite agreement with employers, employees and the government. In June 2010, the government announced that it will halt all payments towards pension contributions and that the state will no longer finance the existing pension schemes. In 2012, employers' contributions will be reduced by 10% and it is estimated that further reductions up to 25% will apply by 2015. Additionally, the government charged pensioners earning more than €1,400 (monthly) a 3–7% 'solidarity tax' (LAFKA/ΛΑΦΚΑ) on first-pillar pensions in order to finance its own contributions towards social assistance supplements. Essentially, this tax is not an additional measure of government spending, but is replacing the government's contributions, thus reducing government total budgetary payments and possibly borrowing needs.

In October 2011, and in order for the Greek government to secure the 'sixth support package', it introduced a new pension reform, which curtails:

- 40% of the pension entitlement of retirees younger than 55 years old;
- 20% of all pension income that exceeds €1,200;
- 30% of any occupational pension that exceeds €150; and
- a minimum of 15% on all public sector lump sum payments (retrospectively since 1 January 2010).

At the same time, the government increased the 'solidarity tax' from 3% up to 14% of pension income in excess of €1,400, while for pensioners younger than 60 years old, an additional tax of 6% up to 10% will apply (Ministry of Finance, 2011). Additional new charges (2%) will be applied to public sector pensioners in order to fund future lump sum payments. In terms of eligibility changes, the government increased the requirement for early retirement from 35 to 37 contribution years.

Amid the cuts, the government introduced a plan for a basic pension of €360, to be introduced in 2018 and funded from general tax revenue and privatisations. This entitlement will be linked partly to the changes in GDP and price indexation in 2014 (INE–GSEE, 2010). So far, there is uncertainty as to who will be eligible for this basic pension but one cannot fail to admit that the model envisioned by the current government resembles a residual model (Venieris, forthcoming). Further to this, occupational pension schemes are under huge pressure, not least due to lower wages and employment rates that do not channel enough contributions to the funds. The government has reduced occupational schemes' institutional role through lower replacement rates, ceilings on contributions and the removal of state guarantees for occupational scheme entitlements. What emerges here is the government's intention to minimise the role of occupational pensions following the planned changes in collective bargaining. This conclusion is further supported by the fact that occupational pension funds have been forced to buy Greek state bonds in the past, a political act that essentially transferred pensioners' money to the government budget. According to the 26 October 2011 proposals, social insurance funds will be forced to accept a 50% 'haircut' in the value of the Greek bonds they own, and will most likely face solvency issues or even be taken over by the state, the very state that historically obliged them to buy its bonds.

Impact on economy and society

What was presented earlier represents only a selection from the plethora of austerity measures enacted and implemented since 2010. The PASOK government's aim was to meet the target of reducing the deficit to 8.5% of GDP by the end of 2011 with further substantial reductions in 2012; the ambition being to eliminate the deficit by 2013 and even generate some modest primary surplus. So far, these measures have had a devastating impact on the Greek economy, plunging it into a deep recession from which no end is yet visible. Since the beginning of the crisis in 2009, Greek GDP has contracted by nearly 15%, while just for 2011 the Greek GDP contracted by 6.9% (IOBE, 2012). Subsequently, public debt as a percentage of GDP increased spectacularly (see Figure 10.1) and is expected to increase even more as Greece continues to use its loans to solely serve its lenders while failing to revive its economy or drastically improve trade account balances. A confidential report on the sustainability of Greece's debt (IMF/EC/ECB, 2011; see also Eurobank Research, 2011) estimated that the debt will reach 172.7% of GDP in 2012 (approximately €373 billion) from 120% in 2009, the year prior to the IMF/EC/ECB 'bailout' loan. The rather over-optimistic estimations of the government for 2012 anticipated a further contraction of GDP by 2.5%, putting in serious doubt whether there will be any return to positive rates of GDP growth from 2013 onwards. Rapid decline in domestic demand, industrial output and bank savings, the collapse of consumer confidence, and dramatic increases in unemployment were to a large extent the results of the state taking billions of Euros out of the Greek economy by means of relentless taxation and substantial reductions in pensions and wages. In this respect, and regardless of the original causes of the Greek crisis, it is clear that the measures taken so far have failed spectacularly – as admitted by key ministers who oversaw their introduction and implementation (Chrissochoides, 2011; Venizelos, 2011) – and in fact led to the dramatic worsening of the crisis. This evaluation assumes of course that the measures' original aim was to assist Greece in recovering from the crisis with reforms that were to help the economy instead of primarily securing the interests of investors and banks, domestic and international; for, so far, these interests have been served remarkably well.

Nevertheless, more measures are planned for the very near future, which include further reductions in the wages of public sector employees, further tax increases, as well as the redundancies of thousands of public sector employees, and some are already being implemented. However, the 'jewel' in the crown of the measures demanded by the IMF/EC/ECB 'troika' as a prerequisite for the, twice-postponed, sixth tranche of the loan involves extensive privatisations and the selling of numerous public assets and government stakes in companies (the railway company, Hellenic Defense Systems, the port of Piraeus, Hellenic Postbank, the telephone company, motorways, Athens airport and the Greek lottery and related group of companies), which, by 2015, should raise €50 billion. As the German magazine *Der Spiegel* (2011) put it, this is nothing short of the ultimate 'selling off the Family Silver'.

For most Greeks, the reality under the austerity measures signalled 'the end of the world' as they knew it. The official unemployment rate more than doubled – from 7.7% in May 2008 to 17.7% in 2011 (Eurostat, 2012) – with women and especially young people hit particularly hard. For the latter, migration emerges as the main exit route to find employment. By 2010, official statistics recorded 27.7% of the population as at risk of poverty, the highest percentage among the EU15 (ELSTAT, 2012). Of children aged 0–17 years old, 23% were estimated to be at risk of poverty in 2010 while, in early 2012, the British media reported that increasing numbers of financially desperate Greek parents were giving their children to charities or institutions run by the Greek Church as they were unable to provide for their care (BBC World Service, 2012). At the same time, while businesses are either closing down or firing their employees, job creation has stagnated to bottom levels both in the private and public sector. Since January 2009 and up to August 2011, 68,000 businesses (15% of the total) have gone bust (*Kathimerini*, 2011) while thousands more (approximately 10% of the remaining total) reported severe difficulties in meeting their credit obligations (ICAP, 2011). According to statistics from the National Bank of Greece (2011), the distribution of private debt among household and business debt reached 59.2% and 60.2% of GDP, respectively. The same report highlighted serious delays in the payment of mortgages while non-payment of consumer loans had reached 20%. More recent surveys in the Athens area reported that six out of 10 households find it very hard to meet their tax obligations, loans and utility bills, while 52% reported difficulties in meeting even their basic everyday needs (IME-GSEBEE, 2012).

Apart from a small minority, most Greek families have experienced a dramatic decrease in their well-being and their socio-economic security, as repeated surveys in subjective economic hardship reveal. Gallup's ongoing Global Wellbeing Survey reported that 60% of Greeks were 'struggling' with their current life in 2011, with the percentage of those reported as 'thriving' collapsing from 44% in 2007 to 16% in 2011. Further, 'the percentage of Greeks who rate[d] their lives so poorly that they are considered "suffering" has more than tripled to 25% in 2011, from 7% in 2007' (Gallup, 2011a), the highest percentage among the Eurozone countries. Using questions measuring the Index of Personal Economic Distress (IPED), a recent epidemiological study conducted by the Athens University Research Institute for Psychiatric Health found that 16.5% of respondents reported very high economic distress in 2011, an increase of approximately 20.4% in comparison to 2009 (URIPH, 2011). The same study recorded substantial increases in feelings of melancholy, symptoms of clinical depression, suicidal thoughts and self-reported suicidal attempts. Regarding the latter, approximately 1.5% of the sample reported having made a suicide attempt when the respective figure for 2008 was 0.6%. Against this background, it comes as no surprise that the reported number of suicides attributed to economic hardship increased by 40% in the first five months of 2011 – the vast majority of which were males aged 35 to 60 – while the total number of suicides doubled in the years of the crisis (Violantzis, 2011). These are unprecedented figures for Greece, a country that traditionally recorded one of the lowest suicide rates in the EU.

At the same time, a large number of publicly provided services and sectors (eg hospitals, schools, universities, welfare services) are facing a double challenge. On the one hand, they have to offer their services under serious economic constraints, reduced staff and budgetary cuts as the state withdraws its funding. On the other hand, it is reasonable to assume that they will face substantial rises in the demand for their services given that large parts of the middle classes will begin withdrawing from private services as their incomes diminish, and, further, that the demand on the voluntary and non-governmental sector to fill the gap will intensify as some newspaper reports already indicate (*Eleftherotypia*, 2011).

Conclusion

The promises of a bright economic future that accompanied Greece's entry into the Eurozone in 2001 proved unfounded. Nine years later, Greece finds itself in a dire fiscal state, having surrendered substantial parts of its national economic sovereignty and having to implement very harsh austerity measures under the surveillance of its lenders. So far, the reforms prescribed by the ECB/EC/IMF and, to a large extent, implemented by Greek governments have done nothing to alleviate the crisis. Instead, they have severely reduced socio-economic security, undermined social cohesion and sunk the Greek economy into the deepest and most prolonged recession in recent memory, with no end in sight.

Similar to other nation states (Farnsworth and Irving, 2011), employment and social policy (especially pensions) were at the heart of the structural reforms. Although the character and direction of these reforms were similar to those attempted before the crisis, the adoption of the austerity measures accelerated their pace, and paved the way for even more reforms that previously met the resistance of the electorate, unions and many socio-professional groups. At the same time, in order to supposedly boost competitiveness and exports, both the PASOK government and the tri-party government of national accord that was in place at the time of writing – led by Mr Papademos, an unelected ex-banker – opted for a dual strategy of 'internal devaluation' and indiscriminate taxation of the working population and pensioners; that is, a strategy of severely reducing wages and labour costs, cutting welfare benefits, services and pensions, and increasing taxation regardless of ability to pay. It appears that the solution that these governments opted for was to transfer the risk, the cost and the responsibility of the economic crisis to the easy targets – the salariat working population and pensioners, in both the public and private sectors – and attack the main pillar of their socio-economic security – small private property – while keeping other sectors and practices protected. Instead of revisiting the role of the banking sector and the lack of investment in the real economy or seriously tackling tax evasion and corruption, endemic at the elite level in both the private and public sectors, or taking the reorganisation of the state seriously, both governments picked a different enemy: social and employment security, wage and pension incomes, and working standards.

Taking as a starting point that even after two years of austerity the Greek economy is in a weaker position, there is not much scope for any optimism regarding welfare futures. In political terms, the policies of the PASOK government came in striking contrast with its electoral promises of centre-left inspiration back in 2009 by putting forward one of the harshest and most punitive packages of pro-market austerity measures in recent European history. They have culminated in an anti-social policy that wreaked havoc upon Greek society, forcing large parts of the population into severe insecurity. With many households and family businesses indebted and unemployment soaring, the middle and working classes are experiencing a free fall in their living standards and their faith in the politico-economic institutions, domestic and European, has understandably been seriously challenged. In a 2011 Gallup poll, 77% of Greek respondents said that they had no confidence in the national government and 78% said that they had no confidence in financial institutions or banks (Gallup, 2011b). Further, in a 2011 Eurobarometer survey, 83% declared that they did not trust the government, 82% that they did not trust the parliament and 67% that they did not trust the EU (compared with an EU average of 47%), while 75% said that the EU was not effective in combating the crisis (Eurobarometer, 2011). Hence, our assertion that the crisis is not only economic, but deeply politico-economic, signalling the end of the post-dictatorship politico-economic regime in Greece while seriously questioning the direction of EU integration and the role of national democratic politics within it. We would expect a radicalisation of political opinion and behaviour to reaffirm territorial and political control over the Greek economy, but any misfortune will directly spark rifts with the EU. Still, as a consolation, Greeks do not seem to be all alone in the EU in questioning both their domestic regimes and the direction and scope of the further politico-economic integration of the Eurozone. Countries in the EU periphery are undergoing very similar 'treatments' and, if Greece is to be taken as the testing ground, they will also face pressures for substantial reductions in their national economic sovereignty. As Mark Mazower (2011), historian of modern Greece, put it:

> The European Union was supposed to shore up a fragmented Europe, to consolidate its democratic potential and to transform the continent into a force capable of competing on the global stage. It is perhaps fitting that one of Europe's oldest and most democratic nation-states should be on the new front line, throwing all these achievements into question. For we are all small powers

now, and once again Greece is in the forefront of the fight for the future.

Note

[1] The so-called spread represents the difference in the interest that financial market institutions are willing to charge in order to buy Greek government bonds over the interest they are willing to charge in order to buy German government bonds. A CDS is a financial instrument resembling, to some extent, a traditional insurance policy where, for a fee, the issuer of the CDS promises to pay the face value of the loan that the buyer of the CDS had issued in the case of loan default. However, there is a fundamental difference between a CDS and the classic insurance policy. A CDS can also be purchased by a buyer who has no exposure to the loan for which the CDS was issued. This so-called *naked* CDS is effectively a speculative bet where the buyer gains when the loan that s/he is not exposed to defaults. Even well-known figures of the financial world described *naked* CDSs as 'toxic' and called for their strict regulation (Soros, 2009).

References

Allen, J., Barlow, J., Leal, J., Maloutas, T. and Padovani, L. (2004) *Housing and welfare in Southern Europe*, Oxford: Blackwell.

Barclays Capital (2011) 'Global rates weekly', 17 June.

BBC World Service (2012) 'The Greek parents "too poor" to care for their children', 10 January. Available at: http://www.bbc.co.uk/news/magazine-16472310

Bordo, M.D., Cavallo, A.F. and Meissner, C.M. (2010) 'Sudden stops: determinants and output effects in the first era of globalisation 1880–1913', *Journal of Development Economics*, vol 91, pp 227–41.

Calvo, G.A. (1998) 'Capital flows and capital-market crises: the simple economics of sudden stops', *Journal of Applied Economics*, vol 1, no 1, pp 35–54.

Catao, L. (2006) 'Sudden stops and currency drops: a historical look', IMF Working Paper 06/133.

Chissochoides, M. (2011) 'Interview in Skai TV', 19 December. Available at: http://www.chrisohoidis.gr/el/ μπο ρ ούσ α μ ε –ν α– α π ο φύγ ο υ μ ε –τ ο–μ ν η μόν ι ο

Der Spiegel (2011) 'A fatally flawed recovery plan – Greece back on the brink', 6 June. Available at: http://www.spiegel.de/international/europe/0,1518,766809,00.html

Dizard, J. (2010) 'The Greek debt drama would be better played sooner', *Financial Times*, 2 November.

Eleftherotypia (2011) 'The surge in poverty drives many citizens in the soup kitchens of the municipalities of Attica', 11 December (in Greek). Available at: http://www.enet.gr/?i=news.el.article&id=331155, accessed 20 November 2011.

Eliadakis, T. (2011) *External borrowing in the birth and evolution of the New Greek State, 1824–2009*, Athens: Batsioulas (in Greek).

ELSTAT (2012) 'Research on income and living conditions of households for 2010 – Risk poverty', Greek Statistical Office, January 2012. Available at: www.statistics.gr/portal/page/portal/ESYE/BUCKET/A0802/PressReleases/A0802_SFA10_DT_AN_00_2010_01_F_GR.pdf, accessed on 5 May 2012.

Eurobank Research (2011) 'Greece macro monitor – latest macro & market developments', 24 October.

Eurobarometer (2011) 'Standard Eurobarometer Survey No 75', Spring.

European Commission (2011c) 'The Greek loan facility'. Available at: http://ec.europa.eu/economy_finance/eu_borrower/greek_loan_facility/index_en.htm

Eurostat (2012) Unemployment statistics, European Commission. Available at: http://epp.eurostat.ec.europa.eu/statistics_explained/index.php/Unemployment_statistics, accessed on 5 April 2012.

Farnsworth, K. and Irving, Z. (2011) 'Varieties of crisis', in K. Farnsworth and Z. Irving (eds) *Social policy in challenging times: economic crisis and welfare systems*, Bristol: Policy Press.

Featherstone, K. (2011) 'The Greek sovereign debt crisis and EMU: a failing state in a skewed regime', *Journal of Common Market Studies*, vol 49, no 2, pp 193–217.

Fotopoulos, T. (1985) *Dependent development: the case of Greece*, Athens: Exantas.

Fotopoulos, T. (1993) *The neo-liberal consensus and the crisis of the growth economy*, Athens: Gordios.

Gallup (2011a) 'In Greece, "suffering" up sharply to 25% – Greeks expect their lives in five years to be worse than they are today', 25 September. Available at: http://www.gallup.com/poll/149675/Greece-Suffering-Sharply.aspx

Gallup (2011b) 'Greece's government faces deficit in public trust', 4 November. Available at: http://www.gallup.com/poll/150578/Greece-Government-Faces-Deficit-Public-Trust.aspx

GGG (*Gazette of Greek Government*) (2010) 'Part III – changes in the memorandum of financial and economic policies, first issue', *Gazette of Greek Government*, 65. Available at http://apografi.gov.gr/wp-content/uploads/downloads/2012/02/N3845_2010.pdf,(accessed 5 April 2012).

Gibson, D.H., Hall, S.G. and Tavlas, G.S. (2011) *The Greek financial crisis: growing imbalances and sovereign spreads, Working Paper No 124*, Athens: Bank of Greece.

ICAP – Business Services Group (2011) '58% increase on businesses inconsistent loan payments', Business Report, 15 June (in Greek).

IME-GSEBEE (2012) *Income and household expenditure survey report, January 11*, Athens: IME-GSEBEE (in Greek).

IMF (International Monetary Fund) (2011) 'World economic outlook database', Washington DC: IMF.

IMF, EC (European Commission) and ECB (European Central Bank) (2011) 'Strictly confidential report – Greece: debt sustainability analysis', 21 October.

INE-GSEE (Institute of Employment of the General Confederation of Workers) (2008) *The Greek economy and employment, annual study*, Athens: INE-GSEE (in Greek).

INE-GSEE (2010) *The Greek economy and employment, annual study*, Athens: INE-GSEE (in Greek).

INE-GSEE (2011) *The Greek economy and employment, annual study*, Athens: INE-GSEE (in Greek).

IOBE (Foundation for Economic and Industrial Research) (2012) 'The Greek Economy 1/12', *Quarterly Bulletin*, No 67, March 2012. Available at: www.iobe.gr/media/engoik/112eng.pdf, accessed on 5 April 2012.

Karamesini, M. (2008) 'Continuity and change in the Southern European social model', *International Labour Review*, vol 147, p 1.

Karantinos, D. (2006) *European Employment Observatory contribution to the EEO, Autumn Review 2006 'Flexicurity'*, Athens: National Centre of Social Research.

Kathimerini (2011) 'The national confederation of Greek Commerce warns for further 58,000 business closures', 9 September (in Greek).

Katsimi, M. and Moutos, T. (2010) 'EMU and the Greek crisis: the political-economy perspective', *European Journal of Political Economy*, vol 26, no 4, pp 568–76.

Kofas, V.J. (1989) *Intervention and underdevelopment: Greece during the cold war*, Pennsylvania, PA: Pennsylvania State University Press.

Kostarelou, E. (2010) 'The eight wounds of the IMF memo', *Eleytherotypia Daily Newspaper*, 8 May (in Greek).

Kouvelakis, S. (2011) 'The Greek cauldron', *New Left Review* 72, November–December.

Lapavitsas, C. (2011) 'Euro exit strategy crucial for Greeks', *The Guardian*, 21 June.

Lapavitsas, C., Kaltenbrunner, A., Lambrinidis, G., Lindo, D., Meadway, J., Michell, J., Painceira, J.P., Pires, E., Powell, J., Stenfors, A. and Teles, N. (2010) 'The Eurozone between austerity and default', RMF occasional report.

Lazaretou, S. (2010) 'Financial crises and financial market regulation: the long record of an "emerger"', Bank of Greece Working Paper 140, October 2011. Available at: www.bankofgreece.gr/BogEkdoseis/Paper2011140.pdf, accessed on 5 April 2012.

Levandis, J.A. (1944) *The Greek foreign debt and the great powers, 1821–1898*, New York, NY: Columbia University Press.

LFA (Loan Facility Agreement) (2010) published by the Greek Ministry of Finance, 3 May. Available at: www.minfin.gr/content-api/f/binaryChannel/minfin/datastore/30/2d/05/302d 058d2ca156bc35b0e268f9446a71c92782b9/application/pdf/sn_ kyrwtikoimf_2010_06_04_A.pdf, accessed on 5 April 2012.

Mansori, K. (2011) 'Why Greece, Spain, and Ireland aren't to blame for Europe's woes', *The New Republic*, 11 October. Available at: www. tnr.com/article/economy/95989/eurozone-crisis-debt-dont-blame-greece

Mazower, M. (2011) 'Democracy's cradle, rocking the world', *The New York Times*, 29 June. Available at: /www.nytimes.com/2011/06/30/opinion/30mazower.html

Megas, C. (2010) 'The timetable of attack on industrial relations and social insurance', *Eleftherotypia Newspaper*, 5 May (in Greek). Available at: www.enet.gr/?i=news.el.article&id=158778, accessed on 20 November 2011.

Michael-Matsas, S. (2010) 'A Greek stage? All the world's a stage', *Radical Socialist*. Available at: www.radicalsocialist.in/articles/world-politics/P171-greece-and-the-world-capitalist-crisis, accessed on 5 April 2012.

Ministry of Finance (2011) 'Explanatory report: pension reforms, single wage policy, labour reserve, and other parameters for the application of the medium-term fiscal strategy 2012–2015', 6 October, Athens (in Greek).

National Bank of Greece (2011) 'Bulletin of conjectural indicators', Number 138, July–August 2011 (in Greek).

Nelson, R., Belkin P. and Mix, D. (2011) 'Greece's debt crisis: overview, policy responses, and implications', CRS Report for Congress, Congressional Research Service. Available at: www.fas.org/sgp/crs/row/R41167.pdf

Office of National Statistics (2010) *United Kingdom national accounts – the blue book*, Basingstoke: Palgrave Macmillan.

Panagopoulos, G. (2011) 'Labour law in Greece has been abolished', 6 October (in Greek). Available at: www.capital.gr/news.asp?id=1299089

Papadopoulos, T. (2006) 'Support for the unemployed in a familistic welfare regime: the case of Greece', in E. Mossialos and M. Petmesidou (eds) *Social policy developments in Greece*, Aldershot: Ashgate.

Papadopoulos, T. and Roumpakis, A. (2009) 'Familistic welfare capitalism in crisis: the case of Greece', ERI working paper series, WP-09-14.

Papadimitriou, D.B. and Wray, L.R. (2011) 'Confusion in Euroland', Levy Institute One-Pager No.20, November 23. Available at: www.levyinstitute.org/pubs/op_20.pdf, accessed on 5 April 2012.

Petmesidou, M. (1991) 'Statism, social policy and the middle classes in Greece', *Journal of European Social Policy*, vol 1, no 1, pp 31–48.

Petmesidou, M. (forthcoming) 'What future for the middle classes and "inclusive solidarity" in South Europe?' *Global Social Policy*, 11.

Polychroniou, C.J. (2011) 'An unblinking glance at a national catastrophe and the potential dissolution of the Eurozone', University of Massachusetts Amherst, Political Economy Research Institute, Research Brief, September.

PricewaterhouseCoopers (2010) 'PwC projects total UK public and private debt to hit £10 trillion by 2015', 9 November. Available at: www.ukmediacentre.pwc.com/News-Releases/PwC-projects-total-UK-public-and-private-debt-to-hit-10-trillion-by-2015-f84.aspx

Reuters (2011) 'Euro zone pushing for tougher policing of Greece', 18 October. Available at: www.reuters.com/article/2011/10/18/eu-greece-taskforce-idUSB5E7L501J20111018

Reuters (2012) 'EU/IMF aid schedule for Greece pushed back 3 months', 5 January. Available at: www.reuters.com/article/2012/01/05/eu-greece-loans-idUSL6E8C52JC20120105

SIPRI (Stockholm International Peace Research Institute) (2011) The SIPRI Military Expenditure Database. Available at http://milexdata.sipri.org/, accessed on 5 April 2012.

Soros, G. (2009) 'Opinion: one way to stop bear raids', *Wall Street Journal*, 24 March.

The Economist (2011) 'Greek statistics – numbers in action', 29 November.

URIPH (University Research Institute for Psychiatric Health) (2011) 'Results of national survey of psychiatric health', *Eleftherotypia Newspaper*, 5 October (in Greek). Available at: www.enet.gr/?i=news. el.ellada&id=315386, accessed on 20 November 2011.

Venieris, D. (1997) 'Dimensions of social policy in Greece', in M. Rhodes (ed) *Southern European welfare states: Between crisis and reform*, London: Frank Cass and Co.

Venieris, D. (forthcoming) *Economic crisis and social policy deregulation: the new 'Greece minor disaster' 2010–11, Greek Review of Social Sciences*, Athens: National Centre of Social Research (in Greek).

Venizelos, E. (2011) 'The DNA of the memorandum of understanding is leading us to a deadlock', 13 December (in Greek). Available at: www. inews.gr/143/antimnimoniakos-kai-o-exouthenomenos-venizelos-to-DNA-tou-mnimoniou-mas-odigei-se-adiexodo.htm

Violantzis, A. (2011) 'Surge in economic suicides', Interview in TVXS, 22 September (in Greek). Available at: http://tvxs.gr/news/ ε λ λάδ α/ εξαρση-στις«οικονομικές»αυτοκτονίες

ELEVEN

From opportunity to austerity: crisis and social policy in Spain

Javier Ramos-Díaz and Albert Varela

Introduction

Despite experiencing more than a decade of rapid growth and achieving a relatively healthy fiscal position, Spain has been hit hard by the financial crisis and is struggling to recover. The collapse of the housing bubble, which largely drove the so-called Spanish Miracle through high levels of corporate and household debt, led to a sharp increase in unemployment rates and put a share of the banking sector under significant strain.

The crisis was seen as an opportunity to implement a change of productive model towards a more productive knowledge-based economy with which to fund the future of the Spanish welfare model. The Spanish government initially reacted with an expansionary programme aiming to reduce unemployment, restore the credit flow and reinforce social protection. These measures, alongside declining public revenues (see Figure 11.1) and increased public spending, led to higher government debt (from 36.2% of Gross Domestic Product [GDP] in 2007 to 60.1% in 2010), but it is still well below the 85.5% average of the EU-17 (Eurostat, 2011a). The weak growth prospects, however, made financial markets wary of Spain's capacity to repay these debts and start demanding increasingly higher yields, while international institutions pressurised the government to introduce austerity measures.

The magnitude of the crisis and the pressures to enact austerity measures forced the government to turn its back on its initial plans. Impetus was then given to a programme of adjustment, deficit reduction and financial stabilisation to ensure medium-term budget sustainability and to placate markets. This is having both direct and indirect negative impacts on the welfare state, as austerity is leading to social spending cuts, and the loss of revenue and growing public deficits are hampering

Figure 11.1: Tax revenue (millions €)

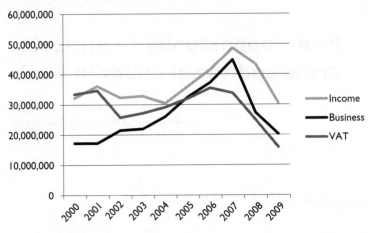

Source: INE (2011a).

the efforts to develop the limited Spanish welfare state into a much more comprehensive and universalistic model.

The Spanish Miracle and the crisis

Since the late 1990s and until the unfolding of the post-2008 crisis, Spain had experienced a remarkable decade of economic growth, hailed by many as an economic miracle. A booming economy, expanding at a faster pace than the EU average, Spain finally appeared to be catching up with the wealthier Northern European economies (see Figure 11.2). This process of convergence was attributed to the implementation by both Socialist and Conservative governments of labour market deregulation, liberalisation, privatisation and public spending reforms since the mid-1990s. Furthermore, the application of orthodox budgetary policy during the Conservative government from 1996 to 2004, in strict compliance with the EU Stability and Growth Pact, coupled with increases in employment rates and revenue from taxation and privatisation operations were identified as the drivers of the historically low levels of public debt and deficit. In fact, government budgets reached fiscal surpluses for three consecutive years prior to the crisis (see Figure 11.3).

While these reforms had a significant impact in facilitating growth, the role of Spain's integration into the EU is even more important to understanding the development of the economy. Access to Structural

Figure 11.2: Annual GDP growth, 1994–2010 (%)

Figure 11.3: Financial balances as a percentage of GDP, (+) surplus (–) deficit

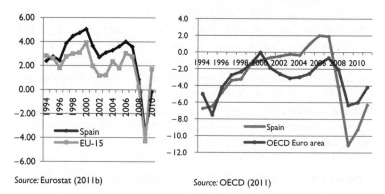

Source: Eurostat (2011b)

Source: OECD (2011)

Funds encouraged the process of convergence with Europe. Spain received €118 billion between 1986 and 2006, which contributed 1.5% of GDP every year between 1994 and 1999. These funds contributed to the modernisation of the Spanish economy and eased the painful process of industrial transformation (Ramos et al, forthcoming), which resulted in the dismantling of uncompetitive industries and the expansion of the service and construction sectors. This change was, nonetheless, only partially effective in modernising Spain's industry, as it failed to turn it into an advanced, highly productive and competitive economy.

Since 1987, GDP per capita grew at an average rate of 2.5%, while productivity barely increased by 1% on average, and at a meagre 0.6% from 2000 onwards (Doménech, 2008). Growth was mainly driven by high internal demand and increased employment rates, rather than by a rise in productivity. The large share of the market occupied by small- and medium-sized enterprises (SMEs), high regulatory costs, and low investment in research and development (R&D) and human capital are key causes for the large gap between Spain and the most productive economies. Huerta Arribas and García Olaverri (2008) have also shown that widespread deficiencies in organisational and human capital, such as excessively hierarchical management, the lack of internal flexibility, conflictual industrial relations in the workplace as well as insufficient lifelong learning programmes, also held back the productivity of Spanish businesses.

Additionally, Spain's poor record in innovation is a key factor behind this lack of competitiveness. Although R&D expenditure has grown in the past 15 years, it is still below the EU average as a percentage of

GDP. A breakdown of R&D investment since the mid-1990s reveals an interesting picture. Government spending in R&D has grown dramatically[1] from barely 50% to 101% of the EU average and higher education has experienced a less sharp but converging trend towards European levels. The main gap in expenditure is to be found in the private sector, which was spending less than 40% of the EU average in the mid-1990s and has not grown sufficiently in more than a decade (see Figure 11.4). It is clear that the private sector was much more inclined to make profits from the booming housing sector than to make a corresponding effort in innovation, thus contributing decisively to perpetuating a model based on low productivity.

Figure 11.4: Expenditure on R&D as a percentage of average EU-15

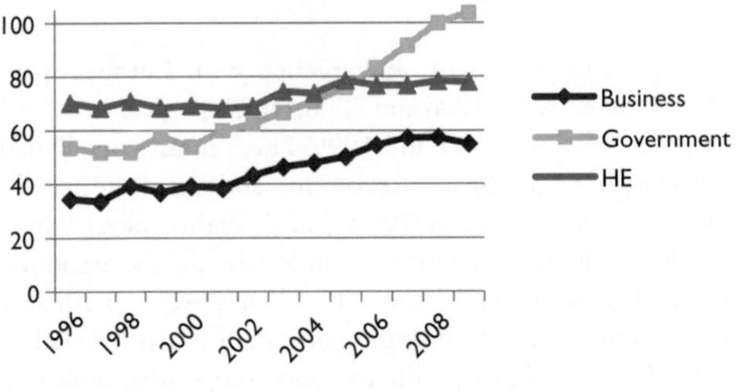

Source: Eurostat (2011c).

If there was ever a 'miracle' in Spain's growth, it was manifested in its capacity to grow very quickly on the basis of both low competitiveness and low productivity. Spain had run consistently high trade deficits during the boom, and between 2007 and 2008, current account deficits reached more than 10% of GDP, making it one of the most imbalanced economies in the world. As Etxezarreta et al (2011) have suggested, this performance would not have been possible outside the Economic and Monetary Union (EMU). The EMU quickly developed into a dual system, with central economies running current account surpluses and exporting heavily to peripheral economies, which would, in turn, run current account deficits. Peripheral economies would finance those trade deficits through increased borrowing from core economies. The expansionary money supply measures initially devised by the European Central Bank (ECB) to stimulate a weak Eurozone facilitated this phenomenon. Thus, instead of activating national demand in slower continental economies, low interest rate policies fuelled Spain's trade deficit and, most importantly, the housing boom. Wolf (2007) anticipated that as the position of the Eurozone members improved, and the money supply tightened, Spain would struggle to adjust. Not having invested sufficiently in the past decade in productivity, innovation and competitiveness, especially in the private sector, would prevent Spain from drawing on increased foreign demand to compensate for a large foreign-credit-fuelled current account deficit.

Likewise, the performance of the Spanish labour market and the significant growth of employment in the period 2000–07 (see Figure 11.5) can be explained to a large extent by easy access to cheap credit, expansionary real estate and services sectors in a context of increasing domestic demand, and the widespread use of temporary employment, which constitutes 32% of total employment and involves 66.6% of workers between the ages of 16 and 24. The expansion of these and other forms of atypical employment contracts, such as part-time work and self-employment, was made possible by a number of labour market reforms from the 1980s pushing for the flexibilisation of labour market regulations in a specific context of uncertainty and institutional rigidity (Polavieja, 2006).

Figure 11.5: Unemployment rates (%)

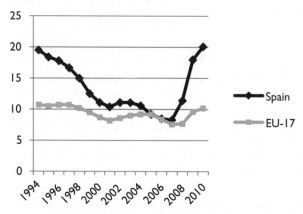

The key characteristics of the Spanish model of flexibility are: (a) its short-termist approach to reforms due to the economic urgencies of the country; and (b) the systematic use of temporary and casual contracts as a mechanism for managing staff, as opposed to mechanisms of internal or management flexibility (Rodriguez-Pinero Royo, 2004, p 217).

These developments have made the Spanish labour market segmented – with a small and shrinking core of protected workers and a growing periphery of unprotected workers with atypical contracts in the informal economy. The decade before the crisis saw employment grow very quickly, but it also led to an increasingly dual structure of the labour market in which precarious employment, characterised by job insecurity and/or low pay, made up an exceedingly large share of the labour market by European standards (Ramos, 2004).

The welfare state under the Spanish Miracle

In the context of growth and healthy public finances, the Socialist government gave impetus to one of the potentially most important social policy reforms since the transition to democracy. The Spanish welfare state is traditionally classed as part of the Southern European (Latin Rim) welfare cluster, characterised by a combination of corporatist social policies focused on status-maintenance and liberal social policies based on residualist principles (Ferrera, 1996). This welfare state underpins a strongly segmented labour market, with low levels of commodification for 'protected' workers (typically permanent full-time workers in the industrial and services sectors) and high levels of commodification for 'non-protected' ones (mainly temporary low-wage workers in low-skilled sectors).

Spain has relatively low levels of welfare expenditure, most of which is dedicated to old-age pensions, health care and unemployment compensation (see Table 11.1). In contrast, social services and family policy are the least developed pillars of the Spanish welfare state.

The household is the most important safety net for the non-protected, which must cope with high dependency with scarce public and private support. This explains the high degree of intergenerational dependency of children and pensioners. Yet there is a wide consensus that, until recently, family policy had not yet found its way into the political agenda, reflected in very low child benefit levels, limited day care provision for children under three and almost negligible policies to reconcile family life and employment (Flaquer, 2000; Naldini, 2003). Families, and more specifically women (IMSERSO, 2005), have borne the financial and practical burden of caring for their dependent relatives (Sarasa and Mestres, 2007). Therefore, although female employment rates have increased rapidly in the last two decades, from 31.5% in 1992 to their highest point ever at 54.9% in 2008, these are below the EU-27 average at the time of 59.1% (Eurostat, 2011e).

Table 11.1: Social expenditure by function as a percentage of GDP, 2007

	Spain	EU-27
Health	6.4	7.4
Old-age	6.5	10.0
Disability	1.6	2.0
Widowhood	1.9	1.7
Unemployment	2.4	1.3
Family and childcare	1.2	2.0
Housing	0.2	0.6
Social exclusion	0.3	0.3
Total	20.5	25.2

Source: Eurostat (2011d).

In order to correct the 'underperformance' of the Spanish welfare system, the Socialist government introduced a number of reforms fostering gender equality and pension adequacy from the mid-2000s.[2] But the most important of these new measures was the introduction of the 2006 Law to Promote Personal Autonomy and Care for Dependent People (39/2006), widely known as the Dependency Law (henceforth, DL), which would progressively overhaul the historically weak fourth pillar of the Spanish welfare state and provide services and benefits to people in need of support due to illness, disability or old age; thus, for the first time, the right of dependent citizens to receive appropriate care was recognised as a public responsibility.

The significance of this new legislation lay in its aim to drive Spain away from a typically Mediterranean welfare model and closer to the patterns of provision of continental welfare states. It is not, however, free from problems. Despite having universalist ambitions, the overall coverage of the DL is still low 'and thus the space left to familialism by default large' (Saraceno, 2010, p 37). Furthermore, the decentralised structure of the Spanish state results in uneven coverage across regions due to problems of administrative coordination (Kahale Carrillo, 2009), funding and implementation (Observatorio de la Dependencia, 2011) and enables some regional governments to partially veto and/or delay the execution of the measures contained in the DL.

In addition, the DL aimed to become a sustainable source of quality employment creation and a mechanism to regularise undeclared work. Importantly, it also introduced an allowance for 'non-professional carers', that is, for individuals who care for their dependent relatives.

The government expected the implementation of these measures to bring about more than 400,000 new jobs and to contribute decisively to tackling the shadow economy of care. Recent evidence shows that between the period of 2008 and 2009, when Spain's unemployment figures doubled, jobs in the social services sector grew significantly, unemployment rates barely increased and large numbers of informal carers became registered in the social insurance system (Rodriguez Castedo and Jímenez Lara, 2010, pp 26–30). Yet the growth in employment was not as high as the government expected.

On the one hand, the crisis is weakening the capacity of regional governments to fund the services as they apply their own austerity plans. On the other hand, despite the fact that the allowance for non-professional carers was initially conceived as an exceptional measure (Kahale Carrillo, 2009), that it has become the most popular of all the available services has been a source of concern for businesses and government, since it does not directly lead to employment creation and greater tax revenue (*El País*, 2010b).

The collapse of the housing bubble and its economic effects

While international institutions (OECD, 2005), economic commentators (*The Economist*, 2003; Wolf, 2007) and inspectors of the Spanish Central Bank (*El País*, 2011a) warned of the excessive growth of housing prices, ministers, both Conservative and Socialist, businessmen and experts were sceptical or they simply denied the existence of a real estate bubble (*El País*, 2008; García-Montalvo, 2008, pp 209–23). Since recent evidence suggests the important role of housing in leading the business cycle in Spain (Álvarez and Cabrero, 2010) and the strong contribution of the construction sector to economic growth (Bellod Redondo, 2007), it is easy to see why.

Garriga (2010, pp 249–50) highlights three structural changes behind the housing boom: a) demographic growth and an increase in activity rates, mainly due to immigration; b) a sharp drop in interest rates due to entering the EMU, from 12% in 1995 to 3.5% in 2003 to 5% in 2007; and c) the deregulation of land use, which led to a 28% increase in land made available for construction. The extent to which fundamentals singlehandedly drove the boom is unclear though (Case and Shiller, 2003). Fernández-Kranz and Hon (2006) suggest that income growth alone cannot satisfactorily explain the explosion in housing prices, and that in 2003, these were already between 24% and 34% above the long-term equilibrium level.

Recent research shows that expectations about housing market performance (García-Montalvo, 2006) and speculative behaviour (Bellod Redondo, 2011) are also key factors explaining the bubble. Local and regional authorities also had strong incentives to facilitate construction by emitting increasingly more building permits (see Figure 11.6), since tax revenue was strongly linked to land use (García, 2010). Finally, fiscal policies that made first-home mortgages tax deductible also played a role. These tax breaks incentivised home-ownership, an estimated 83.2% of the housing market by 2004 (Andrews and Caldera Sánchez, 2011, p 9), reduced tax revenue by €5,520 million in 2007, and favoured middle- to higher-income households (Rodríguez Méndez et al, 2010). They most importantly liberated disposable household income, which, in turn, allowed families to pay for up to 8.6% more expensive properties (García-Montalvo, 2005) than they would have otherwise bought, hence pushing up both prices and household debt.

Figure 11.6: Annual new mortgages, annual building permits (dwelling units) and average house prices (in € per m²)

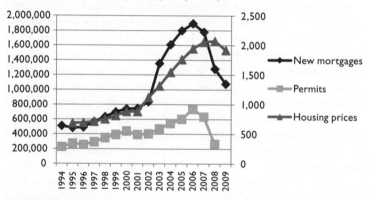

Source: INE (2011b).

The role of the Spanish banking sector in feeding the bubble was also crucial. It is important to underline that Spain is unique in having a banking sector roughly split between a few large commercial banks and a large heterogeneous number of savings banks or *cajas de ahorros*. The historical function fulfilled by *cajas*, which are private foundations with no formal ownership, was the extension of credit availability to, essentially local and regional, households, small businesses and governments. In the 1970s, the sector was deregulated and *cajas* quickly expanded beyond both retail banking and their natural regional boundaries, becoming involved in commercial operations and larger financial operations throughout Spain, as well as relying increasingly on wholesale credit markets (IMF, 2010). The regulation of *cajas* is, however, more fragmented and less effective than that of banks, and their governance arrangements are often highly politicised and clientelistic, which makes them often lacking in transparency.

In the run-up to the crisis, *cajas* engaged in riskier lending activities, most importantly, through large loans extended to construction companies and real estate developers, leaving Spain with one of the highest levels of non-financial corporate debt in Europe, second only to Ireland, and a higher than average household debt (IMF, 2011, p 6; MEH, 2011). Banking institutions thus became highly exposed to the fate of the housing market.[3] As the bubble collapsed, *cajas* found themselves with balance sheets flooded by bad loans and unable to repay mortgage-backed bonds and other securities sold to investors at the height of the property boom (*El País*, 2010a; *Financial Times*, 2010). This, coupled with the drop in interbank lending, led to a credit drought.[4]

Whatever the causes, in 2006, there were already signs of a slowdown in both prices and the turnaround of properties. Many commentators (*Financial Times*, 2006) were already warning of the consequences of an abrupt 'rise in interest rates, higher unemployment, a drop in demand for new homes, fewer tourists'. While the global financial crisis did not cause the Spanish recession, the loss of confidence and the ensuing credit drought acted as a catalyst for the collapse of the housing bubble.

The impact of the collapse of the housing bubble has been hard, creating: (a) higher unemployment, as many workers in construction and related sectors were made redundant (1 million workers, or 5% of total employment; see Figure 11.7); (b) pressure on banks, as mortgage credit and construction and real estate credit constitutes around 60% of bank loans; and (c) weaker public finances, as revenue that resulted from escalating asset prices and transactions was brought to a halt (IMF, 2009, p 18).

The crisis as an opportunity: the stimulus package

As explained earlier, the global financial crisis did not have an immediate effect on Spain's financial situation and the government was reluctant to publicly acknowledge the incoming problems before the 2008 general

Figure 11.7: Unemployment by economic sector in Spain since 2008 (in thousands of people)

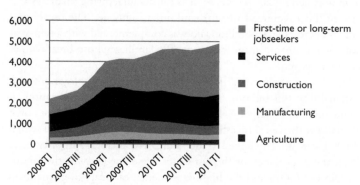

Source: INE (2011c).

election. In fairness, while other European countries were already experiencing slower growth and taking radical measures to stabilise their economies, Spanish macroeconomic indicators did not seem particularly troubling. The comparatively tighter regulation of Spanish banks, particularly the mechanism of 'dynamic loan-loss provisioning' by which banks were forced to use part of the revenue to increase their capital reserves during times of plenty, was heralded as the key factor for that success. The IMF (2009, p 19) estimated that dynamic provisioning in Spain 'bought banks about two years worth of cushion (€24 billion)'. This model was presented as a sound mechanism to curb excessive risk-taking and ensure the solvency of financial sector institutions in times of crisis (World Bank, 2009).

Still free from the pressures of international financial markets and the oncoming Eurozone debt crisis, the Spanish government saw the crisis as an opportunity to change the economic model that had underpinned the boom. The first plan of economic stimulus aimed at reducing unemployment and restoring the credit flow, while reinforcing social protection.

The Plan E (Spanish Plan for Economic Stimulus and Employment)[5] enacted via Decree-Law 9/2008, is the most important counter-cyclical package implemented during the last three years. It consists of 99 measures intended to soften the impact of the crisis for businesses, by facilitating access to credit and increasing liquidity, and households, by boosting disposable income and financing employment creation. For businesses, mainly SMEs, the Plan opened new lines of credit

(€29 billion) and reduced taxes (€17 billion), as well as providing funds to support certain key sectors such as car manufacturing (Plan VIVE),[6] tourism (Plan Renove Tourism)[7] and other industries. The fiscal boost for families reached €14 billion and was complemented with a two-year moratorium on mortgage payments for families whose breadwinner was unemployed.

The Local Authorities' Investment Fund for Employment and Sustainability (€8 billion) was launched to finance the creation of employment in 10 target sectors.[8] According to the government's own calculations, the Local Investment Fund created 400,000 jobs, of which 280,000 were directly linked to the Fund, in 8,000 local authority areas. Given the importance of the construction sector (11% of the labour force and of GDP) and the high dependency of local government on it, an important part of the financed projects (61%) were devoted to renovation and improvements of public spaces and basic facilities and infrastructures. Therefore, the Local Investment Fund was accused of just helping the construction sector to get its breath back for a while.

Plan Avanza 2 (2009), itself part of Plan E, sought to promote a change in the economic model through information and communication technologies (ICTs) and sustainable growth for the period 2010–15. It is included within the framework of different European initiatives (mainly Europa-2020 and e-2010) and consists of five action areas: infrastructures; trust and security; technological training; digital content and services; and ICT sector development. It had a budget of €9 billion and focused on achieving the following 10 objectives:

1. promoting innovative ICT processes in public administration;
2. spreading ICT in health care and welfare;
3. modernising the education and training model through the use of ICTs;
4. spreading telecommunication networks and increasing their capacity;
5. spreading trustworthy ICT among citizens and enterprises;
6. increasing the advanced use of ICT solutions among citizens;
7. spreading the use of ICT business solutions in enterprises;
8. developing technological skills in the ICT sector;
9. strengthening the digital content sector and intellectual property rights in the current technological context and within the Spanish and European legal framework; and
10. developing green ICT.

Overall, Plan E amounted to 1.1% of GDP in 2008, 2.3% in 2009 and 2.6% in 2010, making it the second-greatest stimulus effort in the EU. If other social measures adopted to mitigate the effects of the crisis are taken into consideration, the total fiscal effort amounts to 4.9% of GDP.

Conservative and neo-liberal commentators accused the Plan of being a new episode of inefficiency embedded in demand-side solutions of Keynesian inspiration. They referred to an oft-quoted Keynesian motto 'it is preferable to pay workers to dig holes in the ground, and fill them in again, rather than deprive the economy of the multiplier effect of their wages' to illustrate how they saw the Plan. From their standpoint, these plans did not address Spain's structural problems because they lacked a deeper overhaul of the 'rigid' labour market. Instead of increasing the public deficit, the government should cut public spending, introduce tax breaks and deregulate the labour market, which would reduce unemployment (20.3% in 2011) and stop the fiscal deterioration, which turned from a 2.2% surplus in 2007 to an 11% deficit in 2010. The Spanish Business Confederation (CEOE) proposed reducing the high variety of existing contracts into a single wide-ranging one (*Contrato Único*), aimed at reducing redundancy compensation and costs.[9]

Spain under pressure: austerity and reforms

As the stimulus package was implemented, the Eurozone was under increasing pressure. The debt crises of Greece, Ireland and Portugal, and the subsequent bailouts by the International Monetary Fund (IMF) and the EU, had put Spain in the spotlight. Although Spain's ratio of debt to GDP has moved up from 36.1% in 2007 to 60.0% in 2010, it is still among the lowest of the major Western economies. This low level of public debt should imply lower interest payments and the relief of some pressure on refinancing needs. Yet the high rates of private debt and growing public deficits and unemployment rates have been frequently invoked by rating agencies to downgrade the reliability of the Spanish economy and, by extension, to increase interest rates on Spanish bonds (see Figure 11.8).

De Grauwe (2011) highlights the paradox that while the UK has significantly worse prospects for both its sovereign debt and deficit than Spain, it is the yield on Spanish government bonds that has increased strongly relative to the UK's. This phenomenon is caused by Spain's issuing debt in a currency over which it has no control. Membership of the Eurozone makes Spain vulnerable to the attacks of financial markets because the debt crisis leads to a liquidity crisis and increased

Figure 11.8: Interest rates on 10-year bonds (Spain and Germany)

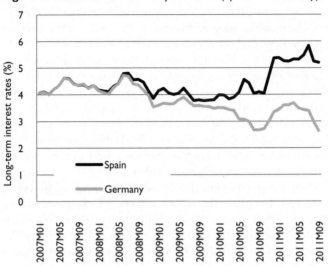

risk of default. In addition, it can force Spain 'into a bad equilibrium, characterised by austerity programs that fail to reduce budget deficits because they lead to a downward economic spiral and punishing interest rates' (de Grauwe, 2011, p 9).

For Krugman (2011), too, all of Spain's problems eventually revert back to its membership in an EMU 'without fiscal and labour market integration'. The Spanish boom led to an over-appreciation of wages relative to the more advanced European economies, which, in turn, were financing that boom. The bust led, first, to a surge in unemployment, with significant barriers to finding jobs in other EU countries, and, second, the inability of Spain to export its way out of its high current account deficit. Loss of revenue, increased spending and lack of competitiveness coupled with the drop in demand resulting from the austerity packages being implemented in Spain and elsewhere makes that impossible. Since currency devaluation is no longer an option, the only way to boost competitiveness would be, as Rodrik (2010) shows, to 'engineer a one-time across-the-board reduction in nominal wages and prices for utilities and services', but strict anti-inflationary policies by the ECB make that impossible, leaving Spain and other countries facing the choice between a long spell of low growth and high unemployment, or a default on their debts.

Adjustment, discipline and stabilisation

The government reacted with a programme of economic adjustment and investment discipline to ensure medium-term budget sustainability and placate the financial markets.The government budget for 2010 forecasts a reduction of the public deficit of 6% of GDP in 2011, in contrast with the 3% of GDP target imposed by the European Stability and Growth Pact for 2012. According to government estimations, the public debt level will stabilise at around 70% of GDP in 2012 and 2013, below the current and expected debt-to-GDP ratio of the Eurozone.

In order to restore market confidence and avoid bank-runs, the government's efforts to strengthen bank balance sheets have focused on guaranteeing bank loans and debts, increasing guarantees for private deposits, buying toxic assets and restricting short-selling. Furthermore, a process of reorganisation of the banking sector was initiated with the creation in 2009 of the Fund for Orderly Bank Restructuring (FROB). The main function of this Fund is to support (through capital injections) integration processes and mergers between *cajas*, as well as to take over the administration of weaker institutions to facilitate restructuring.

A complementary measure was the enacting of two decree-laws, in 2010 and 2011, reforming the Savings Banks Law.This new legislation allowed *cajas* to pursue their activity through commercial banks to tap capital markets and improve their position, emphasised governance reform and professionalisation, and introduced 8% to 10% capital ratios to improve solvency.The Banco de España (BdE), following that mandate, organised a series of mergers, processes of private and public capital injection, the nationalisation of three institutions (€4.75 billion), and conversions to commercial banks (IMF, 2010, p 79; BdE, 2011a). By the end of September 2011, the first stage of recapitalisation of the banking sector had been completed, with an estimated €7.55 billion contributed by the FROB and €5.84 billion in private capital.The key results are an overall €105 billion balance sheet write-down, the dramatic downsizing of the banking sector (45 to 15 institutions) and improved governance arrangements (BdE, 2011b). And yet, despite these reforms, the extent to which more waves of recapitalisation and nationalisation will be needed (*El País*, 2011b) and lending to business and families will resume again (*El País*, 2011c) remains unclear.

Other important measures included in this plan of adjustment are: (i) a reduction in public investment and development; (ii) a reduction in the wages of public sector workers of an average of 5% and a pay freeze in 2011; (iii) the suspension of pension adjustments in 2011, with the exception of minimum and non-contributory pensions; (iv) a rationalisation in health-related expenditure; and (v) the elimination of the birth allowance.

In January 2010, a reform of the social security system was approved, which consisted of increasing the retirement age from 65 to 67 years from 2013, increasing the minimum retirement age and an increase in the years of contributions required for benefit entitlement. Contributions to obtain full pension benefits have increased from 35 to 37 years – with a minimum of 15 years to obtain 50% of the full pension. Eligibility for early retirement is now possible only after 33 years of contribution and it is delayed from 61 to 63 years. A penalisation of 7.5% per year is applied to early retirement, whereas the voluntary extension of working life is encouraged. For careers below 25 years, a year of delay implies a 2% increase in the pension benefit, for careers between 25 and 37 years, the reward is 2.75%, and for careers over 37 years, the pension benefit increases by 4%. The pension reforms also included an improvement of minimum pension benefits for pensioners living alone. According to government estimates, the reform will imply savings for the pension system of around 3.5% of GDP in 2050 (2.8% in 2040 and 1.4% in 2030).

Despite efforts to curb the deficit, the government also enacted long-term measures to continue to support a change in the economic model, albeit this time focusing on the supply side. The Sustainable Economic Law 2011 (SEL) was passed to foster: (i) the modernisation of the regulatory framework of the Spanish economy, in particular the simplification of procedures for the creation of new businesses; (ii) the reduction of administrative burdens on businesses; (iii) fiscal sustainability, more specifically, improving the transparency of local authorities' budgeting process and establishing stricter limits to the renegotiation of and amendments to construction and concession contracts; (iv) the improvement in the regulation of network industries (bolstering efficiency and competitiveness in network industries that may spill over to industry and services activities in general); and (v) a more market-oriented model for vocational training and the elimination of the historical fiscal and regulatory bias in favour of housing investments.

It is expected that the application of the SEL will save money and time due to the simplification of procedures for the creation of companies, which will potentially increase GDP by about 0.07% during the next decade. The impact of the improvement of professional education alone, through a shift from low-skill to high-skill workers, will amount to an increase of up to 1.3% of GDP by 2020.

At the end of the summer of 2011, a number of measures were approved. The most significant is the introduction of a constitutional cap on the structural public deficit, supported by both main parties, Socialist and Conservative, and opposed by all other smaller parties. The amendment foresees a gradual reduction of deficit limits throughout this decade, which would culminate in a maximum structural deficit of 0.4% by the year 2020 (*The Guardian*, 2011). Despite being welcomed by the IMF and international markets, many economists have shown their unease about a reform that essentially restricts fiscal policy, the only tool left to the Spanish government to pursue long-term public investment. Furthermore, given that consensus on what makes an optimum deficit level is lacking, this reform essentially enshrines ideology in the constitution (*El País*, 2011e).

The wealth tax was reintroduced in September 2011 (Decree-Law 13/2011) after having been disabled in 2008. In 2007, it raised €2.12 billion, 72% of which was paid for by the richest 9.6% of taxpayers. It was then argued by the government that it had a regressive impact, as it taxed middle-class households. In addition, monthly VAT returns were introduced. The government estimated that this would bring a stimulus to the economy of an estimated €7.8 billion for 2009. When the tax was reintroduced in 2011, it was approved without opposition, as no party could afford to oppose taxing the wealthy before the election in late November (*El País*, 2011d). The government argued that it would raise €1 billion,[10] and would lead to the creation of 3,000 jobs, but critics suggested that the new reformed wealth tax had lost revenue power and that, given the problems associated with identifying the wealthy, it would have a relatively low impact. It was also strongly criticised by the CEOE (*El País*, 2011e), which accused the wealth tax of being a populist electoral gimmick.

Labour market reforms

A number of labour market reforms were introduced in the period from 2009 to 2011 seeking to clarify the grounds for objective dismissals, to increase internal flexibility, to adapt collective bargaining to the changing economic circumstances and to increase productivity through more efficient training programmes. An initial package of measures was introduced to reduce unemployment by subsidising jobs. Tax relief (5%) was given to small businesses with fewer than 25 employees and with a turnaround smaller than €5 million to hire unemployed people. It also brought in a bonus of €125 per month to top up the social security contributions for employers who hired unemployed people with family dependants until 31 December 2010. These measures also applied to self-employed workers, who maintained or expanded their staff. Measures to boost part-time work were also implemented. Reductions in social security contributions (30%) were devoted to firms creating new part-time jobs for workers less than 30 years of age and the long-term unemployed.

Dismissal payments were reduced from 45 days per year to 33 or 20 days. The advanced notice required in cases of objective dismissals was reduced from 30 to 15 days. In cases of objective dismissal, eight days of salary per year is paid by a fund paid for by employers' contributions. The reform sets limits on the duration of fixed-term contracts and increases their termination costs to 12 days per year of employment. Internal flexibility gains relevance in the reform. At least 5% of total working hours can now be distributed according to business needs, allowing companies to increase working hours during periods of increasing demand and peaks of production.

The modification of the collective bargaining framework has attracted most attention because social agents, mainly employers' associations, have repeatedly postponed the agreement. The reform has focused on fostering flexibility for companies to adapt to their specific circumstances, with a stronger link between productivity and salaries. Under the new legislation, an agreement between workers and managers is sufficient to opt out of a collective bargaining agreement. Failure to reach an agreement can lead to a mediation process lasting for a maximum of one month.

Bargaining at the workplace level is incentivised over sector-level agreements in relation to wages, the structure of collective bargaining, the distribution of working hours and the adoption by businesses of the professional classification system. Noticeably, collective bargaining agreements can now be changed if economic conditions change with respect to the existing conditions at the time of signature. In order to encourage renegotiations, a maximum negotiation period is established to get a new agreement – eight months for agreements lasting two years or less and 14 months for agreements over two years. A wages clause was established to allow wage adjustment if the wage level reduces the competitive position of the firm or if a sustained decrease of the firm's revenues is proved. Finally, the reform eliminated existing restrictions on for-profit employment agencies, so that they were authorised from January 2011.

A specific plan of training and research programmes was implemented to stimulate growth in productivity and improve the labour prospects of trainers and researchers. Companies hiring young workers for training now have to contribute to the social security system. The period to benefit from training contracts was extended from four to five years and the age of beneficiaries was raised to 24. Salary conditions were improved for apprentices and trainees, who would now earn 100% of the minimum wage in the second year. This is applied preferentially to unemployed, unskilled workers up to the age of 30, long-term unemployed workers over 45, workers with disabilities and female victims of domestic violence.

Furthermore, a training programme for unemployed graduates was started in 2009, with a budget of €70 million. The government would subsidise the enrolment of unemployed benefit claimants between the ages of 25 and 40 into official master's degrees provided by public universities.

Activation programmes for the unemployed have also been reinforced. Those unemployed who no longer receive unemployment benefits should actively follow an individualised programme of labour market integration in order to get further additional benefits. Public employment services are obliged to guide and monitor the unemployed in this process of integration.

Conclusions

By 2008, the Spanish economy had been growing robustly for more than a decade, thus converging with its European counterparts. Employment, income and public finances were at all-time highs. This economic conjuncture was used by the government to introduce a number of reforms in the welfare state, most importantly, the Dependency Law, which aimed to push Spain away from the Mediterranean welfare model and closer to Continental and Northern European standards.

Spain's prosperity was not, however, supported by rising productivity, but was rather stimulated by the inflows of European Structural Funds, low interest rates in the Eurozone and increased internal demand. Indeed, the main engine of the so-called Spanish Miracle was a housing bubble fed by cheap credit, the deregulation of land use, speculation and fiscal policy.

Despite the banking sector showing signs of resilience in the face of the first wave of the global financial crisis, the decline in confidence and the credit crunch brought the housing bubble to an end. The labour market, public revenue and, ultimately, the banking sector followed suit. The government saw this crisis as an opportunity to kick-start a much-needed process of economic transformation, but soon markets started targeting the country for its weak growth prospects due to the sharp decline in competitiveness during the boom. Thus, the initial stimulus packages aiming to reduce unemployment, restore the credit flow and reinforce social protection gave way to a programme of adjustment, deficit reduction and financial stabilisation to ensure medium-term budget sustainability and to placate the markets.

The current financial crisis is having both direct and indirect negative impacts on the welfare state. Loss of revenue and the growing public deficit are preventing the development of the welfare state into a much more comprehensive and universalistic model. Austerity is forcing the government to turn its back on its initial plans to push for the modernisation of the economy and embrace a knowledge-based, highly productive model with which to fund the future of Spanish welfare.

A lack of competitiveness, the decentralised nature of the state and membership in an uncoordinated EMU experiencing a crisis of governance are challenging the capacity of Spain to recover. It is difficult to foresee the problems that the new Conservative government will have to cope with and the measures it will be able to enact. Given that new problems are unfolding, and that instability is rife, as we finish this article it is thus difficult to foresee the future developments of this crisis. It seems clear, however, that policies will continue to be heavily shaped by the pressure of financial markets, particularly as long as the Eurozone fails to consolidate a model of fiscal governance.

Notes

[1] Before the crisis, the Socialist government gave R&D spending the largest boost in the budget (a 260% increase) and augmented funding dedicated to scholarships, which resulted in an increase in both the number of students covered and the amount received.

[2] For example: (i) the Law for Effective Equality between Men and Women (including paternity leave and improvements in maternity services); (ii) the creation of a Basic Income programme to foster the emancipation of young people; (iii) increased funding in education (historically high 5% of GDP) and coverage for childcare and early years education; (iv) a 40% funding increase in health care; (v) a minimum wage increase (from 460 to 600 Euros per month); and (vi) an increase in pensions, particularly the lowest, and dramatic improvement in the provision of the Social Security Fund.

[3] By 2011, housing-related companies had an accumulated debt of more than €413 billion (Cinco Días, 2011) and default rates had increased to over 17%.

[4] In just three years, from 2007 to 2010, the proportions of loan applications by businesses that failed or were only partially successful increased sharply from 3% and 9.7% to 13.2% and 27.8%, respectively, while fully successful applications collapsed from 87.3% to 59.1%. Meanwhile, the annual number of bankruptcy filings have soared from barely a thousand in 2005 to around 6,000 in 2010 (INE, 2011).

[5] The Plan E was divided into five main targets: (i) supporting families; (ii) supporting companies; (iii) raising employment rates; (iv) financial and budget measures; and (v) economic modernisation.

[6] The purpose of the Plan was to reduce the number of contaminating vehicles on the roads and, at the same time, give a boost to the automobile sector. Those who wanted to obtain a new car worth less than €20,000 and exchanging a car that was at least 15 years old could save interest payments of €2,000 per car. The new vehicle, however, must have a CO_2 emission level of less than 120g/km.

[7] The Plan sought to establish a competitive and sustainable tourism sector by 2020 by offering low-interest loans for tourist companies to improve energy savings or the implementation of environmental quality management systems. Up to 90% of investment costs would be financed, up to a maximum of €1 million, and with a fixed interest rate of 1.5% (budgeted at €1 billion).

[8] These were as follows: (i) renovation or improvement of urban public spaces and industrial promotion; (ii) facilities and infrastructures for the road network, sewerage, lighting or telecommunications; (iii) construction, renovation or improvement of social, health care, funeral, educational, cultural or sporting facilities; (iv) environmental protection, prevention of pollution and the promotion of energy efficiency; (v) elimination of architectural barriers; (vi) conservation of local and historic heritage; (vii) construction or improvement of water supply and waste-water treatment facilities; (viii) improvements in road safety and the promotion of sustainable urban mobility; (ix) fire prevention; (x) promotion of tourism.

[9] Instead of the current 45 or 33 days per year of redundancy benefits, they proposed to accumulate rights, starting with eight days per year during the first year of contract and increasing it progressively until it reaches 33 days.

[10] The revenue estimates announced by the government were halved shortly after by Inspectors of the Tax Office.

References

Álvarez, L.J. and Cabrero, A. (2010) 'Does housing really lead the business cycle?', Banco de España Working Papers 1024, Banco de España.

Andrews, D. and Caldera Sánchez, A. (2011) 'Drivers of homeownership rates in selected OECD countries', OECD Economics Department Working Papers, No 849, OECD Publishing.

BdE (2011a) 'Note on the savings bank restructuring process: situation in July 2011', 13 July, Madrid.

BdE (2011b) 'The Banco de España takes stock of the financial system recapitalisation process envisaged under RD-l 2/2011', 30 September, Madrid.

Bellod Redondo, JF (2007) 'Crecimiento y especulación immobiliaria en la economia española', *Principios*, no 8, pp 59–82.

Bellod Redondo, J.F. (2011) 'Detección de burbujas inmobiliarias: el caso español', *Contribuciones a la Economía*, vol 5, May.

Case, K.E. and Shiller, R.J. (2003) 'Is there a bubble in the housing market?', *Brookings Papers on Economic Activity*, vol 2, pp 229–362.

Cinco Días (2011) 'La morosidad del credito al sector del ladrillo alcanza el record del 17%', 19 September.

De Grauwe, P. (2011) *The governance of a fragile Europe*, CEPS Working Document no 346, Brussels: Centre for European Policy Studies,

Domenech, R. (2008) *La evolución de la productividad en España y el capital humano*. Documento de trabajo 141/2008. Madrid: Laboratorio de Alternativas.

El País (2008) '¿Burbuja? ¿Qué burbuja?', 7 July.

El País (2010a) 'Las cajas acaparan el riesgo del ladrillo', 6 February.

El País (2010b) 'Los cuidados en casa frenan el empleo', 3 May.

El País (2011a) 'Los inspectores del Banco de España culparon a Caruana de los problemas de la banca con el "ladrillo"', 21 February.

El País (2011b) 'Cajas nacionalizadas', 1 October.

El País (2011c) 'La oposición critica el impuesto de patrimonio pero no lo frenará', 21 September.

El País (2011d) '¿Impuesto de patrimonio? Seamos serios y no hagamos campaña', 18 September.

El País (2011e) 'Las dudas de los economistas', 25 August.

Etxezarreta, M., Navarro, F., Ribera, R. and Soldevila, V. (2011) 'Boom and (deep) crisis in the Spanish economy: the role of the EU in its evolution', paper presented at the 17th Workshop on Alternative Economic Policy in Europe, Vienna, September.

Eurostat (2011a) Government Finance Statistics,. D.o.i.: http://epp. eurostat.ec.europa.eu/portal/page/portal/government_finance_ statistics/data/main_tables

Eurostat (2011b) National Accounts. D.o.i. http://epp.eurostat. ec.europa.eu/portal/page/portal/national_accounts/data/main_tables

Eurostat (2011c) Science, Technology and Innovation. D.o.i. http:// epp.eurostat.ec.europa.eu/portal/page/portal/science_technology_ innovation/data/main_tables

Eurostat (2011d) Social Indicators. D.o.i. http://epp.eurostat.ec.europa. eu/portal/page/portal/social_protection/data/main_tables

Eurostat (2011e) Employment and Unemployment (LFS). D.o.i. http://epp.eurostat.ec.europa.eu/portal/page/portal/employment_ unemployment_lfs/introduction

Fernández-Kranz, D. and Hon, M.T. (2006) 'A cross-section analysis of the income elasticity of housing demand in Spain: is there a real estate bubble?', *Journal of Real Estate Finance and Economics*, vol 32, pp 449–70.

Ferrara, M. (1996) '"The southern model" of welfare in social Europe', *Journal of European Social Policy*, vol 6, no 1, pp 17–37.

Financial Times (2006) 'Boom time Spain waits for the bubble to burst', 8 June.

Financial Times (2010) 'Spanish take steps to rescue savings banks', 9 May.

Flaquer, L. (2000) 'Family policy and welfare state in Southern Europe', Working Paper, No 185, Institut de Ciéncies Polítiques i Socials Prieto.

García, M. (2010) 'The breakdown of the Spanish urban growth model: social and territorial effects of the global crisis', *International Journal of Urban and Regional Research*, vol 34, no 4, pp 967–80.

García-Montalvo, J. (2005) 'Algunas reflexiones sobre la tributación y las desgravaciones a la vivienda', *Economistas*, Marzo, pp 191–7.

García-Montalvo, J. (2006) 'Deconstruyendo la burbuja inmobiliaria: expectativas de revalorización y precio de la vivienda en España', Papeles de Economía Española, no 109.

García-Montalvo, J. (2008) *De la quimera inmobiliaria al colapso financiero*, Barcelona: Antoni Bosch.

Garriga, C. (2010) 'El papel de la construcción en el auge y la caída de los precios de la vivienda en España' in S. Bentolila et al *La crisis de la economía española*, Madrid: Fedea.

Huerta Arribas, E. and García Olaverri, G. (2008) *La frontera de la innovación: la hora de la empresa española*, Documento de Trabajo 139, Madrid: Laboratorio de Alternativas.

IMF (International Monetary Fund) (2009) *Spain: Article IV consultation – staff report; staff supplement; public information notice on the executive board discussion*, IMF Country Report, No 09/128, Washington, DC: International Monetary Fund.

IMF (2010) *Spain: Article IV consultation – staff statement; staff supplement; staff report; statement by the executive director for Spain; and public information notice on the executive board discussion*, IMF Country Report, No 09/128, Washington, DC: International Monetary Fund.

IMF (2011) *Spain: Staff report for the 2011 Article IV consultation*, IMF Country Report, No 11/215, Washington, DC: International Monetary Fund.

IMSERSO (Instituto de Mayores y Servicios Sociales) (2005) *La Atención a las Personas en Situación de Dependencia en España. Libro Blanco*, Madrid: Ministerio de Trabajo y Asuntos Sociales.

INE (Instituto Nacional de Estadística) (Office for National Statistics) (2011a) Información tributaria: Estadísticas de Impuestos. Available at: http://www.ine.es/jaxi/menu.do?L=0&type=pcaxis&path=%2Ft45/p062&file=inebase

INE (2011b) Estadísticas financieras y monetarias: hipotecas. D.o.i. www.ine.es/jaxi/menu.do?L=0&type=pcaxis&path=%2Ft30%2Fp149&file=inebase

INE (2011c) Encuesta de Población Activa. D.o.i.: http://www.ine.es/jaxi/menu.do?type=pcaxis&path=/t22/e308_mnu&file=inebase&N=&L=0

Kahale Carrillo, D.T. (2009) *La cobertura de la situación de dependencia*, Estudios de Progreso 42/2009, Madrid: Fundación Alternativas.

Krugman, P. (2011) 'Can Europe be saved?', *New York Times*, 16 January.

Ministerio de Administraciones Públicas (2008) *State fund for local investment*, Madrid: MAP.

MEH (Ministerio de Economía y Hacienda) (2010) *The sustainable economy law*, Madrid: MEH.

MEH (2011) 'Private indebtedness: some highlights', 29 July.

Ministerio de Política Territorial (2009) *Informe sobre el fondo estatal de inversión local para el empleo y la sostenibilidad*, Madrid: MPT.

Naldini, M. (2003) *The family in the Mediterranean welfare state*, London: Frank Cass.

Observatorio de la Dependencia (2011) 'Desarrollo e implantación territorial de la ley de promoción de la autonomía personal y atención a las persona en situación de dependencia: Informe de evolución de la ley cuatro años después', Madrid.

OECD (Organisation for Economic Co-operation and Development) (2005) *Economic survey of Spain*, Paris: OECD Publishing.

OECD (2011) OECD.StatExtracts. D.o.i: http://stats.oecd.org/

Polavieja, J. (2006) 'The incidence of temporary employment in advanced economies: why is Spain different?', *European Sociological Review*, vol 22, no 1, pp 61–78.

Ramos, J. (2004) 'Empleo Precario en España: Una Asignatura Pendiente', in V. Navarro (ed) *El Estado del Bienestar en España*, Madrid: Tecnos.

Ramos, J., Chico, D. and Catalán, S. (forthcoming) 'España y el Europeísmo Acrítico: 25 años de integración Española en la UE', *Revista de Historia Actual*.

Rodriguez Castedo, A. and Jímenez Lara, A. (2010) *La atención a la dependencia y el empleo*, Documento de Trabajo 159/2010, Madrid: Fundación Alternativas.

Rodríguez Méndez, M., Picos Sánchez, F. and Rodríguez Márquez, J. (2010) 'El tratamiento fiscal de la vivienda en España y su posible reforma', XVII Encuentro de Economía Pública: Políticas Públicas ante la Crisis, Universidad de Murcia. Available at: www.um.es/dp-hacienda/eep2010/comunicaciones/eep2010-86.pdf (accessed 4 April 2010).

Rodrik, D. (2010) 'Who lost Europe?', *Project Syndicate*, 9 June. Available at: www.project-syndicate.org/commentary/rodrik44/English (accessed 9 October 2001).

Saraceno, C. (2010) 'Social inequalities in facing old-age dependency: a bi-generational perspective', *Journal of European Social Policy*, vol 20, no 1, pp 32–44.

Sarasa, S. and Mestres, J. (2007) 'Women's employment and the adult caring burden', in G. Esping-Andersen (ed) *Family formation and family dilemmas in contemporary Europe*, Bilbao: Fundación BBVA, pp 185–222.

Saurina, J. (2009). 'Dynamic provisioning: The experience of Spain,' Crisis response: Public policy for the private sector, Note Number 7 (July). The World Bank Group.

The Economist (2003) 'House of cards', 9 May.

The Guardian (2011) 'Spain changes constitution to cap budget deficit', 26 August.

Wolf, M. (2007) 'The pain in Spain will follow years of rapid economic gain', *Financial Times*, 28 March.

TWELVE

From financial crisis to welfare retrenchment: assessing the challenges to the Irish welfare state

Mairéad Considine and Fiona Dukelow

Introduction

In 2008, the prolonged economic boom in Ireland came to an end. The global financial crisis collided with a precarious economic growth model and, since then, Ireland has been in almost constant crisis mode. A dramatic drop in economic growth and the insolvency of the banking system precipitated recession and a prolonged programme of austerity, which continues under the European Union (EU)/International Monetary Fund (IMF) loan agreement agreed in late 2010. Crisis has become the new normal, and because the strategy for recovery is seen to be so dependent on external forces and conditions, the situation remains uncertain. This chapter considers the impact of this crisis on the Irish welfare state. It begins by briefly sketching the background to the crisis, focusing in particular on the impact of the banking crisis for which the state has borne an enormous debt burden. The second part analyses the consequent impact on the welfare state and looks at how it has been challenged by the social costs of the recession while its capacity to cope has been weakened by retrenchment. The final part takes stock of the politics of retrenchment and what bearing this may have on the welfare state post-crisis. The assessment offered in this chapter can only be provisional as the Irish situation and the broader condition of the Eurozone has yet to reach a resolution and the contours of a post-crisis phase are still not clearly discernible.

Ireland's economic crisis and recession

Since the late 1950s, Ireland's economic strategy has concentrated on producing goods for export with a heavy emphasis on the participation of foreign industry by incentivising foreign direct investment. By the early 1990s, with the expansion of free trade across the EU through the creation of a single market, this strategy encountered hitherto unseen success as Ireland became an attractive location for new companies seeking a manufacturing base in Europe. Simultaneously, as financialised capitalism grew in significance, Ireland became 'conspicuous in the new financial culture' (Negra, 2010, p 840), gaining a substantial share of investment in financial services when its reputation for light regulation grew to match its established reputation as a low-cost competitive manufacturing centre. Conditions for a bubble economy were fostered when unprecedented economic growth coalesced with increasingly cheap finance in preparation for the transition to Economic and Monetary Union (EMU). This was manifested in a property boom and enormous growth in construction-based private debt. The growth rate and degree of lending to property developers far outstripped loans made to personal mortgage-holders, although these also grew at an unprecedented rate (O'Hearn, 2011).

Ireland's property boom stands apart for being the longest and steepest of the housing booms of this period (André, 2010). Unlike the UK, which had a similar but not quite as large house price bubble, Ireland's property bubble came with an enormous expansion of the construction industry, driving increasingly speculative demand. In 2007, 90,000 houses were completed in Ireland compared with 180,000 in the UK whose population is 13 times greater (O'Brien, 2011). The property and construction boom and related growth in private debt essentially contributed to deep imbalances in what had become a highly neo-liberalised and financialised economy. The property market decline portended the overall instability of the economy, which was realised by how quickly economic trouble accelerated in 2008. Over the latter half of that year, key economic indicators were subject to successive downward revisions as the extent of the economic crisis and the exacerbating role of the international credit crunch became apparent. Ireland was the first Eurozone country to enter recession in September 2008 and the economy continued to contract, by 3% of Gross Domestic Product (GDP) in 2008, 7% in 2009 and 0.4% in 2010 (IMF, 2011a).

National debt levels quickly accelerated. Prior to this point, sovereign debt had decreased steadily over the 1990s and 2000s due to major economic expansion and the fact that successive governments paid down debt amassed during the 1980s (Ó Riain, 2010). Between 1987 and 2007, the debt-to-GDP ratio declined from 117% to 25%. The present crisis, therefore, was not built upon the major accrual of sovereign debt in the period preceding it. This situation has reversed sharply in the last three years. The public finances suffered a major shock as tax revenue fell by approximately one third between 2007 and 2009 (Department of Finance, 2011a). Exchequer income, which had been buoyed up by the property asset bubble, dramatically declined as transactional taxes associated with property and construction fell away. Income tax revenue was also affected by the sharp rise in unemployment from 4.5% in 2007 to over 14% in 2011 (CSO, 2011a), while, on the expenditure side, this increase had a major impact on social protection.

However, the fiscal crisis and escalating government debt cannot be understood in isolation from Ireland's banking crisis and the state's response to it. In September 2008, after an emergency meeting with key banking executives, a decision was made by the government to offer a near-blanket guarantee of Irish banking debt. It appears that this decision was taken as a way of responding to what was understood as a liquidity crisis facing the Irish banking sector in the context of the global credit crunch. However, the obscurity of the detail about how that decision was made and the degree of corporate influence over the state's response to the banking crisis have provoked major controversy. Initially proclaimed as the 'cheapest bailout in the world so far' by the Minister for Finance (Lenihan, cited in *Irish Times*, 2008), the guarantees that transfer private to public debt have come at enormous cost to Irish citizens.

The extent of the losses in the Irish banks became increasingly apparent following the property crash. To date, residential property prices have fallen by 43% from their 2007 peak (CSO, 2011b) while commercial property values have fallen by over 60% (NAMA Wine Lake, 2011). The role that financial institutions played in creating the asset bubble has also come to light as investigations into the banking sector (Honohan, 2010; Regling and Watson, 2010; Commission of Investigation into the Banking Sector in Ireland, 2011) revealed a gamut of governance failures and malpractices within the banking institutions and the main regulatory body. To date, the total cost of state recapitalisation of the banks is €70.3 billion (Department of Finance, 2011a); €63 billion has already been put into the banks and the remainder relates to current estimates of what is needed to recapitalise them (Dáil Éireann, 2011). In all, this amounts to 44.5% of GDP. In addition to bank recapitalisation, a 'bad bank', the National Assets Management Agency (NAMA), set up to purchase the riskiest commercial property loans from the banks has cost €30.2 billion (19% of GDP) but this is not recorded as a cost as it is assumed that it will pay for itself over time (Killian et al, 2011). Leaving NAMA aside, it is estimated that under the current arrangement of guarantees and wider liquidity assistance, €279.3 billion of banking liabilities are 'ultimately backed by the state' (Killian et al, 2011, p 20). This level of exposure is equivalent to 177% of GDP. The fiscal crisis, of which costs incurred by the banking crisis are a major component, has seen general government gross debt escalate from 25% of GDP in 2007 to 95% in 2010 and is anticipated to peak at 118% in 2013 (IMF, 2011a). In comparative terms, Ireland's degree of state support for the banking system has been the costliest by far, as evident in Table 12.1.

The triple problem of economic decline, fiscal crisis and a banking crisis was quickly politically framed as placing Ireland in a vulnerable position in the sovereign debt markets and threatening its international business reputation. This paved the way for Ireland's rapid turn to austerity. Despite this pre-emptive attempt to appease the financial markets, Ireland's sovereign debt rating began being downgraded, while the Irish banks also witnessed severe downgrades in their credit ratings during 2009. As the credit crunch mutated into a deeper debt crisis across Europe, this trend intensified for Ireland and some other highly indebted

Table 12.1: State support for the financial sector as a percentage of GDP (2011)

Country	Direct support
Belgium	5.7
Ireland*	40.6
Germany	13.2
Greece	5.8
Netherlands	14.0
Spain	3.0
United Kingdom	6.7
United States	5.1
Average	6.8

Note: * This figure is based on €63 billion already put into the banking system.

Source: Adapted from IMF (2011b, p 28).

countries in the Eurozone. Although held up internationally as an exemplar of austerity as a solution and holding out the prospect of a supposed expansionary fiscal contraction for neo-liberalists (Adam Smith Institute, 2010), the impact of Ireland's ever-costlier banking crisis meant that in late 2010, it had to resort to the EU/IMF funding set up to deal with the Eurozone crisis. Borrowing this money came with an accelerated programme of austerity, economic reform and privatisation while still adhering to the state bailout of banking debt.

This policy response needs to be understood in conjunction with EMU policy, which has also had a large bearing on the Irish crisis. The

Stability and Growth Pact has been influential in setting parameters on the debate about fiscal discipline with regard to deficit-reduction targets and has limited the fiscal policy options available. Specifically, currency devaluation is not an option, which has been used in the past. Ireland, therefore, has had to resort essentially to a deflationary strategy. Such a policy is counterproductive to economic growth and while indications are that growth might return by late 2011, this can only be attributed to the export sector, as austerity has stymied the domestic economy. The degree of growth required to service debts and end austerity remains a far-off prospect and sovereign debt default is still debated as a risk. Again, however, Ireland is held up as an exemplar of the effectiveness of austerity by the EU and the IMF (*Irish Times*, 2011) and as evidence that this solution can work, as initial targets agreed under the funding programme are met and the economy begins to display some feeble growth. Although the turn to external assistance marks a major rupture point in modern Ireland's history, of equal if not greater significance is the preceding readiness with which the state took responsibility for capital's losses and the similar rapidity with which it embarked on a programme of austerity in the public finances. In doing so, it transferred the cost to Irish society and augmented the social costs and citizen losses created by the crisis in its retrenchment of the welfare sate.

The social costs of the crisis and the impact on the Irish welfare state

In contrast to the complex interventionist response to the banking crisis, the fiscal crisis was met with an unrelenting drive for 'fiscal consolidation' in the form of austerity to be achieved through spending cuts and taxation measures. Attention quickly focused on the need for savings across all government departments, including those involved in attending to the social costs of the crisis. In the first of the 'crisis' budgets, welfare payments were protected, although the Minister for Finance was clear that provision would 'target resources at those in greatest need' (Lenihan, 2008), something universal entitlements did not achieve in his view. This was the first of four budgets (between October 2008 and December 2010) during which time all aspects of state spending came under intense scrutiny (McCarthy, 2009, 2011; Department of Public Expenditure and Reform, 2011), generating greater awareness of all aspects of public expenditure and the 'cost' of the welfare state. The predominant discourse on the crisis, however, tends to conflate the fiscal crisis with profligate public spending, leading to a perception that the welfare state is of itself part of the problem. As Murphy observes, 'it seems recession has been seized as political opportunity by those who want to establish Ireland as an ungenerous social welfare model and a more neoliberal welfare state' (Murphy, 2010).

Much attention has been given to the many justifiable criticisms about the way in which public monies have been utilised, yet there has been little acknowledgement that the precise functions of the welfare state are themselves exemplified in a time of such crisis. The unfolding scale of the crisis, however, made the political conditions for retrenchment more favourable. These conditions have been enhanced by the cultivation of a perception that the Irish welfare state is generous; reference has frequently been made to the 'comparatively generous level of social provision' (Lenihan, 2009) and 'the generosity of the social welfare system' (Fielding, 2010) in public discourse. That the minimum social welfare payment (€188) is now €43.20 below the 2009 at-risk-of-poverty level (EAPN, 2011) is not often considered. Little attention is also given to the fact that Irish public spending had actually remained comparatively low by European standards and that the most substantial increases in expenditure can be accounted for in the growth in health spending over the last decade (Eurostat, 2010). Spending on social protection remained low and relatively stable (6.7% of GDP in 2001 and 8.2% in 2007) prior to the crisis; however, it has since risen rapidly, with 2010 expenditure at 13.5% of GDP (DSP, 2011). It is against this backdrop that the scale, speed and scope of the austerity measures being implemented in the Irish welfare state need to be examined.

The scale of fiscal tightening

An overall fiscal adjustment of €21 billion, over 13% of GDP (Department of Finance, 2011a), was secured between 2008 and 2011, making the scale of the austerity unprecedented in Irish economic history. Expenditure cuts account for almost €13 billion; the composition of the fiscal tightening has, therefore, been approximately one third taxation and two thirds cuts in expenditure. This was an explicit element of the policy response to the fiscal crisis (Government of Ireland, 2010) subsequently endorsed by the EU/IMF through the conditions attached to the loan package for Ireland. Apart from the obvious disenchantment attached to having to resort to a 'bailout', the immediate aftermath of the loan deal precipitated much critical comment on how and in what ways 'it was a bad deal for Ireland'. Trenchant criticism, however, offered no bulwark against the level of austerity contained in the loan agreement.

The distribution of spending and taxation adjustments announced by the current government remains weighted in favour of expenditure cuts for the period ahead. Specifically, a further €7.75 billion in spending cuts is planned, with taxation adjustments of €4.65 billion between 2012 and 2015 (Department of Finance, 2011b). The tax-to-GDP ratio will be raised as a consequence but it will likely remain below the European average given that Ireland's tax-to-GDP ratio was 28.2% in 2009, well below the Eurozone average of 39.1% (Eurostat, 2011). Plans to introduce a property tax in 2014 may mark a departure from the previous approach to taxation, although the detail of this remains to be seen. In the meantime, a new household charge, payable at a flat rate, comes into effect in 2012. The imposition of a flat-rate charge, albeit temporarily, does little to alter the perception that the taxation system is not always fair or redistributive. In relation to wider tax equity issues, some reform of tax expenditures is planned. For example, tax relief for supplementary pensions is to be overhauled and the implementation of this policy will present an important litmus test for tax reform over the longer term. Less visible and rarely the focus of extensive political debate, the top 10 tax expenditures in 2006 implied revenue forgone of over €10 billion or 17.5% of all tax receipts (Collins and Walsh, 2011), its significance in redistributive terms remains under-acknowledged in public discourse.

Taken in this context and against the backdrop of the fiscal imbalances outlined earlier, the policy preference to maintain a low-tax model into the future remains, and is firmly wedded to the dominant pre-crisis economic paradigm (Considine and Dukelow, 2011). How this predilection will bear upon the nature of redistribution in the Irish political economy is considered later; the effects of the preference for and the scale of fiscal contraction are first examined with reference to social protection.

Social protection and austerity

As the largest spending department, the Department of Social Protection (DSP) has been a key target for realising savings. The rapid increase in the demand for its services has made this an impossible objective; there was a 35% increase in the numbers in receipt of weekly payments between 2007 and 2010, with a 38% increase in the number of beneficiaries in respect of whom payments were made over the same period (DSP, 2011). The sharp rise in demand for jobseekers' support accounts for much of the increased expenditure by the DSP, which in delivering on one of its core functions, remains simultaneously under pressure to cut spending.

The austerity measures introduced in social protection combine short-term 'programmatic' cost-cutting with more long-term 'systemic' reform (Pierson, 1994). The more systemic reforms centre around: scaling back universal entitlements; increasing the conditionality attached to qualifying criteria for some social insurance payments; limiting the duration of some entitlements; incremental child age-related reforms of the one-parent family payment; and the phased raising of the state pension qualification age. Other reforms focus on strengthening anti-fraud measures and imposing blanket and indefinite payment rate cuts, which are particularly severe in the case of young unemployed people. However, despite the focus on fraud and other efficiency measures, 44% of the savings to be secured by the department in 2011 will be achieved via the 2011 budget cuts in social welfare rates, while reductions in child benefit rates account for a further 17% (NESC, 2011). The key indicators of retrenchment in social protection are outlined in Table 12.2. The bulk of these cuts have been implemented without reference to any particular policy blueprint on social protection. A more explicit reform agenda has been signalled by the new government, the full detail of which remains to be seen.

The impact of this retrenchment needs to be examined in the broader context of poverty and other forms of economic and social distress that have been hallmarks of this crisis. In terms of poverty, the headline figures published to date may suggest little change, although the cuts imposed in the budgets of 2010 and 2011 are not yet captured in the data. However, it is clear that material deprivation has risen since the onset of the crisis, with two or more forms of enforced deprivation reported at 17.1% in 2009 (13.8% in 2008 and 11.8% in 2007). In addition, consistent poverty (a measure of poverty unique to Ireland, combining as it does the risk of poverty with enforced deprivation), rose from 4.2% in 2008 to 5.5% in 2009 (CSO, 2010). This trend is moving in the wrong direction and the target of reducing levels to between 2% and 4% in 2012 will hardly be realised. In terms of groups whose vulnerability to poverty may potentially be heightened by the imposition of welfare cuts, it is notable that children remain the age group most at risk of consistent poverty (8.7%) while almost 17% of lone-parent households were in consistent poverty in 2009. The reduction in the very high level of income inequality, which declined from 0.32 in 2007 to 0.29 in 2009 (CSO, 2010), as per the broader economic patterns associated with recession, will require ongoing attention and needs to be considered in the wider context of enduring poverty and the emergence of substantial structural unemployment, which will take a massive policy effort to reverse.

Table 12.2: Social protection – main elements of retrenchment (2009–11)

Group	Entitlement	Rate reduction*	Eligibility change
Unemployed people	Jobseekers' supports	10%* (average cut)	Reduction in payments if job offer/activation support not taken up
	Jobseekers' benefit	10% cut	Social insurance contributions required doubled and duration of benefit reduced
	Jobseekers' allowance	18–21 years – 51% cut 22–24 years – 30% cut	Age-related payments introduced (except for those with dependent children)
Families and children	Early childcare supplement	Abolished	Withdrawn and replaced with one year of free pre-school education
	Child benefit	16% cut (based on two children)	Payments for children aged 18 and over in full-time education withdrawn
	One-parent family payment	10% cut*	Upper age limit of children reduced to 14 years for new claimants. Ages of children of existing claimants to be reduced on a phased basis as follows: Aged 17 – 2013 Aged 16 – 2014 Aged 15 – 2015 Aged 14 – 2016
Older people	State pension	'Frozen' since 2009 (effective 1.9% cut)*	Qualification age increase – phased basis as follows: 66 years in 2014 67 years in 2021 68 years in 2028
Long-term welfare schemes	Household allowances	Fuel allowance 16% cut (urban dwellers)	No eligibility change
Older people, carers, people with disabilities		Gas allowance 20% cut Electricity allowance 25% (unit) cut	

Note: * Includes removal of the 'double payment' made in December where relevant.

The rapid rise in unemployment quickly became one of the most serious consequences emanating from the crisis. More than half (53.9%) of those currently unemployed have been out of work for over 12 months (CSO, 2011c). Ireland's track record with regard to employment policy has been relatively weak, with Murphy pointing to 'arrested development and a relatively "frozen landscape" of welfare reform and relative to other countries no significant levels of reform towards an active social policy' (Murphy, 2010). A number of initiatives have been undertaken, including the establishment of the National Employment and Entitlements Service and the development of new schemes that focus on creating opportunities for work experience and training. These initiatives are at various stages of implementation and it is not yet clear precisely how and to what extent these will cohere to act as a system of activation that is responsive to the needs of unemployed people. In addition, the number of places available on the new activation schemes is relatively small when put against the 304,500 people (CSO, 2011c) presently out of work. There are also questions about the impact of the 'disincentive measures' recently introduced for jobseekers that fail to take up offers of employment/activation, which include reductions in welfare payments. Such measures would seem to indicate a shift towards a more coercive mutual obligations approach to activation that places emphasis on sanctions and maintaining incentives to work by ensuring benefit levels are kept low (Murphy, 2010). For low-paid workers, there are also significant issues: 37% of all households at risk of poverty have a job (Social Justice Ireland, 2011). While the new government reversed the decision taken by the previous one to cut the minimum wage, the Universal Social Charge introduced in 2011 applies to all earned income over €4,004 per year and brings the lowest earners into the tax net. Refundable tax credits are not available in Ireland, although this has been advocated as an effective way to protect the working poor (Social Justice Ireland, 2011).

The ramifications of the burst of the housing bubble extend well beyond the economic and fiscal domain; there is a serious level of housing distress evidenced by the sharp increase in the number of households in mortgage arrears (8.1% of residential mortgages were in arrears of over 90 days in September 2011; see Central Bank of Ireland, 2011) and the issue of private debt restructuring is far from resolved. In addition, pressures on the social housing sector, which remained under-resourced throughout the boom years, have intensified, with a 75% increase in demand over the last three years (ICSH, 2011). This presents a massive challenge to local authorities where almost 100,000 households (ICSH,

2011) remain on waiting lists. The need for rent and mortgage interest supplements, where the number of recipients has risen by 63% and 375%, respectively, between 2007 and 2010 (DSP, 2011), is also at an all-time high. This short overview of selected aspects of the social costs of the crisis merely provides a snapshot of the scale of the welfare challenges at this juncture. Whether and how these pressures are responded to will be crucial to the well-being and prospects of very many people. What the responses may signify for the future of the welfare state is yet another question, one to which we now turn.

Retrenchment and prospects for the Irish welfare state

A key point of departure in attempting to understand the implications of the current crisis for the future of the Irish welfare state involves making sense of the momentous degree of welfare retrenchment implemented and the fact that this remains an unfinished project. Informed by the work of Pierson (1994, 1996), the view that welfare retrenchment is a difficult policy to pursue and an unpopular move for governments to make (Starke, 2006) has been influential. This perspective points to political buffers (chiefly the popularity of programmes and the growth of interest groups associated with welfare provision) within welfare systems that support their maintenance. In this context, periods of welfare retrenchment tend to happen in the face of severe economic difficulty and budgetary pressure, which eliminates room for other policy options (Korpi and Palme, 2003) while, at the same time, offering opportunity for blame avoidance for the political actors who implement such measures (Pierson, 1996). Even then, however, welfare states appear to have proven resilient.

These observations and lessons from the past might suggest that once the economic pressure has passed, the current episode of retrenchment in Ireland will not leave a lasting impression on the welfare state. However, debate regarding what constitutes retrenchment has broadened to include ways in which the quality of social rights is altered. This includes consideration of 'the extent to which reforms reinforce or damage different social interests so as to change the context in which welfare state policies are made' (Taylor-Gooby, forthcoming, p 3) and takes account of trends involving the restructuring of welfare programmes, which have been more widespread across welfare states. Furthermore, a significant element of the political dynamics of retrenchment involves the discursive framing of proposals and policies (Cox, 2001; Slothuus,

2007), which can mean more up-front change rather than change by stealth. This framing and pursuit of retrenchment may also pose benefits as opposed to risks to right-leaning political parties, as noted by Giger and Nelson (2010) who suggest that retrenchment is not necessarily a universally unpopular move with voters. Taking these aspects of the retrenchment debate into account, we look at the manner in which the framing and pursuit of retrenchment can be understood with reference to particular elements of Irish political economy that may be salient in determining the future path of the welfare state.

A highly significant factor is the rapidity with which Ireland turned to retrenchment, whereas the more common initial international reaction was to implement stimulus measures and use social protection policy as a tool to alleviate the social costs of the crisis (OECD, 2009; Bonnet et al, 2010). As noted previously, the reaction was framed with reference to the imperative of fiscal discipline in the face of international market constraints, which, if viewed in isolation, could be construed as a blame-avoidance strategy. However, debate about the need for fiscal discipline was heavily informed by the critique of welfare expenditure, which shifted the problems of the crisis to the welfare state domain. A closely related point is the degree to which such action and framing of fiscal austerity and retrenchment has turned out to be politically feasible.

Perhaps the greatest expression of the public's reaction lies in how the political landscape has been transformed by the first election since the crisis unfolded, held in the spring of 2011. The vote of the historically dominant Fianna Fáil party, which had been in power since 1997 as the leader of various coalition governments, imploded. Yet the election of a Fine Gael–Labour coalition appears to be 'transformation without transformation'. Fine Gael experienced its most successful election, reaching a near majority. Its election manifesto revealed continuity with the prevailing ideas about policy goals, problems and solutions, for example, promising to focus on 'budget cuts rather than job destroying tax increases' and to deliver 'smaller better government' (Fine Gael, 2011, pp 4, 6). As the two main parties, until now at least, Fianna Fáil and Fine Gael have tended to compete on the 'pin-head' (Hall, 2011, p 19) of the middle ground. Labour's presence in the current coalition does not significantly alter this picture. Historically, its leadership has had a reputation for being cautious, which is reinforced by its usual pairing in government with the conservative Fine Gael (Puirséil, 2007), and it has not succeeded in offering an alternative narrative of the crisis or to the EU/IMF loan agreement. This may echo its historical experience, and its status as the smaller party in the present coalition. It is also reflective of the wider failure of social democratic politics across Europe to effectively respond to the crisis and puncture the neo-liberal hegemony.

In Irish political discourse, the notion of a common national interest is appealed to over class issues or interests, hence concerns about and the language of social justice and redistribution are absent from debate. Ideas about the generosity of the welfare system, welfare as a lifestyle choice, welfare fraud, the disincentive effects of welfare and the inefficiency of the public sector making it not fit for purpose have become commonplace and relatively uncontested in current political debate. These ideas do not come across as ideologically loaded, but as common-sense, pragmatic definitions of problems and policy solutions.

This situation is bolstered by the relative strengthening of other neo-liberal voices/interests and the contrasting weaker position of left-wing actors and policy advocates, particularly since the crisis took hold. Of significance here is the demise of the social partnership model of policymaking that had been in place since 1987, even though it was considered unsatisfactory in many ways for its consensus-based approach and co-opting what might otherwise be more independent actors critical of government policy (Allen, 2000; Meade, 2005). In its wake, however, trade unions did not turn more combative. Private and public sector pay cuts and job losses have not resulted in major union resistance or strike action. While the lack of union resistance to private sector wage cuts and job losses may reflect the 'steady erosion of union density in the private sector' (Finn, 2011, p 35), the weakened position of the public sector unions is perhaps connected to the wider public sector backlash that emerged in the conflation of the crisis with profligate public spending.

Not unrelated is the proliferation of economic interests in the form of corporate actors and economic commentators in the public discursive sphere. While some brought attention to the policy mistake of the banking guarantee and the punitive terms of the EU/IMF loan agreement, they speak with broad unanimity of the need for retrenchment. This is not to deny the fact that many new civil society movements and campaigns have been active in attempting to rebut the dominant narrative of the crisis and to propose alternative economic and social policies. Gaining legitimacy for alternative ideas is, however, a key problem in the media, which operates 'in a narrowly circumscribed sphere of debate' (Meade, 2008, p 334). As Massey observes for the case of the UK, but which has parallels with the Irish case, when 'ideas from the left do get a hearing they tend to (have to) be argued on the political terrain of existing economic policy' (Massey, 2011, p 35).

Wider attitudes, values and preferences in relation to the Irish welfare state indicate something of an embedding of more individualist attitudes and welfare preferences (Hardiman et al, 2006; Tasc, 2010), raising broader questions about redistribution, the mechanisms to be used and to what purpose, particularly in the current crisis. More broadly, the discursive treatment of taxpayers as 'givers' to the state contrasted with the treatment of benefit recipients as 'takers' is significant (Cook, 1989, in Sinfield, 2011). As Sinfield notes, 'this operation of double standards, not only of discourse but also of respect and reward, has continued to be little challenged' (Sinfield, 2011, p 77), a point that resonates given the predominance of corporate and economic assessments of the Irish crisis. Conflicting attitudes to redistribution are all the more salient given the scale of the revenue collapse, providing evidence of the need to make the tax system more sustainable, equitable and broadly based (Commission on Taxation, 2009). However, this is balanced against expressed concerns that there are limits to the ways in which taxation should be reformed, as illustrated by the former Taoiseach who remarked that:

> it is tempting to claim that all our problems can be solved simply by increasing taxes on the wealthy without the need for contributions from others, or expenditure cutbacks. ... evidence suggests that high marginal tax rates will discourage high-skilled workers from remaining in Ireland, as well as discouraging high-skilled workers from locating here in the first place. (Cowen, 2009)

The measures since imposed have largely not run counter to this view; headline income tax rates remain unchanged, and while tax bands have been reduced, and new levies introduced, there has been no substantive break with the policy preference to keep tight strictures on the parameters of tax reform. Corporation tax is to be maintained at 12.5% and increasing income tax rates has also been ruled out. Aversion to higher taxation remains.

Having never really broken away from its liberal characterisation in any substantive way, even in economically prosperous years, the Irish welfare state retains a complex mix of public entitlement and private provision that now weakens its resilience in the face of the enormous pressure the crisis has imposed. Furthermore, the longer trajectory of a comparatively late and relatively reluctant welfare state, coupled with a 'solidarity without equality' (Ó Riain and O'Connell, 2000, p 339) approach to redistribution, highlights a path-dependency legacy that has yet to be undermined. Many 'middle-class' beneficiaries of the welfare state fail to see themselves as such. Areas such as pensions and health care derived from private provision contain significant subsidies from the state.

The drift to the private sector intensified since the mid-1990s, representing an embedding of what Glennerster identifies as 'mixed modes of funding' where 'as an alternative to raising taxes the state has intervened to encourage or require individuals to fund their own provision' (Glennerster, 2010, p 695). While Ireland does not represent a prototype of such a model, given that public services are available, it does encourage people to supplement public services with their own provision. Prior to the current crisis, the National Economic and Social Council identified a 'deepening dualism' in the welfare state, with many people supplementing public provision 'with additional protection they purchase for themselves' (NESC, 2005, p 163). As against this, others almost wholly reliant on the state face the risk of being 'further removed from the mainstream of Irish society and less likely to experience mobility into it' (NESC, 2005, p 163). Overall, there remains a reluctance to engage explicitly with the solidaristic principles that underpin the distributional objectives of the welfare state in favour of the earlier-mentioned common national interest. The new government has not veered from this path in any significant way. The economic and fiscal response to the crisis remains firmly within an austerity framework, although an electoral commitment to provide free GP care by 2016, for example, signifies how some of their social policy aspirations run counter to the discourse of retrenchment. This suggests that social policy expansion of some kind is envisaged in the post-crisis period, albeit limited and of likely greater significance to middle-class beneficiaries.

Concluding remarks

If, as Sinfield suggests, 'the "legitimacy of welfare" is dependent on "patterns of solidarity" in contributing to the common good' (Sinfield, 2011, p 73), the tax and welfare measures that comprise those patterns, and their impact, need to be the subject of much greater scrutiny and debate. The dominance of the economic, banking and fiscal components of the crisis, and the prescription to them, has had the effect of sidelining and allowing a sidestepping of the more fundamental questions emanating from the social crisis. This, in turn, is reflective of the broader terrain of the political economy of the Irish welfare state and together they have meant that the capacity for collective discursive engagement beyond the horizon of welfare retrenchment has effectively been hindered, for now at least.

Beyond the national context, a major factor looming large in the future of Irish economic and social policy is the fate of the Eurozone and the wider project of European integration. At the time of writing (autumn 2011), it is apparent that the EU/IMF solution of austerity coupled with full debt repayment is not solving the sovereign and banking debt problems across the EU. The crisis has brought Europe to a critical juncture between further integration and fragmentation. As 'the outlier inside' (Hay et al, 2008, p 182), that is, the only liberal economy in the Eurozone, fragmentation might have economic benefits for Ireland over the longer term, giving it greater scope for fiscal policy in line with its economic model, although this would potentially intensify the liberal character of the welfare state. The prospect of greater European integration might reduce national control over social policy, particularly with respect to taxation and distribution. However, what this might mean returns us to the issues of solidarity, welfare and the common good. Palmer's question about 'what political and social values will inspire that integration?' (Palmer, 2011, p 107) would become highly pertinent for the future of all European welfare states, not just the Irish one.

References

Adam Smith Institute (2010) 'Ireland leaves recession'. Available at: http://www.adamsmith.org/blog/tax-and-economy/ireland-leaves-recession/

Allen, K. (2000) *The Celtic tiger: the myth of social partnership in Ireland*, Manchester: Manchester University Press.

André, C. (2010) *A bird's eye view of OECD housing markets*, OECD Economics Department Working Paper No 746, Paris: OECD.

Bonnet, F., Ehmke, E. and Hagemejer, K. (2010) 'Social security in times of crisis', *International Social Security Review*, vol 63, no 2, pp 47–70.

Central Bank of Ireland (2011) 'Latest quarterly mortgage arrears data show 8.1% of mortgage accounts in arrears over 90 days, up from 7.2% at the end of June', press release, 18 November.

Collins, M. and Walsh, M. (2011) 'Tax expenditures: revenue and information forgone – the experience of Ireland', *Trinity Economics Papers*, Working Paper No 1211.

Commission of Investigation into the Banking Sector in Ireland (2011) *Misjudging risk: causes of the systemic banking crisis in Ireland*, Dublin: Government Publications.

Commission on Taxation (2009) *Commission on Taxation report 2009*, Dublin: Stationery Office.

Considine, M. and Dukelow, F. (2011) 'Ireland and the impact of the economic crisis: upholding the dominant policy paradigm', in K. Farnsworth and Z. Irving (eds) *Social policy in challenging times: Economic crisis and welfare systems*, Bristol: The Policy Press, pp 181–98.

Cowen, B. (2009) Statement on the Budget by the Taoiseach Mr. Brian Cowen T.D., Dáil Éireann, Thursday, 10 December, 2009, at 11.00am. Available atL www.taoiseach.gov.ie/irish/An_Preas-Oifig/ Aithisc_an_Taoisigh_2009/Statement_on_the_Budget_by_the_ Taoiseach_Mr_Brian_Cowen_T_D_,_D%C3%A1il_%C3%89irea nn,_Thursday,_10_December_2009,_at_11_00_a_m_.html

Cox, R. (2001) 'The social construction of an imperative: why welfare reform happened in Denmark and the Netherlands but not in Germany', *World Politics*, vol 53, pp 463–98.

CSO (Central Statistics Office) (2010) *Survey on Income and Living Conditions (SILC) 2009*, Dublin: Stationery Office.

CSO (2011a) 'Live register', September 2011, 5 October.

CSO (2011b) 'Residential property price index', August 2011, 26 September.

CSO (2011c) 'Quarterly national household survey', Quarter 2, 2011, 15 September.

Dáil Éireann (2011) 'Written answers – banks recapitalisation', 14 September. Available at: http://debates.oireachtas.ie/ dail/2011/09/14/00106.asp

Department of Finance (2011a) *The Irish economy in perspective*, Dublin: Department of Finance.

Department of Finance (2011b) *Medium-term fiscal statement, November 2011*, Dublin: Stationery Office.

Department of Public Expenditure and Reform (2011) *Public service reform*, Dublin: Department of Public Expenditure and Reform.

DSP (Department of Social Protection) (2011) *Statistical information on social welfare services 2010*, Dublin: Department of Social Protection.

EAPN (European Anti Poverty Network Ireland) (2011) 'Budget 2012 – pre-budget submission, EAPN Ireland Europe 2020 working group'. Available at: http://www.eapn.ie/eapn/pre-budget-submission- 2012#more-2979

Eurostat (2010) *Government finance statistics*, Luxembourg: Eurostat. Available at: http://epp.eurostat.ec.europa.eu/portal/page/portal/ government_finance_statistics/introduction

Eurostat (2011) *Taxation trends in the European Union*, Luxembourg: Eurostat.

Fielding, M. (2010) 'Employers' difficulty in getting Irish workers', ISME blog, 17 October. Available at: http://blog.isme.ie/enterprise/employers-difficulty-in-getting-irish-workers/

Fine Gael (2011) 'Fine Gael manifesto'. Available at: www.finegael2011.com/pdf/Fine%20Gael%20Manifesto%20low-res.pdf

Finn, D. (2011) 'Ireland on the turn?', *New Left Review*, no 67, pp 5–39.

Giger, N. and Nelson, M. (2010) 'The electoral consequences of welfare state retrenchment: blame avoidance or credit claiming in the era of permanent austerity', *European Journal of Political Research*, vol 5, no 1, pp 1–23.

Glennerster, H. (2010) 'The sustainability of Western welfare states', in F. Castles, S. Leibfried, J. Lewis, H. Obinger and C. Pierson (eds) *The Oxford handbook of the welfare state*, Oxford: Oxford University Press, pp 689–702.

Government of Ireland (2010) *The National recovery plan 2011–2014*, Dublin: Stationery Office.

Hall, S. (2011) 'The neo-liberal revolution', *Soundings*, no 48, pp 9–27.

Hardiman, N., McCashin, T. and Payne, D. (2006) 'Understanding Irish attitudes to poverty and wealth', in J. Garry, N. Hardiman and D. Payne (eds) *Irish social and political attitudes*, Liverpool: Liverpool University Press, pp 43–59.

Hay, C., Riiheläinen, J., Smith, N. and Watson, M. (2008) 'Ireland: the outlier inside', in K. Dyson (ed) *The Euro at ten, Europeanization, power and convergence*, Oxford: Oxford University Press, pp 182–203.

Honohan, P. (2010) *The Irish banking crisis regulatory and financial stability policy, 2003–2008 a report to the Minister for Finance by the Governor of the Central Bank*, Dublin: Central Bank.

ICSH (Irish Council for Social Housing) (2011) 'Charity warns government over dramatic increase in social housing need', press release, 19 September.

IMF (International Monetary Fund) (2011a) 'Ireland: third review under the extended arrangement'. Available at: http://www.imf.org/external/pubs/cat/longres.aspx?sk=25223

IMF (2011b) 'IMF fiscal monitor, addressing fiscal challenge to reduce economic risks', September. Available at: http://www.imf.org/external/pubs/ft/fm/2011/02/pdf/fm1102.pdf

Irish Times (2008) 'Irish bailout cheapest in world, says Lenihan', 10 October.

Irish Times (2011) 'IMF issues upbeat review', 5 October.

Killian, S., Garvey, J. and Shaw, F. (2011) *An audit of Irish debt*, Dublin: Debt and Development Ireland Coalition.

Korpi, W. and Palme, J. (2003) 'New politics and class politics in the context of austerity and globalisation: welfare state regress in 18 countries, 1975–1995', *American Sociological Review*, vol 63, no 5, pp 661–87.

Lenihan, B. (2008) 'Financial statement of the Minister for Finance Mr Brian Lenihan TD', 14 October. Available at: http://www.budget.gov. ie/Budgets/2009/FinancialStatement.aspx

Lenihan, B. (2009) 'Financial statement of the Minister for Finance Mr Brian Lenihan TD', 9 December. Available at: www.budget.gov.ie/ budgets/2010/Documents/FINAL%20Speech.pdf

Massey, D. (2011) 'Ideology and economics in the present moment', *Soundings*, no 48, pp 29–39.

McCarthy, C. (2009) *Review of the Special Group on Public Service Numbers and Expenditure Programmes*, Dublin: Government Publications.

McCarthy, C. (2011) *Report of the Review Group on State Assets and Liabilities*, Dublin: Stationery Office.

Meade, R. (2005) 'We hate it here, please let us stay! Irish social partnership and the community/voluntary sector's conflicted experiences of recognition', *Critical Social Policy*, vol 25, no 3, pp 349–73.

Meade, R. (2008) 'Mayday, mayday! Newspaper framing anti-globalisers! A critical analysis of the *Irish Independent*'s anticipatory coverage of the "Day of the Welcomes" demonstrations', *Journalism*, vol 9, no 3, pp 330–52.

Murphy, M. (2010) 'What future lies ahead for the Irish welfare state?', *Irish Journal of Public Policy*, vol 2, no 1. Available at: http://publish.ucc. ie/ijpp/2010/01/murphy/02/en

NAMA Wine Lake (2011) 'Ireland's other commercial property index confirms steep falls in prices in Q2, 2011'. Available at: http:// namawinelake.wordpress.com/2011/07/26/ireland%E2%80%99s- other-commercial-property-index-confirms-steep-falls-in-prices- in-q2-2011/

Negra, D. (2010) 'Urban space, luxury retailing and the new Irishness', *Cultural Studies*, vol 24, no 6, pp 836–53.

NESC (National Economic and Social Council) (2005) *The developmental welfare state*, Dublin: NESC.

NESC (2011) *Supports and services for unemployed jobseekers: challenges and opportunities in a time of recession*, Dublin: NESDO.

O'Brien, D. (2011) 'How low can house prices go?', *Irish Times*, 1 October.

OECD (Organisation for Economic Co-operation and Development) (2009) *Economic outlook interim report*, March, Paris: OECD.

O'Hearn, D. (2011) 'What happened to the "Celtic tiger"?', *Translocations*, vol 7, no 1, pp 1–8.

Ó Riain, S. (2010) 'Addicted to growth: developmental statism and neoliberalism in the Celtic tiger', in M. Bøss (ed) *The nation-state in transformation: the governance, growth and cohesion of small states under globalisation*, Aarhus: Aarhus University Press, pp 163–90.

Ó Riain, S. and O'Connell, P.J. (2000) 'The role of the state in growth and welfare', in B. Nolan, P.J. O'Connell and C.T. Whelan (eds) *Bust to boom? The Irish experience of growth and inequality*, Dublin: IPA, pp 310–39.

Palmer, J. (2011) 'The EU crisis: integration or gradual disintegration?', *Soundings*, no 48, pp 97–108.

Pierson, P. (1994) *Dismantling the welfare state? Reagan, Thatcher, and the politics of retrenchment*, Cambridge: Cambridge University Press.

Pierson, P. (1996) 'The new politics of the welfare state', *World Politics*, vol 48, no 2, pp 143–79.

Puirséil, N. (2007) *The Irish Labour Party*, Dublin: UCD Press.

Regling, K. and Watson, M. (2010) *A preliminary report on the sources of Ireland's banking crisis*, Dublin: Government Publications.

Sinfield, A. (2011) 'Credit crunch, inequality and social policy', in K. Farnsworth and Z. Irving (eds) *Social policy in challenging times: economic crisis and welfare systems,* Bristol: The Policy Press, pp 65–80.

Slothuus, R. (2007) 'Framing deservingness to win support for welfare state retrenchment', *Scandinavian Political Studies*, vol 30, no 3, pp 232–44.

Social Justice Ireland (2011) *Social Justice Ireland policy briefing, budget choices, a fairer future is possible, October 2011*, Dublin: Social Justice Ireland.

Starke, P. (2006) 'The politics of welfare retrenchment: a literature review', *Social Policy and Administration*, vol 40, no 1, pp 104–20.

Tasc (2010) *The solidarity factor: public responses to economic inequality in Ireland*, Dublin: Tasc.

Taylor-Gooby, P. (forthcoming) 'Root and branch restructuring to achieve major cuts: the social policy programme of the 2010 UK Coalition government', *Social Policy and Administration*. D.o.i.:10.1111/j.1467-9515.2011.00797.x.

THIRTEEN

The Great Recession and US social policy: from expansion to austerity

Daniel Béland and Alex Waddan

Introduction

What has become known as the 'Great Recession' began in the US when the crisis that hit investment banking and other key financial institutions through 2008 developed into a wider economic crisis leading to a massive increase in unemployment. For policymakers, this posed a choice of whether to expand social policy programmes in order to protect people suffering in the economic downturn or to turn to radical welfare state retrenchment to remedy the accelerating problems of deficit and debt (Vis et al, 2011). In the US, the historical evidence as to the likely impact of economic crisis on social policy was contradictory. The economic slowdown and stagflation of the late 1970s did help fuel the conservative resurgence, even if the policy change that subsequently resulted was limited in scope (Pierson, 1994). On the other hand, the Depression of the 1930s had led to a period of sustained social policy expansion, as the New Deal era saw the establishment of the first modern federal welfare state programmes like Social Security (Béland, 2005).

The political dynamics at the end of 2008 suggested that existing welfare state structures would be reinforced and some social policy programmes expanded. The presidential and congressional elections that took place in November 2008, just as the full extent of the crisis was emerging, resulted in the Democratic Party taking unified control of the federal governing institutions. Yet expectations that this would lead to a new 'New Deal' were quickly challenged (Skocpol and Jacobs, 2011), as conservative opponents, maintaining their political cohesion in spite of the defeats in the 2008 elections, decried the policy direction of the Obama administration and Democratic Congress while insisting that the growing budget deficit was the greatest long-term threat to the country's future and that dramatic spending cuts – rather than tax increases – were required to balance the books.

When Barack Obama won the presidential election, he promised major changes to reduce the economic insecurity many Americans faced. But three years after the financial meltdown, unemployment remained high amid what was widely described as a 'slow recovery' as evidence emerged of how the downturn had reinforced the long-term socio-economic stagnation of the 'middle class' (Peck, 2011). In this chapter, we discuss the nature of the recent economic crisis in the United States and analyse some of the most prominent social policy changes enacted in the aftermath of the crisis. These changes included the 2010 health care reform and temporary improvements to unemployment insurance benefits. Other measures that temporarily reinforced the social safety net were also included in the American Recovery and Reinvestment Act of 2009. We then turn to examine how that agenda of social policy expansion was challenged by the return to fiscal austerity related to the increase in the size of both federal and state deficits as well as the ideological resurgence of the Right, which began pushing for spending cuts even before the end of the Great Recession. That conservative revival was manifested in institutional terms in the 2010 midterm congressional elections when the Republicans captured 63 seats and took control of the House of Representatives, which was the biggest gain for either party since 1938. The conclusion of the chapter summarises the key changes enacted before speculating about the future of the US welfare state in a new context of fiscal austerity. As argued, the rise in federal deficits and the conservative ideological ascendency converge to legitimise potential benefit cuts while making it harder for the federal and state governments to launch new measures aimed at adapting social programmes to more effectively fight poverty and economic insecurity in the US.

The nature and consequences of the crisis

As early as the summer of 2007, the germs of a full-blown economic crisis became apparent in the US housing sector, with the multiplication of foreclosures (Veiga, 2007). Although the dramatic increase in the number of foreclosures taking place in 2007 and in the first half of 2008 was a powerful warning sign, it was only in September 2008 that the full extent of how that housing crisis had precipitated a banking and economic crisis became apparent. That month, the US witnessed bold government interventions aimed at rescuing the banking and financial sector. The first major move of the Bush administration was to rescue investment banks and the insurance giant AIG as well as Fannie Mae and Freddie Mac. Importantly, Lehman Brothers was allowed to go bankrupt and the disruption caused by that contributed to the deepening of the financial crisis. To prevent further contagion, the Bush administration put forward a major bailout package that was finally enacted and signed into law on 3 October 2008. This legislation created the Troubled Asset Relief Program (TARP), a 700-billion dollar package that allowed the federal government to purchase troubled assets in order to help banks and financial institutions. This massive and controversial programme represented an unprecedented effort on the part of the federal government to rescue a sector vital to the US economy.

In retrospect, it is possible to argue that TARP prevented a greater financial crisis from occurring. Yet the relative success of TARP in securing financial institutions cannot hide the deep nature of the economic recession that hit the US from late 2007 onwards. Moreover, historical evidence suggests that economic crises resulting from a collapse in the financial sector would be longer-lasting and more severe than normal cyclical recessions (Reinhart and Rogoff, 2009). For instance, in the third quarter of 2008, the recession caused a 2.7% contraction in Gross Domestic Product (GDP) measured in constant US dollars. The following quarter, the contraction in GDP was even greater, at a stunning 5.4% (US Bureau of Economic Analysis, 2010a). Unemployment surged from 5.1% in March 2008 to 8.6% a year later. After peaking at 10.1% in October 2009, it remained as high as 9.7% in May 2010 (US Department of Labor, 2010a). A year later, in May 2011, the unemployment rate had declined to 9.1%, but this was still very high by US standards. This reality pointed to a slow recovery, especially as far as the job market was concerned (Lee, 2011). Moreover, these unemployment figures do not tell us anything about the sheer number of *underemployed* citizens (more than 9 million people in March 2010) who worked part time but wanted full-time employment. Perhaps even more alarming was the high number of people facing long-term unemployment. In March 2010, for example, more than 44.1% of the unemployed had been out of work for at least 27 weeks (US Department of Labor, 2010b). Furthermore, reflecting embedded social and economic inequalities ever present in US society, that unemployment rate was much higher among Hispanics (12.6%) and African-Americans (16.5%) than among non-Hispanic whites (8.8%) (US Bureau of Economic Analysis, 2010b).

Overall, the economic crisis was severe and it directly affected large segments of the population, especially minority ethnic groups. It was also long-lasting. Three years after the collapse of Lehman Brothers, the unemployment rate remained at 9.1% with the sluggish nature of the recovery illustrated by the fact that, in aggregate, no new jobs were created in August 2011 (US Department of Labor, 2011). Unsurprisingly, therefore, the recession lowered living standards. Median household income in 2010 was 6.4% lower than in 2007 (and reflecting the uneven nature of economic growth in the 2000s was 7.1% lower than in 1999 when median household income peaked; see US Census Bureau, 2011, p 4). The economic climate also accentuated poverty, as the percentage of people living below the poverty line rose from 12.5% in 2007 to 15.1% in 2010, and matching the inequalities in the labour market, the poverty rate for African-Americans was 27.4% as against 9.9% for non-Hispanic whites (US Census Bureau, 2011, p 14).

Beyond problems like foreclosures and unemployment, the economic crisis had major political consequences. First, because the financial crunch hit the country less than six weeks before the 2008 presidential election, the early stages of the crisis helped Obama secure a victory against Republican candidate John McCain, who seemed out of touch after he declared, immediately after the bankruptcy of Lehman Brothers, that the US economy had strong foundations (Cooper, 2008, p A1). Obama's campaign message about 'change' resonated in the aftermath of the financial crisis, as he promised to help people facing economic hardship. When he was sworn into office in January 2009, the new Democratic president seemed in an excellent position to reshape US economic and social policy, as he faced an extraordinary situation while receiving the support of a freshly elected Democratic majority in each chamber of Congress. Furthermore, these Democrat majorities, while certainly not capable of exercising parliamentary-style discipline, were more politically coherent than previous such majorities (Cook, 2009). Yet, although the new president did deliver a major health care reform, the social policy legacy of his first term in the White House is much more mixed than many observers anticipated. Despite the crisis and a favourable position in Congress, President Obama struggled to push for meaningful changes in the field of health care reform and beyond (Béland and Waddan, 2011). Furthermore, as the administration began to 'own' the economy, the continuing high levels of unemployment and problems in the housing market, with many homeowners remaining 'underwater' (ie suffering from negative equity), so the political tide that had swept Obama and the Democrats to victory in November 2008 turned against them.

Early social policy responses

The rapid increase in unemployment that took place in the aftermath of the 2008 financial crisis exposed the well-known flaws of the US decentralised unemployment insurance system. Created during the New Deal as a consequence of the Social Security Act 1935, this state-operated system is both fragmented and ungenerous, at least by international standards. For instance, under normal conditions, unemployed workers in most states receive benefits for only 26 weeks in total. Yet, when the unemployment rate increases above a certain level (typically 6%), an Extended Benefits programme generally provides 13 extra weeks of unemployment insurance payments. Additionally, under the Temporary Emergency Unemployment Benefits scheme, during exceptional times of high unemployment, like the recent Great Recession, a further period of benefit becomes available to claimants (Dobelstein, 2009, pp 114–16). However, many part-time and low-waged workers are deemed ineligible to claim unemployment benefits after losing their jobs. For example, between 1992 and 2003, 'low-wage workers were almost two-and-a-half times as likely to be out of work as higher-wage workers, but half as likely to receive UI [unemployment insurance] benefits' (US Government Accountability Office, 2007, p 12). Partly because of this, in March 2009, less than 50% of the citizens registered as unemployed were actually collecting unemployment insurance benefits (Hagenbaugh, 2009).

Considering the flaws of the US unemployment insurance system and the sheer scope of the Great Recession, efforts were made at the federal level to improve benefits. This is evident in the stimulus package adopted at the beginning of the Obama presidency as the American Recovery and Reinvestment Act of 2009 (ARRA). ARRA was designed primarily as a stimulus for the ailing economy and at an estimated cost of $787 billion, it was a major commitment from the new administration. When signing ARRA into law in February 2009, President Obama described it as the 'most sweeping economic recovery package in our history' (quoted in Crummy and Sherry, 2009). Yet, while the package was always likely to be judged according to its overall macroeconomic impact, it had important implications for social policy, at least in the short term. Reflecting how US social welfare programmes lacked the so-called automatic stabilisers apparent in Western European nations during an economic downturn that provided protection to people losing income, ARRA set out to maintain and increase certain benefits. This had the dual effect of helping vulnerable households cope with the loss of income while adding to aggregate demand in the economy. For instance, the Act increased benefits by $25 per week for all unemployment insurance recipients while creating 'a special transfer of up to $7 billion in federal monies to state unemployment programs as incentive "payments" for changing certain state UC laws' (Shelton, 2009, p iii). Thus, the federal government made money available to state unemployment insurance schemes that improved the protection offered to the unemployed. Moreover, ARRA offered more federal money to help states temporarily extend the duration of unemployment benefits for 20 more weeks. Although ARRA did not force the states to enact changes to their unemployment insurance systems, many states adapted their rules to provide benefits to more people for a longer period (National Employment Law Project, 2009).

Another aspect of the US welfare state affected by the ARRA was the Supplemental Nutrition Assistance Program known as Food Stamps. Accessible to people with low income and limited assets, Food Stamps are funded by the federal government and co-administrated by the states and the federal US Department of Agriculture. Food Stamps no longer in fact take the form of actual stamps, as the programme has long been digitalised. In this context, recipients can buy items using an electronic card similar to the one issued by banks and credit card companies instead of traditional and much more visible stamps, a situation that may have reduced the stigma attached to Food Stamps. As part of the ARRA, the maximum amount of Food Stamps available to a family of four jumped from $588 to $668 per month. Moreover, the ARRA also temporarily abolished the three-month time limit on Food Stamps receipt for the unemployed (Pavetti and Rosenbaum, 2010, p 9). In part, because the Obama administration encouraged states to enrol all individuals eligible for Food Stamps (DeParle and Gebeloff, 2009), the number of citizens receiving Food Stamps rose dramatically to reach 42 million in August 2010, which constituted an all-time high for the programme. In fact, that number was 'up 58.5% from August 2007, before the recession began' (Murray, 2010). This meant that, in mid-2010, nearly 14% of the population received Food Stamps, a significant number by any means (Murray, 2010). One aspect of early media reporting about the impact of the recession was the concentration on how previously well-off households suddenly became dependent on the social safety net and, in particular, on Food Stamps (see, eg, Black, 2008; DeParle and Gebeloff, 2009). Overall, therefore, as a result of both greater demand stemming from economic hardship and legislative changes to both eligibility rules and benefit levels, the Great Recession favoured a massive expansion of the Food Stamps programme.

ARRA also included some extra funds for the Temporary Assistance to Needy Families (TANF) programme. TANF was established as part of the controversial welfare reform legislation of 1996. It is a time-limited benefit designed to increase the incentives for welfare recipients to move into work and replaced the Aid to Families with Dependent Children programme that had previously provided cash benefits, on a non-time-limited basis, to poor households with children.[1] ARRA created an Emergency Contingency Fund for TANF that states could draw upon if they had an increase in their caseload. Yet, while a number of states did take some of this funding, the evidence suggests that the programme's administrators remained focused on keeping down overall caseload numbers in most states, meaning that TANF was relatively unresponsive to the increased poverty resulting from the recession (Pavetti and Rosenbaum, 2010). Overall, in contrast to the big increase in the use of Food Stamps, between December 2007 and December 2009, a period when unemployment doubled, TANF caseloads rose by only 13% (Pavetti et al, 2011).

The health care debate

Beyond emergency measures, the first 15 months of the Obama presidency were marked by a fierce debate about health care reform that culminated in the passage of the Patient Protection and Affordable Care Act (PPACA) in March 2010 (Jacobs and Skocpol, 2011). Although President Obama was in a favourable position because of the presence of Democratic majorities in both chambers of Congress, the health policy challenge facing the nation was stark, as reform needed to tackle two major issues in the context of a highly fragmented and complex health system that relied extensively on private benefits (Street, 2008). The first issue was the high numbers of Americans living without any health insurance coverage. In 2008, 15.4% of the US population lacked health insurance. The second issue was the cost of the most expensive health care system in the OECD. In 2008 the United States spent 16% of GDP on health care compared to 10.5% in Germany and only 8.7% in the United Kingdom (OECD, 2010). These dual goals of expanding coverage to more of the population while simultaneously reducing projected aggregate spending on health care set up a potentially contrary legislative task. In this context, health care reform was a risky business for Democrats, who faced Republicans unwilling to collaborate with them on reform and who strongly criticised the Obama administration for advocating health care reform in a time of economic recession.

The legislative process proved long and complex and the final PPACA was more compromised than many reform advocates wanted.Yet, even if the long-term impact of the PPACA remains uncertain because changes are being phased in gradually over a number of years, the reform does introduce major changes to the US health care system (Béland and Waddan, forthcoming). In order to significantly reduce the numbers of uninsured, the law creates incentives to encourage employers to purchase health insurance for their employees and also allows children to remain covered by a parent's health insurance until the age of 26. Furthermore, the legislation is to considerably expand Medicaid, the social assistance programme created in 1965 to provide minimum health coverage to specific low-income categories of the population. Starting in 2014, Medicaid will cover everyone earning less than 133% of the federal poverty level.This compares to the situation in 2010 when Medicaid did 'not even cover a majority of the federally defined poverty population' (Olson, 2010, p 226). Overall, by 2019, the new Medicaid rules should bring coverage to 16 million more Americans (CBO, 2010a). In addition, starting in 2014, health insurance exchanges will cater for people not covered through their employer or government programmes such as Medicaid and Medicare. Established by state authorities, these exchanges will work as regulated insurance markets in which federal subsidies should help lower-income people purchase a private insurance plan. By 2019, an estimated 24 million people will get their health insurance through such exchanges (CBO, 2010b). A further, popular, aspect of the PPACA is that insurers are prohibited from refusing to cover people with pre-existing medical conditions.

Since the administration had emphasised that health reform would reduce rather than increase the federal budget deficit, there was a focus on the Congressional Budget Office's (CBO's) scoring of the fiscal impact of reform proposals. In the end, the CBO predicted that the net impact on the federal budget of all the aspects of the PPACA would be a saving of $143 billion between 2010 and 2019 (CBO, 2010b), as the accumulated extra spending involved in expanding Medicaid and subsidising premiums in the health exchanges would be more than offset by savings generated in the Medicare programme and extra revenues like fees on branded drug manufacturers and insurers as well as additional hospital insurance taxes (CBO, 2010b). In addition to reducing the government's direct costs, the PPACA set out to reduce the burden on the wider American economy by introducing incentives for more cost discipline in the private health care market. Furthermore, the law laid out plans to modernise medical care delivery through encouraging greater efficiency and integration.

One important thing to understand in the context of this chapter is that, although a major social policy development enacted in the context of an economic crisis, health care reform was not a direct consequence of the crisis since health reform was a major issue long before the Great Recession. The crisis did help Democrats win the presidency and secure more seats in Congress in the 2008 elections, providing Democrats with the institutional capacity to enact a major health care reform (Hacker, 2011), but seeing it as a direct corollary of the Great Recession is problematic (Béland and Waddan, 2011). Nevertheless, the PPACA's potential impact should not be understated. It will not bring about true universal health coverage, as an estimated 23 million people will remain uninsured in the US in 2019 (CBO, 2010b), but if fully implemented, the PPACA will be the most redistributive social policy measure enacted in the US in a generation (Leonhardt, 2010). The revenues raised by the PPACA will primarily come from an increased Medicare payroll tax on people earning over $200,000; a new tax on unearned income of over $200,000; and taxes and fees on various medical providers including hospitals, physicians and the pharmaceutical industry (Connolly, 2010, pp 169–78). This represents a significant economic transfer from the wealthiest to lower- and middle-income Americans (Jacobs, 2011, p 626).

The return to austerity

If the relationship between the economic crisis and the 2010 health care reform is rather subtle, one of the most direct consequences of the Great Recession and the emergency spending it triggered was a massive increase in federal deficits. In 2011, for example, the White House expected the annual federal deficit for that year to reach $1.65 *trillion*, the equivalent of 10.9% of GDP, 'the largest deficit as a share of the economy since World War II' (Paletta and Boles, 2011). The return of large federal deficits (which had been gradually eliminated during the Clinton era) had already begun during the Bush years in the aftermath of the 2001 and 2003 tax cuts and the wars in Afghanistan and Iraq. Yet, starting in 2008, the Great Recession made things much worse, as the downturn both reduced federal revenues and increased social spending. As the federal deficit kept rising, starting in 2009, Republicans in Congress accused the Obama administration of overspending. Moreover, outside Congress, the growing right-wing populist movement known as the Tea Party asserted that spending was 'out of control' in Washington and that spending cuts were imperative. As the conservative discourse about 'out of control' spending gained momentum, the White House found it increasingly difficult to persuade Congress to finance additional stimulus and social policy efforts. Moreover, a debate over the future of the Bush-era tax cuts raged in 2009 and 2010, as Republicans categorically opposed President Obama's proposal to eliminate the tax cuts for the wealthy while renewing those affecting the middle class. Finally, during the lame duck session of Congress that immediately followed the November 2010 midterms, the President approved a legislative deal with Congress that extended payments to the long-term unemployed while maintaining the soon-to-be-expired Bush tax cuts, including those for the wealthy (Herszenhorn and Calmes, 2010). The administration maintained that securing the extension of unemployment benefits was a priority but the decision of President Obama to renew the Bush tax cuts for the rich illustrated the growing domination of conservative ideas on deficit control, which focused on spending cuts rather than on tax increases traditionally supported by Democrats.

In the late winter of 2010 and early spring of 2011, as the budget debate for the 2012 fiscal year raged, the Republicans increasingly pushed for large-scale spending cuts. The most systematic document put forward by the Republicans, now in charge of the House of Representatives, was the so-called 'Ryan Budget', which was embedded in a logic of fiscal austerity strikingly close to the ideas associated with the Tea Party movement. Formulated by Tea Party supporter and Chairman of the House Committee on the Budget Paul Ryan (Wisconsin), this seemingly radical budget proposal aimed to:

> recommit the nation fully to the timeless principles of American government enshrined in the U.S. Constitution – liberty, limited government, and equality under the rule of law. It seeks to guide policies by those principles, freeing the nation from the crushing burden of debt that is now threatening its future. (House Committee on the Budget, 2011)

As this quote suggests, the document depicted the debt in apocalyptic terms while arguing that the US government had grown out of control.

From this perspective, one could argue that, for many Republicans, the presence of large federal deficits provided an opportunity to push for a reduction in the size of government that they had long supported, regardless of the fiscal climate of the day. Following the 2001 tax cuts, some analysts speculated that the Bush administration was pursuing a 'starve the beast' strategy (Schick, 2003). As it turned out, the Bush era saw increased deficits as revenue reductions were not matched by spending cuts (Béland and Waddan, 2008), but, by 2011, conservatives were insisting that the dire fiscal position of government meant that there was no option but to cut government spending. Hence, conservatives claimed that there was a fiscal imperative to pursue the policies that they had always favoured. In turn, this helps explain why the push for austerity was so strong on the Right, as many Tea Party supporters and House Republicans, who opposed 'big government' in principle, expressed their enthusiasm for budget cuts and their aversion to tax increases. Thus, in the 'Ryan Budget', the focus was on spending cuts affecting programmes like Medicaid as well as a proposal to privatise Medicare by transforming it into a voucher programme.

The Medicare proposal featured in the 'Ryan Budget' was particularly controversial, as liberal commentators like Paul Krugman pointed to the fact that the proposed voucher system to subsidise people to purchase private health insurance coverage would mean the end of the programme as it was known (Krugman, 2011). Although Medicare remains a popular programme that Republicans themselves claimed to defend during the 2009–10 health care debate, this bold proposal reveals how their push for austerity is part of an ambitious plan to downsize the federal government. Clearly, increasingly bleak budget numbers have been successfully used to press for major federal social policy cuts and restructuring. Although only time will tell if these controversial proposals will materialise, by 2011, the Republicans and their Tea Party allies had already succeeded in reframing the federal policy agenda inasmuch as they had pushed to the fore a new politics of austerity that legitimised demands for spending cuts while making it harder for the Obama administration to propose new ways to improve social protection in an era of growing economic insecurity.

The balance of power between those advocating austerity versus those still promoting social spending and economic stimulus was well illustrated during the protracted debate over raising the country's debt ceiling through the summer of 2011 (Calmes, 2011). As the deadline for raising the debt limit approached, the Republicans controlling the House of Representatives pressed for an agreement that meant that any rise in the limit would be accompanied by significant spending cuts. In July 2011, President Obama put forward a so-called 'grand bargain' that proposed a total of $4 trillion in deficit reduction, including cuts to Social Security, Medicare and Medicaid. After some apparent initial interest, Republican leaders rejected the deal because it also included closing tax loopholes that would have affected wealthier Americans (Calmes and Hulse, 2011). Thus, Republicans insisted that austerity measures were to be imposed exclusively through spending cuts with no revenue-raising measures as part of the mix. The eventual debt ceiling agreement settled on over $2 trillion in spending cuts over 10 years with $900 billion agreed at the outset with a newly established bipartisan congressional commission charged with finding a further $1.2 trillion in deficit reduction (Hulse and Cooper, 2011).

After the failure to agree a long-term deficit-reduction deal in the summer of 2011, Standard and Poor's lowered its credit rating for the US from AAA to AA+, with this decision leading Chinese officials to reflect on US profligacy (Alderman, 2011). By the end of November, the special congressional Commission admitted that it could not agree on a deficit-reduction package as Democrats demanded that some new revenues be included in any deal while the Republicans refused to endorse new taxes. But the Democrats had been willing to concede significant spending cuts (Lipton, 2011), suggesting that Republicans were dominating the battle of ideas over the future of federal social policy in the US. Illustrating how the centre of ideational gravity within the Republican Party had shifted to the right, the early stages of the process to find the Republican presidential candidate for 2012 saw all candidates reject any prospect of revenue-raising as part of a package to reduce the budget deficit. At a debate in August 2011, the Republican presidential hopefuls were asked whether they would accept a deficit-reduction deal that was loaded 10 to one in terms of spending cuts versus revenue-raising. All replied that they would reject such a deal because it included tax increases (Cowen, 2011). While this may be dismissed as pandering to a particular section of the Republican core electorate for short-term expediency (and, as such, as no more irresponsible than when Democrats make promises of what they will provide with no detail about how they would pay for it), it is indicative of how conservatives have consolidated around a fundamental anti-tax and correspondingly anti-welfare set of ideas (Hacker and Pierson, 2005). Republican opposition to tax increases remained strong despite the fact that, in 2010, receipts to the federal government stood at 14.9% of GDP, the lowest level since 1950 (Tax Policy Center, 2011).

The fiscal crisis and the state governments (and the future of Medicaid)

Given the federal character of the American state, it is important to look beyond Washington DC and to examine how policymakers at state level adapted to the tightening fiscal constraints, especially as the Great Recession brought about the biggest recorded decline in state revenues. Even as revenues improved slightly at the beginning of 2011, those 'revenues remained roughly 9% below pre-recession levels' (McNichol et al, 2011). In fact, the pressure on state governments was more acute than that on the federal government, given the more limited revenue pools available to states coupled with the fact that nearly all states have some sort of balanced budget requirement (Maynard, 2010). In addition, as revenues declined from 2008 onwards, the demands on state budgets increased, as a greater number of people fell into hardship and turned to state social services for aid. This left states with budget shortfalls that meant they had to use up any 'rainy day' funds or look to cut spending in other areas.

Initially, state governments were helped in their efforts to deal with these problems by Washington, as the ARRA distributed significant funds to help cover state-level budget deficits in education and health, which are the biggest areas of state government spending. Those funds, however, had largely dried up by mid-2011, as many states enacted new budgets at the start of July 2011. At the start of fiscal year 2012, states reported 'shortfalls that total $103 billion with only $6 billion in federal Recovery Act dollars remaining available' (McNichol et al, 2011, p 3). Faced with the choice between raising taxes and making spending cuts, policymakers in most states opted for the latter course of action. In 2011, state general fund spending declined by 6.3%. Austerity measures typically included some cuts that further hurt people already damaged by the recession. For example, for the first time in half a century, a state, Michigan, reduced its state unemployment benefit (Prah, 2011). These cuts sometimes came with expressions of regret. In December 2010, Washington State Governor Chris Gregiore lamented:

> In any other time I would not sign this budget.... It's difficult to support something that goes against all that we have accomplished over the past six years. But these are the circumstances we find ourselves in, and we've been left with few options. (Quoted in Gramlich, 2011)

Elsewhere, especially in the aftermath of the 2010 elections that saw Republican gains in state houses across the country, the spending restrictions were seen as an opportunity to 'starve the beast' and reduce state government activities. Shortly after his inauguration, the new Republican Governor of Wisconsin, Scott Walker, announced that 'Under our administration ... state government will do only what is necessary' (quoted in Gramlich, 2011).

In social policy terms, the programme that best highlighted the problems facing the states was Medicaid, which provides health insurance to very low-income Americans and is jointly funded by the federal and state governments. Reflecting the importance of federal arrangements, states had long shown different commitment levels to Medicaid in terms of expenditure and intensity of efforts to enrol the eligible population (Thompson, 2011, pp 551–2), but all states came under pressure, as the recession and increased unemployment meant that more people turned to public programmes. ARRA did provide support to states' Medicaid funds through 2009 but, by the summer of 2010, it was clear that many states would run into deep fiscal trouble if there was not further significant federal funding; however, reflecting the changing mood in Washington, there was less willingness to fill the gaps in state Medicaid expenditure (Luo and Wheaton, 2010). Hence, by 2011, state governments had become increasingly distressed about paying their share of Medicaid costs (Goldstein and Balz, 2011), with evidence that the pressures of maintaining Medicaid spending was crowding out other areas of important social spending (Orszag, 2011). In fiscal year 2010, Medicaid spending accounted for 21.8% of state government expenditure, meaning that it had overtaken primary and secondary education spending as the biggest single item in states' budgets (National Association of State Budget Officers, 2010, p 2). Yet, by the fall of 2011, even the Obama administration was openly talking of cutting Medicaid payments to the states as part of its deficit-reduction efforts (Pear, 2011). Ironically, these developments were occurring against the backdrop of the expansion of Medicaid proposed in the PPACA (for more on the states and the PPACA, see Greer, 2011; Thompson, 2011).

Conclusion

The depth of the recession and the continuing severity of its impact on millions of Americans was illustrated in September 2011 when the US Census Bureau issued its report on poverty in the country in 2010. The numbers showed a poverty rate of 15.1%, which was the highest since 1993 (US Census Bureau, 2011, p 14). Furthermore, the poorest Americans had become even poorer. Of those below the poverty line, 44.3% lived in 'deep poverty', which is defined as a household income less than half the poverty line. This was the highest level of 'deep poverty' in 36 years (DeParle and Tavernise, 2011).

Yet, even as the report was issued, the debate in Washington was increasingly focusing not on how the government could develop social policy initiatives to alleviate the problems of those Americans hurt by the recession, but on how existing welfare state programmes might be cut back in order to reduce overall government spending (Pear, 2011). This consensus on the likely future retrenchment of social programmes stands in contrast to the expectations that arose when President Obama took office with Democratic majorities in both chambers of Congress in January 2009. The rapid enactment of ARRA, which included important safety-net spending on items such as Medicaid and Food Stamps, followed by the commitment to major health care reform that aimed to provide coverage to millions of uninsured Americans, suggested that the federal government was to meet the recession with an expansionary social policy agenda aimed at protecting vulnerable families and households. But, even before the midterm elections of 2010, that seemed likely to be a short-lived political moment, as voluble protests against health care reform and 'big government' dominated much of the news agenda. Furthermore, conservatives who protested that the PPACA betrayed the wishes of the majority of the public had their position reinforced by the 2010 elections, with some evidence that the health care reform cost Democrats votes (Saldin, 2010).

Moving forward, therefore, the elections of 2012 look critical to the future of social welfare policy in the United States. A revival of the spirit of January 2009 looks most unlikely but if Democrats retain control of the White House and/or one chamber of Congress, then this will possibly slow the process of retrenchment. Most obviously, Republicans are committed to a repeal of the PPACA, as reflected by the vote of the Republican-controlled House to do exactly that shortly after coming to power in 2011. By 2011, even with a Democrat in the White House, the tone of political discourse about social policy indicated a conservative ideological ascendancy. Conservatives claimed that their preference for social spending retrenchment was reinforced by the need for deficit reduction, which included reforms to the so-called 'third rails' ('touch it and die') of American politics, Medicare and Social Security. At the state level as well, the prospects for social policy activism look bleak, as the recovery from the revenue declines witnessed after 2008 are likely to be slow, particularly as the aggregate economic recovery remains stalled, with some states predicting that their revenues by 2020 will not have recovered to pre-recession levels (Goodman, 2011). In these circumstances, in a number of policy areas, conservative social policy goals resulting in diminished public social protection will possibly be advanced. Overall, therefore, the idea of that recession would lead to a politics of austerity (Vis et al, 2011) that favoured retrenchment looks likely to prove the case in the US, but the political road has been a winding one and future elections will still perhaps affect the speed of travel.

Acknowledgements

The authors would like to thank Kevin Farnsworth for his helpful comments and suggestions. They also thank the participants at the 'Global Economic Crisis and the Welfare State' workshop held at the University of Bremen in November 2011 for their feedback on an earlier version of this chapter. Daniel Béland acknowledges support from the Canada Research Chairs program.

Note

[1] The families receiving Aid to Families with Dependent Children and now TANF are mostly single-parent households with a female head of household.

References

Alderman, L. (2011) 'Some concern abroad about U.S. downgrade', *New York Times*, 6 August.

Béland, D. (2005) *Social security: history and politics from the new deal to the privatization debate*, Lawrence, KA: University Press of Kansas.

Béland, D. and Waddan, A. (2008) 'Taking "big government conservatism" seriously? The Bush presidency reconsidered', *The Political Quarterly*, vol 79, no 1, pp 109–18.

Béland, D. and Waddan, A. (2011) 'Social policy and the recent economic crisis in Canada and the United States', in K. Farnsworth and Z. Irving (eds) *Social policy in challenging times: economic crisis and welfare systems*, Bristol: The Policy Press, pp 231–49.

Béland, D. and Waddan, A. (forthcoming) 'The Obama presidency and health insurance reform: assessing continuity and change', *Social Policy & Society*.

Black, J. (2008) 'Americans' food stamp use nears all-time high', *Washington Post*, 26 November.

Calmes, J. (2011) 'Behind battles over debt, a war over government', *New York Times*, 14 July.

Calmes, K, and Hulse, C. (2011) 'Debt ceiling talks collapse as Boehner walks out', *New York Times*, 22 July.

CBO (Congressional Budget Office) (2010a) *The budget and economic outlook: fiscal years 2010 to 2020*, Washington, DC: Congress of the United States. Available at: http://www.cbo.gov/ftpdocs/108xx/doc10871/01-26-Outlook.pdf

CBO (2010b) 'H.R. 4872, Reconciliation Act of 2010', March 18. Available at: http://www.cbo.gov/ftpdocs/113xx/doc11355/hr4872.pdf

Connolly, C. (2010) 'How we got there' in The Washington Post, *Landmark: The inside story of America's new health-care law and what it means for us all*, New York: PublicAffairs.

Cook, R. (2009) 'Not your father's Democratic Congress', *Sabato's Crystal Ball*, 19 February. Available at: http://www.centerforpolitics.org/crystalball/articles/frc2009021901/

Cooper, M. (2008) 'McCain laboring to hit right note on the economy', *New York Times*, 16 September.

Cowen, T. (2011) 'The problem with no new taxes', *New York Times*, 1 October.

Crummy, K. and Sherry, A. (2009) 'Obama signs Stimulus Bill', *The Denver Post*, 18 February.

DeParle, J. and Gebeloff, R. (2009) 'Food stamp use soars, and stigma fades', *New York Times*, 29 November.

DeParle, J. and Tavernise, S. (2011) 'Poor are still getting poorer, but downturn's punch varies, census data show', *New York Times*, 15 September.

Dobelstein, A. (2009) *Understanding the Social Security Act: the foundation of social welfare for America in the twenty-first century*, New York, NY: Oxford University Press.

Goldstein, A. and Balz, D. (2011) 'Governors differ on extent of flexibility for Medicaid', *Washington Post*, 27 February.

Goodman, J. (2011) 'State budget outlook: the worst isn't over', *Stateline*, 19 January. Available at: www.stateline.org/live/details/story?contentId=541781

Gramlich, J. (2011) 'As state budgets, payrolls shrink, so do ambitions', *Stateline*, 10 January. Available at: www.stateline.org/live/details/story?contentId=540492

Greer, S. (2011) 'The states' role under the Patient Protection and Affordable Care Act', *Journal of Health Policy, Politics and Law*, vol 36, no 3, pp 469–73.

Hacker, J. (2011) 'Why reform happened', *Journal of Health Policy, Politics and Law*, vol 36, no 3, pp 437–41.

Hacker, J. and Pierson, P. (2005) *Off center: the Republican revolution and the erosion of American democracy*, New Haven, CT: Yale University Press.

Hagenbaugh, B. (2009) 'Many of the jobless get no unemployment benefits', *USA Today*, 10 April.

Herszenhorn, D. and Jackie C. (2010), 'Tax Deal suggests New Path for Obama', *New York Times*, 6 December.

House Committee on the Budget (2011) 'The path to prosperity: restoring America's promise', April, Washington, DC.

Hulse, C. and Cooper, H. (2011) 'Obama and leaders reach debt deal', *New York Times*, 31 July.

Jacobs, L.R. (2011) 'America's critical juncture: the Affordable Care Act and its reverberations', *Journal of Health Politics, Policy and Law*, vol 36, no 3, pp 625–31.

Jacobs, L.R. and Skocpol, T. (2011) *Health care reform and American politics: what everyone needs to know*, New York, NY: Oxford University Press.

Krugman, P. (2011) 'Vouchercare is not Medicare', *New York Times*, 6 June, A21.

Lee, D. (2011) 'Unemployment notches up to 9.1% in May as employers add just 54,000 to payrolls', *LA Times*, 3 June. Available at: http://www.latimes.com/business/la-fi-jobs-report-20110604,0,3594048.story

Leonhardt, D. (2010) 'In Health Bill, Obama attacks wealth inequality', *New York Times*, 23 March.

Lipton, E. (2011) 'Lawmakers trade blame as deficit talks crumble', *New York Times*, 21 November.

Luo, M. and S. Wheaton (2010) 'Aid to States may be lost as Jobs Bill stalls', *New York Times*, 26 June.

Maynard, M. (2010) 'State budget cuts: across the board, and at cross-purposes,' Stateline.org, 23 June. Available at: www.stateline.org/live/details/story?contentId=493525

McNichol, E., Oliff, P. and Johnson, N. (2011) *States continue to feel recession's impact*, Washington, DC: Center for Budget and Policy Priorities.

Murray, S. (2010) 'In U.S., 14% rely on food stamps', *Wall Street Journal*, 4 November. Available at: http://blogs.wsj.com/economics/2010/11/04/some-14-of-us-uses-food-stamps/

National Association of State Budget Officers (2010) 'Summary: NASBO state expenditure's report', December. Available at: http://www.nasbo. org/LinkClick.aspx?fileticket=HSlQhWvejXA%3d&tabid=38

National Employment Law Project (2009) 'Federal stimulus funding produces unprecedented wave of state unemployment insurance reforms'. Available at: http://www.nelp.org/page/-/UI/UIMA. Roundup.June.09.pdf?nocdn=1

OECD (2010) Directorate for Employment, Labour and Social Affairs, *OECD Health Data for 2010*. Available at: www.oecd.org/document /16/0,3343,en_2649_34631_2085200_1_1_1_1,00.html

Olson, L.K. (2010) *The politics of Medicaid*, New York, NY: Columbia University Press.

Orszag, P. (2011) 'How health care can save or sink America', *Foreign Affairs*, vol 90, no 4, pp 42–56.

Paletta, D. and Boles, C. (2011) 'White House expects deficit to spike to $1.65 trillion', *Wall Street Journal*, 14 February.

Pavetti, L. and Rosenbaum, D. (2010) *Creating a safety net that works when the economy doesn't: the role of the Food Stamp and TANF Programs*, Washington, DC: Center on Budget and Policy Priorities. Available at: www.cbpp.org/cms/index.cfm?fa=view&id=3096

Pavetti, L., Trisi, D. and Schott, L. (2011) *TANF responded unevenly during downturn*, Washington, DC: Center on Budget and Policy Priorities. Available at: www.cbpp.org/files/1-25-11tanf.pdf

Pear, R. (2011) 'Democrats see perils on path to health cuts', *New York Times*, 13 September.

Peck, D. (2011) 'Can the middle class be saved?', *The Atlantic*, vol 308, no 2, pp 60–78.

Pierson, P. (1994) *Dismantling the welfare state? Reagan, Thatcher, and the politics of retrenchment*, New York, NY: Cambridge University Press.

Prah, P. (2011) 'States balance budgets with cuts, not taxes', *Stateline*, 16 June. Available at: www.stateline.org/live/details/ story?contentId=581343

Reinhart, C. and Rogoff, K. (2009) 'The aftermath of financial crises', *American Economic Review*, vol 99, no 2, pp 466–72.

Saldin, R. (2010) 'Healthcare reform: a prescription for the 2010 Republican landslide?', *The Forum*, vol 8, no 4, Article 10.

Schick, A. (2003) 'Bush's budget problem', in F. Greenstein (ed) *The George W Bush presidency: an early assessment*, Baltimore, MD: Johns Hopkins University Press.

Shelton, A.M. (2009) 'Unemployment insurance provisions in the American Recovery and Reinvestment Act of 2009', Federal Publications, Paper 618. Available at: http://digitalcommons.ilr.cornell. edu/key_workplace/618

Skocpol, T. and Jacobs, L. (2011) *Reaching for a new deal: ambitious governance, economic meltdown, and polarized politics in Obama's first two years*, New York, NY: Russell Sage Foundation.

Street, D. (2008) 'Balancing act: the public–private mix in health care systems', in D. Béland and B. Gran (eds) *Public and private social policy: health and pension policies in a new era*, Houndmills: Palgrave Macmillan, pp 15–44.

Tax Policy Center (2011) 'Historical federal receipt and outlay summary'. Available at: www.taxpolicycenter.org/taxfacts/Content/PDF/ fed_receipt_sum_historical.pdf

Thompson, F. (2011) 'The Medicaid platform: can the termites be kept at bay?', *Journal of Health Policy, Politics and Law*, vol 36, no 3, pp 549–53.

US Bureau of Economic Analysis (2010a) 'National economic accounts: Gross Domestic Product, percent change from preceding period'. Available at: www.bea.gov/national/index.htm#gdp

US Bureau of Economic Analysis (2010b) 'Employment situation news release', April. Available at: www.bls.gov/news.release/archives/ empsit_04022010.htm

US Census Bureau (2011) *Income, poverty and health insurance coverage in the United States 2010*, Washington, DC: US Department of Commerce.

US Department of Labor (2010a) *Labor force statistics from the current population survey*, Washington, DC: UDSL. Available at: http://data. bls.gov/PDQ/servlet/SurveyOutputServlet?data_tool=latest_ numbers&series_id=LNS14000000

US Department of Labor (2010b) *The employment situation March 2010*, Washington, DC: Bureau of Labor Statistics, USDL. Available at: www. bls.gov/news.release/pdf/empsit.pdf

US Department of Labor (2011) *Employment situation summary*, Washington, DC: Bureau of Labor Statistics. Available at: www.bls. gov/news.release/empsit.nr0.htm

US Government Accountability Office (2007) *Unemployment insurance: low wage and part time workers continue to experience low rates of receipt*, Washington, DC: USGAO.

Veiga, A. (2007) 'Number of US homes facing foreclosure doubles', *USA Today*, 1 November.

Vis, B., Van Kersbergen, K. and Hylands, T. (2011) 'To what extent did the financial crisis intensify the pressure to reform the welfare state?', *Social Policy and Administration*, vol 45, no 4, pp 338–53.

FOURTEEN

Seeking refuge in the Nordic model: social policy in Iceland after 2008

Zoë Irving

Introduction

As a small island state, Iceland has not figured prominently in comparative analysis or welfare state modelling and has only recently gained popular notoriety as a result of its economic and environmental volatility. Notwithstanding the parallels between the global effects of volcanic ash clouds and the ballooning detritus of international finance, this chapter focuses on the Icelandic experience of 21st-century financial crisis, and what this might reveal about the development of social policy. Iceland's position as the earliest country to face post-2008 economic collapse is significant in terms of lessons to be drawn regarding financial regulation and the political process. The post-crisis Icelandic welfare trajectory is even more significant, however, in considering both the challenge (or not) to neo-liberal hegemony posed by the global economic crisis and the extent to which welfare states are bound (or not) to particular patterns of national response. The chapter begins with some commentary on the place of small (island) states in global context, and outlines some of the key historical and socio-political features that have shaped the Icelandic welfare state. After setting out how Iceland came to be at the centre of the financial crisis, the chapter goes on to explore social policy development since 2008. The discussion in the final section reflects on the extent to which the post-crisis response in Iceland represents an alternative vision giving lasting change, or a variant of the social and economic triage represented in the responses of other advanced economies.

Small island states: just extras on the world stage?

Academic literature on small states, and more particularly small island states, is mainly found in the disciplines of economics, international relations and development studies, complemented by long-standing anthropological and sociological insight gained from the study of the organisation of bounded, homogeneous population groups (eg Cohen, 1987; Goffman, 1990 [1959]; Benedict, 1993 [1934]; Malinowski, 2002 [1922]). Until very recently, notably with the UNRISD[1] 'Social policy in small states' project (2007–9), social development and welfare arrangements in small states have not been of significant interest in comparative social policy studies. This partly reflects the analytical dismissal of 'size' as a factor within the traditional concerns of welfare regime theory (Irving, 2011a), but also the wider assumptions regarding the characteristics of small (island) states and their place in the world system. For small island states, apparent peripheral status is assumed due to both geography and size. Environmental precariousness and remoteness, and the economic disadvantages that these features suggest (eg resource paucity and import reliance), combine with a numeric obstacle to military might that bars entry to the corridors of world power. However, this stereotypical view belies the various dimensions of what has been called the 'traditional paradox in international relations concerning the strength of the weak' (Katzenstein, 1985, p 21). This strength is manifested in various ways either through the use of 'vulnerable' country status to achieve preferential treatment in multilateral trade agreements and economic aid (Prasad, 2007) or through collective action. Alliances of small states and/or small island states are active participants in regional and international policy arenas such as the European Union (EU) and United Nations (UN) (Baldacchino, 2004). An illustrative example of small states 'thinking big' is the prominent role played by Iceland within the UN group of Small Island Developing States in negotiations relating to the Kyoto Protocol,[2] which then Prime Minister Halldór Asgrímsson was keen to point out in his speech on this topic. He concluded with the claim that 'We are a small state, that is true, but we are not a microstate. There is a difference' (Asgrímsson, 2004). More recently, in November 2011, Iceland again demonstrated its ability to think big in becoming the first country in Western Europe to recognise Palestine as an independent state, despite the resistance of the US and other UN Security Council members to this development.[3] These examples give an indication of the capacity of small island states to go against the grain of international pressure, which in the case of Iceland, is particularly significant in the context of the economic crisis.

In the sociological study of small island states, a tension derives from what has been called the 'New Guinea effect'. Selwyn (1980), for example, is critical of what he regards as the ascription of 'oddity' status to island states, which clouds recognition of the ways in which these states are subject to the same highs and lows of development experienced by all small states. Nevertheless, while the particular effect of 'islandness' is more empirically indeterminate, size is significant, as Katzenstein's (1985) work on the political economy of small European states has demonstrated, and as subsequent studies of politics and economics have also shown. To take an observation made from the study of biology, although size is simply a 'property', 'It is the supreme and universal determinant of what any organism can be and do' (Tyler Bonner, 2006, pp 3, 147), and while laws of nature are the same for all organisms, their significance is mediated through size. Similarly, while the operation of social, political and economic life may adhere to certain universals, the size of a social organisation makes an important difference to the form of that operation. A range of literature suggests, for example, that patterns of political discourse differ between small and large states (Schmidt, 2003): that 'small' is more democratic, more socio-politically tolerant (Dommen, 1980; Ott, 2000; Srebrnik, 2004) and more economically open and flexible (Read, 2004). Where positive qualities in either economic or socio-political development are identified, one question that arises is whether big can learn from small. This question underlay Katzenstein's original investigation of why the small European economies 'did better' than the US in the 1980s and forms part of the title of a recent work further exploring the fortunes of small welfare states since the 1970s (Obinger et al, 2010). The case of Iceland set out in the following discussion explores the progress of a potentially 'crucial test case' (as Obinger et al [2010] posit small states to be) for building alternative futures in the aftermath of first-order crisis. As noted in one early commentary on Iceland's troubles compared to those of other liberal economies, 'They differ only in scale, but not substance' (*The Economist*, 2008).

The Icelandic welfare state before 2008

Iceland claims to be Northern Europe's oldest 'democracy' with 1,100 years of settlement (Karlsson, 2000), but it is an island of modern settlers, which in development terms, has seen most change since attaining independence from Denmark in 1944. The strength of the social democratic/socialist parties at the critical welfare-building period during the 1930s and 1940s had ensured that provision established in the late 1800s was extended in the form of insurance against unemployment, sickness and invalidity, as well as health provision, pensions and social assistance. Nevertheless, in the decades following independence, the strength of the liberal/conservative Independence (IP) and Progressive (PP) parties similarly ensured that welfare expansion did not conform to the Nordic model associated with Iceland's neighbours (Karlsson, 2000; Jonsson, 2001; Ólafsson, 2005). There is no sense in which Iceland can be considered a Nordic 'laggard' in its welfare state development, which embodies elements of both hybridity – Iceland forged strong ties with the US following occupation during the 1940s – and exceptionalism. This latter characteristic stems from the specific concerns of a small society with great geopolitical significance, limited but desirable natural resources, and an overriding desire for the maintenance of national sovereignty. Icelanders value 'independence' far more highly than other qualities, for example (and far more highly than other European respondents; see European Commission, 2005, p 142), and, it is argued (Ólafsson, 2003, p 7), exhibit the 'populist culture' and values shared among settler societies, which are 'rugged, materialistic and achievement-oriented'.

In terms of social indicators, Iceland's achievements have been exceptional, particularly in health and education where mean years of schooling increased from 7.4 to 10.4 between 1980 and 2010, life expectancy rose from 76.6 to 81.7, and Gross National Income (GNI) per capita rose by 37% in the same period (UNDP, 2011). Iceland topped the Human Development Index ranking in 2007/08, having been within the highest-scoring nations during the early to mid-2000s. However, it is clear that Iceland's success in welfare outcomes is more related to consistently high levels of employment than a redistributive impulse on the part of the state. Combined employment rates have been over 76% since 1991, peaking at 81.7% in 2001, and while full-time male employment rates were above 90% during 2003–08, women's full-time rates also exceeded 62% during this period. Labour force participation rates among older workers (aged 55–64) have also been consistently well above the Organisation for Economic Co-operation and Development (OECD) average, peaking at 88.4% compared with an average of 51.6% in 2002 (55.0% in the UK) for example.[4] In the pre-crisis 2000s, the effective age of retirement (68.9 for men) has also exceeded all OECD countries in the global North bar Japan. Security through employment has thus maintained living standards and reduced pressure for the development of citizenship-based rather than insurance-led social protection.

In the years following independence, welfare arrangements have been characterised by liberal tendencies that reflect what might be regarded as the 'Icelandic' Lutheran heritage – the institutionalisation of the value of work (Kahl, 2009) but in the context of a relatively uncompetitive domestic labour market, and a less-articulated need to avoid selectivism in the quest for class integration. Social cohesion has perhaps been expressed in other ways, such as strong popular support for national ownership of resources and industry (Inglehart, 1997).[5] The liberal features include the restriction of the scope of benefit entitlements, the increasing prevalence of means-testing and the lack of benefit generosity, combined with greater reliance on private provision, particularly for retirement. Throughout the 1990s, second-tier compulsory occupational pensions outstripped the value of public pensions, which themselves declined in value vis-à-vis wages, and participation in third-tier individual pensions is comparatively high at 60% of wage-earners (Ólafsson, 2009). Health provision expanded and shifted from a municipal insurance-based to a tax-financed system in the early 1970s, but continued to involve elements of insurance for hospital services, co-payment, user charges and private provision, particularly in adult dental care. Social care developed largely as a voluntary sector activity and it too has seen an expansion of private sector involvement, for example, in residential care. In other areas of family policy and childcare, Iceland's gender arrangements resemble those of other Nordic countries more closely, such as provisions for shared parental leave, but, at the same time, both child benefits[6] and childcare subsidies are means-tested and lone-parent entitlements privilege larger families. Thus, in Siaroff's (1994) analysis, Iceland scored highly on the 'protestant' female work desirability indicators but less well on those of family welfare orientation.

Housing policy also illustrates the more contradictory dimensions of Iceland's welfare arrangements, with a shift towards social housing provision in the 1980s (Sveinsson, 1996) in contrast to its residualisation in the UK. The most unusual element of housing policy is the existence of the state mortgage lender, the Housing Financing Fund (HFF), which was intended to promote 'social owner-occupation' through the nationalisation of mortgage lending in the mid-1980s. By the end of the decade, the HFF was responsible for 85% of housing credit (Jonsson, 2001). Not surprisingly, the HFF has been a target for liberalisation in advice offered by the OECD for some time (OECD, 2005), but despite the rapidly expanding market competition for housing finance in the 2000s, the HFF has retained a central role.

In contrast to the mix of social policies introduced between the 1940s and 1980s, under the premiership of self-avowed Friedmanite Davíð Oddsson (1991–2004), the 1990s were a period of neo-liberal ascendance in Iceland. Both the public and private sectors were subject to a series of liberalising reforms, including privatisation within tertiary education, marketisation of public services and administration, health sector reorganisation, and, most importantly for Iceland's subsequent crisis, the privatisation of banking in 2003. In terms of raising its profile in the global market, these reforms appeared to achieve the government's expansionist ideals. Between 1995 and 2005, the economy grew by 50% in real terms and Oddsson's successor in 2004, Halldor Asgrímsson, was able to declare Iceland the fifth most competitive global economy (Asgrímsson, 2005). In 2004, Iceland's level of foreign equity investment was the second largest of 122 countries, only outpaced by the United Arab Emirates (Sighvatsson et al, 2011). This transformation from 'extra' to 'leading role' on the world stage was the result of a politically driven desire to maximise Iceland's comparative advantage. As is the case for many small island states, the global financial sector is one area where this can be achieved given limited human and natural resources. In an effort to secure inward investment, corporate tax was lowered from 51% to 18% and Iceland's three largest banks (Glitnir, Kaupthing and Landsbanki) were able to expand at a rate previously unknown in international finance. The so-called 'viking' investors were able to stake claims in a diverse range of international retail operations (eg food, aviation, toys and jewellery[7]) but in doing so exposed the nation to liabilities far beyond its capacity to guarantee (see Irving, 2011b). In the words of one commentator, Iceland had become 'a caricature of US-style casino capitalism' (Hannibalsson, 2011): inter-bank and intra-bank[8] borrowing to finance foreign acquisitions using foreign credit, the further accumulation of external debt via high interest payments to lure foreign deposits, and the inability of the Central Bank of Iceland to meet its obligations as a lender of last resort resulted in Iceland becoming the first nation-state to face outright bankruptcy in the wake of the US sub-prime crisis. Iceland's three largest banks collapsed in October 2008 with estimated losses of US$100 billion leaving Iceland with net debts equivalent to 210% of GDP (Sighvatsson et al, 2011).

In retrospect, the failings of bank regulation, the oligarchical control and political cronyism exercised by Iceland's wealthy elites, and the reaction of the UK, as well as popular euphoria emanating from the credit boom, are all implicated in Iceland's crisis or *Kreppan* – 'the pinch' as it is referred to in Iceland (Boyes, 2009; Jónsson, 2009; Special Investigation Committee, 2010). In more general terms, as the current Finance Minister described events: 'These politicians and ideologists ... in many ways turned Iceland into a neoliberal laboratory. And the experiment had a terrible ending' (*The Guardian*, 2009). The 'terrible ending' included the necessity for an International Monetary Fund (IMF) loan (the Stand By Arrangement, henceforth SBA) of US$2.1 billion with a further IMF-supported US$2.5 billion in bilateral arrangements with the Nordic countries, the Faroe Islands and Poland. At the time of the collapse, household debt was reported to represent 213% of disposable income compared to 169% in the UK (*The Economist*, 2008). Many households in Iceland held loans and mortgages in foreign currencies and, thus, the massive depreciation of the Krona (by 40%[9] immediately following the bank collapse) combined with subsequent job losses, reductions in social security payments and price increases has had a significant impact on social and economic welfare.

Possibilities for welfare state 'regime change'

The events in September 2008 also had a significant political impact on Iceland. The failure of the IP-led coalition to address the ensuing economic turmoil resulted in national protests and the eventual resignation of the government. Following this so-called 'pot and pan revolution', a general election in April 2009 returned the first leftist coalition government in Iceland's history, with the Social Democratic Alliance (SDA) gaining 29.8% of the vote and the Left–Green Movement (LGM) 21.7%. Iceland also gained its first woman Prime Minister, Johanna Sigurðardóttir. This was a historic change in Icelandic politics, since although parties of the Left had formed part of coalition governments from independence up until the 1960s, divisions within these parties had prevented them gaining significant power, and where improvements in welfare provision have occurred, they have been argued to be more a result of collective bargaining than government action (Ólafsson, 1993; Jonsson, 2001). In its initial address to the electorate, the government stated that it aimed to create 'a Nordic welfare society in Iceland, where collective interests take precedence over particular interests'.[10] In social policy terms, there was clearly a conflict between surfacing collectivist values and external pressures to introduce austerity measures, both through the IMF's SBA conditions and more broadly through international messages about the need to restore market confidence. With an initial ratio of 25% tax increases to 75% spending cuts in 2011, and a 'difficult, even painful but unavoidable' tagline (Sigfússon, 2010), the Icelandic austerity plan had superficial similarity to those of many of the other advanced European economies. However, there are two important dimensions to the Icelandic response that differentiate it from those of other countries: a political emphasis on the commitment to welfare and acts of resistance to both international and 'market' pressures.

A commitment to welfare

The coalition government has expressed its ideological commitment to ensuring the protection of those worst affected by the crisis in the short term and, in the long term, to transforming Icelandic society. In its policy statement 'Iceland 2020' (representing the government's 'vision for the future') the opening sentence states that 'Iceland aims to become a dynamic society capable of protecting its welfare in a manner that is sustainable and serves all members of the community by the year 2020' (Prime Minister's Office, 2011). On achieving office in 2009, the government prioritised key areas of welfare policy development. First, progression of reforms to the system of social security that had been undertaken from 2007, when the SDA had joined the IP in coalition. In their entirety (the final bill to parliament will be presented in Spring 2012[11]), these reforms target system complexity but also intend to remove inequalities created by the means-testing of social pensions, and create an activation-led system of sickness and disability benefits based on the Norwegian model (Ólafsson, 2009). In a related effort to reverse the neoliberal drift in social policy, the new government also abolished the hospital user charges introduced immediately prior to the election and abandoned the previous administration's plans for health sector reorganisation in favour of the development of new plans including cost-savings drawn from reductions in doctors' pay rather than labour-shedding (Ólafsson, 2009). Second, the long-term 'consolidation of administration' is a core strategy for cost-saving reform, involving ministry mergers and a nationwide reorganisation of public sector operations. It is also presented as a safeguarding strategy as far as the negative effects of austerity measures are concerned (Sigfússon, 2010), a view shared by 'The Welfare Watch' committee of ministers and social partners tasked with monitoring social and economic change in the aftermath of 2008. The policy proposals contained in its initial report (The Welfare Watch, 2010) reinforce the government's desire to ensure that those most disadvantaged remain protected within the context of spending cuts, and that reforms constituting 'emergency measures', rather than a politically defined policy package, should be reversible come better times. This 'reversibility' is confirmed in the 2011 Budget Proposal:[12]

> The objective is a sustainable growth of the economy that is based on realistic production of valuable goods and services instead of debt accumulation.... In this way, the Treasury and the municipalities' revenue base will grow, there will be less need for austerity measures and expenditure cuts, and it will subsequently be possible to begin retiring debt and to regain social welfare services that need to be scaled back for the time being.

Iceland is of course shouldering a huge gross debt as a result of the bank failures, estimated at its highest at 100% of GDP in 2011 (IMF, 2011b), reducing to 81% by 2012 according to the Ministry of Finance. The 'crunch' year was 2010/11 as far as economic forecasts have been concerned, when negative indicators were set to peak and the impact of both the crisis and its related austerity measures were predicted to hit hardest within the population. However, the '2011 budget proposal' (Ministry of Finance, 2011) estimated that the economy would be in surplus by 2012, with revenue increases expected to represent a third of the amount to be cut in expenditure. The progressiveness of personal income tax has been increased and inheritance tax was raised from 5% to 10%, but VAT at 25% (in the second band) remains the highest in Europe. Payroll taxes were also increased by 1.6% in 2009 and 2010 and social security contributions thus increased as a proportion of revenue from 9.5% in 2007 to 14.6% in 2010. Less progressive measures, such as raising the levels of income at which means-tested benefits are paid, halving payments for Childbirth Leave and reductions in child benefit and mortgage interest rebates, have been framed as a means to protect the most vulnerable groups (older people and those with disabilities) and front-line services. In tandem with these measures, wage agreements over the years to 2013 have been secured amounting to a 3.5% increase for 2012 in the public sector, with further increases for those on low earnings. At face value, the level of cuts set out in Table 14.1 suggest that a political desire to build a 'welfare society' would be beset by more limitations than possibilities in practice. However, given the detail of the ways in which the cuts will be implemented and the principles by which they are underpinned, the figures alone do 'camouflage more than they reveal'.

Table 14.1 Cuts planned in Iceland's 2011 budget

Area of spending	Current spending (billion Krona)	% reduction
Transportation, economic and unemployment affairs	82.0	10.5%
Health	115.4	4.7%
Social security and welfare	132.8	4.9%
Education	47.8	5.6%
General public services	27.2	6.7%
Public order and safety	20.9	6.8%
Culture, sport and religion	15.3	8.5%
Housing and distribution system	4.9	3.8%
Total	446.3	6.3%

Source: Ministry of Finance (2011)

Politics in Iceland have always been more than the sum of Right–Left difference. In determining the course of policy development, there are 'shorter distances and deeper links' between political actors as much as 'economic agents' (Read, 2004, p 370) and popular mobilisation is a significant catalyst in the policy process. The more recent budget proposal for 2012 was subject to substantial revisions during several rounds of parliamentary discussion and some disquiet within the coalition (various reports in *Iceland Review*[13] detail the proposal's progress and its critics). Areas benefiting from less severe cuts than originally proposed included education and health, pensions and disability benefits, and interest relief for indebted households, which is to include contributions from financial institutions. Much policy effort has been put into protecting the incomes of indebted households (eg write-offs and assistance with restructuring and rescheduling, changes in the legislation on foreclosures, and the establishment of a new Debtors' Ombudsman's Office). In contrast to popular demand for further action on debt relief, however, the IMF has indicated that measures should now be allowed to 'work through' to 'contain expectations of further relief' (IMF, 2011a) and this area will, thus, provide an illuminating example of how a battle of ideas between indebted advanced nations and their International Governmental Organisation creditors is played out.

The huge rise in unemployment since 2009 (up from 1.6% in 2008 to 8% in 2009) accounts for the greatest challenge to Iceland's post-crisis 'Nordic' welfare trajectory. This is partly because unemployment is obviously linked to diswelfare in numerous ways, but also because measures to counter unemployment are a relatively undeveloped area of policy in Iceland. The direct link between income and social and job security has represented its core economic strength and its route to the 'good society' but other than some policy discussion around the activation of those claiming disability benefits in the early 2000s, there was little necessity to devote attention to active labour-market policies in the pre-crisis condition of fractional unemployment (see Figure 14.1). In their 2010 report, The Welfare Watch drew particular attention to labour-market exclusion among younger age groups, as, in common with the problems of unemployment in many of the other 'most-affected' nations, youth unemployment poses the greatest risks to current social stability and future growth. One of the problems specific to Iceland's meteoric economic rise and fall is that during the period of prosperity, many young people were able to secure relatively high-wage jobs with little education or training investment, but these jobs have disappeared in the current climate. These changes reflect not only the recessionary impact of the crisis on sectors such as construction, but also the impact of the credit freeze and capital control measures on small businesses. Much of the migrant labour force departed in the aftermath of 2008 but with no residue of job vacancies. Re-entry to education has become a key strategy and activation measures introduced from 2010 include the opening of secondary schools to under 25s who wish to complete their education (30% of those aged between 20 and 66 have no formal secondary education), provisions for job retraining, subsidised 'trial hiring' and volunteer work. The Directorate of Labour has estimated that 50% of participants in such programmes have secured employment in the subsequent months (IMF, 2011b) but the OECD (2011), while supportive of the success of the 'internship' measure, is less convinced of the effectiveness of the total package of activation measures. This is also important because one of the indices on which Iceland has consistently bettered other OECD countries is the rate of long-term unemployment, which was 0.25% of the labour force in 2007. This rate had increased to 3% by 2011 and is worrying since structural unemployment was a core problem following the crisis experienced by the other Nordic countries in the 1990s (OECD, 2011). On the demand side, the government has also introduced a number of counter-recessionary measures to assist businesses small and large, including, for example, collaboration with pension funds in the financing of large-scale investment projects and personal income tax and VAT rebates on maintenance work.

Although the IMF expressed some concern regarding unemployment in its final SBA review (IMF, 2011b), the government is less pessimistic because the rate has declined from 2010/11 (Ministry of Finance, 2010b). However, the conditions that have assisted in decelerating the rise of unemployment (expansion of part-time employment, wage freezes and reductions, and outward migration of both Icelandic nationals and migrant workers) do not equate to good welfare outcomes, particularly given that unemployment benefit at around 50% of average earnings after three months (Ólafsson, 2009) is comparatively low. The government intends to halve unemployment from 8.3% in 2011 to 4.8% by 2014 and also reduce unemployment-related spending in that period by 40%. This will prove a considerable challenge.

Figure 14.1: Unemployment as a percentage of the labour force, 1980–2009

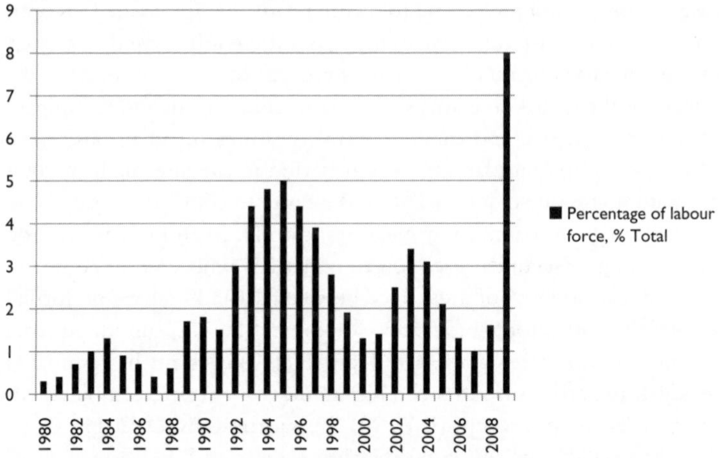

Source: Figure created from data available at http://www.statice.is

Since 2003, part-time employment has decreased as a proportion of women's employment but from 2008 to 2010 has increased its share by 3% to 37.8%. The pattern for men is broadly similar, although a 4.1% increase from 2008 to 2010 is higher, taking the part-time share total to 14.1%. The significance of part-time employment in the post-crisis labour market differs according to age as the rate among 16–24 year olds has dropped markedly from 40.4% to 27.4% during 2008–10 while the rate for 25–54 year olds has increased from 15.4% to 24%. The increasing significance of (involuntary) part-time work has led the government to extend unemployment benefit entitlements to these workers alongside a more general extension of the total period of unemployment benefit entitlement from three to four years, but also to consider the place of part-time employment in expanding opportunities for the relatively high proportion of the population in receipt of disability benefits (6.9%). While not necessarily adopting the Dutch model (Visser, 2002), a progressive development of part-time employment is one potential route to the achievement of the government's 2020 gender employment objectives. In policy terms, the future of job creation and growth has been located in the development of hi-tech services (financial services still accounted for 26% of GDP in 2011) with an emphasis on education, science research and innovation, and, given the political priorities of the LGM, 'eco-innovation and its products' (Prime Minister's Office, 2011). Iceland's size and geography do present advantages in this vision (see Irving, 2011b, pp 214–15).

With reliance on a new economic model for growth, it is intended that Iceland will become a 'fully fledged member of the group of Nordic welfare states, which guarantee social security and the equality of citizens' (Prime Minister's Office, 2011, p 7). In her recent speech on Icelandic National Day (17 June 2011), Johanna Sigurðardóttir again emphasised the values she sees as underpinning Iceland's recovery and future:

> It is no coincidence that Nordic welfare societies are, by most measures, the world's most economically successful societies, which serve as models for other nations because welfare and economic prowess go hand-in-hand. This is not least the case in small societies such as that of Iceland. Such societies simply fail to thrive when inequality gets out of bounds.... By increasing equality, they will ensure additional triumphs for Icelandic society, while healing the wounds left by the collapse and inequality of the past decade on the economy and society.[14]

Inequality, and its sharp increase during the period of 'prosperity' prior to 2008 ('Iceland 2020' reports that between 1993 and 2007, the Gini coefficient increased by 103%), is thus admitted as the core social problem and there is a government commitment to reducing the Gini coefficient to 25 by 2020. An indicative attempt to move in this direction is the increase in the net wealth tax to 1.25%, and the 10.5% salary tax on financial institutions, insurance companies and pension funds introduced in the budget for 2012. The wealth tax was an explicitly redistributive measure, introduced because 'In recent years, substantial monetary assets have accumulated in the hands of a small group of people' (Ministry of

Finance, 2011, p 16). Long-term tax reform is also on the policy agenda as the means to 'guarantee Nordic welfare' (Prime Minister's Office, 2011, p 28). Taken as a whole, these examples of post-crisis policy reform demonstrate that within the national context, and in the case of Iceland with austerity imposed rather than chosen, welfare retrenchment does not necessarily imply either the abandonment of state guarantees or the permanency of changes. The following section considers Iceland's response in the international context.

Acts of resistance

In contrast to other countries, the Icelandic response to the collapse of its three largest banks was to write off foreign liabilities altogether and, instead, establish three replacement domestic banks using the domestic assets of the failed banks to cover creditors' claims. Given the complexity of what is owed by who to whom, even the Central Bank of Iceland's report (Sighvatsson et al, 2011) is unable to provide a definitive assessment of the size and scope of Iceland's debt. It estimates that the final net debt pertaining to the largest failed banks would be between 38% and 48% of GDP, but there are a number of 'uncertainties' that may alter this figure. For example, Actavis, a multinational pharmaceutical company registered in Iceland, is reported as owing its foreign owner the equivalent of 70% of Icelandic GDP, and several other small banks and a number of holding companies are subject to 'winding-up proceedings'. The report suggests that, directly and indirectly, the financial collapse has added debt worth around 60% of GDP to the public sector but that 'net external public sector debt will never exceed more than one fourth of GDP' (Sighvatsson et al, 2011, pp 6, 36).

The biggest 'uncertainty' is the outcome of legal proceedings relating to the 'Icesave' debacle, which has shown not only that 'debt' is a slippery concept, but also that as far as 'the logic of no alternative' is concerned, resistance is not futile. Icesave was the online operation of Landsbanki, which offered high interest rates to savers and had accrued deposits from thousands of UK and Dutch investors, including some high-profile organisations in the UK.[15] Since the dramatic use of UK anti-terrorism legislation in reaction to the bankruptcy of Landsbanki, the pressure upon Iceland to secure the risks of foreign investors has been immense. This pressure from both the UK and Dutch treasuries, international organisations (eg IMF, 2008) and 'the markets' has been met with extreme hostility among Icelanders who have continued to refute their accountability for the 'foreign debts of reckless people' (as then Chair of the Central Bank Davíð Oddsson referred to the problem in 2008). This hostility is well founded given that the liabilities would render the population hopelessly indebted for generations. Despite the resolution of the dispute (ie an Icelandic promise to pay out) being regarded as a measure of Iceland's economic rehabilitation and restoration of its international standing, the final national referendum on the issue in April 2011 returned a resounding 'no' to this option. Resolution will now come as a result of judicial proceedings in the EFTA[16] Surveillance Authority court. Iceland has committed to the payment of interest accrued in the meantime (around 0.5% of GDP according to Sighvatsson et al [2011]) but Prime Minister Sigurðardóttir believes that over 90% of priority claims will be covered by the bank's assets[17] and the OECD (2011) has indicated that uncertainty is not affecting the IMF agreement. Following the referendum, all three key ratings agencies reviewed Iceland's status and despite assumptions that a 'no' vote would damage Iceland's international reputation, it was removed from Standard and Poor's 'credit watch' list and moved from 'negative' to 'stable' in the assessment of Fitch. What is significant is that against the warning that 'the markets' would punish Iceland were it not prepared to pick up the debt, the people and government took a stand against the power of financial capital, put welfare first and the sky did not fall in.

Despite its seemingly vulnerable global position, Iceland has, thus, continued to exercise strength and independence in its international relationships after 2008. Although it submitted to an IMF loan and associated conditionalities, the coalition government has met the conditions within its own frame of reference and the IMF has been surprisingly indulgent in response to the government's desire to 'protect the most vulnerable', publicly expressing admiration for Iceland's consensual decision-making (IMF, 2009). By August 2011, the IMF had approved all six tranches of the loan payment, and while raising concerns about slower-than-expected progress in some areas of economic reform (eg private sector debt restructuring), the organisation's evaluation of the government's actions has been positive. In fact, on economic measures, Iceland's recovery does appear encouraging, as the Minister of Finance (2010a) reports: lower-than-predicted contraction, increasing domestic production, a surplus in the balance of trade, inflation down from 17.8% in 2009 to 5.3% in 2011, GDP growth of 2.5% in 2011 and an appreciating Icelandic Krona. Witness to the recovery was a successful US$1 billion issue of government bonds in summer 2011 that was 100% oversubscribed according to the Ministry of Finance[18] and represented an 'investors' reward' according to the *Wall Street Journal* (Barley, 2011).

In the wake of the crisis, one element of Iceland's relocation in the international domain was its rapidly submitted application to join the EU. This was an interesting volte face since, prior to 2008, potential EU membership had been a source of division between those who felt that Iceland would benefit from the protection and stability that accession would bring, and those who privileged national sovereignty and feared not only a loss of nationhood, but also a loss of control of Iceland's key resources. This debate has recurred since the 1970s and, as Thorhallsson (2002) notes, the predilection for membership has been much greater among the general population than within the political elite, but the crisis altered both perceptions of safety in an insecure world[19] and national priorities. The IMF has supported membership and the OECD (2011) advises that should Iceland accede, it should also adopt the Euro 'as quickly as possible'. As Iceland's recovery proceeds, however, the possibility of its ever-closer union with Europe is looking increasingly unlikely. Accession discussions continued throughout 2011[20] and, in its progress report in October, the European Commission confirmed that the necessary political and economic conditions for membership had been met. However, popular and political appetite for accession has waned considerably. The Left–Green and Independence Parties are opposed to accession, with the Progressive Party also likely to follow suit. Ultimately, the decision to join will be agreed (or not) via a referendum and it seems that despite Iceland's continuing insecurities, the overriding desire to maintain sovereignty (including its own currency) has re-emerged as the means to achieve a Nordic social model.

Conclusions

Although many commentators within Iceland write with a continued feeling of pessimism regarding the possibilities for change, from the perspective of states where the revitalisation rather than the 'non-death' of neo-liberalism is both apparent in political discourse and felt through the assault on public welfare, the rejection of ratings agency-led social policy has much appeal. The fact that Davíð Oddsson is now editor of the conservative daily newspaper *Morgunblaðið*, despite having played a central role in Iceland's downfall, is disheartening but should not distract attention from the enduring and positive accomplishments of policy reform, which have prevented the return to business as usual that has occurred in countries such as the UK and Ireland. The inadequacies of the democratic process in Iceland have been exposed and despite the initial 'revolution', the changes necessary to redistribute power are proving incremental, but at least their necessity is recognised. What is demonstrated in the Icelandic response to the crisis is that a social policy based on what 'the market' will tolerate is not the only solution. The lack of capitulation on the Icesave question and the declining support for the market security offered by EU membership are testament to the strength of the weak in determining a future that is based on an alternative set of values. Whether it will provide an 'incentive for other countries ravaged by the asset bubble to hang their own bondholders out to dry' (Jónsson, 2009, p 211) remains to be seen, but protests over the summer of 2011 in Spain have been linked to the Icelandic response, and the Greek government's agony over the conflicting pressures of the markets and the people suggests that the 'welfare state' cannot yet be consigned to an anomaly of post-war history. There are of course many features of the Icelandic experience that are specific and outside the realm of possibility for larger states, but if there is one lesson to be learned, it is that in order to oppose the hegemony of austerity, there has to be a counterfactual, and Iceland is convincing in this regard. Perhaps Iceland should retain its crisis role as 'canary in a coalmine' (*Reykjavik Grapevine*, 2009) whose post-crisis voice should be heard by states big and small.

Notes

[1] United Nations Research Institute for Social Development project, available at: www.unrisd.org/research/spd/smallstates

[2] The international agreement on climate change that, after lengthy negotiations begun in 1997, came into force in 2005 (see: http://unfccc.int/kyoto_protocol/items/2830.php).

[3] See: www.guardian.co.uk/world/2011/nov/30/iceland-recognises-palestinian-state/

[4] Labour Force Survey by sex and age, available at: http://stats.oecd.org/Index.aspx?DataSetCode=LFS_SEXAGE_I_R

[5] In the 1990 World Values Survey, 38% of Icelandic respondents supported this, which is far higher than any other nation – the next highest was South Africa at 7%.

[6] Although the under-seven child supplement is not means-tested.

[7] Many of which, with familiar names in the UK, have since gone into receivership or been taken over (Woolworths and Somerfield are two examples).

[8] Both the Special Investigation Commission report (2010) and the Central Bank of Iceland report (Sighvatsson et al, 2011) suggest that via complex and dubious means, the three largest banks financed their own foreign borrowing.

[9] See: www.sedlabanki.is/?pageid=552&itemid=5d8b67bd-f82d-49a2-a57f-35118b8154a8&nextday=6&nextmonth=2

[10] Prime Minister's Office, see: http://eng.forsaetisraduneyti.is/news-and-articles/nr/3706

[11] Personal Communication, Department of Social and Labour Market Affairs, Ministry of Welfare, 5 November 2011.

[12] Available at: http://eng.fjarmalaraduneyti.is/media/Fjarlog/Fiscal_consolidation_plan_2011.pdf

[13] Available at: http://icelandreview.com/icelandreview/daily_news/?cat_id=16567&ew_0_a_id=371420

[14] Address of the Prime Minister on 17 June 2011. Available at: http://eng.forsaetisraduneyti.is/minister/JS_speeches/nr/6811

[15] For example, local and police authorities and the Audit Commission.

[16] European Free Trade Association.

[17] In an article in *The Guardian* on 13 April 2011, available at: www.guardian.co.uk/commentisfree/2011/apr/13/icesave-referendum-uk-payments

[18] Available at: http://eng.fjarmalaraduneyti.is/publications/news/nr/14376

[19] To part-paraphrase Zygmunt Bauman (2001).

[20] See Ministry of Finance, available at: www.mfa.is/speeches-and-articles/nr/6467

References

Asgrímsson, H. (2004) 'Why small states must think big', Prime Minister's Opening Address to Workshop on Small States, Reykjavik, 17 September. Available at: http://eng.forsaetisraduneyti.is/minister/Speeches_HA/nr/1517

Asgrímsson, H. (2005) 'The Icelandic economy', Prime Minister's speech, Landsbanki Islands, 14 March. Available at: http://eng.forsaetisraduneyti.is/minister/Speeches_HA/nr/1732

Bauman, Z. (2001) *Community: Seeking safety in an insecure world*, Cambridge: Polity Press.

Baldacchino, G. (2004) 'Editorial introduction', *World Development*, vol 32, no 2, p 327.

Barley, R. (2011) 'Investors reward Iceland's steady progress', *Wall Street Journal Online*, 10 June. Available at: http://online.wsj.com/article/SB10001424052702304259304576375340039763606-search.html?KEYWORDS=Richard+Barley&COLLECTION=wsjie/6month

Benedict, R. (1993 [1934]) *Patterns of culture*, Boston, MA: Houghton Mifflin.

Boyes, R. (2009) *Meltdown Iceland*, London: Bloomsbury.

Cohen, A.P. (1987) *Whalsay: symbol, segment and boundary in a Shetland Island community*, Manchester: Manchester University Press.

Dommen, E. (1980) 'Some distinguishing characteristics of island states', *World Development*, no 8, pp 931-43.

European Commission (2005) 'Social values, science and technology', Special Eurobarometer No. 225. Available at: http://ec.europa.eu/public_opinion/archives/ebs/ebs_225_report_en.pdf

Goffman, E. (1990 [1959]) *The presentation of self in everyday life*, London: Penguin.

Hannibalsson, J.B. (2011) 'To be or not to be – a republic at the crossroads', *Reykjavik Grapevine*, no 1.

IMF (International Monetary Fund) (2008) 'IMF Executive Board approves US$2.1 billion stand-by arrangement for Iceland', press release No 08/296, 19 November. Available at: www.imf.org/external/np/sec/pr/2008/pr08296.htm

IMF (2009) 'Statement by the IMF mission to Iceland', press release 09/76, 13 March. Available at: www.imf.org/external/np/sec/pr/2009/pr0976.htm

IMF (2011a) 'IMF completes fourth review under the stand-by arrangement for Iceland', press release No 11/5, 11 January. Available at: www.imf.org/external/np/sec/pr/2011/pr1105.htm

IMF (2011b) 'Iceland: fifth review under the stand-by arrangement', IMF Country Report No 11/125, June. Available at: http://eng.efnahagsraduneyti.is/Publications/nr/3249

Inglehart, R. (1997) *Modernization and postmodernization, cultural, economic and political change in 43 societies*, Princeton, NJ: Princeton University Press.

Irving, Z. (2011a) 'Curious cases: small island states' exceptionalism and its contribution to comparative welfare theory', in M. Benson and R. Munro (eds) *Sociological Routes and Political Roots, The Sociological Review*, special issue, vol 58, no 2, pp 225–45 (also published as (2011) *The sociological review monograph series*, Oxford: Wiley-Blackwell).

Irving, Z. (2011b) 'Waving not drowning: Iceland *kreppan* and alternative social policy futures', in K. Farnsworth and Z. Irving (eds) *Social policy in challenging times, economic crisis and welfare systems*, Bristol: The Policy Press.

Jónsson, Á. (2009) *Why Iceland? How one of the world's smallest countries became the meltdown's biggest casualty*, New York, NY: McGraw Hill.

Jonsson, G. (2001) 'The Icelandic welfare state in the twentieth century', *Scandinavian Journal of History*, vol 26, no 3, pp 249–67.

Kahl, S. (2009) 'Religious doctrines and poor relief: a different causal pathway', in K. Van Kersbergen and P. Manow (eds) *Religion, class coalitions and welfare states*, Cambridge: Cambridge University Press.

Karlsson, G. (2000) *Iceland's 1100 years*, London: Hurst and Company.

Katzenstein, P. (1985) *Small states in world markets, industrial policy in Europe*, Ithaca, NY: Cornell University Press.

Malinowski, B. (2002 [1922]) *Argonauts of the western Pacific*, London: Routledge.

Ministry of Finance (2010a) '2011 fiscal budget proposal', October. Available at: http://eng.fjarmalaraduneyti.is/government-finance/fiscal-budget/nr/13674

Ministry of Finance (2010b) 'Budget proposal 2011', Chapter 3, Available at: http://eng.fjarmalaraduneyti.is/media/Fjarlog/Fiscal_consolidation_plan_2011.pdf

Ministry of Finance (2011) 'Treasury finances January–August 2011'. Available at: http://eng.fjarmalaraduneyti.is/government-finance/treasury/nr/14703

Obinger, H., Starke, P., Moser, J., Bogedan, C., Gindulis, E. and Leibfried, S. (eds) (2010) *Transformations of the welfare state: small states big lessons*, Oxford: Oxford University Press.

OECD (Organisation for Economic Co-operation and Development) (2005) *Economic survey of Iceland, 2005*, Policy Brief, OECD Observer, February, Paris: OECD.

OECD (2011) *Economic surveys Iceland June 2011 overview*, Paris: OECD.

Ólafsson, S. (1993) 'Variations within the Scandinavian model: Iceland in the Scandinavian perspective', *International Journal of Sociology*, vol 22, no 4, pp 61-88.

Ólafsson, S. (2003) 'Contemporary Icelanders – Scandinavian or American?', *Scandinavian Review*, vol 91, no 1, pp 6–14.

Ólafsson, S. (2005) 'Normative foundations of the Icelandic welfare state: on the gradual erosion of citizenship-based welfare rights', in S. Kuhnle and N. Kildal (eds) *Normative foundations of the Nordic welfare states*, London: Routledge.

Ólafsson, S. (2009) 'Pensions, health and long-term care, Iceland', Annual Report, Analytical Support on the Socio-Economic Impact of Social Protection Reforms (ASISP), European Commission, DG Employment, Social Affairs and Equal Opportunities.

Ott, D. (2000) *Small is democratic, an examination of state size and democratic development*, New York, NY: Garland Publishing.

Prasad, N. (2007) 'Research proposal and project document: social policies in small states', a joint project of the Commonwealth Secretariat and United Nations Research Institute for Social Development (UNRISD).

Prime Minister's Office (2011) 'Iceland 2020 – governmental policy statement for the economy and community', January. Available at: http://eng.forsaetisraduneyti.is/iceland2020/31.

Read, R. (2004) 'The implications of increasing globalization and regionalism for the economic growth of small island states', *World Development*, vol 32, no 2, pp 365-78.

Reykjavik Grapevine (2009) '2008 politics in 30 minutes', vol 1, no 1.

Schmidt, V. (2003) 'How, where and when does discourse matter in small states' welfare state adjustment?', *New Political Economy*, vol 8, no 1, pp 127–46.

Selwyn, P. (1980) 'Smallness and islandness', *World Development*, vol 8, no 12, pp 945-51.

Siaroff, A. (1994) 'Work, welfare and gender equality: A new typology' in D. Sainsbury, *Gendering welfare states,* London, Sage.

Sigfússon, S. (2010) 'Rising from the ruins', parts 1, 6, 22 September. Available at: http://eng.fjarmalaraduneyti.is/minister/sjs/nr/13560

Sighvatsson, A., Sighvatsson, A., Daníelsson, A., Svavarsson, D., Hermannsson, F., Gunnarsson, G., Helgadóttir, H., Bjarnadóttir R. and Ríkarðsson, R.B. (2011) 'What does Iceland owe?', Economic Affairs No 4, February, Reykjavik, The Central Bank of Iceland. Available at: www.sedlabanki.is/lisalib/getfile.aspx?itemid=8713

Special Investigation Commission (2010) 'Report of the SIC', delivered to Althingi, 12 April. Available at: http://sic.althingi.is/

Srebrnik, H. (2004) 'Small island nations and democratic values', *World Development*, vol 32, no 2, pp 329–41.

Sveinsson, J.R. (1996) 'Main trends of Icelandic housing in the 1980s and 1990s', *Scandinavian Housing and Planning Research*, vol 13, pp 215–20.

The Economist (2008) 'Kreppanomics, how a banking crisis brought down a small economy', 9 October.

The Guardian (2009) 'Iceland one year on: small island in big trouble', 28 September. Available at: http://www.guardian.co.uk/business/2009/sep/28/iceland-crisis-one-year-on

The Welfare Watch (2010) *Report to the Althingi,* Ministry of Social Affairs and Social Security, Iceland, January 2010

Thorhallsson, B. (2002) 'The skeptical political elite versus the pro-European public: the case of Iceland', *Scandinavian Studies*, vol 74, no 3, pp 349–78.

Tyler Bonner, J. (2006) *Why size matters, from bacteria to blue whales*, Princeton, NJ: University of Princeton Press.

UNDP (United Nations Development Programme) (2011) 'Human development report 2011, explanatory note on 2011 HDR composite indices, Iceland', United Nations Development Programme. Available at: http://hdrstats.undp.org/images/explanations/ISL.pdf

Visser, J. (2002) 'The first part-time economy in the world: a model to be followed?', *Journal of European Social Policy*, vol 12, no 1, pp 23–42.

Index

Page references for notes are followed by n

U

V

W

Y

Z